THE HISTORY

OF ENGLAND

from the Invasion of Julius Caesar

to The Revolution in 1688

IN SIX VOLUMES

BY DAVID HUME, ESQ.

VOLUME IV

Based on the Edition of 1778, with the Author's

Last Corrections and Improvements

Liberty*Classics*

Liberty*Classics* is a publishing imprint of Liberty Fund, Inc., a foundation established to encourage study of the ideal of a society of free and responsible individuals.

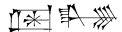

The cuneiform inscription that serves as the design motif for our end-papers is the earliest-known written appearance of the word "freedom" (*ama-gi*), or "liberty." It is taken from a clay document written about 2300 B.C. in the Sumerian city-state of Lagash.

This Liberty*Classics* edition is based on the edition of 1778, containing the author's last corrections and improvements. The only two recorded sets of that edition in the United States were consulted. One is a complete set at the Humanities Research Center of the University of Texas at Austin. The other is an incomplete set in the Boston Public Library. The publisher acknowledges with thanks the cooperation of both institutions as well as the advice of Professors William B. Todd and David Levy.

Design by Martin Lubin/Betty Binns Graphics, New York, New York.
Editorial services provided by Harkavy Publishing Service, New York, New York.

Library of Congress Cataloging in Publication Data

Hume, David, 1711–1776.
   The history of England.

   "Based on the edition of 1778, with the author's last corrections and improvements."
   Reprint. Originally published: London: T. Cadell, 1778. With new foreword.
   1. Great Britain—History—To 1485. 2. Great Britain—History—Tudors, 1485–1603. 3. Great Britain—History—Stuarts, 1603–1714. I. Title.
DA30.H9 1984   942   82–25868
ISBN 0–86597–019–X (series)
ISBN 0–86597–020–3 (pbk. series)
ISBN 0–86597–030–0 (Volume IV)
ISBN 0–86597–031–9 (Volume IV pbk.)

10 9 8 7 6 5 4 3 2

CONTENTS

OF THE FOURTH VOLUME

Confederacy against the protestants –
Murder of Rizzio – A parliament –
Murder of Darnley – Queen of Scots
marries Bothwel – Insurrections in Scotland –
Imprisonment of Mary – Mary flies into
England – Conferences at York
and Hampton Court

X L

Character of the puritans –
Duke of Norfolk's conspiracy – Insurrection
in the north – Assassination of the earl
of Murray – A parliament – Civil wars
of France – Affairs of the Low Countries –
New conspiracy of the duke of Norfolk – Trial
of Norfolk – His execution – Scots affairs –
French affairs – Massacre of Paris –
French affairs – Civil wars of the
Low Countries – A parliament

X L I

Scots affairs – Spanish affairs –
Sir Francis Drake – A parliament –
Negociations of marriage with the duke
of Anjou – Scots affairs – Letter of queen Mary
to Elizabeth – Conspiracies in England –

XLIV

APPENDIX III

THE HISTORY

OF ENGLAND

VOLUME IV

XXXVIII

ELIZABETH

*Queen's popularity – Re-establishment
of the protestant religion – A parliament –
Peace with France – Disgust between the queen
and Mary queen of Scots – Affairs of
Scotland – Reformation in Scotland –
Civil wars in Scotland – Interposal
of the queen in the affairs of Scotland –
Settlement of Scotland – French affairs –
Arrival of Mary in Scotland – Bigotry
of the Scotch Reformers – Wise
government of Elizabeth*

I N A NATION so divided as the English, it could scarcely be ex-   *1558.*
pected, that the death of one sovereign, and the accession of
another, who was generally believed to have embraced opposite
principles to those which prevailed, could be the object of universal satisfaction: Yet so much were men displeased with the present
conduct of affairs, and such apprehensions were entertained of   *Queen's*
futurity, that the people, overlooking their theological disputes,   *popu-*
expressed a general and unfeigned joy that the scepter had passed   *larity.*
into the hand of Elizabeth. That princess had discovered great
prudence in her conduct during the reign of her sister; and as men
were sensible of the imminent danger, to which she was every

moment exposed, compassion towards her situation, and concern for her safety, had rendered her, to an uncommon degree, the favourite of the nation. A parliament had been assembled a few days before Mary's death; and when Heathe, archbishop of York, then chancellor, notified to them that event, scarcely an interval of regret appeared; and the two houses immediately resounded with the joyful acclamations of "God save queen Elizabeth: Long and happily may she reign." The people, less actuated by faction, and less influenced by private views, expressed a joy still more general and hearty on her proclamation; and the auspicious commencement of this reign prognosticated that felicity and glory, which, during its whole course, so uniformly attended it.[a]

Elizabeth was at Hatfield when she heard of her sister's death; and after a few days she went thence to London through crowds of people, who strove with each other in giving her the strongest testimony of their affection. On her entrance into the Tower, she could not forbear reflecting on the great difference between her present fortune and that which a few years before had attended her, when she was conducted to that place as a prisoner, and lay there exposed to all the bigotted malignity of her enemies. She fell on her knees, and expressed her thanks to Heaven, for the deliverance, which the Almightly had granted her from her bloody persecutors; a deliverance, she said, no less miraculous than that which Daniel had received from the den of lions. This act of pious gratitude seems to have been the last circumstance, in which she remembered any past hardships and injuries. With a prudence and magnanimity truly laudable, she buried all offences in oblivion, and received with affability even those who had acted with the greatest malevolence against her. Sir Harry Bennifield himself, to whose custody she had been committed, and who had treated her with severity, never felt, during the whole course of her reign, any effects of her resentment.[b] Yet was not the gracious reception, which she gave, prostitute and undistinguishing. When the bishops came in a body to make their obeisance to her, she expressed to all of them sentiments of regard; except to Bonner, from whom she turned aside, as from a man polluted with blood, who was a just object of horror to every heart susceptible of humanity.[c]

[a] Burnet, vol. ii. p. 373.   [b] Burnet, vol. ii. p. 374.   [c] Ibid. Heylin, p. 102.

CHAPTER XXXVIII

After employing a few days in ordering her domestic affairs, Elizabeth notified to foreign courts, her sister's death, and her own accession. She sent Lord Cobham to the Low Countries, where Philip then resided; and she took care to express to that monarch, her gratitude for the protection which he had afforded her, and her desire of persevering in that friendship which had so happily commenced between them. Philip, who had long foreseen this event, and who still hoped, by means of Elizabeth, to obtain that dominion over England, of which he had failed in espousing Mary, immediately dispatched orders to the duke of Feria, his ambassador at London, to make proposals of marriage to the queen; and he offered to procure from Rome a dispensation for that purpose. But Elizabeth soon came to the resolution of declining the proposal. She saw, that the nation had entertained an extreme aversion to the Spanish alliance during her sister's reign; and that one great cause of the popularity, which she herself enjoyed, was the prospect of being freed, by her means, from the danger of foreign subjection. She was sensible, that her affinity with Philip was exactly similar to that of her father with Catherine of Arragon; and that her marrying that monarch was, in effect, declaring herself illegitimate, and incapable of succeeding to the throne. And though the power of the Spanish monarchy might still be sufficient, in opposition to all pretenders, to support her title, her masculine spirit disdained such precarious dominion, which, as it would depend solely on the power of another, must be exercised according to his inclinations. [d] But while these views prevented her from entertaining any thoughts of a marriage with Philip, she gave him an obliging, though evasive, answer; and he still retained such hopes of success, that he sent a messenger to Rome, with orders to solicit the dispensation.

The queen too, on her sister's death, had written to Sir Edward Carne, the English ambassador at Rome, to notify her accession to the pope; but the precipitate nature of Paul broke through all the cautious measures concerted by this young princess. He told Carne, that England was a fief of the holy see; and it was great temerity in Elizabeth to have assumed, without his participation, the title and authority of queen: That being illegitimate, she could

[d] Camden in Kennet, p. 370. Burnet, vol. ii. p. 375.

not possibly inherit that kingdom; nor could he annul the sentence pronounced by Clement VII. and Paul III. with regard to Henry's marriage: That were he to proceed with rigour, he should punish this criminal invasion of his rights, by rejecting all her applications; but being willing to treat her with paternal indulgence, he would still keep the door of grace open to her: And that if she would renounce all pretensions to the crown, and submit entirely to his will, she should experience the utmost lenity, compatible with the dignity of the apostolic see.[e] When this answer was reported to Elizabeth, she was astonished at the character of that aged pontiff; and having recalled her ambassador, she continued with more determined resolution to pursue those measures, which already she had secretly embraced.

The queen, not to alarm the partizans of the catholic religion, had retained eleven of her sister's counsellors; but in order to balance their authority, she added eight more, who were known to be inclined to the protestant communion; the marquis of Northampton, the earl of Bedford, Sir Thomas Parry, Sir Edward Rogers, Sir Ambrose Cave, Sir Francis Knolles, Sir Nicholas Bacon, whom she created lord keeper, and Sir William Cecil, secretary of state.[f] With these counsellors, particularly Cecil, she frequently deliberated concerning the expediency of restoring the protestant religion, and the means of executing that great enterprise. Cecil told her, that the greater part of the nation had, ever since her father's reign, inclined to the reformation; and though her sister had constrained them to profess the ancient faith, the cruelties, exercised by her ministers, had still more alienated their affections from it: That happily the interests of the sovereign here concurred with the inclinations of the people; nor was her title to the crown compatible with the authority of the Roman pontiff: That a sentence, so solemnly pronounced by two popes against her mother's marriage, could not possibly be recalled, without inflicting a mortal wound on the credit of the see of Rome; and even if she were allowed to retain the crown, it would only be on an uncertain and dependant footing: That this circumstance alone counterbalanced all dangers whatsoever; and these dangers themselves, if narrowly examined, would be found very little formidable: That the curses

Re-estab-lishment of the protestant religion.

[e] Father Paul, lib. 5.   [f] Strype's Ann. vol. i. p. 5.

and execrations of the Romish church, when not seconded by military force, were, in the present age, more an object of ridicule than of terror, and had now as little influence in this world as in the next: That though the bigotry or ambition of Henry or Philip might incline them to execute a sentence of excommunication against her, their interests were so incompatible, that they never could concur in any plan of operations; and the enmity of the one would always ensure to her the friendship of the other: That if they encouraged the discontents of her catholic subjects, their dominions also abounded with protestants, and it would be easy to retaliate upon them: That even such of the English as seemed at present zealously attached to the catholic faith, would, most of them, embrace the religion of their new sovereign; and the nation had of late been so much accustomed to these revolutions, that men had lost all idea of truth and falsehood in such subjects: That the authority of Henry VIII. so highly raised by many concurring circumstances, first enured the people to this submissive defer-ence; and it was the less difficult for succeeding princes to continue the nation in a track, to which it had so long been accustomed: And that it would be easy for her, by bestowing on protestants all pre-ferment in civil offices and the militia, the church and the univer-sities, both to ensure her own authority, and to render her religion entirely predominant. [g]

The education of Elizabeth, as well as her interest, led her to favour the reformation; and she remained not long in suspence with regard to the party, which she should embrace. But though determined in her own mind, she resolved to proceed by gradual and secure steps, and not to imitate the example of Mary, in en-couraging the bigots of her party to make immediately a violent invasion on the established religion. [h] She thought it requisite, however, to discover such symptoms of her intentions, as might give encouragement to the protestants, so much depressed by the late violent persecutions. She immediately recalled all the exiles, and gave liberty to the prisoners, who were confined on account of religion. We are told of a pleasantry of one Rainsford on this occasion, who said to the queen, that he had a petition to present

[g] Burnet, vol. ii. p. 377. Camden, p. 370.   [h] Burnet, vol. ii. p. 378. Camden, p. 371.

her in behalf of other prisoners called Matthew, Mark, Luke, and John: She readily replied, that it behoved her first to consult the prisoners themselves, and to learn of them whether they desired that liberty, which he demanded for them.[i]

Elizabeth also proceeded to exert, in favour of the reformers, some acts of power which were authorized by the extent of royal prerogative, during that age. Finding, that the protestant teachers, irritated by persecution, broke out in a furious attack on the ancient superstition, and that the Romanists replied with no less zeal and acrimony, she published a proclamation, by which she inhibited all preaching without a special licence;[k] and though she dispensed with these orders in favour of some preachers of her own sect, she took care, that they should be the most calm and moderate of the party. She also suspended the laws so far as to order a great part of the service; the litany, the Lord's prayer, the creed, and the gospels; to be read in English. And having first published injunctions, that all the churches should conform themselves to the practice of her own chapel, she forbade the hoste to be any more elevated in her presence; an innovation, which, however frivolous it may appear, implied the most material consequences.[l]

These declarations of her intention, concurring with preceding suspicions, made the bishops foresee with certainty a revolution in religion. They therefore refused to officiate at her coronation; and it was with some difficulty, that the bishop of Carlisle was at last prevailed on to perform the ceremony. When she was conducted through London, amidst the joyful acclamations of her subjects, a boy, who personated Truth, was let down from one of the triumphal arches, and presented to her a copy of the Bible. She received the book with the most gracious deportment; placed it next her bosom; and declared, that, amidst all the costly testimonies, which the city had that day given her of their attachment, this present was by far the most precious and most acceptable.[m] Such were the innocent artifices, by which Elizabeth insinuated herself into the affections of her subjects. Open in her address,

[i] Heylin, p. 103.   [k] Heylin, p. 104. Strype, vol. i. p. 41.   [l] Camden, p. 371. Heylin, p. 104. Strype, vol. i. p. 54. Stowe, p. 635.   [m] Burnet, vol. ii. p. 380. Strype, vol. i. p. 29.

CHAPTER XXXVIII

gracious and affable in all public appearances, she rejoiced in the concourse of her subjects, entered into all their pleasures and amusements, and without departing from her dignity, which she knew well how to preserve, she acquired a popularity beyond what any of her predecessors or successors ever could attain. Her own sex exulted to see a woman hold the reins of empire with such prudence and fortitude: And while a young princess of twenty-five years (for that was her age at her accession) who possessed all the graces and insinuation, though not all the beauty of her sex, courted the affection of individuals by her civilities, of the public by her services, her authority, though corroborated by the strictest bands of law and religion, appeared to be derived entirely from the choice and inclination of the people.

A sovereign of this disposition was not likely to offend her subjects by any useless or violent exertions of power; and Elizabeth, though she threw out such hints as encouraged the protestants, delayed the entire change of religion till the meeting of the parliament, which was summoned to assemble. The elections had gone entirely against the catholics, who seem not indeed to have made any great struggle for the superiority;[n] and the houses met, in a disposition of gratifying the queen in every particular, which she could desire of them. They began the session with an unanimous declaration, "that queen Elizabeth was, and ought to be, as well by the word of God, as the common and statute laws of the realm, the lawful, undoubted, and true heir to the crown, lawfully descended from the blood-royal, according to the order of succession, settled in the 35th of Henry VIII."[o] This act of recognition was probably dictated by the queen herself and her ministers; and she shewed her magnanimity, as well as moderation, in the terms, which she employed on that occasion. She followed not Mary's practice in declaring the validity of her mother's marriage, or in expresly repealing the act formerly made against her own legitimacy: She knew, that this attempt must be attended with reflec-

A parliament.

---

[n] Notwithstanding the byass of the nation towards the protestant sect, it appears, that some violence, at least according to our present ideas, was used in these elections: Five candidates were nominated by the court to each borough and three to each county; and by the sheriff's authority the members were chosen from among these candidates. *See state papers collected by Edward earl of Clarendon,* p. 92.   [o] 1 Eliz. cap. 3.

tions on her father's memory, and on the birth of her deceased sister; and as all the world was sensible, that Henry's divorce from Anne Boleyn was merely the effect of his usual violence and caprice, she scorned to found her title on any act of an assembly, which had too much prostituted its authority by its former variable, servile, and iniquitous decisions. Satisfied therefore in the general opinion entertained with regard to this fact, which appeared the more undoubted, the less anxiety she discovered in fortifying it by votes and enquiries; she took possession of the throne, both as her birthright, and as ensured to her by former acts of parliament; and she never appeared anxious to distinguish these titles.[p]

The first bill brought into parliament with a view of trying their disposition on the head of religion, was that for suppressing the monasteries lately erected, and for restoring the tenths and first-fruits to the queen. This point being gained without much difficulty, a bill was next introduced, annexing the supremacy to the crown; and though the queen was there denominated *governess,* not *head,* of the church, it conveyed the same extensive power, which, under the latter title, had been exercised by her father and brother. All the bishops who were present in the upper house strenuously opposed this law; and as they possessed more learning than the temporal peers, they triumphed in the debate; but the majority of voices in that house, as well as among the commons, was against them. By this act the crown, without the concurrence, either of the parliament or even of the convocation, was vested with the whole spiritual power; might repress all heresies, might establish or repeal all canons, might alter every point of discipline, and might ordain or abolish any religious rite or ceremony.[q] In determining heresy, the sovereign was only limited (if that could be called a limitation) to such doctrines as had been adjudged heresy, by the authority of the Scripture, by the first four general councils, or by any general council, which followed the Scripture as their rule, or to such other doctrines as should hereafter be denominated heresy by the parliament and convocation. In order to exercise this authority, the queen, by a clause of the act, was

[p] Camden, p. 372. Heylin, p. 107, 108.   [q] 1 Eliz. cap. 1. This last power was anew recognized in the act of uniformity. 1 Eliz. cap. 2.

CHAPTER XXXVIII

empowered to name commissioners, either laymen or clergymen, as she should think proper; and on this clause was afterwards founded the court of ecclesiastical commission; which assumed large discretionary, not to say arbitrary powers, totally incompatible with any exact boundaries in the constitution. Their proceedings indeed were only consistent with absolute monarchy, but were entirely suitable to the genius of the act on which they were established; an act that at once gave the crown alone all the power, which had formerly been claimed by the popes, but which even these usurping prelates had never been able fully to exercise, without some concurrence of the national clergy.

Whoever refused to take an oath, acknowledging the queen's supremacy, was incapacitated from holding any office; whoever denied the supremacy, or attempted to deprive the queen of that prerogative, forfeited, for the first offence, all his goods and chattels; for the second, was subjected to the penalty of a premunire; but the third offence was declared treason. These punishments, however severe, were less rigorous than those which were formerly, during the reigns of her father and brother, inflicted in like cases.

A law was passed, confirming all the statutes enacted in king Edward's time with regard to religion: ʳ The nomination of bishops was given to the crown without any election of the chapters: The queen was empowered, on the vacancy of any see, to seize all the temporalities, and to bestow on the bishop-elect an equivalent in the impropriations belonging to the crown. This pretended equivalent was commonly much inferior in value; and thus the queen, amidst all her concern for religion, followed the example of the preceding reformers, in committing depredations on the ecclesiastical revenues.

The bishops and all incumbents were prohibited from alienating their revenues, and from letting leases longer than twenty-one years or three lives. This law seemed to be meant for securing the property of the church; but as an exception was left in favour of the crown, great abuses still prevailed. It was usual for the courtiers during this reign, to make an agreement with a bishop or incumbent; and to procure a fictitious alienation to the queen, who

ʳ 1 Eliz. cap. 2.

afterwards transferred the lands to the person agreed on.[s] This method of pillaging the church was not remedied till the beginning of James I. The present depression of the clergy exposed them to all injuries; and the laity never stopped, till they had reduced the church to such poverty, that her plunder was no longer a compensation for the odium incurred by it.

A solemn and public disputation was held during this session, in presence of lord keeper Bacon, between the divines of the protestant and those of the catholic communion. The champions, appointed to defend the religion of the sovereign, were, as in all former instances, entirely triumphant; and the popish disputants, being pronounced refractory and obstinate, were even punished by imprisonment.[t] Emboldened by this victory, the protestants ventured on the last and most important step, and brought into parliament a bill[u] for abolishing the mass, and re-establishing the liturgy of king Edward. Penalties were enacted, as well against those who departed from this mode of worship, as against those who absented themselves from the church and the sacraments. And thus in one session, without any violence, tumult, or clamour, was the whole system of religion altered, on the very commencement of a reign, and by the will of a young woman, whose title to the crown was by many thought liable to great objections: An event, which, though it may appear surprising to men in the present age, was every where expected on the first intelligence of Elizabeth's accession.

The commons also made a sacrifice to the queen, more difficult to obtain than that of any articles of faith: They voted a subsidy of four shillings in the pound on land, and two shillings and eight pence on moveables, together with two fifteenths.[w] The house in no instance departed from the most respectful deference and complaisance towards the queen. Even the importunate address which they made her on the conclusion of the session, to fix her choice of a husband, could not, they supposed, be very disagreeable to one of her sex and age. The address was couched in the most respectful expressions; yet met with a refusal from the queen. She told the speaker, that, as the application from the house was con-

[s] Strype, vol. i. p. 79.   [t] Ibid. p. 95.   [u] 1 Eliz. cap. 2.   [w] See note [A] at the end of the volume.

ceived in general terms, only recommending marriage, without pretending to direct her choice of a husband, she could not take offence at the address, or regard it otherwise than as a new instance of their affectionate attachment to her: That any farther interposition on their part would have ill become either them to make as subjects, or her to hear as an independent princess: That even while she was a private person, and exposed to much danger, she had always declined that engagement, which she regarded as an incumbrance; much more, at present, would she persevere in this sentiment, when the charge of a great kingdom was committed to her, and her life ought to be entirely devoted to promoting the interests of religion and the happiness of her subjects: That as England was her husband, wedded to her by this pledge (and here *1559.* she shewed her finger with the same gold ring upon it, with which she had solemnly betrothed herself to the kingdom at her inauguration) so all Englishmen were her children; and while she was employed in rearing or governing such a family, she could not deem herself barren, or her life useless and unprofitable: That if she ever entertained thoughts of changing her condition, the care of her subjects' welfare would still be uppermost in her thoughts; but should she live and die a virgin, she doubted not but divine Providence, seconded by their counsels and her own measures, would be able to prevent all dispute with regard to the succession, and secure them a sovereign, who, perhaps better than her own issue, would imitate her example, in loving and cherishing her people: And that for her part, she desired that no higher character, or fairer remembrance of her should be transmitted to posterity, than to have this inscription engraved on her tomb-stone, when she should pay the last debt to nature; "Here lies Elizabeth, who lived and died a maiden queen."[x]

After the prorogation of the parliament,[y] the laws, enacted with *8th* regard to religion, were put in execution, and met with little oppo- *May.* sition from any quarter. The liturgy was again introduced in the

---

[x] Camden, p. 375. Sir Simon d'Ewes.   [y] It is thought remarkable by Camden, that though this session was the first of the reign, no person was attainted; but on the contrary, some restored in blood by the parliament. A good sympton of the lenity, at least of the prudence, of the queen's government; and that it should appear remarkable, is a proof of the rigour of preceding reigns.

vulgar tongue, and the oath of supremacy was tendered to the clergy. The number of bishops had been reduced to fourteen by a sickly season, which preceded; and all these, except the bishop of Landaffe, having refused compliance, were degraded from their sees: But of the inferior clergy throughout all England, where there are near 10,000 parishes, only eighty rectors and vicars, fifty prebendaries, fifteen heads of colleges, twelve archdeacons, and as many deans, sacrificed their livings to their religious principles.[z] Those in high ecclesiastic stations, being exposed to the eyes of the public, seem chiefly to have placed a point of honour in their perseverance; but on the whole; the protestants, in the former change introduced by Mary, appear to have been much more rigid and conscientious. Though the catholic religion, adapting itself to the senses, and enjoining observances, which enter into the common train of life, does at present lay faster hold on the mind than the reformed, which, being chiefly spiritual, resembles more a system of metaphysics; yet was the proportion of zeal, as well as of knowledge, during the first ages after the reformation, much greater on the side of the protestants. The catholics continued, ignorantly and supinely, in their ancient belief, or rather their ancient practices: But the reformers, obliged to dispute on every occasion, and inflamed to a degree of enthusiasm by novelty and persecution, had strongly attached themselves to their tenets; and were ready to sacrifice their fortunes and even their lives, in support of their speculative and abstract principles.

The forms and ceremonies, still preserved in the English liturgy, as they bore some resemblance to the ancient service, tended farther to reconcile the catholics to the established religion; and as the queen permitted no other mode of worship, and at the same time struck out every thing that could be offensive to them in the new liturgy,[a] even those who were addicted to the Romish communion made no scruple of attending the established church. Had Elizabeth gratified her own inclinations, the exterior appearance, which is the chief circumstance with the people, would have been still more similar between the new and the ancient form of worship. Her love of state and magnificence, which she affected in

[z] Camden, p. 376. Heylin, p. 115. Strype, vol. i. p. 73, with some small variations. [a] Heylin, p. 111.

CHAPTER XXXVIII

every thing, inspired her with an inclination towards the pomp of the catholic religion; and it was merely in compliance with the prejudices of her party, that she gave up either images or the addresses to saints, or prayers for the dead.[b] Some foreign princes interposed to procure the Romanists the privilege of separate assemblies in particular cities, but the queen would not comply with their request; and she represented the manifest danger of disturbing the national peace by a toleration of different religions.[c]

While the queen and parliament were employed in settling the public religion, the negociations for a peace were still conducted, first at Cercamp, then at Cateau-Cambresis, between the ministers of France, Spain, and England; and Elizabeth, though equally prudent, was not equally successful in this transaction. Philip employed his utmost efforts to procure the restitution of Calais, both as bound in honour to indemnify England, which, merely on his account, had been drawn into the war; and as engaged in interest to remove France to a distance from his frontiers in the Low Countries. So long as he entertained hopes of espousing the queen, he delayed concluding a peace with Henry; and even after the change of religion in England deprived him of all such views, his ministers hinted to her a proposal, which may be regarded as reasonable and honourable. Though all his own terms with France were settled, he seemed willing to continue the war, till she should obtain satisfaction; provided she would stipulate to adhere to the Spanish alliance, and continue hostilities against Henry, during the course of six years:[d] But Elizabeth, after consulting with her ministers, wisely rejected this proposal. She was sensible of the low state of her finances; the great debts contracted by her father, brother, and sister; the disorders introduced into every part of the administration; the divisions by which her people were agitated; and she was convinced that nothing but tranquillity during some years could bring the kingdom again into a flourishing condition, or enable her to act with dignity and vigour, in her transactions with foreign nations. Well acquainted with the value which Henry put upon Calais, and the impossibility, during the present emergence, of recovering it by treaty, she was willing rather to suffer that loss,

Peace with France.

[b] Burnet, vol. ii. p. 376, 397. Camden, p. 371. [c] Camden, p. 378. Strype, vol. i. p. 150, 370. [d] Forbes's Full View, vol. i. p. 59.

than submit to such a dependence on Spain, as she must expect to fall into, if she continued pertinaciously in her present demand. She ordered, therefore, her ambassadors, lord Effingham, the bishop of Ely, and Dr. Wotton, to conclude the negociation, and to settle a peace with Henry, on any reasonable terms. Henry offered to stipulate a marriage between the eldest daughter of the dauphin, and the eldest son of Elizabeth; and to engage for the restitution of Calais as the dowry of that princess;[e] but as the queen was sensible, that this treaty would appear to the world a palpable evasion, she insisted upon more equitable, at least, more plausible conditions. It was at last agreed, that Henry should restore Calais at the expiration of eight years; that, in case of failure, he should pay five hundred thousand crowns, and the queen's title to Calais still remain; that he should find the security of seven or eight foreign merchants, not natives of France, for the payment of this sum; that he should deliver five hostages till that security were provided; that if Elizabeth broke the peace with France or Scotland during the interval, she should forfeit all title to Calais; but if Henry made war on Elizabeth, he should be obliged immediately to restore that fortress.[f] All men of penetration easily saw, that these stipulations were but a colourable pretence for abandoning Calais; but they excused the queen on account of the necessity of her affairs; and they even extolled her prudence, in submitting, without farther struggle, to that necessity. A peace with Scotland was a necessary consequence of that with France.

Philip and Henry terminated hostilities by a mutual restitution of all places taken during the course of the war; and Philip espoused the princess Elizabeth, eldest daughter of France, formerly betrothed to his son Don Carlos. The duke of Savoy married Margaret, Henry's sister, and obtained a restitution of all his dominions of Savoy and Piedmont, except a few towns, retained by France. And thus, general tranquillity seemed to be restored to Europe.

Disgust between the queen, and Mary queen of Scots. But, though peace was concluded between France and England, there soon appeared a ground of quarrel, of the most serious nature, and which was afterwards attended with the most important consequences. The two marriages of Henry VIII. that with

[e] Forbes, vol. i. p. 54.   [f] Forbes, p. 68. Rymer, tom. xv. p. 505.

CHAPTER XXXVIII

Catherine of Arragon, and that with Anne Boleyn, were incompatible with each other; and it seemed impossible, that both of them could be regarded as valid and legal: But still the birth of Elizabeth lay under some disadvantages, to which that of her sister, Mary, was not exposed. Henry's first marriage had obtained the sanction of all the powers, both civil and ecclesiastical, which were then acknowledged in England; and it was natural, for protestants as well as Romanists, to allow, on account of the sincere intention of the parties, that their issue ought to be regarded as legitimate. But his divorce and second marriage had been concluded in direct opposition to the see of Rome; and though they had been ratified by the authority both of the English parliament and convocation, those who were strongly attached to the catholic communion, and who reasoned with great strictness, were led to regard them as entirely invalid, and to deny altogether the queen's right of succession. The next heir of blood was the queen of Scots, now married to the dauphin; and the great power of that princess, joined to her plausible title, rendered her a formidable rival to Elizabeth. The king of France had secretly been soliciting at Rome a bull of excommunication against the queen; and she had here been beholden to the good offices of Philip, who, from interest more than either friendship or generosity, had negociated in her favour, and had successfully opposed the pretensions of Henry. But the court of France was not discouraged with this repulse: The duke of Guise, and his brothers, thinking, that it would much augment their credit, if their niece should bring an accession of England, as she had already done of Scotland, to the crown of France, engaged the king not to neglect the claim; and, by their persuasion, he ordered his son and daughter-in-law to assume openly the arms as well as title of England, and to quarter these arms on all their equipages, furniture, and liveries. When the English ambassador complained of this injury, he could obtain nothing but an evasive answer; that as the queen of Scots was descended from the blood royal of England, she was entitled, by the example of many princes, to assume the arms of that kingdom. But besides that this practice had never prevailed without permission being first obtained, and without making a visible difference between the arms; Elizabeth plainly saw, that this pretension had not been advanced during the reign of her sister Mary; and that, therefore, the king of France intended, on the first opportunity, to dispute her legitimacy, and her title to the crown. Alarmed at the danger, she thenceforth conceived a violent jealousy against the queen of Scots; and was determined, as far as possible, to incapacitate Henry from the execution of his project. The sudden death of that monarch, who was killed in a tournament at Paris, while celebrating the espousals of his sister with the duke of Savoy, altered not her views. Being informed that his successor, Francis II. still continued to assume, without reserve, the title of king of England, she began to consider him and his queen as her mortal enemies; and the present situation of affairs in Scotland afforded her a favourable opportunity, both of revenging the injury, and providing for her own safety.

Affairs of Scotland. The murder of the cardinal-primate at St. Andrews had deprived the Scottish catholics of a head, whose severity, courage, and capacity had rendered him extremely formidable to the innovators in religion; and the execution of the laws against heresy began thenceforth to be more remiss. The queen-regent governed the kingdom by prudent and moderate counsels; and as she was not disposed to sacrifice the civil interests of the state to the bigotry or interests of the clergy, she deemed it more expedient to temporize, and to connive at the progress of a doctrine, which she had not power entirely to repress. When informed of the death of Edward, and the accession of Mary to the crown of England, she entertained hopes, that the Scottish reformers, deprived of the countenance which they received from that powerful kingdom, would lose their ardour with their prospect of success, and would gradually return to the faith of their ancestors. But the progress and revolutions of religion are little governed by the usual maxims of civil policy; and the event much disappointed the expectations of the regent. Many of the English preachers terrified with the severity of Mary's government, took shelter in Scotland, where they found more protection, and a milder administration; and while they propagated their theological tenets, they filled the whole kingdom with a just horror against the cruelties of the bigotted catholics, and showed their disciples the fate, which they must expect, if ever their adversaries should attain an uncontrouled authority over them.

A hierarchy, moderate in its acquisitions of power and riches, may safely grant a toleration to sectaries; and the more it softens the zeal of innovators by lenity and liberty, the more securely will it possess those advantages, which the legal establishments bestow upon it. But where superstition has raised a church to such an exorbitant height as that of Rome, persecution is less the result of bigotry in the priests, than of a necessary policy; and the rigour of law is the only method of repelling the attacks of men, who, besides religious zeal, have so many motives, derived both from public and private interest, to engage them on the side of innovation. But though such overgrown hierarchies may long support themselves by these violent expedients, the time comes, when severities tend only to enrage the new sectaries, and make them break through all bounds of reason and moderation. This crisis was now visibly approaching in Scotland; and whoever considers merely the transactions resulting from it, will be inclined to throw the blame equally on both parties; whoever enlarges his view, and reflects on the situations, will remark the necessary progess of human affairs, and the operation of those principles, which are inherent in human nature.

Some heads of the reformers in Scotland, such as the earl of Argyle, his son lord Lorne, the earls of Morton, and Glencarne, Erskine of Dun, and others, observing the danger to which they were exposed, and desirous to propagate their principles, entered privately into a bond or association; and called themselves the *Congregation* of the Lord, in contradistinction to the established church, which they denominated the congregation of Satan. The tenor of the bond was as follows: "We perceiving how Satan, in his members, the antichrist of our time, do cruelly rage, seeking to overthrow and to destroy the gospel of Christ and his congregation, ought, according to our bounden duty, to strive, in our master's cause, even unto the death, being certain of the victory in him. We do therefore promise, before the majesty of God and his congregation, that we, by his grace, shall with all diligence continually apply our whole power, substance, and our very lives, to maintain, set forward, and establish the most blessed word of God and his congregation; and shall labour, by all possible means, to have faithful ministers, truly and purely to minister Christ's gospel and sacraments to his people: We shall maintain them, nourish them, and defend them, the whole congregation of Christ, and

Reformation in Scotland.

every member thereof, by our whole power, and at the hazard of our lives, against Satan, and all wicked power, who may intend tyranny and trouble against the said congregation: Unto which holy word and congregation we do join ourselves; and we forsake and renounce the congregation of Satan, with all the superstitious abomination and idolatry thereof; and moreover shall declare ourselves manifestly enemies thereto, by this faithful promise before God, testified to this congregation by our subscriptions. At Edinburgh, the third of December, 1557."[g]

Had the subscribers of this zealous league been content only to demand a toleration of the new opinions; however incompatible their pretensions might have been with the policy of the church of Rome, they would have had the praise of opposing tyrannical laws, enacted to support an establishment prejudicial to civil society: But it is plain, that they carried their views much farther; and their practice immediately discovered the spirit by which they were actuated. Supported by the authority, which, they thought, belonged to them as the congregation of the Lord, they ordained, that prayers in the vulgar tongue[h] should be used in all the parish churches of the kingdom; and that preaching, and the interpretation of the scriptures should be practised in private houses, till God should move the prince to grant public preaching by faithful and true ministers.[i] Such bonds of association are always the forerunners of rebellion; and this violent invasion of the established religion was the actual commencement of it.

Before this league was publicly known or avowed, the clergy, alarmed with the progress of the reformation, attempted to recover their lost authority by a violent exercise of power, which tended still farther to augment the zeal and number of their enemies. Hamilton, the primate, seized Walter Mill, a priest of an irreproachable life, who had embraced the new doctrines; and having tried him at St. Andrews, condemned him to the flames for heresy. Such general aversion was entertained against this barbarity, that it was some time before the bishops could prevail on any one to act the part of a civil judge, and pronounce sentence upon Mill; and even after the time of his execution was fixed, all the

[g] Keith, p. 66. Knox, p. 101.   [h] The reformers used at that time king Edward's liturgy in Scotland. Forbes, p. 155.   [i] Keith, p. 66. Knox, p. 101.

CHAPTER XXXVIII

shops of St. Andrews being shut, no one would sell a rope to tie him to the stake, and the primate himself was obliged to furnish this implement. The man bore the torture with that courage, which, though usual on these occasions, always appears supernatural and astonishing to the multitude. The people, to express their abhorrence against the cruelty of the priests, raised a monument of stones on the place of his execution; and as fast as the stones were removed by order of the clergy, they were again supplied from the voluntary zeal of the populace.[k] It is in vain for men to oppose the severest punishment to the united motives of religion and public applause; and this was the last barbarity of the kind, which the catholics had the power to exercise in Scotland.

Some time after, the people discovered their sentiments in such a manner as was sufficient to prognosticate to the priests the fate, which was awaiting them. It was usual on the festival of St. Giles, the tutelar saint of Edinburgh, to carry in procession the image of that saint; but the protestants, in order to prevent the ceremony, found means, on the eve of the festival, to purloin the statue from the church; and they pleased themselves with imagining the surprise and disappointment of his votaries. The clergy, however, framed hastily a new image, which, in derision, was called by the people young St. Giles; and they carried it through the streets, attended by all the ecclesiastics in the town and neighbourhood. The multitude abstained from violence so long as the queen-regent continued a spectator, but the moment she retired, they invaded the idol, threw it in the mire, and broke it in pieces. The flight and terror of the priests and friars, who, it was remarked, deserted, in his greatest distress, the object of their worship, was the source of universal mockery and laughter.

Encouraged by all these appearances the congregation proceeded with alacrity in openly soliciting subscriptions to their league; and the death of Mary of England, with the accession of Elizabeth, which happened about this time, contributed to encrease their hopes of final success in their undertaking. They ventured to present a petition to the regent, craving a reformation of the church, and of the *wicked, scandalous,* and *detestable* lives of the prelates and ecclesiastics.[l] They framed a petition, which they in-

[k] Knox, p. 122.   [l] Knox, p. 121.

tended to present to parliament, and in which, after premising, that they could not communicate with the damnable idolatry, and intolerable abuses of the papistical church, they desired, that the laws against heretics, should be executed by the civil magistrate alone, and that the scripture should be the sole rule in judging of heresy.[m] They even petitioned the convocation, and insisted, that prayers should be said in the vulgar tongue, and that bishops should be chosen with the consent of the gentry of the diocese, and priests with the consent of the parishioners.[n] The regent prudently temporized between these parties; and as she aimed at procuring a matrimonial crown for her son-in-law, the dauphin, she was, on that as well as other accounts, unwilling to come to extremities with either of them.

But after this concession was obtained, she received orders from France, probably dictated by the violent spirit of her brothers, to proceed with rigour against the reformers, and to restore the royal authority by some signal act of power.[o] She made the more eminent of the protestant teachers be cited to appear before the council at Stirling; but when their followers were marching thither in great multitudes, in order to protect and countenance them, she entertained apprehensions of an insurrection, and, it is said, dissipated the people by a promise,[p] that nothing should be done to the prejudice of the ministers. Sentence, however, was passed, by which all the ministers were pronounced rebels on account of their not appearing. A measure which enraged the people, and made them resolve to oppose the regent's authority by force of arms, and to proceed to extremities against the clergy of the established religion.

In this critical time, John Knox arrived from Geneva, where he had passed some years in banishment, and where he had imbibed, from his commerce with Calvin, the highest fanaticism of his sect, augmented by the native ferocity of his own character. He had been invited back to Scotland by the leaders of the reformation; and mounting the pulpit at Perth, during the present ferment of men's minds, he declaimed with his usual vehemence against the idolatry and other abominations of the church of Rome, and in-

11th May.

---

[m] Ibid. p. 123.   [n] Keith, p. 78, 81, 82.   [o] Melvil's Memoirs, p. 24. Jeb, vol. ii. p. 446.   [p] See note [B] at the end of the volume.

cited his audience to exert their utmost zeal for its subversion. A priest was so imprudent after this sermon, as to open his repository of images and reliques, and prepare himself to say mass. The audience, exalted to a disposition for any furious enterprize, were as much enraged as if the spectacle had not been quite familiar to them: They attacked the priest with fury, broke the images in pieces, tore the pictures, overthrew the altars, scattered about the sacred vases; and left no implement of idolatrous worship, as they termed it, entire or undefaced. They thence proceeded, with additional numbers and augmented rage, to the monasteries of the grey and black friars, which they pillaged in an instant: The Carthusians underwent the same fate: And the populace, not content with robbing and expelling the monks, vented their fury on the buildings which had been the receptacles of such abomination; and in a little time nothing but the walls of these edifices were left standing. The inhabitants of Couper in Fife soon after imitated the example.[q]

The queen-regent, provoked at these violences, assembled an army, and prepared to chastise the rebels. She had about two thousand French under her command, with a few Scottish troops; and being assisted by such of the nobility as were well affected to her, she pitched her camp within ten miles of Perth. Even the earl of Argyle, and lord James Stuart, prior of St. Andrews, the queen's natural brother, though deeply engaged with the reformers, attended the regent in this enterprise, either because they blamed the fury of the populace, or hoped by their own influence and authority to mediate some agreement between the parties. The congregation, on the other hand, made preparations for defence; and being joined by the earl of Glencarne from the west, and being countenanced by many of the nobility and gentry, they appeared formidable from their numbers, as well as from the zeal by which they were animated. They sent an address to the regent, where they plainly insinuated, that, if they were pursued to extremities, by the *cruel beasts* the churchmen, they would have recourse to foreign powers for assistance; and they subscribed themselves her faithful subjects in all things not repugnant to God, assuming, at the same time, the name of the faithful congregation of Christ

Civil wars in Scotland.

[q] Spotswood, p. 121. Knox, p. 127.

Jesus.[r] They applied to the nobility attending her, and maintained, that their own past violences were justified by the word of God, which commands the godly to destroy idolatry, and all the monuments of it; and though all civil authority was sacred, yet was there a great difference between the authority and the persons who exercised it;[s] and that it ought to be considered, whether or not those abominations, called by the pestilent papists, Religion, and which they defend by fire and sword, be the true religion of Christ Jesus. They remonstrated with such of the queen's army as had formerly embraced their party, and told them, "That as they were already reputed traitors by God, they should likewise be excommunicated from their society, and from the participation of the sacraments of the church, which God by his mighty power had erected among them; whose ministers have the same authority which Christ granted to his apostles in these words, *Whose sins ye shall forgive shall be forgiven, and whose sins ye shall retain shall be retained.*"[t] We may here see, that these new saints were no less lofty in their pretensions than the ancient heirarchy: No wonder they were enraged against the latter as their rivals in dominion. They joined to all these declarations an address to the established church; and they affixed this title to it: "To the generation of antichrist, the pestilent prelates and their *shavelings*[u] in Scotland, the congregation of Christ Jesus within the same sayeth." The tenor of the manifesto was suitable to this title. They told the ecclesiastics, "As ye by tyranny intend not only to destroy our bodies, but also by the same to hold our souls in bondage of the devil, subject to idolatry; so shall we, with all the force and power which God shall grant unto us, execute just vengeance and punishment upon you: Yea, we shall begin the same war which God commanded Israel to execute against the Canaanites; that is, contract of peace shall never be made, till you desist from your open idolatry, and cruel persecution of God's children. And this, in the name of the eternal God, and of his son Christ Jesus, whose verity we profess, and Gospel we have preached, and holy sacraments rightly administered, we signify unto you, to be our intent, so far as God will assist us to withstand your idolatry. Take this for warning, and be not deceived."[w] With these outrageous symptoms, commenced in

[r] Knox, p. 129.   [s] Knox, p. 131.   [t] Ibid. p. 133.   [u] A contemptuous term for a priest.   [w] Keith, p. 85, 86, 87. Knox, p. 134.

CHAPTER XXXVIII

Scotland that cant, hypocrisy, and fanaticism, which long infested that kingdom, and which, though now mollified by the lenity of the civil power, is still ready to break out on all occasions.

The queen regent, finding such obstinate zeal in the rebels, was content to embrace the counsels of Argyle and the prior of St. Andrews, and to form an accommodation with them. She was received into Perth, which submitted, on her promising an indemnity for past offences, and engaging not to leave any French garrison in the place. Complaints, very ill founded, immediately arose concerning the infraction of this capitulation. Some of the inhabitants, it was pretended, were molested on account of the late violences; and some companies of Scotch soldiers, supposed to be in French pay, were quartered in the town; which step, though taken on very plausible grounds, was loudly exclaimed against by the congregation.[x] It is asserted that the regent, to justify these measures, declared, that princes ought not to have their promises too strictly urged upon them; nor was any faith to be kept with heretics: And that for her part, could she find as good a colour, she would willingly bereave all these men of their lives and fortunes.[y] But it is no wise likely, that such expressions ever dropped from this prudent and virtuous princess. On the contrary, it appears, that all these violences were disagreeable to her; that she was in this particular over-ruled by the authority of the French counsellors placed about her; and that she often thought, if the management of those affairs had been entrusted wholly to herself, she could easily, without force, have accommodated all differences.[z]

The congregation, inflamed with their own zeal, and enraged by these disappointments, remained not long in tranquillity. Even before they left Perth, and while as yet they had no colour to complain of any violation of treaty, they had signed a new covenant, in which, besides their engagements to mutual defence, they vowed, in the name of God, to employ their whole power in destroying every thing that dishonoured his holy name; and this covenant was subscribed, among others, by Argyle and the prior of St. Andrews.[a] These two leaders now desired no better pretence for deserting the regent and openly joining their associates, than the complaints, however doubtful, or rather false, of her breach of

[x] Knox, p. 139.   [y] Ibid. Spotswood, p. 123.   [z] See note [C] at the end of the volume.   [a] Keith, p. 89. Knox, p. 138.

promise. The congregation also, encouraged by this accession of force, gave themselves up entirely to the furious zeal of Knox, and renewed at Crail, Anstruther, and other places in Fife, like depredations on the churches and monasteries with those formerly committed at Perth and Couper. The regent, who marched against them with her army, finding their power so much encreased, was glad to conclude a truce for a few days, and to pass over with her forces to the Lothians. The reformers besieged and took Perth; proceeded thence to Stirling, where they exercised their usual fury; and finding nothing able to resist them, they bent their march to Edinburgh, the inhabitants of which, as they had already anticipated the zeal of the congregation against the churches and monasteries, gladly opened their gates to them. The regent, with the few forces which remained with her, took shelter in Dunbar, where she fortified herself, in expectation of a reinforcement from France.

Meanwhile, she employed her partizans in representing to the people the dangerous consequences of this open rebellion; and she endeavoured to convince them, that the lord James, under pretence of religion, had formed the scheme of wresting the sceptre from the hands of the sovereign. By these considerations many were engaged to desert the army of the congregation; but much more by the want of pay or any means of subsistence; and the regent, observing the malcontents to be much weakened, ventured to march to Edinburgh, with a design of suppressing them. On the interposition of the duke of Chatelrault, who still adhered to her, she agreed to a capitulation, in which she granted them a toleration of their religion, and they engaged to commit no farther depredations on the churches. Soon after they evacuated the city; and before they left it, they proclaimed the articles of agreement; but they took care to publish only the articles favourable to themselves, and they were guilty of an imposture, in adding one to the number, namely, that idolatry should not again be erected in any place where it was at that time suppressed.[b]

An agreement, concluded while men were in this disposition, could not be durable; and both sides endeavoured to strengthen themselves as much as possible, against the ensuing rupture,

[b] See note [D] at the end of the volume.

CHAPTER XXXVIII

which appeared inevitable. The regent, having got a reinforcement of 1000 men from France, began to fortify Leith; and the
congregation seduced to their party the duke of Chatelrault, who
had long appeared inclined to join them, and who was at last
determined by the arrival of his son, the earl of Arran, from
France, where he had escaped many dangers, from the jealousy, as
well as bigotry, of Henry and the duke of Guise. More French
troops soon after disembarked under the command of La Brosse,
who was followed by the bishop of Amiens, and three doctors of
the Sorbonne. These last were supplied with store of syllogisms,
authorities, citations, and scholastic arguments, which they intended to oppose to the Scottish preachers, and which, they justly
presumed, would acquire force, and produce conviction, by the
influence of the French arms and artillery.[c]

The constable Montmorency had always opposed the marriage
of the Dauphin with the queen of Scots, and had foretold, that, by
forming such close connexions with Scotland, the ancient league
would be dissolved; and the natives of that kingdom, jealous of a
foreign yoke, would soon become, instead of allies, attached by
interest and inclination, the most inveterate enemies to the French
government. But though the event seemed now to have justified
the prudence of that aged minister, it is not improbable, considering the violent counsels, by which France was governed, that the
insurrection was deemed a favourable event; as affording a pretence, for sending over armies, for entirely subduing the country,
for attainting the rebels,[d] and for preparing means thence to invade England, and support Mary's title to the crown of that kingdom. The leaders of the congregation, well acquainted with these
views, were not insensible of their danger, and saw that their only
safety consisted in the vigour and success of their measures. They
were encouraged by the intelligence received of the sudden death
of Henry II.; and having passed an act from their own authority,
depriving the queen-dowager of the regency, and ordering all the
French troops to evacuate the kingdom, they collected forces to
put their edict in execution against them. They again became
masters of Edinburgh; but found themselves unable to keep long

[c] Spotswood, p. 134. Thuan, lib. xxiv. c. 10.   [d] Forbes, vol. i. p. 139.
Thuan, lib. xxiv. c. 13.

possession of that city. Their tumultuary armies, assembled in haste, and supported by no pay, soon separated upon the least disaster, or even any delay of success; and were incapable of resisting such veteran troops as the French, who were also seconded by some of the Scottish nobility, among whom the earl of Bothwel distinguished himself. Hearing that the marquis of Elbeuf, brother to the regent, was levying an army against them in Germany, they thought themselves excusable for applying, in this extremity, to the assistance of England; and as the sympathy of religion, as well as regard to national liberty, had now counterbalanced the ancient animosity against that kingdom, this measure was the result of inclination, no less than of interest.[e] Maitland of Lidington, therefore, and Robert Melvil, were secretly dispatched by the congregation to solicit succours from Elizabeth.

Interposition of the queen in Scotch affairs.
The wise council of Elizabth did not long deliberate in agreeing to this request, which concurred so well with the views and interests of their mistress. Cecil in particular represented to the queen, that the union of the crowns of Scotland and France, both of them the hereditary enemies of England, was ever regarded as a pernicious event; and her father, as well as protector Somerset, had employed every expedient, both of war and negociation, to prevent it: That the claim, which Mary advanced to the crown, rendered the present situation of England still more dangerous, and demanded, on the part of the queen, the greatest vigilance and precaution: That the capacity, ambition, and exorbitant views of the family of Guise, who now governed the French counsels, were sufficiently known; and they themselves made no secret of their design to place their niece on the throne of England: That deeming themselves secure of success, they had already, somewhat imprudently and prematurely, taken off the mask; and Throgmorton, the English ambassador at Paris, sent over, by every courier, incontestible proofs of their hostile intentions:[f] That they only waited till Scotland should be entirely subdued; and having thus deprived the English of the advantages, resulting from their situation and naval power, they prepared means for subverting the queen's authority: That the zealous catholics in England, discontented with the present government, and satisfied in the legality of

[e] See note [E] at the end of the volume. [f] Forbes, vol. i. p. 134, 136, 149, 150, 159, 165, 181, 194, 229, 231, 235–241, 253.

CHAPTER XXXVIII

Mary's title, would bring them considerable reinforcement, and would disturb every measure of defence against that formidable power: That the only expedient for preventing these designs was to seize the present opportunity, and take advantage of a like zeal in the protestants of Scotland; nor could any doubt be entertained with regard to the justice of a measure, founded on such evident necessity, and directed only to the ends of self-preservation: That though a French war, attended with great expence, seemed the necessary consequence of supporting the malcontents in Scotland, that power, if removed to the continent, would be much less formidable; and a small disbursement at present would in the end be found the greatest frugality: And that the domestic dissentions of France, which every day augmented, together with the alliance of Philip, who, notwithstanding his bigotry and hypocrisy, would never permit the entire conquest of England, were sufficient to secure the queen against the dangerous ambition and resentment of the house of Guise.[g]

Elizabeth's propensity to caution and economy was, though with some difficulty,[h] overcome by these powerful motives; and she prepared herself to support by arms and money the declining affairs of the congregation in Scotland. She equipped a fleet, which consisted of thirteen ships of war; and giving the command of it to Winter, she sent it to the Frith of Forth: She appointed the young duke of Norfolk her lieutenant in the northern counties, and she assembled at Berwic an army of eight thousand men under the command of lord Gray, warden of the east and middle marches. Though the court of France, sensible of the danger, offered her to make immediate restitution of Calais, provided she would not interpose in the affairs of Scotland; she resolutely replied, that she never would put an inconsiderable fishing-town in competition with the safety of her dominions;[i] and she still continued her preparations. She concluded a treaty of mutual defence with the congregation, which was to last during the marriage of the queen of Scots with Francis and a year after; and she promised never to desist till the French had entirely evacuated Scotland.[k] And having thus taken all proper measures for success, and re-

[g] Forbes, vol. i. p. 387. Jebb, vol. i. p. 448. Keith, append. 24.   [h] Forbes, vol. i. p. 454, 460.   [i] Spotswood, p. 146.   [k] Knox, p. 217. Haynes's State Papers, vol. i. p. 153. Rymer, tom. xv. p. 569.

ceived from the Scots six hostages for the performance of articles, she ordered her fleet and army to begin their operations.

1560.
15th
Jan.

The appearance of Elizabeth's fleet in the Frith disconcerted the French army, who were at that time ravaging the county of Fife; and obliged them to make a circuit by Stirling, in order to reach Leith, where they prepared themselves for defence. The English army, reinforced by 5000 Scots,[l] sat down before the place; and after two skirmishes, in the former of which, the English had the advantage, in the latter the French, they began to batter the town; and though repulsed with considerable loss in a rash and ill-conducted assault, they reduced the garrison to great difficulties. Their distress was augmented by two events; the dispersion by a storm of d'Elbeuf's fleet, which carried a considerable army on board,[m] and the death of the queen-regent, who expired about this time in the castle of Edinburgh; a woman endowed with all the capacity which shone forth in her family, but possessed of much more virtue and moderation than appeared in the conduct of the other branches of it. The French, who found it impossible to subsist for want of provisions, and who saw, that the English were

5th
July.

continually reinforced by fresh numbers, were obliged to capitulate: And the bishop of Valence and count Randan, plenipotentiaries from France, signed a treaty at Edinburgh with Cecil and Dr. Wotton, whom Elizabeth had sent thither for that purpose. It

Settle-
ment of
Scotland.

was there stipulated, that the French should instantly evacuate Scotland; that the king and queen of France and Scotland should thenceforth abstain from bearing the arms of England, or assuming the title of that kingdom; that farther satisfaction for the injury already done in that particular should be granted Elizabeth; and that commissioners should meet to settle this point, or if they could not agree, that the king of Spain should be umpire between the crowns. Besides these stipulations, which regarded England, some concessions were granted to the Scots; namely, that an amnesty should be published for all past offences; that none but natives should enjoy any office in Scotland; that the states should name twenty-four persons, of whom the queen of Scots should chuse seven, and the states five, and in the hands of these twelve should the whole administration be placed during their queen's

[l] Haynes, vol. i. p. 256, 259.   [m] Haynes, vol. i. p. 223.

CHAPTER XXXVIII

absence; and that Mary should neither make peace nor war without consent of the states." In order to hasten the execution of this important treaty, Elizabeth sent ships, by which the French forces were transported into their own country.

Thus Europe saw, in the first transaction of this reign, the genius and capacity of the queen and her ministers. She discerned at a distance the danger, which threatened her; and instantly took vigorous measures to prevent it. Making all possible advantages of her situation, she proceeded with celerity to a decision; and was not diverted by any offers, negociations, or remonstrances of the French court. She stopped not till she had brought the matter to a final issue; and had converted that very power, to which her enemies trusted for her destruction, into her firmest support and security. By exacting no improper conditions from the Scottish malcontents even during their greatest distresses, she established an entire confidence with them; and having cemented the union by all the ties of gratitude, interest, and religion, she now possessed an interest over them beyond what remained even with their native sovereign. The regard, which she acquired by this dextrous and spirited conduct, gave her every where, abroad as well as at home, more authority than had attended her sister, though supported by all the power of the Spanish monarchy.º

The subsequent measures of the Scottish reformers tended still more to cement their union with England. Being now entirely masters of the kingdom, they made no farther ceremony or scruple, in fully effecting their purpose. In the treaty of Edinburgh it had been agreed, that a parliament or convention should soon be assembled; and the leaders of the congregation, not waiting till the queen of Scots should ratify that treaty, thought themselves fully entitled, without the sovereign's authority, immediately to summon a parliament. The reformers presented a petition to this assembly; in which they were not contented with desiring the establishment of their doctrine; they also applied for the punishment of the catholics, whom they called vassals to the Roman harlot; and they asserted, that, among all the rabble of the clergy, such is their expression, there was not one lawful minister; but that

---

ⁿ Rymer, vol. xv, p. 593. Keith, p. 137. Spotswood, p. 147. Knox, p. 229.
º Forbes, vol. i. p. 354, 372. Jebb, vol. ii. p. 452.

they were, all of them, thieves and murderers; yea, rebels and traitors to civil authority; and therefore unworthy to be suffered in any reformed commonwealth.[p] The parliament seem to have been actuated by the same spirit of rage and persecution. After ratifying a confession of faith, agreeable to the new doctrines, they passed a statute against the mass, and not only abolished it in all the churches, but enacted, that whoever, any where, either officiated in it or was present at it, should be chastised, for the first offence, with confiscation of goods and corporal punishment, at the discretion of the magistrate; for the second, with banishment; and for the third, with loss of life.[q] A law was also voted for abolishing the papal jurisdiction in Scotland: The presbyterian form of discipline was settled, leaving only at first some shadow of authority to certain ecclesiastics, whom they called Superintendants. The prelates of the ancient faith appeared, in order to complain of great injustice committed on them by the invasion of their property, but the parliament took no notice of them; till at last, these ecclesiastics, tired with fruitless attendance, departed the town. They were then cited to appear; and as nobody presented himself, it was voted by the parliament, that the ecclesiastics were entirely satisfied, and found no reason of complaint.

Sir James Sandilands, prior of St. John, was sent over to France to obtain the ratification of these acts; but was very ill received by Mary, who denied the validity of a parliament, summoned without the royal consent; and she refused her sanction to those statutes. But the protestants gave themselves little concern about their queen's refusal. They immediately put the statutes in execution: They abolished the mass; they settled their ministers; they committed every where furious devastations on the monasteries, and even on the churches, which they thought profaned by idolatry; and deeming the property of the clergy lawful prize, they took possession, without ceremony, of the far greater part of the ecclesiastical revenues. Their new preachers, who had authority sufficient to incite them to war and insurrection, could not restrain their rapacity; and fanaticism concurring with avarice, an incurable wound was given to the papal authority in that country. The protestant nobility and gentry, united by the consciousness of such

[p] Knox, p. 237, 238.   [q] Ibid. p. 254.

unpardonable guilt, alarmed for their new possessions, well acquainted with the imperious character of the house of Guise, saw
no safety for themselves but in the protection of England; and they
dispatched Morton, Glencarne, and Lidington to express their
sincere gratitude to the queen for her past favours, and represent
to her the necessity of continuing them.

Elizabeth, on her part, had equal reason to maintain a union *French*
with the Scottish protestants; and soon found that the house of *affairs.*
Guise, notwithstanding their former disappointments, had not
laid aside the design of contesting her title, and subverting her
authority. Francis and Mary, whose counsels were wholly directed
by them, refused to ratify the treaty of Edinburgh; and showed no
disposition to give her any satisfaction for that mortal affront,
which they had put upon her, by their openly assuming the title
and arms of England. She was sensible of the danger attending
such pretensions; and it was with pleasure she heard of the violent
factions, which prevailed in the French government, and of the
opposition, which had arisen against the measures of the duke of
Guise. That ambitious prince, supported by his four brothers, the
cardinal of Lorraine, the duke of Aumale, the marquis of Elbeuf,
and the grand prior, men no less ambitious than himself, had
engrossed all the authority of the crown; and as he was possessed
of every quality, which could command the esteem or seduce the
affections of men, there appeared no end of his acquisitions and
pretensions. The constable, Montmorency, who had long balanced
his credit, was deprived of all power: The princes of the blood, the
king of Navarre, and his brother, the prince of Condé, were entirely excluded from offices and favour: The queen-mother, herself, Catherine de Medicis, found her influence every day declining: And as Francis, a young prince, infirm both in mind and
body, was wholly governed by his consort, who knew no law but the
pleasure of her uncles, men despaired of ever obtaining freedom
from the dominion of that aspiring family. It was the contests of
religion, which first inspired the French with courage openly to
oppose their unlimited authority.

The theological disputes, first started in the north of Germany,
next in Switzerland, countries at that time wholly illiterate, had
long ago penetrated into France, and as they were assisted by the
general discontent against the court and church of Rome, and by

the zealous spirit of the age, the proselytes to the new religion were secretly encreasing in every province. Henry II. in imitation of his father Francis, had opposed the progress of the reformers; and though a prince addicted to pleasure and society, he was transported by a vehemence, as well as bigotry, which had little place in the conduct of his predecessor. Rigorous punishments had been inflicted on the most eminent of the protestant party; and a point of honour seemed to have arisen, whether the one sect could exercise, or the other suffer most barbarity. The death of Henry put some stop to the persecutions; and the people, who had admired the constancy of the new preachers, now heard with favour their doctrines and arguments. But the cardinal of Lorraine, as well as his brothers, who were possessed of the legal authority, thought it their interest to support the established religion; and when they revived the execution of the penal statutes, they necessarily drove the malcontent princes and nobles to embrace the protection of the new religion. The king of Navarre, a man of mild dispositions, but of a weak character, and the prince of Condé, who possessed many great qualities, having declared themselves in favour of the protestants, that sect acquired new force from their countenance; and the admiral, Coligni, with his brother Andelot, no longer scrupled to make open profession of their communion. The integrity of the admiral, who was believed sincere in his attachment to the new doctrine, and his great reputation both for valour and conduct, for the arts of peace as well as of war, brought credit to the reformers; and after a frustrated attempt of the malcontents to seize the king's person at Amboise, of which Elizabeth had probably some intelligence,[r] every place was full of distraction, and matters hastened to an open rupture between the parties. But the house of Guise, though these factions had obliged them to remit their efforts in Scotland, and had been one chief cause of Elizabeth's success, were determined not to relinquish their authority in France, or yield to the violence of their enemies. They found an opportunity of seizing the king of Navarre and the prince of Condé; they threw the former into prison; they obtained a

---

[r] Forbes, vol. i. p. 214. Throgmorton, about this time, unwilling to entrust to letters the great secrets committed to him, obtained leave, under some pretext, to come over to London.

CHAPTER XXXVIII

sentence of death against the latter; and they were proceeding to put the sentence in execution, when the king's sudden death saved the noble prisoner, and interrupted the prosperity of the duke of Guise. The queen-mother was appointed regent to her son Charles IX. now in his minority: The king of Navarre was named lieutenant-general of the kingdom: The sentence against Condé was annulled: The constable was recalled to court: And the family of Guise, though they still enjoyed great offices and great power, found a counterpoise to their authority.

4th Dec. 1561.

Elizabeth was determined to make advantage of these events against the queen of Scots, whom she still regarded as a dangerous rival. She saw herself freed from the perils attending a union of Scotland with France, and from the pretensions of so powerful a prince as Francis; but she considered, at the same time, that the English catholics, who were numerous, and who were generally prejudiced in favour of Mary's title, would now adhere to that princess with more zealous attachment, when they saw, that her succession no longer endangered the liberties of the kingdom, and was rather attended with the advantage of effecting an entire union with Scotland. She gave orders, therefore, to her ambassador, Throgmorton, a vigilant and able minister, to renew his applications to the queen of Scots, and to require her ratification of the treaty of Edinburgh. But though Mary had desisted, after her husband's death, from bearing the arms and title of queen of England, she still declined gratifying Elizabeth in this momentous article; and being swayed by the ambitious suggestions of her uncles, she refused to make any formal renunciation of her pretensions.

Meanwhile, the queen-mother of France, who imputed to Mary all the mortifications, which she had met with during Francis's life-time, took care to retaliate on her by like injuries; and the queen of Scots, finding her abode in France disagreeable, began to think of returning to her native country. Lord James, who had been sent in deputation from the states to invite her over, seconded these intentions; and she applied to Elizabeth, by D'Oisel, for a safe conduct, in case she should be obliged to pass through England:[s] But she received for answer, that, till she had given

[s] Goodall, vol. i. p. 175.

satisfaction, by ratifying the treaty of Edinburgh, she could expect no favour from a person, whom she had so much injured. This denial excited her indignation; and she made no scruple of expressing her sentiments to Throgmorton, when he reiterated his applications to gratify his mistress in a demand, which he represented as so reasonable. Having cleared the room of her attendants, she said to him; "How weak I may prove, or how far a woman's fraility may transport me, I cannot tell: However, I am resolved not to have so many witnesses of my infirmity as your mistress had at her audience of my ambassador D'Oisel. There is nothing disturbs me so much, as the having asked, with so much importunity, a favour which it was of no consequence for me to obtain. I can, with God's leave, return to my own country without *her* leave; as I came to France, in spite of all the opposition of her brother, king Edward: Neither do I want friends both able and willing to conduct me home, as they have brought me hither; though I was desirous rather to make an experiment of your mistress's friendship than of the assistance of any other person. I have often heard you say, that a good correspondence between her and myself would conduce much to the security and happiness of both our kingdoms: Were she well convinced of this truth, she would hardly have denied me so small a request. But, perhaps, she bears a better inclination to my rebellious subjects than to me, their sovereign, her equal in royal dignity, her near relation, and the undoubted heir of her kingdoms. Besides her friendship, I ask nothing at her hands: I neither trouble her, nor concern myself in the affairs of her state: Not that I am ignorant, that there are now in England a great many malcontents, who are no friends to the present establishment. She is pleased to upbraid me as a person little experienced in the world: I freely own it; but age will cure that defect. However, I am already old enough to acquit myself honestly and courteously to my friends and relations, and to encourage no reports of your mistress, which would misbecome a queen and her kinswoman. I would also say, by her leave, that I am a queen as well as she, and not altogether friendless: And, perhaps, I have as great a soul too; so that methinks we should be upon a level in our treatment of each other. As soon as I have consulted the states of my kingdom, I shall be ready to give her a reasonable answer; and I am the more intent on my journey, in order to make the quicker dispatch in this affair. But she, it seems, intends to stop my journey; so that either she will not let me give her satisfaction, or is resolved not to be satisfied; perhaps, on purpose to keep up the disagreement between us. She has often reproached me with my being young; and I must be very young, indeed, and as ill advised, to treat of matters of such great concern and importance, without the advice of my parliament. I have not been wanting in all friendly offices to her; but she disbelieves or overlooks them. I could heartily wish, that I were,as nearly allied to her in affection as in blood: For that, indeed, would be a most valuable alliance."[l]

Such a spirited reply, notwithstanding the obliging terms interspersed in it, was but ill fitted to conciliate friendship between these rival princesses, or cure those mutual jealousies which had already taken place. Elizabeth equipped a fleet, on pretence of pursuing pyrates, but probably with an intention of intercepting the queen of Scots in her return homewards. Mary embarked at Calais; and passing the English fleet in a fog, arrived safely at Leith, attended by her three uncles, the duke of Aumale, the grand prior, and the marquess of Elbeuf, together with the marquess of Damville, and other French courtiers. This change of abode and situation was very little agreeable to that princess. Besides her natural prepossessions in favour of a country in which she had been educated from her earliest infancy, and where she had borne so high a rank, she could not forbear both regretting the society of that people, so celebrated for their humane disposition, and their respectful attachment to their sovereign, and reflecting on the disparity of the scene which lay before her. It is said, that, after she was embarked at Calais, she kept her eyes fixed on the coast of France, and never turned them from that beloved object, till darkness fell, and intercepted it from her view. She then ordered a couch to be spread for her in the open air; and charged the pilot, that, if in the morning the land were still in sight, he should awake her, and afford her one parting view of that country, in which all her affections were centered. The weather proved calm, so that the ship made little way in the night-time: And Mary had once more an opportunity of seeing the French coast. She sat up on her couch, and still looking towards the land, often repeated these words: "Farewell, France, farewell; I shall never see thee more."[u]

19th Aug. Arrival of Mary in Scotland.

---

[l] Caballa, p. 374. Spotswood, p. 177.   [u] Keith, p. 179. Jebb, vol. ii. p. 483.

The first aspect, however, of things in Scotland was more favour-able, if not to her pleasure and happiness, at least to her repose and security, than she had reason to apprehend. No sooner did the French gallies appear off Leith, than people of all ranks, who had long expected their arrival, flocked towards the shore, with an earnest impatience to behold and receive their young sovereign. Some were led by duty, some by interest, some by curiosity; and all combined to express their attachment to her, and to insinuate themselves into her confidence, on the commencement of her administration. She had now reached her nineteenth year; and the bloom of her youth and amiable beauty of her person were farther recommended by the affability of her address, the politeness of her manners, and the elegance of her genius. Well accomplished in all the superficial, but engaging graces of a court, she afforded, when better known, still more promising indications of her character; and men prognosticated both humanity from her soft and obliging deportment, and penetration from her taste in all the refined arts of music, eloquence, and poetry.[w] And as the Scots had long been deprived of the presence of their sovereign, whom they once de-spaired ever more to behold among them, her arrival seemed to give universal satisfaction; and nothing appeared about the court, but symptoms of affection, joy, and festivity.

The first measures, which Mary embraced, confirmed all the prepossessions entertained in her favour. She followed the advice given her in France by D'Oisel and the bishop of Amiens, as well as her uncles; and she bestowed her confidence entirely on the leaders of the reformed party, who had greatest influence over the people, and who, she found, were alone able to support her gov-ernment. Her brother, lord James, whom she soon after created earl of Murray, obtained the chief authority; and after him Lid-ington, secretary of state, a man of great sagacity, had a principal share in her confidence. By the vigour of these men's measures she endeavoured to establish order and justice in a country, divided by public factions and private feuds; and that fierce, intractable peo-ple, unacquainted with laws and obedience, seemed, for a time, to submit peaceably to her gentle and prudent administration.

---

[w] Buchan, lib. xvii. c. 9. Spotswood, p. 178, 179. Keith, p. 180. Thuan, lib. xxix. c. 2.

CHAPTER XXXVIII

But there was one circumstance, which blasted all these promising appearances, and bereaved Mary of that general favour,
which her agreeable manners and judicious deportment gave her
just reason to expect. She was still a papist; and though she published, soon after her arrival, a proclamation, enjoining every one
to submit to the established religion, the preachers and their adherents could neither be reconciled to a person polluted with so
great an abomination, nor lay aside their jealousies of her future
conduct. It was with great difficulty she could obtain permission
for saying mass in her own chapel; and had not the people apprehended, that, if she had here met with a refusal, she would instantly have returned to France, the zealots never would have
granted her even that small indulgence. The cry was, "Shall we
suffer that idol to be again erected within the realm?" It was
asserted in the pulpit, that one mass was more terrible than
ten thousand armed men landed to invade the kingdom:[x] Lord
Lindesey, and the gentlemen of Fife, exclaimed, "That the idolater
should die the death;" such was their expression. One that carried
tapers for the ceremony of that worship, was attacked and insulted
in the court of the palace. And if lord James, and some popular
leaders, had not interposed, the most dangerous uproar was justly
apprehended, from the ungoverned fury of the multitude.[y] The
usual prayers in the churches were to this purpose: That God
would turn the queen's heart, which was obstinate against him
and his truth; or if his holy will be otherwise, that he would
strengthen the hearts and *hands* of the elect, stoutly to oppose the
rage of all tyrants.[z] Nay, it was openly called in question, whether
that princess, being an idolatress, was entitled to any authority,
even in civil matters?[a]

The helpless queen was every moment exposed to contumely,
which she bore with benignity and patience. Soon after her arrival
she dined in the castle of Edinburgh; and it was there contrived,
that a boy, six years of age, should be let down from the roof,
and should present her with a bible, a psalter, and the keys of the
castle. Lest she should be at a loss to understand this insult on her
as a papist; all the decorations expressed the burning of Corah,

[x] Knox, p. 287.   [y] Ibid. p. 284, 285, 287. Spotswood, p. 179.   [z] Keith,
p. 179.   [a] Ibid. p. 202.

Dathan, and Abiram, and other punishments inflicted by God upon idolatry.[b] The town council of Edinburgh had the assurance, from their own authority, to issue a proclamation banishing from their district, "all the wicked rabble of antichrist, the pope, such as priests, monks, friars, together with adulterers and fornicators."[c] And because the privy-council suspended the magistrates for their insolence, the passionate historians[d] of that age have inferred, that the queen was engaged, by a sympathy of manners, to take adulterers and fornicators under her protection. It appears probable, that the magistrates were afterwards reinstated in their office, and that their proclamation was confirmed.[e]

But all the insolence of the people was inconsiderable in comparison of that which was exercised by the clergy and the preachers, who took a pride in vilifying, even to her face, this amiable princess. The assembly of the church framed an address, in which, after telling her, that her mass was a bastard service of God, the fountain of all impiety, and the source of every evil which abounded in the realm; they expressed their hopes, that she would, ere this time, have preferred truth to her own preconceived opinion, and have renounced her religion, which, they assured her, was nothing but abomination and vanity. They said, that the present abuses of government were so enormous, that, if a speedy remedy were not provided, God would not fail in his anger to strike the head and the tail, the disobedient prince and sinful people. They required, that severe punishment should be inflicted on adulterers and fornicators. And they concluded with demanding for themselves some addition both of power and property.[f]

The ringleader in all these insults on majesty was John Knox; who possessed an uncontrouled authority in the church, and even in the civil affairs of the nation, and who triumphed in the contumelious usage of his sovereign. His usual appellation for the queen was Jezabel; and though she endeavoured, by the most gracious condescension, to win his favour, all her insinuations could gain nothing on his obdurate heart. She promised him access to her whenever he demanded it; and she even desired him, if he found her blameable in any thing, to reprehend her freely in

[b] Ibid. p. 189.   [c] Ibid. p. 192.   [d] Knox, p. 292. Buchan, lib. xvii. c. 20. Haynes, vol. i. p. 372.   [e] Keith, p. 202.   [f] Knox, p. 311, 312.

CHAPTER XXXVIII

private, rather than vilify her in the pulpit before the whole people: But he plainly told her, that he had a public ministry entrusted
to him; that if she would come to church, she should there hear the
gospel of truth; and that it was not his business to apply to every
individual, nor had he leisure for that occupation.[g] The political
principles of the man, which he communicated to his brethren,
were as full of sedition as his theological were of rage and bigotry.
Though he once condescended so far as to tell the queen, that he
would submit to her, in the same manner as Paul did to Nero;[h] he
remained not long in this dutiful strain. He said to her, that "Sam-
uel feared not to slay Agag, the fat and delicate king of Amalek,
whom king Saul had saved: Neither spared Elias Jezabel's false
prophets, and Baal's priests, though King Ahab was present. Phi-
neas," added he, "was no magistrate; yet feared he not to strike
Cosbie and Zimri in the very act of filthy fornication. And so,
Madam, your grace may see, that others than chief magistrates
may lawfully inflict punishment on such crimes as are condemned
by the law of God."[i] Knox had formerly, during the reign of Mary
of England, written a book against female succession to the crown:
The title of it is, *The first blast of the trumpet against the monstrous
regimen of women*. He was too proud either to recant the tenets of
this book, or even to apologize for them; and his conduct shewed,
that he thought no more civility than loyalty due to any of the
female sex.

The whole life of Mary was, from the demeanour of these men,
filled with bitterness and sorrow. This rustic apostle scruples not,
in his history, to inform us, that he once treated her with such
severity, that she lost all command of temper, and dissolved in
tears before him: Yet so far from being moved with youth, and
beauty, and royal dignity reduced to that condition, he persevered
in his insolent reproofs; and when he relates this incident, he
discovers a visible pride and satisfaction in his own conduct.[k] The
pulpits had become mere scenes of railing against the vices of
the court; among which were always noted as the principal, feasting, finery, dancing, balls, and whoredom, their necessary attendant.[l] Some ornaments, which the ladies at that time wore upon

[g] Knox, p. 310.   [h] Ibid. p. 288.   [i] Ibid. p. 326.   [k] Knox, p. 332, 333.
[l] Ibid. p. 322.

their petticoats, excited mightily the indignation of the preachers; and they affirmed, that such vanity would provoke God's vengeance, not only against these foolish women, but against the whole realm.[m]

Mary, whose age, condition, and education invited her to liberty and cheerfulness, was curbed in all amusements, by the absurd severity of these reformers; and she found every moment reason to regret her leaving that country, from whose manners she had in her early youth received the first impressions.[n] Her two uncles, the duke of Aumale, and the grand prior, with the other French nobility, soon took leave of her: The marquis of Elbeuf remained some time longer; but after his departure, she was left to the society of her own subjects; men unacquainted with the pleasures of conversation, ignorant of arts and civility, and corrupted, beyond their usual rusticity, by a dismal fanaticism, which rendered them incapable of all humanity or improvement. Though Mary had made no attempt to restore the ancient religion, her popery was a sufficient crime: Though her behaviour was hitherto irreproachable, and her manners sweet and engaging, her gaiety and ease were interpreted as signs of dissolute vanity: And to the harsh and preposterous usage, which this princess met with, may, in part, be ascribed those errors of her subsequent conduct, which seemed so little of a piece with the general tenor of her character.

There happened to the marquis of Elbeuf, before his departure, an adventure, which, though frivolous, might enable him to give Mary's friends in France a melancholy idea of her situation. This nobleman, with the earl of Bothwel, and some other young courtiers, had been engaged, after a debauch, to pay a visit to a woman called Alison Craig, who was known to be liberal of her favours; and because they were denied admittance, they broke the windows, thrust open the door, and committed some disorders, in searching for the damsel. It happened, that the assembly of the church was sitting at that time, and they immediately took the matter under their cognizance. In conjunction with several of the nobility, they presented an address to the queen, which was introduced with this awful prelude. "To the queen's majesty, and to her secret and great council, her grace's faithful and obedient subjects,

---

[m] Ibid. p. 330.   [n] Ibid. p. 294.

CHAPTER XXXVIII

the professors of Christ Jesus's holy evangil, with the spirit of righteous judgment." The tenor of the petition was, that the fear of God, the duty which they owed her grace, and the terrible threatenings, denounced by God against every city or country where horrible crimes were openly committed, compelled them to demand the severe punishment of such as had done what in them lay to kindle the wrath of God against the whole realm: That the iniquity, of which they complained, was so heinous and so horrible, that they should esteem themselves accomplices in it, if they had been engaged by worldly fear, or servile complaisance, to pass it over in silence, or bury it in oblivion: That as they owed her grace obedience in the administration of justice, so were they entitled to require of her, in return, the sharp and condign punishment of this enormity, which, they repeated it, might draw down the vengeance of God on the whole kingdom: And that they maintained it to be her duty to lay aside all private affections towards the actors in so heinous a crime, and so enormous a villany, and without delay bring them to a trial, and inflict the severest penalties upon them. The queen gave a gracious reception to this peremptory address; but because she probably thought, that breaking the windows of a brothel merited not such severe reprehension, she only replied, that her uncle was a stranger, and that he was attended by a young company: But she would put such order to him and to all others, that her subjects should henceforth have no reason to complain. Her passing over this incident so slightly was the source of great discontent, and was regarded as a proof of the most profligate manners.[o] It is not to be omitted, that Alison Craig, the cause of all the uproar, was known to entertain a commerce with the earl of Arran, who, on account of his great zeal for the reformation, was, without scruple, indulged in that enormity.[p]

Some of the populace of Edinburgh broke into the queen's chapel during her absence, and committed outrages; for which two of them were indicted, and it was intended to bring them to a trial. Knox wrote circular letters to the most considerable zealots of the party, and charged them to appear in town, and protect their brethren. The holy sacraments, he there said, are abused by profane papists; the mass has been said; and in worshipping that idol,

[o] Knox, p. 302, 303, 304. Keith, p. 509.   [p] Knox, Ibid.

the priests have omitted no ceremony, not even the conjuring of
their accursed water, that had ever been practised in the time of
the greatest blindness. These violent measures for opposing justice
were little short of rebellion; and Knox was summoned before the
council to answer for his offence. The courage of the man was
equal to his insolence. He scrupled not to tell the queen, that the
pestilent papists, who had inflamed her against these holy men,
were the sons of the devil; and must therefore obey the directions
of their father, who had been a liar and a manslayer from the
beginning. The matter ended with the full acquittal of Knox.[q]
Randolph, the English ambassador in Scotland, had reason to
write to Cecil, speaking of the Scottish nation: "I think marvelously
of the wisdom of God, that gave this unruly, inconstant, and cum-
bersome people no more power nor substance: For they would
otherwise run wild."[r]

We have related these incidents at greater length, than the
necessity of our subject may seem to require: But even trivial
circumstances, which show the manners of the age, are often more
instructive, as well as entertaining, than the great transactions of
wars and negociations, which are nearly similar in all periods and
in all countries of the world.

The reformed clergy in Scotland had, at that time, a very natural reason for their ill-humour, namely, the poverty or rather
beggary, to which they were reduced. The nobility and gentry had
at first laid their hands on all the property of the regular clergy,
without making any provision for the friars and nuns, whom they
turned out of their possessions. The secular clergy of the catholic
communion, though they lost all ecclesiastical jurisdiction, still
held some of the temporalities of their benefices; and either became laymen themselves, and converted them into private property, or made conveyance of them at low prices to the nobility, who
thus enriched themselves by the plunder of the church. The new
teachers had hitherto subsisted chiefly by the voluntary oblations
of the faithful; and in a poor country, divided in religious sentiments, this establishment was regarded as very scanty and very
precarious. Repeated applications were made for a legal settlement to the preachers; and though almost every thing in the

[q] Knox, p. 336, 342.   [r] Keith, p. 202.

CHAPTER XXXVIII

kingdom was governed by their zeal and caprice, it was with difficulty that their request was at last complied with. The fanatical
spirit which they indulged, and their industry in decrying the
principles and practices of the Romish communion, which placed
such merit in enriching the clergy, proved now a very sensible
obstacle to their acquisitions. The convention, however, passed a
vote,[s] by which they divided all the ecclesiastical benefices into
twenty-one shares: They assigned fourteen to the ancient pos-
sessors: Of the remaining seven they granted three to the crown;
and if that were found to answer the public expences, they bestowed the overplus on the reformed ministers. The queen was
empowered to levy all the seven; and it was ordained, that she
should afterwards pay to the clergy what should be judged to
suffice for their maintenance. The necessities of the crown, the
rapacity of the courtiers, and the small affection which Mary bore
to the protestant ecclesiastics, rendered their revenues contemptible as well as uncertain; and the preachers, finding that they could
not rival the gentry, or even the middling rank of men, in opulence
and plenty, were necessitated to betake themselves to other expedients for supporting their authority. They affected a furious zeal
for religion, morose manners, a vulgar and familiar, yet mysterious cant; and though the liberality of subsequent princes
put them afterwards on a better footing with regard to revenue,
and thereby corrected in some degree those bad habits; it must be
confessed, that, while many other advantages attend presbyterian
government, these inconveniences are not easily separated from
the genius of that ecclesiastical polity.

The queen of Scots, destitute of all force, possessing a narrow
revenue, surrounded with a factious turbulent nobility, a bigotted
people, and insolent ecclesiastics, soon found, that her only expedient for maintaining tranquillity was to preserve a good correspondence with[t] Elizabeth, who, by former connexions and services,
had acquired such authority over all these ranks of men. Soon after
her arrival in Scotland, secretary Lidington was sent to London, in
order to pay her compliments to the queen, and express her desire
of friendship and a good correspondence; and he received a commission from her, as well as from the nobility of Scotland, to de-

---

[s] Knox, p. 296. Keith, p. 210.   [t] Jebb, vol. ii. p. 456.

mand, as a means of cementing this friendship, that Mary should,
by act of parliament or by proclamation (for the difference between these securities was not then deemed very considerable) be
declared successor to the crown. No request could be more unreasonable, or made at a more improper juncture. The queen replied,
that Mary had once discovered her intention not to wait for the
succession, but had openly, without ceremony or reserve, assumed
the title of queen of England, and had pretended a superior right
to her throne and kingdom: That though her ambassadors, and
those of her husband, the French king, had signed a treaty, in
which they renounced that claim, and promised satisfaction for so
great an indignity, she was so intoxicated with this imaginary right,
that she had rejected the most earnest solicitations, and even, as
some endeavoured to persuade her, had incurred some danger in
crossing the seas, rather than ratify that equitable treaty: That her
partizans every where had still the assurance to insist on her title,
and had presumed to talk of her own birth as illegitimate: That
while affairs were on this footing; while a claim thus openly made,
so far from being openly renounced, was only suspended till a
more favourable opportunity, it would in her be the most egregious imprudence to fortify the hands of a pretender to her crown,
by declaring her the successor: That no expedient could be worse
imagined for cementing friendship than such a declaration; and
kings were often found to bear no good will to their successors,
even though their own children; much more when the connexion
was less intimate, and when such cause of disgust and jealousy had
already been given, and indeed was still continued, on the part of
Mary: That though she was willing, from the amity which she bore
her kinswoman, to ascribe her former pretensions to the advice of
others, by whose direction she was then governed; her present
refusal to relinquish them could proceed only from her own prepossessions, and was a proof that she still harboured some dangerous designs against her: That it was the nature of all men to be
disgusted with the present, to entertain flattering views of futurity,
to think their services ill rewarded, to expect a better recompence
from the successor; and she should esteem herself scarcely half a
sovereign over the English, if they saw her declare her heir, and
arm her rival with authority against her own repose and safety:
That she knew the inconstant nature of the people; she was ac-

quainted with the present divisions in religion; she was not ignorant, that the same party, which expected greater favour during
the reign of Mary, did also imagine, that the title of that princess
was superior to her own: That for her part, whatever claims were
advanced, she was determined to live and die queen of England;
and after her death, it was the business of others to examine who
had the best pretensions, either by the laws or by right of blood, to
the succession: That she hoped the claim of the queen of Scots
would then be found solid; and considering the injury, which she
herself had received, it was sufficient indulgence, if she promised,
in the mean time, to do nothing which might, in any respect,
weaken or invalidate it: And that Mary, if her title were really
preferable, a point, which, for her own part, she had never enquired into, possessed all advantages above her rivals; who, destitute both of present power, and of all support by friends, would
only expose themselves to inevitable ruin, by advancing any weak,
or even doubtful pretensions."

These views of the queen were so prudent and judicious, that
there was no likelihood of her ever departing from them: But that
she might put the matter to a fuller proof, she offered to explain
the words of the treaty of Edinburgh, so as to leave no suspicion of
their excluding Mary's right of succession;" and in this form, she
again required her to ratify that treaty. Matters at last came to this
issue, that Mary agreed to the proposal, and offered to renounce
all present pretensions to the crown of England, provided Elizabeth would agree to declare her the successor.* But such was the
jealous character of this latter princess, that she never would consent to strengthen the interest and authority of any claimant, by
fixing the succession; much less would she make this concession in
favour of a rival queen, who possessed such plausible pretensions
for the present, and who, though she might verbally renounce
them, could easily resume her claim on the first opportunity.
Mary's proposal, however, bore so specious an appearance of
equity and justice, that Elizabeth, sensible that reason would, by
superficial thinkers, be deemed to lie entirely on that side, made no
more mention of the matter; and though farther concessions were

" Buchanan, lib. xvii. c. 14–17. Camden, p. 385. Spotswood, p. 180, 181.
" Ibid. p. 181.   * Haynes, vol. i. p. 377.

never made by either princess, they put on all the appearances of a cordial reconciliation and friendship with each other.

Wise govern-ment of Elizabeth. The queen observed, that, even without her interposition, Mary was sufficiently depressed by the mutinous spirit of her own subjects; and instead of giving Scotland, for the present, any inquietude or disturbance, she employed herself, more usefully and laudably, in regulating the affairs of her own kingdom, and promoting the happiness of her people. She made some progress in paying those great debts which lay upon the crown; she regulated the coin, which had been much debased by her predecessors; she furnished her arsenals with great quantities of arms from Germany and other places; engaged her nobility and gentry to imitate her example in this particular; introduced into the kingdom the art of making gun-powder and brass cannon; fortified her frontiers on the side of Scotland; made frequent reviews of the militia; encouraged agriculture by allowing a free exportation of corn; promoted trade and navigation; and so much encreased the shipping of her kingdom, both by building vessels of force herself, and suggesting like undertakings to the merchants, that she was justly stiled the restorer of naval glory, and the queen of the northern seas.[y] The natural frugality of her temper, so far from incapacitating her from these great enterprizes, only enabled her to execute them with greater certainty and success; and all the world saw in her conduct the happy effects of a vigorous perseverance in judicious and well concerted projects.

It is easy to imagine, that so great a princess, who enjoyed such singular felicity and renown, would receive proposals of marriage from every one, that had any likelihood of succeeding; and though she had made some public declarations in favour of a single life, few believed, that she would persevere for ever in that resolution. The archduke Charles, second son of the emperor,[z] as well as Casimir, son of the elector Palatine, made applications to her; and as this latter prince professed the reformed religion, he thought himself, on that account, better entitled to succeed in his addresses. Eric, king of Sweden, and Adolph, duke of Holstein, were encouraged by the same views to become suitors: And the earl of Arran, heir to the crown of Scotland, was, by the states of that

[y] Camden, p. 388. Strype, vol. i. p. 230, 336, 337.   [z] Haynes, vol. i. p. 233.

kingdom, recommended to her as a suitable marriage. Even some of her own subjects, though they did not openly declare their pretensions, entertained hopes of success. The earl of Arundel, a person declining in years, but descended from an ancient and noble family, as well as possessed of great riches, flattered himself with this prospect; as did also Sir William Pickering, a man much esteemed for his personal merit. But the person most likely to succeed, was a younger son of the late duke of Northumberland, lord Robert Dudley, who, by means of his exterior qualities, joined to address and flattery, had become, in a manner, her declared favourite, and had great influence in all her counsels. The less worthy he appeared of this distinction, the more was his great favour ascribed to some violent affection, which could thus seduce the judgment of this penetrating princess; and men long expected, that he would obtain the preference above so many princes and monarchs. But the queen gave all these suitors a gentle refusal, which still encouraged their pursuit; and she thought, that she should the better attach them to her interests, if they were still allowed to entertain hopes of succeeding in their pretensions. It is also probable, that this policy was not entirely free from a mixture of female coquetry; and that, though she was determined in her own mind never to share her power with any man, she was not displeased with the courtship, solicitation, and professions of love, which the desire of acquiring so valuable a prize procured her from all quarters.

What is most singular in the conduct and character of Elizabeth, is, that, though she determined never to have any heir of her own body, she was not only very averse to fix any successor to the crown; but seems also to have resolved, as far as it lay in her power, that no one, who had pretensions to the succession, should ever have any heirs or successors. If the exclusion given by the will of Henry VIII. to the posterity of Margaret, queen of Scotland, was allowed to be valid, the right to the crown devolved on the house of Suffolk; and the lady Catharine Gray, younger sister to the lady Jane, was now the heir of that family. This lady had been married to lord Herbert, son of the earl of Pembroke; but having been divorced from that nobleman, she had made a private marriage with the earl of Hertford, son of the protector; and her husband, soon after consummation, travelled into France. In a little time she

appeared to be pregnant, which so enraged Elizabeth, that she
threw her into the Tower, and summoned Hertford to appear, in
order to answer for his misdemeanor. He made no scruple of
acknowledging the marriage, which, though concluded without
the queen's consent, was entirely suitable to both parties; and for
this offence he was also committed to the Tower. Elizabeth's severity stopped not here: She issued a commission to enquire into the
matter; and as Hertford could not, within the time limited, prove
the nuptials by witnesses, the commerce between him and his
consort was declared unlawful, and their posterity illegitimate.
They were still detained in custody; but by bribing their keepers,
they found means to have farther intercourse; and another child
appeared to be the fruit of their commerce. This was a fresh source
of vexation to the queen; who made a fine of fifteen thousand
pounds be set on Hertford by the star-chamber, and ordered his
confinement to be thenceforth more rigid and severe. He lay in
this condition for nine years, till the death of his wife, by freeing
Elizabeth from all fears, procured him his liberty.[a] This extreme
severity must be accounted for, either by the unrelenting jealousy
of the queen, who was afraid lest a pretender to the succession
should acquire credit by having issue; or by her malignity, which,
with all her great qualities, made one ingredient in her character,
and which led her to envy in others those natural pleasures of love
and posterity, of which her own ambition and desire of dominion
made her renounce all prospect for herself.

There happened, about this time, some other events in the
royal family, where the queen's conduct was more laudable:
Arthur Pole, and his brother, nephews to the late cardinal, and
descended from the duke of Clarence, together with Anthony
Fortescue, who had married a sister of these gentlemen, and some
other persons, were brought to their trial for intending to withdraw into France, with a view of soliciting succours from the
duke of Guise, of returning thence into Wales, and of proclaiming
Mary queen of England, and Arthur Pole duke of Clarence. They
confessed the indictment, but asserted, that they never meant
to execute these projects during the queen's life-time: They had
only deemed such precautions requisite in case of her demise,

[a] Haynes, vol. i. p. 369, 378, 396. Camden, p. 389. Heylin, p. 154.

which, some pretenders to judicial astrology had assured them, they might with certainty look for before the year expired. They were condemned by the jury; but received a pardon from the queen's clemency.[b]

[b] Strype, vol. i. p. 333. Heylin, p. 154.

XXXIX

*State of Europe – Civil wars of
France – Havre de Grace put in possession
of the English – A parliament – Havre lost –
Affairs of Scotland – The queen
of Scots marries the earl of Darnley –
Confederacy against the protestants –
Murder of Rizzio – A parliament –
Murder of Darnley – Queen of Scots marries
Bothwel – Insurrection in Scotland –
Imprisonment of Mary – Mary flies into England –
Conferences at York and Hampton Court*

1562.
State of
Europe.
AFTER THE COMMENCEMENT of the religious wars in France,
which rendered that flourishing kingdom, during the course
of near forty years, a scene of horror and devastation, the great
rival powers in Europe were Spain and England; and it was not
long before an animosity, first political, then personal, broke out
between the sovereigns of these countries.

Philip II. of Spain, though he reached not any enlarged views
of policy, was endowed with great industry and sagacity, a remarkable caution in his enterprizes, an unusual foresight in all his
measures; and as he was ever cool and seemingly unmoved by
passion, and possessed neither talents nor inclination for war, both

his subjects and his neighbours had reason to expect justice, happiness, and tranquillity, from his administration. But prejudices had on him as pernicious effects as ever passion had on any other monarch; and the spirit of bigotry and tyranny, by which he was actuated, with the fraudulent maxims which governed his counsels, excited the most violent agitation among his own people, engaged him in acts of the most enormous cruelty, and threw all Europe into combustion.

After Philip had concluded peace at Cateau-Cambresis, and had remained some time in the Netherlands, in order to settle the affairs of that country, he embarked for Spain; and as the gravity of that nation, with their respectful obedience to their prince, had appeared more agreeable to his humour, than the homely familiar manners, and the pertinacious liberty of the Flemings, it was expected, that he would for the future reside altogether at Madrid, and would govern all his extensive dominions by Spanish ministers and Spanish counsels. Having met with a violent tempest on his voyage, he no sooner arrived in harbour, than he fell on his knees; and after giving thanks for his deliverance, he vowed, that his life, which was thus providentially saved, should thenceforth be entirely devoted to the extirpation of heresy.[c] His subsequent conduct corresponded to these professions. Finding that the new doctrines had penetrated into Spain, he let loose the rage of persecution against all who professed them, or were suspected of adhering to them; and by his violence he gave new edge, even to the usual cruelty of priests and inquisitors. He threw into prison Constantine Ponce, who had been confessor to his father, the emperor Charles; who had attended him during his retreat; and in whose arms that great monarch had terminated his life: And after this ecclesiastic died in confinement, he still ordered him to be tried and condemned for heresy, and his statue to be committed to the flames. He even deliberated, whether he should not exercise like severity against the memory of his father, who was suspected, during his later years, to have indulged a propensity towards the Lutheran principles: In his unrelenting zeal for orthodoxy, he spared neither age, sex, nor condition: He was present, with an inflexible countenance, at the most barbarous executions: He is-

[c] Thuanus, lib. xxiii. cap. 14.

sued rigorous orders, for the prosecution of heretics, in Spain, Italy, the Indies, and the Low Countries: And having founded his determined tyranny on maxims of civil policy, as well as on principles of religion, he made it apparent to all his subjects, that there was no method, except the most entire compliance, or most obstinate resistance, to escape or elude the severity of his vengeance.

During that extreme animosity, which prevailed between the adherents of the opposite religions, the civil magistrate, who found it difficult, if not impossible, for the same laws to govern such enraged adversaries, was naturally led, by specious rules of prudence, in embracing one party, to declare war against the other, and to exterminate, by fire and sword, those bigots, who, from abhorrence of his religion, had proceeded to an opposition of his power, and to a hatred of his person. If any prince possessed such enlarged views as to foresee, that a mutual toleration would in time abate the fury of religious prejudices, he yet met with difficulties in reducing this principle to practice; and might deem the malady too violent to await a remedy, which, though certain, must necessarily be slow in its operation. But Philip, though a profound hypocrite, and extremely governed by self-interest, seems also to have been himself actuated by an imperious bigotry; and as he employed great reflection in all his conduct, he could easily palliate the gratification of his natural temper under the colour of wisdom, and find in this system no less advantage to his foreign than his domestic politics. By placing himself at the head of the catholic party, he converted the zealots of the ancient faith into partizans of Spanish greatness; and by employing the powerful allurement of religion, he seduced every where the subjects from that allegiance which they owed to their native sovereign.

The course of events, guiding and concurring with choice, had placed Elizabeth in a situation diametrically opposite; and had raised her to be the glory, the bulwark, and the support of the numerous, though still persecuted protestants, throughout Europe. More moderate in her temper than Philip, she found, with pleasure, that the principles of her sect required not such extreme severity in her domestic government, as was exercised by that monarch; and having no object but self-preservation, she united her interests in all foreign negociations with those who were every where struggling under oppression, and guarding themselves

CHAPTER XXXIX

against ruin and extermination. The more virtuous sovereign was thus happily thrown into the more favourable cause; and fortune, in this instance, concurred with policy and nature.

During the life-time of Henry II. of France, and of his successor, the force of these principles was somewhat restrained, though not altogether overcome, by motives of a superior interest; and the dread of uniting England with the French monarchy, engaged Philip to maintain a good correspondence with Elizabeth. Yet even during this period he rejected the garter which she sent him; he refused to gratify the ancient league between the house of Burgundy and England;[d] he furnished ships to transport French forces into Scotland; he endeavoured to intercept the earl of Arran, who was hastening to join the malcontents in that country; and the queen's wisest ministers still regarded his friendship as hollow and precarious.[e] But no sooner did the death of Francis II. put an end to Philip's apprehensions with regard to Mary's succession, than his animosity against Elizabeth began more openly to appear; and the interests of Spain and those of England were found opposite in every negociation and transaction.

The two great monarchies of the continent, France and Spain, being possessed of nearly equal force, were naturally antagonists; and England, from its power and situation, was intitled to support its own dignity, as well as tranquillity, by holding the balance between them. Whatever incident, therefore, tended too much to depress one of these rival powers, as it left the other without controul, might be deemed contrary to the interests of England: Yet so much were these great maxims of policy over-ruled, during that age, by the disputes of theology, that Philip found an advantage in supporting the established government and religion of France; and Elizabeth in protecting faction and innovation.

The queen-regent of France, when reinstated in authority by the death of her son, Francis, had formed a plan of administration more subtle than judicious; and balancing the catholics with the hugonots, the duke of Guise with the prince of Condé, she endeavoured to render herself necessary to both, and to establish her own dominion on their constrained obedience.[f] But the equal

Civil wars of France.

---

[d] Digges's Complete Ambassador, p. 369. Haynes, p. 585. Strype, vol. iv. No. 246.   [e] Haynes, vol. i. p. 280, 281, 283, 284.   [f] Davila, lib. ii.

counterpoise of power, which, among foreign nations, is the source of tranquillity, proves always the ground of quarrel between domestic factions; and if the animosity of religion concur with the frequent occasions, which present themselves, of mutual injury, it is impossible, during any time, to preserve a firm concord in so delicate a situation. The constable, Montmorency, moved by zeal for the ancient faith, joined himself to the duke of Guise: The king of Navarre, from his inconstant temper, and his jealousy of the superior genius of his brother, embraced the same party: And Catherine, finding herself depressed by this combination, had recourse to Condé and the hugonots, who gladly embraced the opportunity of fortifying themselves by her countenance and protection.[g] An edict had been published, granting a toleration to the protestants; but the interested violence of the duke of Guise, covered with the pretence of religious zeal, broke through this agreement; and the two parties, after the fallacious tranquillity of a moment, renewed their mutual insults and injuries. Condé, Coligni, Andelot, assembled their friends, and flew to arms: Guise and Montmorency got possession of the king's person, and constrained the queen-regent to embrace their party: Fourteen armies were levied and put in motion in different parts of France:[h] each province, each city, each family, was agitated with intestine rage and animosity. The father was divided against the son; brother against brother; and women themselves, sacrificing their humanity as well as their timidity to the religious fury, distinguished themselves by acts of ferocity and valour.[i] Wherever the hugonots prevailed, the images were broken, the altars pillaged, the churches demolished, the monasteries consumed with fire: Where success attended the catholics, they burned the bibles, re-baptized the infants, constrained married persons to pass anew through the nuptial ceremony: And plunder, desolation, and bloodshed attended equally the triumph of both parties. The parliament of Paris itself, the seat of law and justice, instead of employing its authority to compose these fatal quarrels, published an edict, by which it put the sword into the hands of the enraged multitude, and empowered the catholics every where to massacre the hugo-

[g] Davila, lib. iii.   [h] Father Paul, lib. vii.   [i] Ibid.

CHAPTER XXXIX

nots:[k] And it was during this period, when men began to be somewhat enlightened, and in this nation, renowned for polished manners, that the theological rage, which had long been boiling in men's veins, seems to have attained its last stage of virulence and ferocity.

Philip, jealous of the progress which the hugonots made in France, and dreading that the contagion would spread into the Low Country provinces, had formed a secret alliance with the princes of Guise, and had entered into a mutual concert for the protection of the ancient faith, and the suppression of heresy. He now sent six thousand men, with some supply of money, to reinforce the catholic party; and the prince of Condé, finding himself unequal to so great a combination, countenanced by the royal authority, was obliged to dispatch the Vidame of Chartres and Brieguemaut to London, in order to crave the assistance and protection of Elizabeth. Most of the province of Normandy was possessed by the hugonots: And Condé offered to put Havre de Grace into the hands of the English; on condition, that, together with three thousand men for the garrison of that place, the queen should likewise send over three thousand to defend Dieppe and Rouen, and should furnish the prince with a supply of a hundred thousand crowns.[l]

Havre de Grace put in possession of the English.

Elizabeth, besides the general and essential interest of supporting the protestants, and opposing the rapid progress of her enemy the duke of Guise, had other motives which engaged her to accept of this proposal. When she concluded the peace at Cateau-Cambresis, she had good reason to foresee, that France never would voluntarily fulfil the article, which regarded the restitution of Calais; and many subsequent incidents had tended to confirm this suspicion. Considerable sums of money had been expended on the fortifications; long leases had been granted of the lands; and many inhabitants had been encouraged to build and settle there, by assurances that Calais should never be restored to the English.[m] The queen, therefore, wisely concluded, that, could she get possession of Havre, a place, which commanded the mouth of the Seine, and was of greater importance than Calais, she should easily con-

20th Sept.

---

[k] Ibid. Haynes, p. 391.   [l] Forbes, vol. ii, p. 48.   [m] Forbes, p. 54, 257.

strain the French to execute the treaty, and should have the glory of restoring to the crown that ancient possession, so much the favourite of the nation.

No measure could be more generally odious in France, than the conclusion of this treaty with Elizabeth. Men were naturally led to compare the conduct of Guise, who had finally expelled the English, and had debarred these dangerous and destructive enemies from all access into France, with the treasonable politics of Condé, who had again granted them an entrance into the heart of the kingdom. The prince had the more reason to repent of this measure, as he reaped not from it all the advantage which he expected. Three thousand English immediately took possession of Havre and Dieppe, under the command of Sir Edward Poinings; but the latter place was found so little capable of defence, that it was immediately abandoned.[n] The siege of Rouen was already formed by the catholics, under the command of the king of Navarre and Montmorency; and it was with difficulty that Poinings could throw a small reinforcement into the place. Though these English troops behaved with gallantry,[o] and though the king of Navarre was mortally wounded during the siege; the catholics still continued the attack of the place, and carrying it at last by assault, put the whole garrison to the sword. The earl of Warwic, eldest son of the late duke of Northumberland, arrived soon after at Havre, with another body of three thousand English, and took on him the command of the place.

It was expected, that the French catholics, flushed with their success at Rouen, would immediately have formed the siege of Havre, which was not as yet in any condition of defence; but the intestine disorders of the kingdom soon diverted their attention to another enterprise. Andelot, seconded by the negociations of Elizabeth, had levied a considerable body of protestants in Germany; and having arrived at Orleans, the seat of the hugonots' power, he enabled the prince of Condé and the admiral to take the field, and oppose the progress of their enemies. After threatening Paris during some time, they took their march towards Normandy, with a view of engaging the English to act in conjunction with them, and of fortifying themselves by the farther assistance,

[n] Ibid. vol. ii. p. 199.   [o] Ibid. p. 161.

CHAPTER XXXIX

which they expected from the zeal and vigour of Elizabeth.[p] The catholics, commanded by the constable, and under him by the duke of Guise, followed on their rear; and overtaking them at Dreux, obliged them to give battle. The field was fought with great obstinacy on both sides: And the action was distinguished by this singular event, that Condé and Montmorency, the commanders of the opposite armies, fell both of them prisoners into the hands of their enemies. The appearances of victory remained with Guise; but the admiral, whose fate it ever was to be defeated, and still to rise more terrible after his misfortunes, collected the remains of the army; and inspiring his own unconquerable courage and constancy into every breast, kept them in a body, and subdued some considerable places in Normandy. Elizabeth, the better to support his cause, sent him a new supply of a hundred thousand crowns; and offered, if he could find merchants to lend him the money, to give her bond for another sum of equal amount.[q]

The expences, incurred by assisting the French hugonots, had emptied the queen's exchequer; and in order to obtain supply, she found herself under a necessity of summoning a parliament: An expedient, to which she never willingly had recourse. A little before the meeting of this assembly, she had fallen into a dangerous illness, the small-pox; and as her life, during some time, was despaired of, the people became the more sensible of their perilous situation, derived from the uncertainty, which, in case of her demise, attended the succession of the crown. The partizans of the queen of Scots, and those of the house of Suffolk, already divided the nation into factions; and every one foresaw, that, though it might be possible at present to determine the controversy by law, yet, if the throne were vacant, nothing but the sword would be able to fix a successor. The commons, therefore, on the opening of the session, voted an address to the queen; in which, after enumerating the dangers attending a broken and doubtful succession, and mentioning the evils which their fathers had experienced from the contending titles of York and Lancaster, they entreated the queen to put an end to their apprehensions, by choosing some husband, whom, they promised, whoever he were, gratefully to receive, and faithfully to serve, honour, and obey: Or if she had entertained

1563. January 12. A parliament.

---

[p] Forbes, p. 320. Davila, lib. iii.   [q] Forbes, vol. ii. p. 322, 347.

any reluctance to the married state, they desired, that the lawful successor might be named, at least appointed, by act of parliament. They remarked, that, during all the reigns which had passed since the conquest, the nation had never before been so unhappy, as not to know the person, who, in case of the sovereign's death, was legally entitled to fill the vacant throne. And they observed, that the fixed order, which took place in inheriting the French monarchy, was one chief source of the usual tranquillity, as well as of the happiness, of that kingdom.[r]

This subject, though extremely interesting to the nation, was very little agreeable to the queen; and she was sensible, that great difficulties would attend every decision. A declaration in favour of the queen of Scots would form a settlement perfectly legal; because that princess was commonly allowed to possess the right of blood; and the exclusion given by Henry's will, deriving its weight chiefly from an act of parliament, would lose all authority, whenever the queen and parliament had made a new settlement, and restored the Scottish line to its place in the succession. But she dreaded giving encouragement to the catholics, her secret enemies, by this declaration. She was sensible that every heir was, in some degree, a rival; much more one who enjoyed a claim for the present possession of the crown; and who had already advanced, in a very open manner, these dangerous pretensions. The great power of Mary, both from the favour of the catholic princes, and her connections with the house of Guise, not to mention the force and situation of Scotland, was well known to her; and she saw no security, that this princess, if fortified by a sure prospect of succession, would not revive claims, which she could never yet be prevailed on formally to relinquish. On the other hand, the title of the house of Suffolk was supported by the more zealous protestants only; and it was very doubtful, whether even a parliamentary declaration in its favour would bestow on it such validity as to give satisfaction to the people. The republican part of the constitution had not yet acquired such an ascendant as to controul, in any degree, the ideas of hereditary right; and as the legality of Henry's will was still disputed, though founded on the utmost authority which a parliament could confer; who could be assured, that a

[r] Sir Simon D'Ewes's Journ. p. 81.

CHAPTER XXXIX

more recent act would be acknowledged to have greater validity? In the frequent revolutions, which had of late taken place, the right of blood had still prevailed over religious prejudices; and the nation had ever shewn itself disposed rather to change its faith than the order of succession. Even many protestants declared themselves in favour of Mary's claim of inheritance;[s] and nothing would occasion more general disgust, than to see the queen, openly and without reserve, take part against it. The Scottish princess also, finding herself injured in so sensible a point, would thenceforth act as a declared enemy; and uniting together her foreign and domestic friends, the partizans of her present title and of her eventual succession, would soon bring matters to extremities against the present establishment. The queen, weighing all these inconveniences, which were great and urgent, was determined to keep both parties in awe, by maintaining still an ambiguous conduct; and she rather chose, that the people should run the hazard of contingent events, than that she herself should visibly endanger her throne, by employing expedients, which, at best, would not bestow entire security on the nation. She gave, therefore, an evasive answer to the applications of the commons; and when the house, at the end of the session, desired, by the mouth of their speaker, farther satisfaction on that head, she could not be prevailed on to make her reply more explicit. She only told them, contrary to her declarations in the beginning of her reign, that she had fixed no absolute resolution against marriage; and she added, that the difficulties, attending the question of the succession, were so great, that she would be contented, for the sake of her people, to remain some time longer in this vale of misery; and never should depart life with satisfaction, till she had laid some solid foundation for their future security.[t]

The most remarkable law passed this session was that which bore the title of *Assurance of the queen's royal power over all states and subjects within her dominions.*[u] By this act, the asserting twice, by writing, word, or deed, the pope's authority, was subjected to the penalties of treason. All persons in holy orders were bound to take the oath of supremacy; as also, all who were advanced to any degree, either in the universities or in common law; all school-

[s] Keith, p. 322.   [t] Sir Simon D'Ewes's Journal, p. 75.   [u] 5 Eliz. c. 1.

masters, officers in court, or members of parliament: And the penalty of their second refusal was treason. The first offence, in both cases, was punished by banishment and forfeiture. This rigorous statute was not extended to any of the degree of a baron; because it was not supposed, that the queen could entertain any doubt with regard to the fidelity of persons possessed of such high dignity. Lord Montacute made opposition to the bill; and asserted in favour of the catholics, that they disputed not, they preached not, they disobeyed not the queen, they caused no trouble, no tumults among the people.[w] It is, however, probable, that some suspicions of their secret conspiracies had made the queen and parliament encrease their rigour against them; though it is also more than probable, that they were mistaken in the remedy.

There was likewise another point, in which the parliament, this session, shewed more the goodness of their intention than the soundness of their judgment. They passed a law against fond and fantastical prophecies, which had been observed to seduce the people into rebellion and disorder:[x] But at the same time they enacted a statute, which was most likely to encrease these and such like superstitions: It was levelled against conjurations, enchantments, and witchcraft.[y] Witchcraft and heresy are two crimes, which commonly encrease by punishment, and never are so effectually suppressed as by being totally neglected. After the parliament had granted the queen a supply of one subsidy and two fifteenths, the session was finished by a prorogation. The convocation likewise voted the queen a subsidy of six shillings in the pound, payable in three years.

While the English parties exerted these calm efforts against each other, in parliamentary votes and debates, the French factions, enflamed to the highest degree of animosity, continued that cruel war, which their intemperate zeal, actuated by the ambition of their leaders, had kindled in the kingdom. The admiral was successful in reducing the towns of Normandy, which held for the king; but he frequently complained, that the numerous garrison of Havre, remained totally inactive, and was not employed in any military operation against the common enemy. The queen, in taking possession of that place, had published a manifesto,[z] in which

---

[w] Strype, vol. i. p. 260.   [x] 5 Eliz. c. 15.   [y] Ibid. c. 16.   [z] Forbes, vol. ii.

she pretended, that her concern for the interests of the French king had engaged her in that measure, and that her sole intention was to oppose her enemies of the house of Guise, who held their prince in captivity, and employed his power to the destruction of his best and most faithful subjects. It was chiefly her desire to preserve appearances, joined to the great frugality of her temper, which made her, at this critical juncture, keep her soldiers in garrison, and restrain them from committing farther hostilities upon the enemy.[a] The duke of Guise, meanwhile, was aiming a mortal blow at the power of the hugonots; and had commenced the siege of Orleans, of which Andelot was governor, and where the constable was detained prisoner. He had the prospect of speedy success in this undertaking; when he was assassinated by Poltrot, a young gentleman, whose zeal, instigated (as is pretended, though without any certain foundation) by the admiral and Beza, a famous preacher, led him to attempt that criminal enterprize. The death of this gallant prince was a sensible loss to the catholic party; and though the cardinal of Lorraine, his brother, still supported the interests of the family, the danger of their progress appeared not so imminent either to Elizabeth or to the French protestants. The union, therefore, between these allies, which had been cemented by their common fears, began thenceforth to be less intimate; and the leaders of the hugonots were persuaded to hearken to terms of a separate accommodation. Condé and Montmorency held conferences for settling the peace; and as they were both of them impatient to relieve themselves from captivity, they soon came to an agreement with regard to the conditions. The character of the queen-regent, whose ends were always violent, but who endeavoured, by subtilty and policy, rather than force, to attain them, led her to embrace any plausible terms; and in spite of the protestations of the admiral, whose sagacity could easily discover the treachery of the court, the articles of agreement were finally settled between the parties. A toleration, under some restrictions, was anew granted to the protestants; a general amnesty was published; Condé was reinstated in his offices and governments; and after money was advanced for the payment of arrears due to the German troops, they were dismissed the kingdom.

[a] Forbes, vol. ii. p. 276, 277.

By the agreement between Elizabeth and the prince of Condé it had been stipulated,[b] that neither party should conclude peace without the consent of the other; but this article was at present but little regarded by the leaders of the French protestants. They only comprehended her so far in the treaty, as to obtain a promise, that, on her relinquishing Havre, her charges and the money which she had advanced them, should be repaid her by the king of France, and that Calais, on the expiration of the term, should be restored to her. But she disdained to accept of these conditions; and thinking the possession of Havre a much better pledge for effecting her purpose, she sent Warwic orders to prepare himself against an attack from the now united power of the French monarchy.

The earl of Warwic, who commanded a garrison of six thousand men, besides seven hundred pioniers, had no sooner got possession of Havre, than he employed every means for putting it in a posture of defence;[c] and after expelling the French from the town, he encouraged his soldiers to make the most desperate defence against the enemy. The constable commanded the French army; the queen-regent herself, and the king, were present in the camp; even the prince of Condé joined the king's forces, and gave countenance to this enterprize; the admiral and Andelot alone, anxious still to preserve the friendship of Elizabeth, kept at a distance, and prudently refused to join their ancient enemies in an attack upon their allies.

From the force, and dispositions, and situation of both sides, it was expected, that the siege would be attended with some memorable event; yet did France make a much easier acquisition of this important place, than was at first apprehended. The plague creeped in among the English soldiers; and being encreased by their fatigue and bad diet (for they were but ill supplied with provisions[d]) it made such ravages, that sometimes a hundred men a day died of it, and there remained not at last fifteen hundred in a condition to do duty.[e] The French, meeting with such feeble resistance, carried on their attacks successfully; and having made two breaches, each of them sixty feet wide, they prepared for a general assault, which must have terminated in the slaughter of

[b] Forbes, vol. ii. p. 79.   [c] Ibid. p. 158.   [d] Forbes, vol. ii. p. 377, 498.
[e] Ibid. p. 450, 458.

65

CHAPTER XXXIX

the whole garrison.*/* Warwic, who had frequently warned the English council of the danger, and who had loudly demanded a supply of men and provisions, found himself obliged to capitulate, and to content himself with the liberty of withdrawing his garrison. The articles were no sooner signed, than lord Clinton, the admiral, who had been detained by contrary winds, appeared off the harbour with a reinforcement of three thousand men; and found the place surrendered to the enemy. To encrease the misfortune, the infected army brought the plague with them into England, where it swept off great multitudes, particularly in the city of London. Above twenty thousand persons, there, died of it in one year.*g* *Havre lost. 28th July.*

Elizabeth, whose usual vigour and foresight had not appeared in this transaction, was now glad to compound matters; and as the queen-regent desired to obtain leisure, in order to prepare measures for the extermination of the hugonots, she readily hearkened to any reasonable terms of accommodation with England.*h* It was agreed, that the hostages, which the French had given for the restitution of Calais, should be restored for 220,000 crowns; and that both sides should retain all their claims and pretensions. *2d April.*

The peace still continued with Scotland; and even a cordial friendship seemed to have been cemented between Elizabeth and Mary. These princesses made profession of the most entire affection; wrote amicable letters every week to each other; and had adopted, in all appearance, the sentiments as well as style of sisters. Elizabeth punished one Hales, who had published a book against Mary's title;*i* and as the lord keeper Bacon was thought to have encouraged Hales in this undertaking, he fell under her displeasure, and it was with some difficulty he was able to give her satisfaction, and recover her favour.*k* The two queens had agreed in the foregoing summer to an interview at York;*l* in order to remove all difficulties with regard to Mary's ratification of the treaty of Edinburgh, and to consider of the proper method for settling the succession of England: But as Elizabeth carefully avoided touching on this delicate subject, she employed a pretence of the wars in France, which, she said, would detain her in London; and she delayed till next year the intended interview. It is also *Scotch affairs.*

f Ibid. p. 498.   *g* See note [F] at the end of the volume.   *h* Davila, lib. 3.
i Keith, p. 252.   *k* Ibid. p. 253.   *l* Haynes, p. 388.

probable, that, being well acquainted with the beauty and address and accomplishments of Mary, she did not chuse to stand the comparison with regard to those exterior qualities, in which she was eclipsed by her rival; and was unwilling, that a princess, who had already made great progress in the esteem and affections of the English, should have a farther opportunity of encreasing the number of her partizans.

Mary's close connections with the house of Guise, and her devoted attachment to her uncles, by whom she had been early educated and constantly protected, was the ground of just and unsurmountable jealousy to Elizabeth, who regarded them as her mortal and declared enemies, and was well acquainted with their dangerous character and ambitious projects. They had made offer of their niece to Don Carlos, Philip's son; to the king of Sweden, the king of Navarre, the archduke Charles, the duke of Ferrara, the Cardinal of Bourbon, who had only taken deacon's orders, from which he might easily be freed by a dispensation; and they were ready to marry her to any one, who could strengthen their interests, or give inquietude and disturbance to Elizabeth.[m] Elizabeth on her part was equally vigilant to prevent the execution of their schemes, and was particularly anxious, lest Mary should form any powerful foreign alliance, which might tempt her to revive her pretensions to the crown, and to invade the kingdom on the side where it was weakest and lay most exposed.[n] As she believed, that the marriage with the archduke Charles was the one most likely to have place, she used every expedient to prevent it; and besides remonstrating against it to Mary herself, she endeavoured to draw off the archduke from that pursuit, by giving him some hopes of success in his pretensions to herself, and by inviting him to a renewal of the former treaty of marriage.[o] She always told the queen of Scots, that nothing would satisfy her but her espousing some English nobleman, who would remove all grounds of jealousy, and cement the union between the kingdoms; and she offered on this condition to have her title examined, and to declare her successor to the crown.[p] After keeping the matter in these general terms during a twelvemonth, she at last named lord Robert

[m] Forbes, vol. ii. p. 287. Strype, vol. i. p. 400.   [n] Keith, p. 247, 284. [o] Melvil, p. 41.   [p] Keith, p. 243, 249, 259, 265.

CHAPTER XXXIX

Dudley, now created earl of Leicester, as the person on whom she desired that Mary's choice should fall.

The earl of Leicester, the great and powerful favourite of Elizabeth, possessed all those exterior qualities, which are naturally alluring to the fair sex; a handsome person, a polite address, an insinuating behaviour; and by means of these accomplishments, he had been able to blind even the penetration of Elizabeth, and conceal from her the great defects, or rather odious vices, which attended his character. He was proud, insolent, interested, ambitious; without honour, without generosity, without humanity; and atoned not for these bad qualities, by such abilities or courage, as could fit him for that high trust and confidence, with which she always honoured him. Her constant and declared attachment to him had naturally emboldened him to aspire to her bed; and in order to make way for these nuptials, he was universally believed to have murdered, in a barbarous manner, his wife, the heiress of one Robesart. The proposal of espousing Mary was by no means agreeable to him; and he always ascribed it to the contrivance of Cecil, his enemy; who, he thought, intended by that artifice to make him lose the friendship of Mary from the temerity of his pretensions, and that of Elizabeth from jealousy of his attachments to another woman.[q] The queen herself had not any serious intention of effecting this marriage; but as she was desirous, that the queen of Scots should never have any husband, she named a man, who, she believed, was not likely to be accepted of; and she hoped, by that means, to gain time, and elude the project of any other alliance. The earl of Leicester was too great a favourite to be parted with; and when Mary, allured by the prospect of being declared successor to the crown, seemed at last to hearken to Elizabeth's proposal, this princess receded from her offers, and withdrew the bait, which she had thrown out to her rival.[r] This duplicity of conduct, joined to some appearance of an imperious superiority, assumed by her, had drawn a peevish letter from Mary; and the seemingly amicable correspondence between the two queens was, during some time, interrupted. In order to make up the breach, the queen of Scots dispatched Sir James Melvil to London; who

[q] Camden, p. 396.   [r] Keith, p. 269, 270. Appendix, p. 158. Strype, vol. i. p. 414.

has given us in his memoirs a particular account of his negotiation.

Melvil was an agreeable courtier, a man of address and conversation; and it was recommended to him by his mistress, that,
besides grave reasonings concerning politics and state-affairs, he
should introduce more entertaining topics of conversation, suitable to the sprightly character of Elizabeth; and should endeavour
by that means to insinuate himself into her confidence. He succeeded so well, that he threw that artful princess entirely off her
guard,[s] and made her discover the bottom of her heart, full of all
those levities and follies and ideas of rivalship, which possess the
youngest and most frivolous of her sex. He talked to her of his
travels, and forgot not to mention the different dresses of the
ladies in different countries, and the particular advantages of each,
in setting off the beauties of the shape and person. The queen said,
that she had dresses of all countries; and she took care thenceforth
to meet the ambassador every day apparelled in a different habit:
Sometimes she was dressed in the English garb, sometimes in the
French, sometimes in the Italian; and she asked him, which of
them became her most? He answered, the Italian; a reply, that, he
knew, would be agreeable to her, because that mode showed to
advantage her flowing locks, which, he remarked, though they
were more red than yellow, she fancied to be the finest in the
world. She desired to know of him what was reputed the best
colour of hair: She asked whether his queen or she had the finest
hair: She even enquired which of them he esteemed the fairest
person: A very delicate question, and which he prudently eluded,
by saying that her majesty was the fairest person in England, and
his mistress in Scotland. She next demanded which of them was
tallest: He replied, his queen: Then is she too tall, said Elizabeth:
For I myself am of a just stature. Having learned from him, that his
mistress sometimes recreated herself by playing on the harp-
sichord, an instrument on which she herself excelled, she gave
orders to lord Hunsdon, that he should lead the ambassador, as it
were casually, into an apartment, where he might hear her perform; and when Melvil, as if ravished with the harmony, broke into
the queen's apartment, she pretended to be displeased with his

1564.

---

[s] Haynes, p. 447.

intrusion; but still took care to ask him whether he thought Mary or her the best performer on that instrument.[t] From the whole of her behaviour, Melvil thought he might, on his return, assure his mistress, that she had no reason ever to expect any cordial friendship from Elizabeth, and that all her professions of amity were full of falsehood and dissimulation.

After two years had been spent in evasions and artifices,[u] Mary's subjects and counsellors, and probably herself, began to think it full time, that some marriage were concluded, and lord Darnley, son of the earl of Lenox, was the person, in whom most men's opinions and wishes centered. He was Mary's cousin-german, by the lady Margaret Douglas, niece to Harry VIII. and daughter of the earl of Angus, by Margaret, queen of Scotland. He had been born and educated in England, where the earl of Lenox had constantly resided, since he had been banished by the prevailing power of the house of Hamilton: And as Darnley was now in his twentieth year, and was a very comely person, tall and delicately shaped, it was hoped, that he might soon render himself agreeable to the queen of Scots. He was also by his father a branch of the same family with herself; and would, in espousing her, preserve the royal dignity in the house of Stuart: He was, after her, next heir to the crown of England; and those who pretended to exclude her on account of her being a foreigner, had endeavoured to recommend his title, and give it the preference. It seemed no inconsiderable advantage, that she could, by marrying him, unite both their claims; and as he was by birth an Englishman, and could not, by his power or alliances, give any ground or suspicion to Elizabeth, it was hoped, that the proposal of this marriage would not be unacceptable to that jealous princess.

Elizabeth was well informed of these intentions;[w] and was secretly not displeased, with the projected marriage between Darnley and the queen of Scots.[x] She would rather have wished, that Mary had continued for ever in a single life: But finding little probability of rendering this scheme effectual, she was satisfied with a choice, which freed her at once from the dread of a foreign alliance, and from the necessity of parting with Leicester, her

[t] Melvil, p. 49, 50.   [u] Keith, p. 264.   [w] Keith, p. 261.   [x] Ibid. p. 280, 282.
Jebb, vol. ii. p. 46.

favourite. In order to pave the way to Darnley's marriage, she secretly desired Mary to invite Lenox into Scotland, to reverse his attainder, and to restore him to his honours and fortune.[y] And when her request was complied with, she took care, in order to preserve the friendship of the Hamiltons and her other partizans in Scotland, to blame openly this conduct of Mary.[z] Hearing that the negotiation for Darnley's marriage advanced apace, she gave that nobleman permission, on his first application, to follow his father into Scotland: But no sooner did she learn, that the queen of Scots was taken with his figure and person, and that all measures were fixed for espousing him, than she exclaimed against the marriage; sent Throgmorton to order Darnley immediately, upon his allegiance, to return to England; threw the countess of Lenox and her second son into the Tower, where they suffered a rigorous confinement; seized all Lenox's English estate; and, though it was impossible for her to assign one single reason for her displeasure,[a] she menaced, and protested, and complained, as if she had suffered the most grievous injury in the world.

28th
July.

The politics of Elizabeth, though judicious, were usually full of duplicity and artifice; but never more so than in her transactions with the queen of Scots, where there entered so many little passions and narrow jealousies, that she durst not avow to the world the reasons of her conduct, scarcely to her ministers, and scarcely even to herself. But besides a womanish rivalship and envy against the marriage of this princess, she had some motives of interest for feigning a displeasure on the present occasion. It served her as a pretence for refusing to acknowledge Mary's title to the succession of England; a point to which, for good reasons, she was determined never to consent. And it was useful to her for a purpose, still more unfriendly and dangerous, for encouraging the discontents and rebellion of the Scottish nobility and ecclesiastics.[b]

Nothing can be more unhappy for a people than to be governed by a sovereign, attached to a religion different from the established; and it is scarcely possible that mutual confidence can ever, in such a situation, have place between the prince and his subjects. Mary's conduct had been hitherto, in every respect, un-

---

[y] Keith, p. 255, 259, 272.   [z] Melvil, p. 42.   [a] Keith, p. 274, 275.   [b] Ibid. p. 290.

exceptionable, and even laudable; yet had she not made such   *1565.*
progress in acquiring popularity, as might have been expected
from her gracious deportment and agreeable accomplishments.
Suspicions every moment prevailed on account of her attachment
to the catholic faith, and especially to her uncles, the open and
avowed promoters of the scheme for exterminating the professors
of the reformed religion throughout all Europe. She still refused
to ratify the acts of parliament which had established the reformation; she made attempts for restoring to the catholic bishops some
part of their civil jurisdiction;[c] and she wrote a letter to the council
of Trent, in which, besides professing her attachment to the catholic faith, she took notice of her title to succeed to the crown of
England, and expressed her hopes of being able, in some period,
to bring back all her dominions to the bosom of the church.[d] The
zealots among the protestants were not wanting, in their turn, to
exercise their insolence against her, which tended still more to
alienate her from their faith. A law was enacted, making it capital,
on the very first offence, to say mass any where, except in the
queen's chapel;[e] and it was with difficulty that even this small
indulgence was granted her: The general assembly importuned
her anew to change her religion; to renounce the blasphemous
idolatry of the mass, with the tyranny of the Roman Antichrist; and
to embrace the true religion of Christ Jesus.[f] As she answered with
temper, that she was not yet convinced of the falsity of her religion
or the impiety of the mass; and that her apostacy would lose her
the friendship of her allies on the continent; they replied, by assur-
ing her, that their religion was undoubtedly the same which had
been revealed by Jesus Christ, which had been preached by the
apostles, and which had been embraced by the faithful in the
primitive ages; that neither the religion of Turks, Jews, nor Papists
was built on so solid a foundation as theirs; that they alone, of all
the various species of religionists, spread over the face of the earth,
were so happy as to be possessed of the truth; that those who hear,
or rather who gaze on the mass, allow sacrilege, pronounce blas-
phemy, and commit most abominable idolatry; and that the
friendship of the King of Kings was preferable to all the alliances
in the world.[g]

[c] Spotswood, p. 198.   [d] Father Paul, lib. vii.   [e] Keith, p. 268.   [f] Ibid.
p. 545. Knox, p. 374.   [g] Keith, p. 550, 551.

The queen of Scots marries the earl of Darnley.   The marriage of the queen of Scots had kindled afresh the zeal of the reformers, because the family of Lenox was believed to adhere to the catholic faith; and though Darnley, who now bore the name of King Henry, went often to the established church, he could not, by this exterior compliance, gain the confidence and regard of the ecclesiastics. They rather laid hold of the opportunity to insult him to his face; and Knox scrupled not to tell him from the pulpit, that God, for punishment of the offences and ingratitude of the people, was wont to commit the rule over them to boys and women.[h] The populace of Edinburgh, instigated by such doctrines, began to meet and to associate themselves against the government.[i] But what threatened more immediate danger to Mary's authority, were the discontents which prevailed among some of the principal nobility.

The duke of Chatelrault was displeased with the restoration, and still more with the aggrandizement of the family of Lenox, his hereditary enemies; and entertained fears lest his own eventual succession to the crown of Scotland should be excluded by his rival, who had formerly advanced some pretensions to it. The earl of Murray found his credit at court much diminished by the interest of Lenox, and his son; and began to apprehend the revocation of some considerable grants, which he had obtained from Mary's bounty. The earls of Argyle, Rothes, and Glencairne, the lords Boyde and Ochiltry, Kirkaldy of Grange, Pittarow, were instigated by like motives; and as these were the persons who had most zealously promoted the reformation, they were disgusted to find, that the queen's favour was entirely ingrossed by a new cabal, the earls of Bothwel, Athole, Sutherland, and Huntley; men who were esteemed either lukewarm in religious controversy, or inclined to the catholic party. The same ground of discontent, which, in other courts, is the source of intrigue, faction, and opposition, commonly produced in Scotland, either projects of assassination, or of rebellion; and besides mutual accusations of the former kind, which it is difficult to clear up,[k] the malcontent lords, as soon as they saw the queen's marriage entirely resolved on, entered into a confederacy for taking arms against their sovereign. They met at

[h] Ibid. p. 546. Knox, p. 381.   [i] Knox, p. 377.   [k] See note [G] at the end of the volume.

CHAPTER XXXIX

Stirling; pretended an anxious concern for the security of religion; framed engagements for mutual defence; and made applications to Elizabeth for assistance and protection.[l] That princess, after publishing the expressions of her displeasure against the marriage, had secretly ordered her ambassadors Randolf and Throgmorton, to give in her name some promises of support to the malcontents; and had even sent them a supply of ten thousand pounds, to enable them to begin an insurrection.[m]

Mary was no sooner informed of the meeting at Stirling, and the movements of the lords, than she summoned them to appear at court, in order to answer for their conduct; and having levied some forces to execute the laws, she obliged the rebels to leave the low countries, and take shelter in Argyleshire. That she might more effectually cut off their resources, she proceeded with the king to Glasgow, and forced them from their retreat. They appeared at Paisley in the neighbourhood with about a thousand horse; and passing the queen's army, proceeded to Hamilton, thence to Edinburgh, which they entered without resistance. They expected great reinforcements in this place, from the efforts of Knox and the seditious preachers; and they beat their drums, desiring all men to enlist, and receive wages for the defence of God's glory.[n] But the nation was in no disposition for rebellion: Mary was esteemed and beloved: Her marriage was not generally disagreeable to the people: And the interested views of the malcontent lords were so well known, that their pretence of zeal for religion had little influence even on the ignorant populace.[o] The king and queen advanced to Edinburgh at the head of their army: The rebels were obliged to retire into the south; and being pursued by a force which now amounted to eighteen thousand men,[p] they found themselves under a necessity of abandoning their country, and of taking shelter in England.

Elizabeth, when she found the event so much to disappoint her expectations, thought proper to disavow all connexions with the Scottish malcontents, and to declare every where, that she had never given them any encouragement, nor any promise of countenance or assistance. She even carried farther her dissimulation and

[l] Keith, p. 293, 294, 300, 301.　[m] Knox, p. 380. Keith, Append. p. 164. Anderson, vol. iii. p. 194.　[n] Knox, p. 381.　[o] Ibid. p. 380, 385.　[p] Ibid. p. 388.

hypocrisy. Murray had come to London, with the abbot of Kil-winning, agent for Chatelrault; and she seduced them, by secret assurances of protection, to declare, before the ambassadors of France and Spain, that she had nowise contributed to their insur-rection. No sooner had she extorted this confession from them, than she chased them from her presence, called them unworthy traitors, declared that their detestable rebellion was of bad exam-ple to all princes, and assured them, that, as she had hitherto given them no encouragement, so should they never thenceforth receive from her any assistance or protection.[q] Throgmorton alone, whose honour was equal to his abilities, could not be prevailed on to conceal the part, which he had acted in the enterprise of the Scot-tish rebels; and being well apprised of the usual character and conduct of Elizabeth, he had had the precaution to obtain an order of council to authorize the engagements, which he had been obliged to take with them.[r]

The banished lords, finding themselves so harshly treated by Elizabeth, had recourse to the clemency of their own sovereign; and after some solicitation and some professions of sincere re-pentence, the duke of Chatelrault obtained his pardon, on condi-tion that he should retire into France. Mary was more implacable against the ungrateful earl of Murray and the other confederates, on whom she threw the chief blame of the enterprize; but as she was continually plied with applications from their friends, and as some of her most judicious partizans in England thought, that nothing would more promote her interests in that kingdom, than the gentle treatment of men so celebrated for their zeal against the catholic religion; she agreed to give way to her natural temper, which inclined not to severity, and she seemed determined to re-store them to favour.[s] In this interval, Rambouillet arrived as am-bassador from France, and brought her advice from her uncle, the cardinal of Lorraine, to whose opinion she always paid an extreme deference, by no means to pardon these protestant leaders, who had been engaged in a rebellion against her.[t]

The two religions, in France, as well as in other parts of Europe, were rather irritated than tired with their acts of mutual violence;

[q] Melvil, p. 57. Knox, p. 388. Keith, p. 319. Crawford, p. 62, 63.   [r] Melvil, p. 60.   [s] Ibid. p. 59, 60, 61, 62, 63. Keith, p. 322.   [t] Keith, p. 325. Melvil, p. 63.

CHAPTER XXXIX

and the peace granted to the hugonots, as had been foreseen by
Coligni, was intended only to lull them asleep, and prepare the way
for their final and absolute destruction. The queen-regent made a
pretence of travelling through the kingdom, in order to visit the
provinces, and correct all the abuses arising from the late civil war;
and after having held some conferences on the frontiers with the
duke of Lorraine and the duke of Savoy, she came to Bayonne,
where she was met by her daughter, the queen of Spain, and the
duke of Alva. Nothing appeared in the congress of these two splendid courts, but gaiety, festivity, love, and joy; but amidst these
smiling appearances were secretly fabricated schemes the most
bloody, and the most destructive to the repose of mankind, that
had ever been thought of in any age or nation. No less than a total
and universal extermination of the protestants by fire and sword
was concerted by Philip and Catherine of Medicis; and Alva, agreeably to his fierce and sanguinary dispostion, advised the queen-
regent to commence the execution of this project, by the immediate massacre of all the leaders of the hugonots.[u] But that princess,
though equally hardened against every humane sentiment, would
not forego this opportunity of displaying her wit and refined politics; and she purposed, rather by treachery and dissimulation,
which she called address, to lead the protestants into the snare, and
never to draw the sword, till they were totally disabled from resistance. The cardinal of Lorraine, whose character bore a greater
affinity to that of Alva, was a chief author of this barbarous association against the reformers; and having connected his hopes of
success with the aggrandizement of his niece, the queen of Scots,
he took care, that her measures should correspond to those violent
counsels, which were embraced by the other catholic princes. In
consequence of this scheme, he turned her from the road of clemency, which she intended to have followed; and made her resolve
on the total ruin of the banished lords.[w] A parliament was summoned at Edinburgh for attainting them; and as their guilt was
palpable and avowed, no doubt was entertained but sentence
would be pronounced against them. It was by a sudden and violent
incident, which, in the issue, brought on the ruin of Mary herself,
that they were saved from the rigour of the law.

*Confed-
eracy
against
the
protes-
tants.*

1566.

[u] Davila, lib. iii. [w] Melvil, p. 63. Keith Append. p. 176.

The marriage of the queen of Scots with lord Darnley was so natural, and so inviting in all its circumstances, that it had been precipitately agreed to by that princess and her council; and while she was allured by his youth, and beauty, and exterior accomplishments, she had at first overlooked the qualities of his mind, which nowise corresponded to the excellence of his outward figure. Violent, yet variable in his resolutions; insolent, yet credulous and easily governed by flatterers; he was destitute of all gratitude, because he thought no favours equal to his merit; and being addicted to low pleasures, he was equally incapable of all true sentiments of love and tenderness.[x] The queen of Scots, in the first effusions of her fondness, had taken a pleasure in exalting him beyond measure: She had granted him the title of king; she had joined his name with her own in all public acts; she intended to have procured him from the parliament a matrimonial crown: But having leisure afterwards to remark his weakness and vices, she began to see the danger of her profuse liberality, and was resolved thenceforth to proceed with more reserve in the trust, which she should confer upon him. His resentment against this prudent conduct served but the more to encrease her disgust; and the young prince, enraged at her imagined neglects, pointed his vengeance against every one whom he deemed the cause of this change in her measures and behaviour.

Murder of Rizzio. There was in the court, one David Rizzio, who had of late obtained a very extraordinary degree of confidence and favour with the queen of Scots. He was a Piedmontese, of mean birth, son of a teacher of music, himself a musician; and finding it difficult to subsist by his art in his own country, he had followed into Scotland an ambassador; whom the duke of Savoy sent thither to pay his compliments to Mary, some time after her first arrival. He possessed a good ear, and a tolerable voice; and as that princess found him useful to complete her band of music, she retained him in her service after the departure of his master. Her secretary for French dispatches having, some time after, incurred her displeasure, she promoted Rizzio to that office, which gave him frequent opportunities of approaching her person, and insinuating himself into her favour. He was shrewd and sensible, as well as

[x] Keith, p. 287, 329. Append. p. 163.

aspiring, much beyond his rank and education; and he made so good use of the access which fortune had procured him, that he was soon regarded as the chief confident and even minister of the queen. He was consulted on all occasions; no favours could be obtained but by his intercession; all suitors were obliged to gain him by presents and flattery; and the man, insolent from his new exaltation, as well as rapacious in his acquisitions, soon drew on himself the hatred of the nobility and of the whole kingdom.[y] He had at first employed his credit to promote Darnley's marriage; and a firm friendship seemed to be established between them: But on the subsequent change of the queen's sentiments, it was easy for Henry's friends to persuade him, that Rizzio was the real author of her indifference, and even to rouze in his mind jealousies of a more dangerous nature. The favourite was of a disagreeable figure, but was not past his youth;[z] and though the opinion of his criminal correspondence with Mary might seem of itself unreasonable, if not absurd, a suspicious husband could find no other means of accounting for that lavish and imprudent kindness, with which she honoured him. The rigid austerity of the ecclesiastics, who could admit of no freedoms, contributed to spread this opinion among the people; and as Rizzio was universally believed to be a pensionary of the pope's, and to be deeply engaged in all schemes against the protestants, any story, to his and Mary's disadvantage, received an easy credit among the zealots of that communion.

Rizzio, who had connected his interests with the Roman catholics, was the declared enemy of the banished lords; and by promoting the violent prosecution against them, he had exposed himself to the animosity of their numerous friends and retainers. A scheme was also thought to be formed for revoking some exorbitant grants made during the queen's minority; and even the nobility, who had seized the ecclesiastical benefices, began to think themselves less secure in the possession of them.[a] The earl of Morton, chancellor, was affected by all these considerations, and still more by a rumour spread aboard, that Mary intended to appoint Rizzio chancellor in his place, and to bestow that dignity on a mean and upstart foreigner, ignorant of the laws and language

[y] Keith, p. 282, 302. Crawford's Memoirs, p. 5. Spotswood, p. 193.   [z] See note [H] at the end of the volume.   [a] Keith, p. 326. Melvil, p. 64.

of the country.[b] So indiscreet had this princess been in her kindness to Rizzio, that even that strange report met with credit, and
proved a great means of accelerating the ruin of the favourite.
Morton, insinuating himself into Henry's confidence, employed
all his art to inflame the discontent and jealousy of that prince; and
he persuaded him, that the only means of freeing himself from the
indignities under which he laboured, was to bring the base
stranger to the fate, which he had so well merited, and which was
so passionately desired by the whole nation. George Douglas, natural brother to the countess of Lenox, concurred in the same
advice; and the lords of Ruthven and Lindesey, being consulted,
offered their assistance in the enterprize; nor was even the earl of
Lenox, the king's father, averse to the design.[c] But as these conspirators were well acquainted with Henry's levity, they engaged
him to sign a paper, in which he avowed the undertaking, as
tending to the glory of God and advancement of religion, and
promised to protect them against every consequence, which might
ensue upon the assassination of Rizzio.[d] All these measures being
concerted, a messenger was dispatched to the banished lords, who
were hovering near the borders; and they were invited by the king
to return to their native country.

9th
March.

This design, so atrocious in itself, was rendered still more so by
the circumstances which attended its execution. Mary, who was in
the sixth month of her pregnancy, was supping in private, and had
at table the countess of Argyle, her natural sister, with Rizzio, and
others of her servants. The king entered the room by a private
passage, and stood at the back of Mary's chair: Lord Ruthven,
George Douglas, and other conspirators, being all armed, rushed
in after him; and the queen of Scots terrified with the appearance,
demanded of them the reason of this rude intrusion. They told
her, that they intended no violence against her person; but meant
only to bring that villain, pointing to Rizzio, to his deserved punishment. Rizzio, aware of the danger, ran behind his mistress, and
seizing her by the waist, called aloud to her for protection; while
she interposed in his behalf, with cries, and menaces, and entreat-

[b] Buchanan, lib. xvii, c. 60. Crawford, p. 6. Spotswood, p. 194. Knox,
p. 393. Jebb, vol. i. p. 456.   [c] Crawford, p. 7.   [d] Goodall, vol. i. p. 266.
Crawford, p. 7.

CHAPTER XXXIX

ies. The impatient assassins, regardless of her efforts, rushed upon their prey, and by overturning every thing which stood in their way, encreased the horror and confusion of the scene. Douglas, seizing Henry's dagger, stuck it in the body of Rizzio, who, screaming with fear and agony, was torn from Mary by the other conspirators, and pushed into the antichamber, where he was dispatched with fifty-six wounds.[e] The unhappy princess, informed of his fate, immediately dried her tears, and said, She would weep no more; she would now think of revenge. The insult, indeed, upon her person; the stain attempted to be fixed on her honour; the danger to which her life was exposed, on account of her pregnancy; were injuries so atrocious, and so complicated, that they scarcely left room for pardon, even from the greatest lenity and mercy.

The assassins, apprehensive of Mary's resentment, detained her prisoner in the palace; and the king dismissed all who seemed willing to attempt her rescue, by telling them, that nothing was done without his orders, and that he would be careful of the queen's safety. Murray and the banished lords appeared two days after; and Mary, whose anger was now engrossed by injuries more recent and violent, was willingly reconciled to them; and she even received her brother with tenderness and affection. They obtained an acquittal from parliament, and were re-instated in their honours and fortunes. The accomplices also in Rizzio's murder applied to her for a pardon; but she artfully delayed compliance, and persuaded them, that so long as she was detained in custody, and was surrounded by guards, any deed, which she should sign, would have no validity. Meanwhile, she had gained the confidence of her husband, by her persuasion and caresses; and no sooner were the guards withdrawn, than she engaged him to escape with her in the night-time, and take shelter in Dunbar. Many of her subjects here offered her their services; and Mary, having collected an army, which the conspirators had no power to resist, advanced to Edinburgh, and obliged them to fly into England, where they lived in great poverty and distress. They made applications however to the

[e] Melvil, p. 64. Keith, p. 330, 331. Crawford, p. 9.   [f] Melvil, p. 75, 76. Keith, p. 334. Knox, p. 398.   [g] Goodall, vol. i. p. 280. Keith Append. p. 167.

earl of Bothwel, a new favourite of Mary's; and that nobleman, desirous of strengthening his party by the accession of their interest, was able to pacify her resentment; and he soon after procured them liberty to return into their own country.[f]

The vengeance of the queen of Scots was implacable against her husband alone, whose person was before disagreeable to her, and who, by his violation of every tie of gratitude and duty, had now drawn on him her highest resentment. She engaged him to disown all connections with the assassins, to deny any concurrence in their crime, even to publish a proclamation containing a falsehood so notorious to the whole world;[g] and having thus made him expose himself to universal contempt, and rendered it impracticable for him ever to acquire the confidence of any party, she threw him off with disdain and indignation.[h] As if she had been making an escape from him, she suddenly withdrew to Alloa, a seat of the earl of Marre's; and when Henry followed her thither, she suddenly returned to Edinburgh; and gave him every where the strongest proofs of displeasure; and even of antipathy. She encouraged her courtiers in their neglect of him; and she was pleased, that his mean equipage and small train of attendants should draw on him the contempt of the very populace. He was permitted, however, to have apartments in the castle of Edinburgh, which Mary had chosen for the place of her delivery. She there brought forth a son; and as this was very important news to England, as well as to Scotland, she immediately dispatched Sir James Melvil to carry intelligence of the happy event to Elizabeth. Melvil tells us, that this princess, the evening of his arrival in London, had given a ball to her court at Greenwich, and was displaying all that spirit and alacrity, which usually attended her on these occasions: But when news arrived of the prince of Scotland's birth, all her joy was damped: She sunk into melancholy; she reclined her head upon her arm; and complained to some of her attendants, that the queen of Scots was mother of a fair son, while she herself was but a barren stock. Next day, however, at the reception of the ambassador, she resumed her former dissimulation, put on a joyful countenance, gave Melvil thanks for the haste he had made in conveying to her the agreeable intelligence,

19th June.

[h] Melvil, p. 66, 67.

CHAPTER XXXIX

and expressed the utmost cordiality and friendship to her sister.[i]
Some time after, she dispatched the earl of Bedford, with her
kinsman George Cary, son of lord Hunsdon, in order to officiate
at the baptism of the young prince; and she sent by them some
magnificent presents to the queen of Scots.

The birth of a son gave additional zeal to Mary's partizans in
England;[k] and even men of the most opposite parties began to cry
aloud for some settlement of the succession. These humours broke
out with great vehemence in a new session of parliament, held
after six prorogations. The house of peers, which had hitherto
forborne to touch on this delicate point, here took the lead; and
the house of commons soon after imitated the zeal of the lords.
Molineux opened the matter in the lower house, and proposed
that the question of the succession and that of supply should go
hand in hand; as if it were intended to constrain the queen to a
compliance with the request of her parliament.[l] The courtiers
endeavoured to elude the debate: Sir Ralph Sadler told the house,
that he had heard the queen positively affirm, that, for the good
of her people, she was determined to marry. Secretary Cecil and
Sir Francis Knollys gave their testimony to the same purpose; as
did also Sir Ambrose Cave, chancellor of the dutchy, and Sir Edward Rogers, comptroller of the household.[m] Elizabeth's ambition
and masculine character was so well known, that few members
gave any credit to this intelligence; and it was considered merely as
an artifice, by which she endeavoured to retract that positive declaration, which she had made in the beginning of her reign, that
she meant to live and die a virgin. The ministers, therefore, gained
nothing farther by this piece of policy, than only to engage the
house, for the sake of decency, to join the question of the queen's
marriage with that of a settlement of the crown; and the commons
were proceeding with great earnestness in the debate, and had
even appointed a committee to confer with the lords, when express
orders were brought them from Elizabeth not to proceed farther
in the matter. Cecil told them, that she pledged to the house the
word of a queen for her sincerity in her intentions to marry; that
the appointment of a successor would be attended with great danger to her person; that she herself had had experience, during the

30th Sept. A parlia- ment.

[i] Ibid. p. 69, 70. [k] Camden, p. 397. [l] D'Ewes, p. 129. [m] Ibid. p. 124.

reign of her sister, how much court was usually paid to the next heir, and what dangerous sacrifices men were commonly disposed to make of their present duty to their future prospects; and that she was therefore determined to delay, till a more proper opportunity, the decision of that important question."[n] The house was not satisfied with these reasons, and still less with the command, prohibiting them all debate on the subject. Paul Wentworth, a spirited member, went so far as to question whether such a prohibition were not an infringement of the liberties and privileges of the house.[o] Some even ventured to violate that profound respect, which had hitherto been preserved to the queen; and they affirmed that she was bound in duty, not only to provide for the happiness of her subjects during her own life, but also to pay regard to their future security, by fixing a successor; that, by an opposite conduct, she showed herself the stepmother, not the natural parent, of her people, and would seem desirous that England should no longer subsist than she should enjoy the glory and satisfaction of governing it; that none but timorous princes, or tyrants, or faint-hearted women, ever stood in fear of their successors; and that the affections of the people were a firm and impregnable rampart to every sovereign, who, laying aside all artifice or bye-ends, had courage and magnanimity to put his sole trust in that honourable and sure defence.[p] The queen, hearing of these debates, sent for the speaker, and after reiterating her former prohibition, she bade him inform the house, that, if any member remained still unsatisfied, he might appear before the privy council, and there give his reasons.[q] As the members showed a disposition, notwithstanding these peremptory orders, still to proceed upon the question, Elizabeth thought proper, by a message, to revoke them, and to allow the house liberty of debate.[r] They were so mollified by this gracious condescension, that they thenceforth conducted the matter with more calmness and temper; and they even voted her a supply, to be levied at three payments, of a subsidy and a fifteenth, without annexing any condition to it. The queen soon after dissolved the parliament, and told them, with some sharpness in the conclusion, that their proceedings had con-

2d January, 1567.

[n] D'Ewes, p. 127, 128. [o] Ibid. p. 128. [p] Camden, p. 400. [q] D'Ewes, p. 128. [r] Ibid. p. 130.

tained much dissimulation and artifice; that under the plausible pretences of marriage and succession, many of them covered very malevolent intentions towards her; but that, however, she reaped this advantage from the attempts of these men, that she could now distinguish her friends from her enemies. "But do you think," added she, "that I am unmindful of your future security, or will be negligent in settling the succession? That is the chief object of my concern; as I know myself to be liable to mortality. Or do you apprehend, that I meant to encroach on your liberties? No: It was never my meaning; I only intended to stop you before you approached the precipice. All things have their time; and though you may be blessed with a sovereign more wise or more learned than I, yet I assure you, that no one will ever rule over you, who shall be more careful of your safety. And therefore, henceforward, whether I live to see the like assembly or no, or whoever holds the reins of government, let me warn you to beware of provoking your sovereign's patience, so far as you have done mine. But I shall now conclude, that, notwithstanding the disgust I have received (for I mean not to part with you in anger) the greater part of you may assure themselves that they go home in their prince's good graces."[s]

Elizabeth carried farther her dignity on this occasion. She had received the subsidy without any condition; but as it was believed, that the commons had given her that gratuity with a view of engaging her to yield to their requests, she thought proper, on her refusal, voluntarily to remit the third payment; and she said, that money in her subjects' purses was as good to her as in her own exchequer.[t]

But though the queen was able to elude, for the present, the applications of parliament, the friends of the queen of Scots multiplied every day in England; and besides the catholics, many of whom kept a treasonable correspondence with her, and were ready to rise at her command,[u] the court itself of Elizabeth was full of her avowed partizans. The duke of Norfolk, the earls of Leicester, Pembroke, Bedford, Northumberland, Sir Nicholas Throgmorton, and most of the considerable men in England, except Cecil, seemed convinced of the necessity of declaring her the

[s] D'Ewes, p. 116, 117.   [t] Camden, p. 400.   [u] Haynes, p. 446, 448.

successor. None but the more zealous protestants adhered either to the countess of Hertford, or to her aunt, Eleanor, countess of Cumberland; and as the marriage of the former seemed liable to some objections, and had been declared invalid, men were alarmed, even on that side, with the prospect of new disputes concerning the succession. Mary's behaviour also, so moderate towards the protestants, and so gracious towards all men, had procured her universal respect;[w] and the public was willing to ascribe any imprudences, into which she had fallen, to her youth and inexperience. But all these flattering prospects were blasted by the subsequent incidents; where her egregious indiscretions, shall I say, or atrocious crimes, threw her from the height of her prosperity, and involved her in infamy and in ruin.

Murder of Darnley. The earl of Bothwel was of a considerable family and power in Scotland; and though not distinguished by any talents either of a civil or military nature, he had made a figure in that party, which opposed the greatness of the earl of Murray, and the more rigid reformers. He was a man of profligate manners; had involved his opulent fortune in great debts, and even reduced himself to beggary, by his profuse expences;[x] and seemed to have no resource but in desperate counsels and enterprizes. He had been accused more than once of an attempt to assassinate Murray; and though the frequency of these accusations on all sides diminished somewhat the credit due to any particular imputation, they prove sufficiently the prevalence of that detestable practice in Scotland, and may in that view serve to render such rumours the more credible. This man had of late acquired the favour and entire confidence of Mary; and all her measures were directed by his advice and authority. Reports were spread of more particular intimacies between them; and these reports gained ground from the continuance or rather encrease of her hatred towards her husband.[y] That young prince was reduced to such a state of desperation, by the neglects which he underwent from his queen and the courtiers, that he had once resolved to fly secretly into France or Spain, and had even provided a vessel for that purpose.[z] Some of the most considerable nobility, on the other hand, observing her rooted aversion to him,

[w] Melvil, p. 53, 61, 74.   [x] Keith, p. 240.   [y] Melvil, p. 66, 77.   [z] Keith, p. 345–348.

CHAPTER XXXIX

had proposed some expedients for a divorce; and though Mary is said to have spoken honourably on the occasion, and to have embraced the proposal no farther than it should be found consistent with her own honour and her son's legitimacy,[a] men were inclined to believe, that the difficulty of finding proper means for effecting that purpose, was the real cause of laying aside all farther thoughts of it. So far were the suspicions against her carried, that, when Henry, discouraged with the continual proofs of her hatred, left the court and retired to Glasgow, an illness of an extraordinary nature, with which he was seized immediately on his arrival in that place, was universally ascribed by her enemies to a dose of poison, which, it was pretended, she had administered to him.

While affairs were in this situation, all those who wished well to her character or to public tranquillity, were extremely pleased, and somewhat surprized, to hear, that a friendship was again conciliated between them, that she had taken a journey to Glasgow on purpose to visit him during his sickness, that she behaved towards him with great tenderness, that she had brought him along with her, and that she appeared thenceforth determined to live with him on a footing more suitable to the connexions between them. Henry, naturally uxorious, and not distrusting this sudden reconciliation, put himself implicitly into her hands, and attended her to Edinburgh. She lived in the palace of Holy-rood-house; but as the situation of the place was low, and the concourse of people about the court was necessarily attended with noise, which might disturb him in his present infirm state of health, these reasons were assigned for fitting up an apartment for him in a solitary house, at some distance, called the Kirk of Field. Mary here gave him marks of kindness and attachment; she conversed cordially with him; and she lay some nights in a room below his; but on the ninth of February, she told him, that she would pass that night in the palace, because the marriage of one of her servants was there to be celebrated in her presence. About two o'clock in the morning the whole town was much alarmed at hearing a great noise; and was still more astonished, when it was discovered that the noise came from the King's house, which was blown up by gun-powder; that his dead body was found at some distance in a neighbouring field; *Feb. 10.*

[a] Camden, p. 404. Goodall's Queen Mary, vol. ii. p. 317.

and that no marks either of fire, contusion, or violence appeared upon it.[b]

No doubt could be entertained but Henry was murdered; and general conjecture soon pointed towards the earl of Bothwel as the author of the crime.[c] But as his favour with Mary was visible, and his power great, no one ventured to declare openly his sentiments; and all men remained in silence and mute astonishment. Voices, however, were heard in the streets, during the darkness of the night, proclaiming Bothwel, and even Mary herself, to be murderers of the king; bills were secretly affixed on the walls to the same purpose; offers were made, that, upon giving proper securities, his guilt should be openly proved: But after one proclamation from the court, offering a reward and indemnity to any one that would discover the author of that villany, greater vigilance was employed in searching out the spreaders of the libels and reports against Bothwel and the queen, than in tracing the contrivers of the king's assassination, or detecting the regicides.[d]

The earl of Lenox, who lived at a distance from court, in poverty and contempt, was rouzed by the report of his son's murder, and wrote to the queen, imploring speedy justice against the assassins; among whom he named the earl of Bothwel, Sir James Balfour, and Gilbert Balfour his brother, David Chalmers, and four others of the queen's household; all of them persons who had been mentioned in the bills affixed to the walls at Edinburgh.[e] Mary took his demand of speedy justice in a very literal sense; and allowing only fifteen days for the examination of this important affair, she sent a citation to Lenox, requiring him to appear in court, and prove his charge against Bothwel.[f] This nobleman, meanwhile, and all the other persons, accused by Lenox, enjoyed their full liberty;[g] Bothwel himself was continually surrounded with armed men;[h] took his place in council;[i] lived during some

[b] It was imagined, that Henry had been strangled before the house was blown up. But this supposition is contradicted by the confession of the criminals; and there is no necessity to admit it in order to account for the condition of his body. There are many instances that men's lives have been saved who had been blown up in ships. Had Henry fallen on water he had not probably been killed.   [c] Melvil, p. 78. Cabbala, p. 136.   [d] Anderson's Collections, vol. ii. p. 38. vol. iv. p. 167, 168. Spotswood, p. 200. Keith, p. 374.   [e] Keith, p. 372. Anderson, vol. ii. p. 3.   [f] Keith, p. 373.   [g] Ibid. p. 374, 375.   [h] Ibid. p. 405.   [i] Anderson, vol. i. p. 38, 40, 50, 52.

time in the house with Mary;[k] and seemed to possess all his wonted
confidence and familiarity with her. Even the castle of Edinburgh,
a place of great consequence in this critical time, was entrusted to
him, and under him, to his creature, Sir James Balfour, who had
himself been publicly charged as an accomplice in the king's
murder.[l] Lenox, who had come as far as Stirling, with a view of
appearing at the trial, was informed of all these circumstances; and
reflecting on the small train which attended him, he began to
entertain very just apprehensions from the power, insolence, and
temerity of his enemy. He wrote to Mary, desiring that the day of
trial might be prorogued; and conjured her, by all the regard
which she bore to her own honour, to employ more leisure and
deliberation in determining a question of such extreme moment.[m]
No regard was paid to his application: The jury was enclosed, of
which the earl of Caithness was chancellor; and though Lenox,
foreseeing this precipitation, had ordered Cunningham, one of his
retinue, to appear in court, and protest in his name, against the
acquittal of the criminal, the jury proceeded to a verdict.[n] The
verdict was such as it behoved them to give, where neither accuser
nor witness appeared; and Bothwel was absolved from the king's
murder. The jury, however, apprehensive that their verdict would
give great scandal, and perhaps expose them afterwards to some
danger, entered a protest, in which they represented the necessity
of their proceedings.[o] It is remarkable, that the indictment was laid
against Bothwel for committing the crime on the ninth of February, not the tenth, the real day on which Henry was assassinated.[p]
The interpretation generally put upon this error, too gross, it was
thought, to have proceeded from mistake, was, that the secret
council, by whom Mary was governed, not trusting entirely to
precipitation, violence, and authority, had provided this plea, by
which they ensured, at all adventures, a plausible pretence for
acquitting Bothwel.

    Two days after this extraordinary transaction, a parliament was
held; and though the verdict in favour of Bothwel was attended
with such circumstances as strongly confirmed, rather than dimin-

*12th
April.*

[k] Ibid. vol. ii, p. 274.   [l] Spotswood, p. 201.   [m] Keith, p. 375. Anderson,
vol. i. p. 52.   [n] Keith, p. 376. Anderson, vol. ii. p. 106. Spotswood, p. 201.
[o] Spotswood, p. 201. Anderson, vol. i., p. 113.   [p] Keith, p. 375. Anderson,
vol. ii. p. 93. Spotswood, p. 201.

ished, the general opinion of his guilt, he was the person chosen
to carry the royal sceptre on the first meeting of that national
assembly.[q] In this parliament, a rigorous act was made against
those who set up defamatory bills; but no notice was taken of the
king's murder.[r] The favour, which Mary openly bore to Bothwel,
kept every one in awe; and the effects of this terror appeared more
plainly in another transaction, which ensued immediately upon
the dissolution of the parliament. A bond or association was
framed; in which the subscribers, after relating the acquittal of
Bothwel by a legal trial, and mentioning a farther offer, which he
had made, to prove his innocence by single combat, oblige themselves, in case any person should afterwards impute to him the
king's murder, to defend him with their whole power against such
calumniators. After this promise, which implied no great assurance in Bothwel of his own innocence, the subscribers mentioned
the necessity of their queen's marriage, in order to support the
government; and they recommended Bothwel to her as a husband.[s] This paper was subscribed by all the considerable nobility
there present. In a country, divided by violent factions, such a
concurrence in favour of one nobleman, no-wise distinguished
above the rest, except by his flagitious conduct, could never have
been obtained, had not every one been certain, at least firmly
persuaded, that Mary was fully determined on this measure.[t] Nor
would such a motive have sufficed to influence men, commonly so
stubborn and untractable, had they not been taken by surprize,
been ignorant of each other's sentiments, and over-awed by the
present power of the court, and by the apprehensions of farther
violence, from persons so little governed by any principles of honour and humanity. Even with all these circumstances, the subscription to this paper may justly be regarded as a reproach to the
nation.

24th
April.

The subsequent measures of Bothwel were equally precipitate
and audacious. Mary having gone to Stirling to pay a visit to her
son, he assembled a body of eight hundred horse, on pretence of
pursuing some robbers on the borders; and having way-laid her on
her return, he seized her person near Edinburgh, and carried her

---

[q] Keith, p. 78. Crawford, p. 14. [r] Keith, p. 380. [s] Ibid. p. 381. [t] See
note [I] at the end of the volume.

CHAPTER XXXIX

to Dunbar, with an avowed design of forcing her to yield to his purpose. Sir James Melvil, one of her retinue, was carried along with her, and says not, that he saw any signs of reluctance or constraint: He was even informed, as he tells us, by Bothwel's officers, that the whole transaction was managed in concert with her.[u] A woman, indeed, of that spirit and resolution, which is acknowledged to belong to Mary, does not usually, on these occasions, give such marks of opposition to *real* violence, as can appear anywise doubtful or ambiguous. Some of the nobility, however, in order to put matters to farther trial, sent her a private message; in which they told her, that, if, in reality, she lay under force, they would use all their efforts to rescue her. Her answer was, that she had indeed been carried to Dunbar by violence, but ever since her arrival had been so well treated, that she willingly remained with Bothwel.[w] No one gave himself thenceforth any concern to relieve her from a captivity, which was believed to proceed entirely from her own approbation and connivance.

This unusual conduct was at first ascribed to Mary's sense of the infamy attending her purposed marriage; and her desire of finding some colour to gloss over the irregularity of her conduct. But a pardon, given to Bothwel a few days after, made the public carry their conjectures somewhat farther. In this deed, Bothwel received a pardon for the violence committed on the queen's person; and for *all other crimes:* A clause, by which the murder of the king was indirectly forgiven. The rape was then conjectured to have been only a contrivance, in order to afford a pretence for indirectly remitting a crime, of which it would have appeared scandalous to make openly any mention.[x]

These events passed with such rapidity, that men had no leisure to admire sufficiently one incident, when they were surprized with a new one, equally rare and uncommon. There still, however, remained one difficulty, which, it was not easy to foresee, how the queen and Bothwel, determined as they were to execute their shameful purpose, could find expedients to overcome. The man, who had procured the subscription of the nobility, recommending him as a husband to the queen, and who had acted this seeming

[u] Melvil, p. 80.　[w] Spotswood, p. 202.　[x] Anderson, vol. iv. part ii. p. 61.

violence on her person, in order to force her consent, had been married two years before to another woman; to a woman of merit, of a noble family, sister to the earl of Huntley. But persons blinded by passion, and infatuated with crimes, soon shake off all appearance of decency. A suit was commenced for a divorce between Bothwel and his wife; and this suit was opened at the same instant in two different, or rather opposite courts; in the court of the archbishop of St. Andrews, which was popish, and governed itself by the canon law; and in the new consistorial or commissariot court, which was protestant, and was regulated by the principles of the reformed teachers. The plea, advanced in each court, was so calculated as to suit the principles which there prevailed: In the archbishop's court, the pretence of consanguinity was employed, because Bothwel was related to his wife in the fourth degree; in the commissariot court, the accusation of adultery was made use of against him. The parties too, who applied for the divorce, were different in the different courts: Bothwel was the person who sued in the former; his wife in the latter. And the suit in both courts was opened, pleaded, examined, and decided with the utmost precipitation; and a sentence of divorce was pronounced in four days.[y]

The divorce being thus obtained, it was thought proper, that Mary should be conducted to Edinburgh, and should there appear before the courts of judicature, and should acknowledge herself restored to entire freedom. This was understood to be contrived in a view of obviating all doubts with regard to the validity of her marriage. Orders were then given to publish in the church the banns between the queen and the duke of Orkney; for that was the title which he now bore; and Craig, a minister of Edinburgh, was applied to for that purpose. This clergyman, not content with having refused compliance, publicly in his sermons condemned the marriage; and exhorted all who had access to the queen, to give her their advice against so scandalous an alliance. Being called before the council, to answer for this liberty, he showed a courage, which might cover all the nobles with shame, on account of their tameness and servility. He said, that, by the rules of the church, the earl of Bothwel, being convicted of adultery, could not be permitted to marry; that the divorce between him and his former wife was

[y] Anderson, vol. ii. p. 280.

CHAPTER XXXIX

plainly procured by collusion, as appeared by the precipitation of the sentence, and the sudden conclusion of his marriage with the queen; and that all the suspicions which prevailed, with regard to the king's murder, and the queen's concurrence in the former rape, would thence receive undoubted confirmation. He therefore exhorted Bothwel, who was present, no longer to persevere in his present criminal enterprizes; and turning his discourse to the other counsellors, he charged them to employ all their influence with the queen, in order to divert her from a measure, which would load her with eternal infamy and dishonour. Not satisfied even with this admonition, he took the first opportunity of informing the public, from the pulpit, of the whole transaction, and expressed to them his fears, that, notwithstanding all remonstrances, their sovereign was still obstinately bent on her fatal purpose. "For himself," he said, "he had already discharged his conscience, and yet again would take heaven and earth to witness, that he abhorred and detested that marriage, as scandalous and hateful in the sight of mankind: But since the Great, as he perceived, either by their flattery or silence, gave countenance to the measure, he besought the Faithful to pray fervently to the Almighty, that a resolution, taken contrary to all law, reason, and good conscience, might, by the divine blessing, be turned to the comfort and benefit of the church and kingdom." These speeches offended the court extremely; and Craig was anew summoned before the council, to answer for his temerity, in thus passing the bounds of his commission. But he told them, that the bounds of his commission were the word of God, good laws; and natural reason; and were the queen's marriage tried by any of these standards, it would appear infamous and dishonourable, and would be so esteemed by the whole world. The council were so over-awed by this heroic behaviour in a private clergyman, that they dismissed him without farther censure or punishment.[z]

But though this transaction might have recalled Bothwel and the queen of Scots from their infatuation, and might have instructed them in the dispositions of the people, as well as in their own inability to oppose them; they were still resolute to rush forward, to their own manifest destruction. The marriage was solem-

[z] Spotswood, p. 203. Anderson, vol. ii. p. 280.

nized by the bishop of Orkney, a protestant, who was afterwards deposed by the church for this scandalous compliance. Few of the nobility appeared at the ceremony: They had, most of them, either from shame or fear, retired to their own houses. The French ambassador, Le Croc, an aged gentleman of honour and character, could not be prevailed on, though a dependant of the house of Guise, to countenance the marriage by his presence.[a] Elizabeth emonstrated, by friendly letters and messages, against the marriage:[b] The court of France made like opposition; but Mary, though on all other occasions she was extremely obsequious to the advice of her relations in that country, was here determined to pay no regard to their opinion.

15th May.

Queen of Scots marries Bothwel.

The news of these transactions, being carried to foreign countries, filled Europe with amazement, and threw infamy, not only on the principal actors in them, but also on the whole nation, who seemed, by their submission and silence, and even by their declared approbation, to give their sanction to these scandalous practices.[c] The Scots, who resided abroad, met with such reproaches, that they durst no where appear in public; and they earnestly exhorted their countrymen at home, to free them from the public odium, by bringing to condign punishment the authors of such atrocious crimes. This intelligence, with a little more leisure for reflection, roused men from their lethargy; and the rumours, which, from the very beginning,[d] had been spread against Mary, as if she had concurred in the king's murder, seemed now, by the subsequent transactions, to have received a strong confirmation and authority. It was every where said, that even though no particular and direct proofs had as yet been produced of the queen's guilt, the whole tenor of her late conduct was sufficient, not only to beget suspicion, but to produce entire conviction against her: That her sudden resolution of being reconciled to her husband, whom before she had long and justly hated; her bringing him to court, from which she had banished him by neglects and rigours; her fitting up separate apartments for him; were all of them circumstances, which, though trivial in themselves, yet, being com-

[a] Spotswood, p. 203. Melvil, p. 82.   [b] Keith, p. 392. Digges, p. 14.
[c] Melvil, p. 82. Keith, p. 402. Anderson, vol. i. p. 128, 134.   [d] Crawford, p. 11. Keith, Pref. p. 9.

pared with the subsequent events, bore a very unfavourable aspect for her: That the least which, after the king's murder, might have been expected in her situation, was a more than usual caution in her measures, and an extreme anxiety to punish the real assassins, in order to free herself from all reproach and suspicion: That no woman, who had any regard to her character, would allow a man, publicly accused of her husband's murder, so much as to approach her presence, far less give him a share in her counsels, and endow him with favour and authority: That an acquittal, merely in the absence of accusers, was very ill-fitted to satisfy the public; especially if that absence proceeded from a designed precipitation of the sentence, and from the terror, which her known friendship for the criminal had infused into every one: That the very mention of her marriage to such a person, in such circumstances, was horrible; and the contrivances of extorting a consent from the nobility, and of concerting a rape, were gross artifices, more proper to discover her guilt than prove her innocence: That where a woman thus shews a consciousness of merited reproach, and, instead of correcting, provides only thin glosses to cover, her exceptionable conduct, she betrays a neglect of fame, which must either be the effect or the cause of the most shameful enormities: That to espouse a man, who had, a few days before, been so scandalously divorced from his wife; who, to say the least, was believed to have, a few months before, assassinated her husband, was so contrary to the plainest rules of behaviour, that no pretence of indiscretion or imprudence could account for such a conduct: That a woman, who, so soon after her husband's death, though not attended with any extraordinary circumstances, contracts a marriage, which might, in itself, be the most blameless, cannot escape severe censure; but one who overlooks, for her pleasure, so many other weighty considerations, was equally capable, in gratifying her appetites, to neglect every regard to honour and humanity: That Mary was not ignorant of the prevailing opinion of the public, with regard to her own guilt, and of the inferences which would every where be drawn from her conduct; and therefore, if she still continued to pursue measures which gave such just offence, she ratified, by her actions, as much as she could by the most formal confession, all the surmizes and imputations of her enemies: That a prince was here murdered in the face of the world; Bothwel alone was suspected and accused; if he were innocent, nothing could absolve him, either in Mary's eyes or those of the public, but the detection and conviction of the real assassin; yet no enquiry was made to that purpose, though a parliament had been assembled; the sovereign and wife was here plainly silent from guilt, the people from terror: That the only circumstance, which opposed all these presumptions or rather proofs, was, the benignity and goodness of her preceding behaviour, which seemed to remove her from all suspicions of such atrocious inhumanity; but that the characters of men were extremely variable, and persons, guilty of the worst actions, were not always naturally of the worst and most criminal dispositions: That a woman who, in a critical and dangerous moment, had sacrificed her honour to a man of abandoned principles, might thenceforth be led blindfolded by him to the commission of the most enormous crimes, and was in reality no longer at her own disposal: And that, though one supposition was still left to alleviate her blame, namely, that Bothwel, presuming on her affection towards him, had of himself committed the crime, and had never communicated it to her, yet such a sudden and passionate love to a man, whom she had long known, could not easily be accounted for, without supposing some degree of preceding guilt; and as it appeared, that she was not afterwards restrained, either by shame or prudence, from incurring the highest reproach and danger, it was not likely that a sense of duty or humanity would have a more powerful influence over her.

These were the sentiments which prevailed throughout Scotland; and as the protestant teachers, who had great authority, had long borne an animosity to Mary, the opinion of her guilt was, by that means, the more widely diffused, and made the deeper impression on the people. Some attempts, made by Bothwel, and, as is pretended, with her consent, to get the young prince into his power, excited the most serious attention; and the principal nobility, even many of those who had formerly been constrained to sign the application in favour of Bothwel's marriage met at Stirling, and formed an association for protecting the prince, and punishing the king's murderers.[e] The earl of Athole himself, a known

[e] Keith, p. 394.

catholic, was the first author of this confederacy: The earls of
Argyle, Morton, Marre, Glencarne, the lords Boyd, Lindesey,
Hume, Semple, Kirkaldy of Grange, Tulibardine, and secretary
Lidington, entered zealously into it. The earl of Murray, foreseeing such turbulent times, and being desirous to keep free of
these dangerous factions, had, some time before, desired and obtained Mary's permission to retire into France.

Lord Hume was first in arms; and leading a body of eight *Insurrec-*
hundred horse, suddenly environed the queen of Scots and Both- *tions in*
wel, in the castle of Borthwic. They found means of making their *Scotland.*
escape to Dunbar; while the confederate lords were assembling
their troops at Edinburgh; and taking measures to effect their
purpose. Had Bothwel been so prudent as to keep within the
fortress of Dunbar, his enemies must have dispersed for want of
pay and subsistance; but hearing that the associated lords were
fallen into distress, he was so rash as to take the field, and advance *15th*
towards them. The armies met at Carberry Hill, about six miles *June.*
from Edinburgh; and Mary soon became sensible, that her own
troops disapproved of her cause, and were averse to spill their
blood in the quarrel.*f* After some bravadoes of Bothwel, where he
discovered very little courage, she saw no resource but that of
holding a conference with Kirkaldy of Grange, and of putting
herself, upon some general promises, into the hands of the confederates. She was conducted to Edinburgh, amidst the insults of the
populace; who reproached her with her crimes, and even held
before her eyes, which way soever she turned, a banner, on which
were painted the murder of her husband, and the distress of her
infant son.*g* Mary, overwhelmed with her calamities, had recourse
to tears and lamentations. Meanwhile, Bothwel, during her conference with Grange, fled unattended to Dunbar; and fitting out
a few small ships, set sail for the Orkneys, where he subsisted
during some time by piracy. He was pursued thither by Grange,
and his ship was taken, with several of his servants, who afterwards
discovered all the circumstances of the king's murder, and were
punished for the crime.*h* Bothwel himself escaped in a boat, and

f Keith, p. 402. Spotswood, p. 207. *g* Melvil, p. 83, 84. *h* Anderson, vol.
ii. p. 165, 166, &c.

found means to get a passage to Denmark, where he was thrown into prison, lost his senses, and died miserably about ten years after: An end worthy of his flagitious conduct and behaviour.

Imprison-
ment of
Mary.

The queen of Scots, now in the hands of an enraged faction, met with such treatment as a sovereign may naturally expect from subjects, who have their future security to provide for, as well as their present animosity to gratify. It is pretended, that she behaved with a spirit very little suitable to her condition, avowed her inviolable attachment to Bothwel,[i] and even wrote him a letter, which the lords intercepted, where she declared, that she would endure any extremity, nay, resign her dignity and crown itself, rather than relinquish his affections.[k] The malcontents, finding the danger to which they were exposed, in case Mary should finally prevail, thought themselves obliged to proceed with rigour against her; and they sent her next day under a guard to the castle of Lochlevin, situated in a lake of that name. The mistress of the house was mother to the earl of Murray; and as she pretended to have been lawfully married to the late king of Scots, she naturally bore an animosity to Mary, and treated her with the utmost harshness and severity.

Elizabeth, who was fully informed of all those incidents, seemed touched with compassion towards the unfortunate queen; and all her fears and jealousies being now laid asleep, by the consideration of that ruin and infamy, in which Mary's conduct had involved her, she began to reflect on the instability of human affairs, the precarious state of royal grandeur, the danger of encouraging rebellious subjects; and she resolved to employ her authority for alleviating the calamities of her unhappy kinswoman. She sent Sir Nicholas Throgmorton ambassador to Scotland, in order to remonstrate both with Mary and the associated lords; and she gave him instructions, which, though mixed with some lofty pretensions, were full of that good sense which was so natural to her, and of that generosity which the present interesting conjuncture had called forth. She empowered him to declare in her name to Mary, that the late conduct of that princess, so enormous, and

---

[i] Keith, p. 419.   [k] Melvil, p. 84. The reality of this letter appears somewhat disputable; chiefly because Murray and his associates never mentioned it in their accusation of her before queen Elizabeth's commissioners.

CHAPTER XXXIX

in every respect so unjustifiable, had given her the highest offence; and though she felt the movements of pity towards her, she had once determined never to interpose in her affairs, either by advice or assistance, but to abandon her entirely, as a person whose condition was totally desperate, and honour irretrievable: That she was well assured, that other foreign princes, Mary's near relations, had embraced the same resolution; but, for her part, the late events had touched her heart with more tender sympathy, and had made her adopt measures more favourable to the liberty and interests of the unhappy queen: That she was determined not to see her oppressed by her rebellious subjects, but would employ all her good offices, and even her power, to redeem her from captivity, and place her in such a condition as would at once be compatible with her dignity, and the safety of her subjects: That she conjured her to lay aside all thoughts of revenge, except against the murderers of her husband; and as she herself was his near relation, she was better entitled than the subjects of Mary to interpose her authority on that head, and she therefore besought that princess, if she had any regard to her own honour and safety, not to oppose so just and reasonable a demand: That after those two points were provided for, her own liberty, and the punishment of her husband's assassins, the safety of her infant son was next to be considered; and there seemed no expedient more proper for that purpose, than sending him to be educated in England: And that, besides the security, which would attend his removal from a scene of faction and convulsions, there were many other beneficial consequences, which it was easy to foresee as the result of his education in that country.[l]

The remonstrances, which Throgmorton was instructed to make to the associated lords, were entirely conformable to these sentiments, which Elizabeth entertained in Mary's favour. She empowered him to tell them, that, whatever blame she might throw on Mary's conduct, any opposition to their sovereign was totally unjustifiable, and incompatible with all order and good government: That it belonged not to them to reform, much less to punish, the mal-administration of their prince; and the only arms, which subjects could in any case lawfully employ against the supreme

[l] Keith, p. 411, 412, &c.

authority, were entreaties, counsels, and representations: That if these expedients failed, they were next to appeal by their prayers to Heaven; and to wait with patience till the Almighty, in whose hands are the hearts of princes, should be pleased to turn them to justice and to mercy. That she inculcated not this doctrine, because she herself was interested in its observance; but because it was universally received in all well governed states, and was essential to the preservation of civil society: That she required them to restore their queen to liberty; and promised, in that case, to concur with them in all proper expedients for regulating the government, for punishing the king's murderers, and for guarding the life and liberty of the infant prince: And that if the services, which she had lately rendered the Scottish nation, in protecting them from foreign usurpation, were duly considered by them, they would repose confidence in her good offices, and would esteem themselves blame-worthy, in having hitherto made no application to her.[m]

Elizabeth, besides these remonstrances, sent, by Throgmorton, some articles of accommodation, which he was to propose to both parties, as expedients for the settlement of public affairs; and though these articles contained some important restraints on the sovereign power, they were in the main calculated for Mary's advantage, and were sufficiently indulgent to her.[n] The associated lords, who determined to proceed with greater severity, were apprehensive of Elizabeth's partiality; and being sensible, that Mary would take courage from the protection of that powerful princess,[o] they thought proper, after several affected delays, to refuse the English ambassador all access to her. There were four different schemes proposed in Scotland, for the treatment of the captive queen: One, that she should be restored to her authority under very strict limitations: The second, that she should be obliged to resign her crown to the prince, be banished the kingdom, and be confined either to France or England; with assurances from the sovereign, in whose dominions she should reside, that she should make no attempts to the disturbance of the established government: The third, that she should be publicly tried for her crimes, of which her enemies pretended to have undoubted proof, and be sentenced to perpetual imprisonment: The fourth was still more

[m] Keith, p. 414, 415, 429.　　[n] Ibid. p. 416.　　[o] Ibid. p. 427.

severe, and required, that, after her trial and condemnation, capital punishment should be inflicted upon her.[p] Throgmorton supported the mildest proposal; but though he promised his mistress's guarantee for the performance of articles, threatened the ruling party with immediate vengeance in case of refusal,[q] and warned them not to draw on themselves, by their violence, the public reproach, which now lay upon their queen; he found, that, excepting secretary Lidington, he had not the good fortune to convince any of the leaders. All counsels seemed to tend towards the more severe expedients; and the preachers, in particular, drawing their examples from the rigorous maxims of the Old Testament, which can only be warranted by particular revelations, inflamed the minds of the people against their unhappy sovereign.[r]

There were several pretenders to the regency of the young prince, after the intended deposition of Mary. The earl of Lenox claimed that authority as grandfather to the prince: The duke of Chatelrault, who was absent in France, had pretensions as next heir to the crown: But the greatest number of the associated lords inclined to the earl of Murray, in whose capacity they had entire trust, and who possessed the confidence of the preachers and more zealous reformers. All measures being therefore concerted, three instruments were sent to Mary, by the hands of lord Lindsey and Sir Robert Melvil; by one of which she was to resign the crown in favour of her son, by another to appoint Murray regent, by the third to name a council, which should administer the government till his arrival in Scotland. The queen of Scots, seeing no prospect of relief, lying justly under apprehensions for her life, and believing, that no deed, which she executed during her captivity, could be valid, was prevailed on, after a plentiful effusion of tears, to sign these three instruments; and she took not the trouble of inspecting any one of them.[s] In consequence of this forced resignation, the young prince was proclaimed king, by the name of James VI. He was soon after crowned at Stirling, and the earl of Morton took in his name the coronation-oath; in which a promise to extirpate heresy was not forgotten. Some republican pretensions, in favour

29th July.

---

[p] Ibid. p. 420.   [q] Keith, p. 428.   [r] Ibid. p. 422, 426.   [s] Melvil, p. 85. Spotswood, p. 211. Anderson, vol. iii. p. 19.

of the people's power, were countenanced in this ceremony;[1] and a coin was soon after struck, on which the famous saying of Trajan was inscribed, *Pro me; si merear, in me:* For me; if I deserve it, against me.[u] Throgmorton had orders from his mistress not to assist at the coronation of the king of Scots.[w]

The council of regency had not long occasion to exercise their authority. The earl of Murray arrived from France, and took possession of his high office. He paid a visit to the captive queen; and spoke to her in a manner which better suited her past conduct than her present condition. This harsh treatment quite extinguished in her breast any remains of affection towards him.[x] Murray proceeded afterwards to break, in a more public manner, all terms of decency with her. He summoned a parliament; and that assembly, after voting, that she was undoubtedly an accomplice in her husband's murder, condemned her to imprisonment, ratified her demission of the crown, and acknowledged her son for king, and Murray for regent.[y] The regent, a man of vigour and abilities, employed himself successfully in reducing the kingdom. He bribed Sir James Balfour to surrender the castle of Edinburgh: He constrained the garrison of Dunbar to open their gates: And he demolished that fortress.

15th Dec.

But though every thing thus bore a favourable aspect to the new government, and all men seemed to acquiesce in Murray's authority; a violent revolution, however necessary, can never be effected without great discontents; and it was not likely, that, in a country, where the government, in its most settled state, possessed a very disjointed authority, a new establishment should meet with no interruption or disturbance. Few considerable men of the nation seemed willing to support Mary, so long as Bothwel was present; but the removal of that obnoxious nobleman had altered the sentiments of many. The duke of Chatelrault, being disappointed of the regency, bore no good will to Murray; and the same sentiments were embraced by all his numerous retainers: Several of the nobility, finding that others had taken the lead among the associators, formed a faction apart, and opposed the prevailing power: And besides their being moved by some remains of duty

---

[1] Keith, p. 439, 440. [u] Ibid. p. 440. Append. p. 150. [w] Ibid. p. 430.
[x] Melvil, p. 87, Keith, p. 445. [y] Anderson, vol. ii. p. 206, & seq.

and affection towards Mary, the malcontent lords, observing every thing carried to extremity against her, were naturally led to embrace her cause, and shelter themselves under her authority. All who retained any propensity to the catholic religion, were induced to join this party; and even the people in general, though they had formerly either detested Mary's crimes, or blamed her imprudence, were now inclined to compassionate her present situation, and lamented, that a person, possessed of so many amiable accomplishments, joined to such high dignity, should be treated with such extreme severity.[z] Animated by all these motives, many of the principal nobility, now adherents to the queen of Scots, met at Hamilton, and concerted measures for supporting the cause of that princess.

While these humours were in fermentation, Mary was employed in contrivances for effecting her escape; and she engaged, by her charms and caresses, a young gentleman, George Douglas, brother to the laird of Lochlevin, to assist her in that enterprize. She even went so far as to give him hopes of espousing her, after her marriage with Bothwel should be dissolved on the plea of force; and she proposed this expedient to the regent, who rejected it. Douglas, however, persevered in his endeavours to free her from captivity; and having all opportunities of access to the house, he was at last successful in the undertaking. He conveyed her in disguise into a small boat, and himself rowed her ashore. She hastened to Hamilton; and the news of her arrival in that place being immediately spread abroad, many of the nobility flocked to her with their forces. A bond of association for her defence was signed by the earls of Argyle, Huntley, Eglington, Crawford, Cassilis, Rothes, Montrose, Sutherland, Errol, nine bishops, and nine barons, besides many of the most considerable gentry.[a] And in a few days an army, to the number of six thousand men, were assembled under her standard.

Elizabeth was no sooner informed of Mary's escape, than she discovered her resolution of persevering in the same generous and friendly measures, which she had hitherto pursued. If she had not employed force against the regent, during the imprisonment of that princess, she had been chiefly withheld by the fear of pushing

1568.

2d
May.

---

[z] Buchanan, lib. xviii, c. 53.   [a] Keith, p. 475.

him to greater extremities against her;[b] but she had proposed to the court of France an expedient, which, though less violent, would have been no less effectual for her service: She desired that France and England should by concert cut off all commerce with the Scots, till they should do justice to their injured sovereign.[c] She now dispatched Leighton into Scotland to offer both her good offices, and the assistance of her forces, to Mary; but as she apprehended the entrance of French troops into the kingdom, she desired that the controversy between the queen of Scots and her subjects might by that princess be referred entirely to her arbitration, and that no foreign succours should be introduced into Scotland.[d]

But Elizabeth had not leisure to exert fully her efforts in favour of Mary. The regent made haste to assemble forces; and notwithstanding that his army was inferior in number to that of the queen of Scots, he took the field against her. A battle was fought at Langside near Glasgow, which was entirely decisive in favour of the regent; and though Murray, after his victory, stopped the bloodshed, yet was the action followed by a total dispersion of the queen's party. That unhappy princess fled southwards from the field of battle with great precipitation, and came, with a few attendants, to the borders of England. She here deliberated concerning her next measures, which would probably prove so important to her future happiness or misery. She found it impossible to remain in her own kingdom: She had an aversion, in her present wretched condition, to return into France, where she had formerly appeared with so much splendour; and she was not, besides, provided with a vessel, which could safely convey her thither: The late generous behaviour of Elizabeth made her hope for protection, and even assistance, from that quarter;[e] and as the present fears from her domestic enemies were the most urgent, she overlooked all other considerations, and embraced the resolution of taking shelter in England. She embarked on board a fishing-boat in Galloway, and landed the same day at Wirkington in Cumberland, about thirty miles from Carlisle; whence she immediately dispatched a messenger to London; notifying her arrival, desiring

15th May.

Mary flies into England.

---

[b] Ibid. p. 463. Cabala, p. 141.   [c] Keith, p. 462.   [d] Keith, p. 473. in the notes. Anderson, vol. iv. p. 26.   [e] Jebb's Collection, vol. i. p. 420.

CHAPTER XXXIX

leave to visit Elizabeth, and craving her protection, in consequence of former professions of friendship, made her by that princess.

Elizabeth now found herself in a situation, when it was become necessary to take some decisive resolution with regard to her treatment of the queen of Scots; and as she had hitherto, contrary to the opinion of Cecil, attended more to the motives of generosity than of policy;[f] she was engaged by that prudent minister to weigh anew all the considerations, which occurred in this critical conjuncture. He represented, that the party, which had dethroned Mary, and had at present assumed the government of Scotland, was always attached to the English alliance, and was engaged, by all the motives of religion and of interest, to persevere in their connections with Elizabeth: That though Murray and his friends might complain of some unkind usage during their banishment in England, they would easily forget these grounds of quarrel, when they reflected, that Elizabeth was the only ally, on whom they could safely rely, and that their own queen, by her attachment to the catholic faith, and by her other connections, excluded them entirely from the friendship of France, and even from that of Spain: That Mary, on the other hand, even before her violent breach with her protestant subjects, was in secret entirely governed by the counsels of the house of Guise; much more, would she implicitly comply with their views, when, by her own ill conduct, the power of that family and of the zealous catholics was become her sole resource and security: That her pretensions to the English crown would render her a dangerous instrument in their hands; and, were she once able to suppress the protestants in her own kingdom, she would unite the Scottish and English catholics, with those of all foreign states, in a confederacy against the religion and government of England: That it behoved Elizabeth, therefore, to proceed with caution in the design of restoring her rival to the throne; and to take care, both that this enterprize, if undertaken, should be effected by English forces alone, and that full securities should beforehand be provided for the reformers and the reformation in Scotland: That above all, it was necessary to guard carefully the person of that princess; lest, finding this unexpected reserve in the English friendship, she should suddenly take the resolution of flying into

[f] Cabala, p. 140.

France, and should attempt by foreign force to recover possession of her authority: That her desperate fortunes and broken reputation fitted her for any attempt; and her resentment, when she should find herself thus deserted by the queen, would concur with her ambition and her bigotry, and render her an unrelenting, as well as powerful, enemy to the English government: That if she were once abroad, in the hands of enterprizing catholics, the attack on England would appear to her as easy as that on Scotland; and the only method, she must imagine, of recovering her native kingdom, would be to acquire that crown, to which she would deem herself equally intitled: That a neutrality in such interesting situations, though it might be pretended, could never, without the most extreme danger, be upheld by the queen; and the detention of Mary was equally requisite, whether the power of England were to be employed in her favour, or against her: That nothing, indeed, was more becoming a great prince than generosity; yet the suggestions of this noble principle could never, without imprudence, be consulted in such delicate circumstances as those in which the queen was at present placed; where her own safety and the interests of her people were ultimately concerned in every resolution which she embraced: That though the example of successful rebellion, especially in a neighbouring country, could no wise be agreeable to any sovereign, yet Mary's imprudence had been so great, perhaps her crimes so enormous, that the insurrection of subjects, after such provocation, could no longer be regarded as a precedent against other princes: That it was first necessary for Elizabeth to ascertain, in a regular and satisfactory manner, the extent of Mary's guilt, and thence to determine the degree of protection, which she ought to afford her against her discontented subjects: That as no glory could surpass that of defending oppressed innocence, it was equally infamous to patronize vice and murder on the throne; and the contagion of such dishonour would extend itself to all who countenanced or supported it: And that, if the crimes of the Scottish princess should, on enquiry, appear as great and certain as was affirmed and believed, every measure against her, which policy should dictate, would thence be justified; or if she should be found innocent, every enterprize, which friendship should inspire, would be acknowledged laudable and glorious.

Agreeably to these views, Elizabeth resolved to proceed in a

CHAPTER XXXIX

seemingly generous, but really cautious manner, with the queen of Scots; and she immediately sent orders to lady Scrope, sister to the duke of Norfolk, a lady who lived in the neighbourhood, to attend on that princess. Soon after, she dispatched to her lord Scrope himself, warden of the marches, and Sir Francis Knolles, vice chamberlain. They found Mary already lodged in the castle of Carlisle; and after expressing the queen's sympathy with her in her late misfortunes, they told her, that her request of being allowed to visit their sovereign, and of being admitted to her presence, could not at present be complied with: Till she had cleared herself of her husband's murder, of which she was so strongly accused, Elizabeth could not without dishonour show her any countenance, or appear indifferent to the assassination of so near a kinsman.[g] So unexpected a check threw Mary into tears; and the necessity of her situation extorted from her a declaration, that she would willingly justify herself to her sister from all imputations, and would submit her cause to the arbitration of so good a friend.[h] Two days after she sent lord Herreis to London with letter to the same purpose.

This concession, which Mary could scarcely avoid, without an acknowledgment of guilt, was the point expected and desired by Elizabeth: She immediately dispatched Midlemore to the regent of Scotland; requiring him both to desist from the farther prosecution of his queen's party, and send some persons to London to justify his conduct with regard to her. Murray might justly be startled at receiving a message, so violent and imperious; but as his domestic enemies were numerous and powerful, and England was the sole ally, which he could expect among foreign nations, he was resolved rather to digest the affront than provoke Elizabeth by a refusal. He also considered, that, though that queen had hitherto appeared partial to Mary, many political motives evidently engaged her to support the king's cause in Scotland; and it was not to be doubted but so penetrating a princess would in the end discover this interest, and would at least afford him a patient and equitable hearing. He therefore replied, that he would himself take a journey to England, attended by other commissioners; and would willingly submit the determination of his cause to Elizabeth.[i]

[g] Anderson, vol. iv. p. 54, 66, 82, 83, 86.   [h] Ibid. p. 10, 55, 87.   [i] Ibid. p. 13–16.

Lord Herreis now perceived, that his mistress had advanced too far in her concessions: He endeavoured to maintain, that Mary could not, without diminution of her royal dignity, submit to a contest with her rebellious subjects before a foreign prince; and he required either present aid from England, or liberty for his queen to pass over into France. Being pressed, however, with the former agreement before the English council, he again renewed his consent; but in a few days he began anew to recoil; and it was with some difficulty that he was brought to acquiesce in the first determination.[k] These fluctuations, which were incessantly renewed, showed his visible reluctance to the measures pursued by the court of England.

The queen of Scots discovered no less aversion to the trial proposed; and it required all the artifice and prudence of Elizabeth to make her persevere in the agreement, to which she had at first consented. This latter princess still said to her, that she desired not, without Mary's consent and approbation, to enter into the question, and pretended only as a friend to hear her justification: That she was confident there would be found no difficulty in refuting all the calumnies of her enemies; and even if her apology should fall short of full conviction, Elizabeth was determined to support her cause, and procure her some reasonable terms of accommodation: And that it was never meant, that she should be cited to a trial on the accusation of her rebellious subjects; but on the contrary, that they should be summoned to appear and to justify themselves for their conduct towards her.[l] Allured by these plausible professions, the queen of Scots agreed to vindicate herself by her own commissioners, before commissioners appointed by Elizabeth.

During these transactions, lord Scrope and Sir Francis Knolles, who resided with Mary at Carlisle, had leisure to study her character, and to make report of it to Elizabeth. Unbroken by her misfortunes, resolute in her purpose, active in her enterprizes, she aspired to nothing but victory; and was determined to endure any extremity, to undergo any difficulty, and to try every fortune, rather than abandon her cause, or yield the superiority to her enemies. Eloquent, insinuating, affable; she had already con-

[k] Anderson, p. 16–20.   [l] Ibid. p. 11, 12, 13, 109, 110.

CHAPTER XXXIX

vinced all those who approached her, of the innocence of her past conduct; and as she declared her fixed purpose to require aid of her friends all over Europe, and even to have recourse to infidels and barbarians, rather than fail of vengeance against her persecutors, it was easy to foresee the danger, to which her charms, her spirit, her address, if allowed to operate with their full force, would expose them.[m] The court of England, therefore, who, under pretence of guarding her, had already, in effect, detained her prisoner, were determined to watch her with still greater vigilance. As Carlisle, by its situation on the borders, afforded her great opportunities of contriving her escape, they removed her to Bolton, a seat of lord Scrope's in Yorkshire: And the issue of the controversy between her and the Scottish nation was regarded as a subject more momentous to Elizabeth's security and interests, than it had hitherto been apprehended.

The commissioners, appointed by the English court for the examination of this great cause, were the duke of Norfolk, the earl of Sussex, and Sir Ralph Sadler; and York was named as the place of conference. Lesley, bishop of Ross, the lords Herreis, Levingstone, and Boyde, with three persons more, appeared as commissioners from the queen of Scots. The earl of Murray, regent, the earl of Morton, the bishop of Orkney, lord Lindesey, and the abbot of Dunfermling were appointed commissioners from the king and kingdom of Scotland. Secretary Lidington, George Buchanan, the famous poet and historian, with some others, were named as their assistants.

4th Octob. Conferences at York and Hamptoncourt.

It was a great circumstance in Elizabeth's glory, that she was thus chosen umpire between the factions of a neighbouring kingdom, which had, during many centuries, entertained the most violent jealousy and animosity against England; and her felicity was equally rare, in having the fortunes and fame of so dangerous a rival, who had long given her the greatest inquietude, now entirely at her disposal. Some circumstances of her late conduct had discovered a byass towards the side of Mary: Her prevailing interests led her to favour the enemies of that princess: The professions of impartiality, which she had made, were open and frequent; and she had so far succeeded, that each side accused her commis-

[m] Anderson, vol. iv. p. 54, 71, 72, 74, 78, 92.

sioners of partiality towards their adversaries.[n] She herself appears, by the instructions given them, to have fixed no plan for the decision; but she knew, that the advantages, which she should reap, must be great, whatever issue the cause might take. If Mary's crimes could be ascertained by undoubted proof, she could for ever blast the reputation of that princess, and might justifiably detain her for ever a prisoner in England: If the evidence fell short of conviction, it was intended to restore her to the throne, but with such strict limitations, as would leave Elizabeth perpetual arbiter of all differences between the parties in Scotland, and render her in effect absolute mistress of the kingdom.[o]

Mary's commissioners, before they gave in their complaints against her enemies in Scotland, entered a protest, that their appearance in the cause should nowise affect the independance of her crown, or be construed as a mark of subordination to England: The English commissioners received this protest, but with a reserve to the claim of England. The complaint of that princess was next read, and contained a detail of the injuries, which she had suffered since her marriage with Bothwel: That her subjects had taken arms against her, on pretence of freeing her from captivity; that when she put herself into their hands, they had committed her to close custody in Lochlevin; had placed her son, an infant, on her throne; had again taken arms against her after her deliverance from prison; had rejected all her proposals for accommodation; had given battle to her troops; and had obliged her, for the safety of her person, to take shelter in England.[p] The earl of Murray, in answer to this complaint, gave a summary and imperfect account of the late transactions: that the earl of Bothwel, the known murderer of the late king, had, a little after committing that crime, seized the person of the queen and led her to Dunbar; that he acquired such influence over her as to gain her consent to marry him, and he had accordingly procured a divorce from his former wife, and had pretended to celebrate his nuptials with the queen; that the scandal of this transaction, the dishonour which it brought on the nation, the danger to which the infant prince was exposed from the attempts of that audacious man, had obliged the nobility

---

[n] Anderson, vol. iv. part 2. p. 40.   [o] Ibid. 14, 15, &c. Goodall, vol. ii. p. 110.
[p] Anderson, vol. iv. part 2. p. 52. Goodall, vol. ii. p. 128. Haynes, p. 478.

CHAPTER XXXIX

to take arms, and oppose his criminal enterprizes; that after Mary, in order to save him, had thrown herself into their hands, she still discovered such a violent attachment to him, that they found it necessary, for their own and the public safety, to confine her person, during a season, till Bothwel and the other murderers of her husband could be tried and punished for their crimes; and that during this confinement, she had voluntarily, without compulsion or violence, merely from disgust at the inquietude and vexations attending power, resigned her crown to her only son, and had appointed the earl of Murray regent during the minority.[q] The queen's answer to this apology was obvious: That she did not know and never could suspect, that Bothwel, who had been acquitted by a jury, and recommended to her by all the nobility for her husband, was the murderer of the king; and she ever was, and still continues desirous, that, if he be guilty, he may be brought to condign punishment; that her resignation of the crown was extorted from her by the well-grounded fears of her life, and even by direct menaces of violence; and that Throgmorton, the English ambassador, as well as others of her friends, had advised her to sign that paper, as the only means of saving herself from the last extremity, and had assured her, that a consent, given under these circumstances, could never have any validity.[r]

So far the queen of Scots seemed plainly to have the advantage in the contest: And the English commissioners might have been surprized, that Murray had made so weak a defence, and had suppressed all the material imputations against that princess, on which his party had ever so strenuously insisted; had not some private conferences previously informed them of the secret. Mary's commissioners had boasted, that Elizabeth, from regard to her kinswoman, and from her desire of maintaining the rights of sovereigns, was determined, how criminal soever the conduct of that princess might appear, to restore her to the throne;[s] and Murray, reflecting on some past measures of the English court, began to apprehend, that there were but too just grounds for these expectations. He believed, that Mary, if he would agree to conceal

[q] Anderson, vol. iv. part 2. p. 64, & seq. Goodall, vol. ii. p. 144.
[r] Anderson, vol. iv. part 2. p. 60, & seq. Goodall, vol. ii. p. 162.
[s] Anderson, vol. iv. part 2. p. 45. Goodall, vol. ii. p. 127.

the most violent part of the accusation against her, would submit
to any reasonable terms of accommodation; but if he once proceeded so far as to charge her with the whole of her guilt, no
composition could afterwards take place; and should she ever be
restored, either by the power of Elizabeth, or the assistance of her
other friends, he and his party must be exposed to her severe and
implacable vengeance.[t] He resolved, therefore, not to venture
rashly on a measure, which it would be impossible for him ever to
recal; and he privately paid a visit to Norfolk and the other English
commissioners, confessed his scruples, laid before them the evidence of the queen's guilt, and desired to have some security for
Elizabeth's protection, in case that evidence should, upon examination, appear entirely satisfactory. Norfolk was not secretly displeased with these scruples of the regent.[u] He had ever been a
partizan of the queen of Scots: Secretary Lidington, who began
also to incline to that party, and was a man of singular address and
capacity, had engaged him to embrace farther views in her favour,
and even to think of espousing her: And though that duke confessed;[w] that the proofs against Mary seemed to him unquestion-
able, he encouraged Murray in his present resolution not to produce them publicly in the conferences before the English
commissioners.[x]

Norfolk, however, was obliged to transmit to court the queries
proposed by the regent. These queries consisted of four particulars: Whether the English commissioners had authority from their
sovereign to pronounce sentence against Mary, in case her guilt
should be fully proved before them? Whether they would promise
to exercise that authority, and proceed to an actual sentence?
Whether the queen of Scots, if she were found guilty, should be
delivered into the hands of the regent, or, at least, be so secured in
England, that she never should be able to disturb the tranquillity
of Scotland? and, Whether Elizabeth would also, in that case,
promise to acknowledge the young king, and protect the regent in
his authority?[y]

[t] Anderson, vol. iv. part 2. p. 47, 48. Goodall, vol. ii. p. 159.   [u] Crawford,
p. 92. Melvil, p. 94, 95. Haynes, p. 574.   [w] Anderson, vol. iv. part 2. p. 77.
[x] Ibid. 57, 77. State Trials, vol. i. p. 76.   [y] Anderson, vol. iv. part 2. p. 55.
Goodall, vol. ii. p. 130.

CHAPTER XXXIX

Elizabeth, when these queries, with the other transactions, were laid before her, began to think, that they pointed towards a conclusion more decisive and more advantageous than she had hitherto expected. She determined, therefore, to bring the matter into full light; and under pretext that the distance from her person retarded the proceedings of her commissioners, she ordered them to come to London, and there continue the conferences. On their appearance, she immediately joined in commission with them some of the most considerable of her council; Sir Nicholas Bacon, lord keeper, the earls of Arundel and Leicester, lord Clinton, admiral, and Sir William Cecil, secretary.[z] The queen of Scots, who knew nothing of these secret motives, and who expected, that fear or decency would still restrain Murray from proceeding to any violent accusation against her, expressed an entire satisfaction in this adjournment; and declared, that the affair, being under the immediate inspection of Elizabeth, was now in the hands where she most desired to rest it.[a] The conferences were accordingly continued at Hampton-Court; and Mary's commissioners, as before, made no scruple to be present at them.

The queen, meanwhile, gave a satisfactory answer to all Murray's demands; and declared, that, though she wished and hoped, from the present enquiry, to be entirely convinced of Mary's innocence, yet if the event should prove contrary, and if that princess should appear guilty of her husband's murder, she should, for her own part, deem her ever after unworthy of a throne.[b] The regent, encouraged by this declaration, opened more fully his charge against the queen of Scots; and after expressing his reluctance to proceed to that extremity, and protesting, that nothing but the necessity of self-defence, which must not be abandoned for any delicacy, could have engaged him in such a measure, he proceeded to accuse her in plain terms of participation and consent in the assassination of the king.[c] The earl of Lenox too appeared before the English commissioners; and imploring vengeance for the murder of his son, accused Mary as an accomplice with Bothwel in that enormity.[d]

[z] Anderson, vol. iv. part 2. p. 99.   [a] Ibid. p. 95. Goodall, vol. ii. p. 177, 179.   [b] Goodall, vol. ii. p. 199.   [c] Anderson, vol. iv. part 2. p. 115, & seq. Goodall, vol. ii. p. 206.   [d] Anderson, vol. iv. part 2. p. 122. Goodall, vol. ii. p. 208.

When this charge was so unexpectedly given in, and copies of it were transmitted to the bishop of Ross, lord Herreis, and the other commissioners of Mary, they absolutely refused to return an answer; and they grounded their silence on very extraordinary reasons: They had orders, they said, from their mistress, if any thing were advanced that might touch her honour, not to make any defence, as she was a sovereign princess, and could not be subject to any tribunal; and they required, that she should previously be admitted to Elizabeth's presence, to whom, and to whom alone, she was determined to justify her innocence.[e] They forgot, that the conferences were at first begun, and were still continued, with no other view than to clear her from the accusations of her enemies; that Elizabeth had ever pretended to enter into them only as her friend, by her own consent and approbation, not as assuming any jurisdiction over her; that this princess had from the beginning refused to admit her to her presence, till she should vindicate herself from the crimes imputed to her; that she had therefore discovered no new signs of partiality by her perseverance in that resolution; and that though she had granted an audience to the earl of Murray and his collegues, she had previously conferred the same honour on Mary's commissioners;[f] and her conduct was so far entirely equal to both parties.[g]

As the commissioners of the queen of Scots refused to give in any answer to Murray's charge, the necessary consequence seemed to be, that there could be no farther proceedings in the conference. But though this silence might be interpreted as a presumption against her, it did not fully answer the purpose of those English ministers, who were enemies to that princess. They still desired to have in their hands the proofs of her guilt; and in order to draw them with decency from the regent, a judicious artifice was employed by Elizabeth. Murray was called before the English commissioners; and reproved by them, in the queen's name, for the atrocious imputations, which he had the temerity to throw upon his sovereign: But though the earl of Murray, they added, and the other commissioners, had so far forgotten the duty of allegiance to their prince, the queen never would overlook what she owed to her

[e] Anderson, vol. iv. part 2. p. 125, & seq. Goodall, vol. ii. p. 184, 211, 217. [f] Lesley's Negociations in Anderson, vol. iii. p. 25. Haynes, p. 487. [g] See note [J] at the end of the volume.

friend, her neighbour, and her kinswoman; and she therefore
desired to know what they could say in their own justification.[h]
Murray, thus urged, made no difficulty in producing the proofs of
his charge against the queen of Scots; and among the rest, some
love-letters and sonnets of her's to Bothwel, written all in her own
hand, and two other papers, one written in her own hand, another
subscribed by her, and written by the earl of Huntley; each of
which contained a promise of marriage with Bothwel, made before
the pretended trial and acquittal of that nobleman.

All these important papers had been kept by Bothwel in a silver
box or casket, which had been given him by Mary, and which had
belonged to her first husband, Francis; and though the princess
had enjoined him to burn the letters as soon as he had read them,
he had thought proper carefully to preserve them, as pledges of
her fidelity, and had committed them to the custody of Sir James
Balfour, deputy-governor of the castle of Edinburgh. When that
fortress was besieged by the associated lords, Bothwel sent a servant to receive the casket from the hands of the deputy-governor.
Balfour delivered it to the messenger; but as he had at that time
received some disgust from Bothwel, and was secretly negociating
an agreement with the ruling party, he took care, by conveying
private intelligence to the earl of Morton, to make the papers be
intercepted by him. They contained incontestible proofs of Mary's
criminal correspondence with Bothwel, of her consent to the king's
murder, and of her concurrence in the violence, which Bothwel
pretended to commit upon her.[i] Murray fortified this evidence by
some testimonies of correspondent facts;[k] and he added, some
time after, the dying confession of one Hubert, or French Paris, as
he was called, a servant of Bothwel's, who had been executed for
the king's murder, and who directly charged the queen with her
being accessary to that criminal enterprize.[l]

Mary's commissioners had used every expedient to ward this
blow, which they saw coming upon them, and against which, it
appears, they were not provided with any proper defence. As soon
as Murray opened his charge, they endeavoured to turn the conferences from an enquiry into a negociation; and though informed

[h] Anderson, vol. iv. part 2. p. 147. Goodall, vol. ii. p. 233. [i] Anderson, vol.
ii, p. 115. Goodall, vol. ii. p. 1. [k] Anderson, vol. ii. part 2. p. 165, &c.
Goodall, vol. ii. p. 243. [l] Anderson, vol. ii. p. 192. Goodall, vol. ii. p. 76.

by the English commissioners, that nothing could be more dishonourable for their mistress, than to enter into a treaty with such undutiful subjects, before she had justified herself from those enormous imputations, which had been thrown upon her, they still insisted, that Elizabeth should settle terms of accommodation between Mary and her enemies in Scotland.[m] They maintained, that, till their mistress had given in her answer to Murray's charge, his proofs could neither be called for nor produced:[n] And finding, that the English commissioners were still determined to proceed in the method which had been projected, they finally broke off the conferences, and never would make any reply. These papers, at least translations of them, have since been published. The objections, made to their authenticity, are in general of small force: But were they ever so specious, they cannot now be hearkened to; since Mary, at the time when the truth could have been fully cleared, did, in effect, ratify the evidence against her, by recoiling from the enquiry at the very critical moment, and refusing to give an answer to the accusation of her enemies.[o]

But Elizabeth, though she had seen enough for her own satisfaction, was determined, that the most eminent persons of her court should also be acquainted with these transactions, and should be convinced of the equity of her proceedings: She ordered her privy-council to be assembled, and that she might render the matter more solemn and authentic, she summoned along with them the earls of Northumberland, Westmoreland, Shrewsbury, Worcester, Huntingdon, and Warwic. All the proceedings of the English commissioners were read to them: The evidences produced by Murray were perused: A great number of letters, written by Mary to Elizabeth, were laid before them, and the hand-writing compared with that of the letters delivered in by the regent: The refusal of the queen of Scots' commissioners to make any reply, was related: And on the whole, Elizabeth told them, that, as she had, from the first, thought it improper, that Mary, after such horrid crimes were imputed to her, should be admitted to her presence, before she had, in some measure, justified herself from

[m] Anderson, vol. ii. part 2. p. 135, 139. Goodall, vol. ii. p. 224. [n] Anderson, vol. iv. part 2. p. 139, 145. Goodall, vol. ii. p. 228. [o] See note [K] at the end of the volume.

CHAPTER XXXIX

the charge; so now, when her guilt was confirmed by so many evidences, and all answer refused, she must, for her part, persevere more steadily in that resolution.[p] Elizabeth next called in the queen of Scots' commissioners, and after observing, that she deemed it much more decent for their mistress to continue the conferences, than to require the liberty of justifying herself in person, she told them, that Mary might either send her reply by a person whom she trusted, or deliver it herself to some English nobleman, whom Elizabeth should appoint to wait upon her: But as to her resolution of making no reply at all, she must regard it as the strongest confession of guilt; nor could they ever be deemed her friends, who advised her to that method of proceeding.[q] These topics she enforced still more strongly in a letter, which she wrote to Mary herself.[r]

The queen of Scots had no other subterfuge from these pressing remonstrances than still to demand a personal interview with Elizabeth: A concession, which, she was sensible, would never be granted;[s] because Elizabeth knew, that this expedient could decide nothing; because it brought matters to extremity, which that princess desired to avoid; and because it had been refused from the beginning, even before the commencement of the conferences. In order to keep herself better in countenance, Mary thought of another device. Though the conferences were broken off, she ordered her commissioners to accuse the earl of Murray and his associates as the murderers of the king:[t] But this accusation coming so late, being extorted merely by a complaint of Murray's, and being unsupported by any proof, could only be regarded as an angry recrimination upon her enemy.[u] She also desired to have copies of the papers given in by the regent; but as she still persisted in her resolution to make no reply before the English commissioners, this demand was finally refused her.[w]

As Mary had thus put an end to the conferences, the regent expressed great impatience to return into Scotland; and he com-

[p] Anderson, vol. iv. part 2. p. 170, &c. Goodall, vol. ii. p. 254.   [q] Anderson, vol. iv. part 2. p. 179, &c. Goodall, vol. ii. p. 268.   [r] Anderson, vol. iv. part 2. p. 183. Goodall, vol. ii. p. 269.   [s] Cabala, p. 157.   [t] Goodall, vol. ii. p. 280.   [u] See note [L] at the end of the volume.   [w] Goodall, vol. ii. p. 253, 283, 289, 310, 311. Haynes, vol. i. p. 492. See note [M] at the end of the volume.

plained, that his enemies had taken advantage of his absence, and had thrown the whole government into confusion. Elizabeth, therefore, dismissed him; and granted him a loan of five thousand pounds, to bear the charges of his journey.[x] During the conferences at York, the duke of Chatelrault arrived at London, in passing from France; and as the queen knew, that he was engaged in Mary's party, and had very plausible pretensions to the regency of the king of Scots, she thought proper to detain him till after Murray's departure. But notwithstanding these marks of favour, and some other assistance which she secretly gave this latter nobleman,[y] she still declined acknowledging the young king, or treating with Murray as regent of Scotland.

Orders were given for removing the queen of Scots from Bolton, a place surrounded with catholics, to Tutbury in the county of Stafford; where she was put under the custody of the earl of Shrewsbury. Elizabeth entertained hopes, that this princess, discouraged by her misfortunes, and confounded by the late transactions, would be glad to secure a safe retreat from all the tempests with which she had been agitated; and she promised to bury every thing in oblivion, provided Mary would agree, either voluntarily to resign her crown, or to associate her son with her in the government; and the administration to remain, during his minority, in the hands of the earl of Murray.[z] But that high-spirited princess refused all treaty upon such terms, and declared that her last words should be those of a queen of Scotland. Besides many other reasons, she said, which fixed her in that resolution, she knew, that, if, in the present emergence, she made such concessions, her submission would be universally deemed an acknowledgment of guilt, and would ratify all the calumnies of her enemies.[a]

Mary still insisted upon this alternative; either that Elizabeth should assist her in recovering her authority, or should give her liberty to retire into France, and make trial of the friendship of other princes: And as she asserted, that she had come voluntarily into England, invited by many former professions of amity, she thought, that one or other of these requests could not, without the

---

[x] Rymer, tom. xv. p. 677.   [y] MS. in the Advocate's library. A. 3. 29. p. 128, 129, 130. from Cott. Lib. Cal. c. 1.   [z] Goodall, vol. ii. p. 295.   [a] Ibid. p. 301.

CHAPTER XXXIX

most extreme injustice, be refused her. But Elizabeth, sensible of
the danger, which attended both these proposals, was secretly resolved to detain her still a captive; and as her retreat into England
had been little voluntary, her claim upon the queen's generosity
appeared much less urgent than she was willing to pretend. Necessity, it was thought, would to the prudent justify her detention:
Her past misconduct would apologize for it to the equitable: And
though it was foreseen, that compassion for Mary's situation,
joined to her intrigues and insinuating behaviour, would, while
she remained in England, excite the zeal of her friends, especially
of the catholics; these inconveniences were deemed much inferior
to those which attended any other expedient. Elizabeth trusted
also to her own address, for eluding all those difficulties: She
purposed to avoid breaking absolutely with the queen of Scots, to
keep her always in hopes of an accommodation, to negotiate perpetually with her, and still to throw the blame of not coming to any
conclusion, either on unforeseen accidents, or on the obstinacy
and perverseness of others.

We come now to mention some English affairs, which we left
behind us, that we might not interrupt our narrative of the events
in Scotland, which form so material a part of the present reign.
The term, fixed by the treaty of Cateau-Cambresis for the restitution of Calais, expired in 1567; and Elizabeth, after making her
demand at the gates of that city, sent Sir Thomas Smith to Paris;
and that minister, in conjunction with Sir Henry Norris, her resident ambassador, enforced her pretensions. Conferences were
held on that head, without coming to any conclusion, satisfactory
to the English. The chancellor, De L'Hospital, told the English
ambassadors, that, though France by an article of the treaty was
obliged to restore Calais on the expiration of eight years, there was
another article of the same treaty, which now deprived Elizabeth
of any right, that could accrue to her by that engagement: That it
was agreed, if the English should, during the interval, commit
hostilities upon France, they should instantly forfeit all claim to
Calais; and the taking possession of Havre and Dieppe, with whatever pretences that measure might be covered, was a plain violation of the peace between the nations: That though these places
were not entered by force, but put into Elizabeth's hands by the
governors, these governors were rebels; and a correspondence

with such traitors was the most flagrant injury, that could be committed on any sovereign: That in the treaty, which ensued upon the expulsion of the English from Normandy, the French ministers had absolutely refused to make any mention of Calais, and had thereby declared their intention to take advantage of the title, which had accrued to the crown of France: And that though a general clause had been inserted, implying a reservation of all claims; this concession could not avail the English, who at that time possessed no just claim to Calais, and had previously forfeited all right to that fortress.[b] The queen was no wise surprized at hearing these allegations; and as she knew, that the French court intended not from the first to make restitution, much less after they could justify their refusal by such plausible reasons, she thought it better for the present to acquiesce in the loss, than to pursue a doubtful title by a war both dangerous and expensive, as well as unseasonable.[c]

Elizabeth entered anew into negociations for espousing the archduke Charles; and she seems, at this time, to have had no great motive of policy, which might induce her to make this fallacious offer: But as she was very rigorous in the terms insisted on, and would not agree, that the archduke, if he espoused her, should enjoy any power or title in England, and even refused him the exercise of his religion, the treaty came to nothing; and that prince, despairing of success in his addresses, married the daughter of Albert, duke of Bavaria.[d]

[b] Haynes, p. 587.   [c] Camden, p. 406.   [d] Ibid. p. 407, 408.

XL

Character of the puritans –
Duke of Norfolk's conspiracy – Insurrections in
the north – Assassination of the earl
of Murray – A parliament – Civil wars of France –
Affairs of the Low Countries – New conspiracy
of the duke of Norfolk – Trial of Norfolk –
His execution – Scots affairs – French affairs –
Massacre of Paris – French affairs –
Civil wars of the Low Countries –
A parliament

O F ALL THE EUROPEAN CHURCHES, which shook off the yoke of papal authority, no one proceeded with so much reason and moderation as the church of England; an advantage, which had been derived partly from the interposition of the civil magistrate in this innovation, partly from the gradual and slow steps, by which the reformation was conducted in that kingdom. Rage and animosity against the catholic religion was as little indulged as could be supposed in such a revolution: The fabric of the secular hierarchy was maintained entire: The ancient liturgy was preserved, so far as was thought consistent with the new principles: Many ceremonies, become venerable from age and preceding use, were retained: The splendor of the Romish worship, though removed, had at least given place to order and decency: The distinctive

1568.
Character
of the
puritans.

habits of the clergy, according to their different ranks, were continued: No innovation was admitted merely from spite and opposition to former usage; And the new religion, by mitigating the
genius of the ancient superstition, and rendering it more compatible with the peace and interests of society, had preserved itself
in that happy medium, which wise men have always sought, and
which the people have so seldom been able to maintain.

But though such in general was the spirit of the reformation in
that country, many of the English reformers, being men of more
warm complexions and more obstinate tempers, endeavoured to
push matters to extremities against the church of Rome, and indulged themselves in the most violent contrariety and antipathy to
all former practices. Among these, Hooper, who afterwards suffered for his religion with such extraordinary constancy, was
chiefly distinguished. This man was appointed, during the reign of
Edward, to the see of Glocester, and made no scruple of accepting
the episcopal office; but he refused to be consecrated in the episcopal habit, the cymarre and rochette, which had formerly, he said,
been abused to superstition, and which were thereby rendered
unbecoming a true christian. Cranmer and Ridley were surprized
at this objection, which opposed the received practice, and even
the established laws; and though young Edward, desirous of promoting a man so celebrated for his eloquence, his zeal and his
morals, enjoined them to dispense with this ceremony, they were
still determined to retain it. Hooper then embraced the resolution,
rather to refuse the bishopric than cloath himself in those hated
garments; but it was deemed requisite, that, for the sake of the
example, he should not escape so easily. He was first confined to
Cranmer's house, then thrown into prison, till he should consent
to be a bishop on the terms proposed: He was plied with conferences, and reprimands, and arguments: Bucer and Peter Martyr,
and the most celebrated foreign reformers were consulted on this
important question: And a compromise, with great difficulty, was
at last made, that Hooper should not be obliged to wear commonly
the obnoxious robes, but should agree to be consecrated in them,
and to use them during cathedral service:[e] A condescension not

_____

[e] Burnet, vol. ii. p. 152. Heylin, p. 90.

CHAPTER XL

a little extraordinary in a man of so inflexible a spirit as this reformer.

The same objection, which had arisen with regard to the episcopal habit, had been moved against the rayment of the inferior clergy; and the surplice in particular, with the tippet and corner cap, was a great object of abhorrence to many of the popular zealots.[f] In vain was it urged, that particular habits, as well as postures and ceremonies, having been constantly used by the clergy, and employed in religious service, acquire a veneration in the eyes of the people, appear sacred in their apprehensions, excite their devotion, and contract a kind of mysterious virtue, which attaches the affections of men to the national and established worship: That in order to produce this effect an uniformity in these particulars is requisite, and even a perseverance, as far as possible, in the former practice: And that the nation would be happy, if, by retaining these inoffensive observances, the reformers could engage the people to renounce willingly what was absurd or pernicious in the ancient superstition. These arguments, which had influence with wise men, were the very reasons, which engaged the violent protestants to reject the habits. They pushed matters to a total opposition with the church of Rome: Every compliance, they said, was a symbolizing with Antichrist.[g] And this spirit was carried so far by some reformers, that, in a national remonstrance, made afterwards by the church of Scotland against these habits, it was asked, "What has Christ Jesus to do with Belial? What has darkness to do with light? If surplices, corner caps, and tippets have been badges of idolaters in the very act of their idolatry; why should the preacher of Christian liberty, and the open rebuker of all superstition partake with the dregs of the Romish beast? Yea, who is there that ought not rather to be afraid of taking in his hand or on his forehead the print and mark of that odious beast?"[h] But this application was rejected by the English church.

There was only one instance, in which the spirit of contradiction to the Romanists took place universally, in England: The altar was removed from the wall, was placed in the middle of the church, and was thenceforth denominated the communion-

---

[f] Strype, vol. i. p. 416.   [g] Ibid. p. 416.   [h] Keith, p. 565. Knox, p. 402.

table. The reason, why this innovation met with such general reception, was, that the nobility and gentry got thereby a pretence for making spoil of the plate, vestures, and rich ornaments which belonged to the altars.[i]

These disputes, which had been started during the reign of Edward, were carried abroad by the protestants, who fled from the persecutions of Mary; and as the zeal of these men had received an encrease from the furious cruelty of their enemies, they were generally inclined to carry their opposition to the utmost extremity against the practices of the church of Rome. Their communication with Calvin and the other reformers, who followed the discipline and worship of Geneva, confirmed them in this obstinate reluctance; and though some of the refugees, particularly those who were established at Frankfort, still adhered to king Edward's liturgy, the prevailing spirit carried these confessors to seek a still farther reformation. On the accession of Elizabeth, they returned to their native country; and being regarded with general veneration, on account of their zeal and past sufferings, they ventured to insist on the establishment of their projected model; nor did they want countenance from many considerable persons in the queen's council. But the princess herself, so far from being willing to despoil religion of the few ornaments and ceremonies which remained in it, was rather inclined to bring the publick worship still nearer to the Romish ritual;[k] and she thought that the reformation had already gone too far in shaking off those forms and observances, which, without distracting men of more refined apprehensions, tend, in a very innocent manner, to allure, and

---

[i] Heylin, preface, p. 3. Hist. p. 106.   [k] *When Nowel, one of her chaplains, had spoken less reverently in a sermon, preached before her, of the sign of the cross, she called aloud to him from her closet window, commanding him to retire from that ungodly digression and to return unto his text. And on the other side, when one of her divines had preached a sermon in defence of the real presence, she openly gave him thanks for his pains and piety.* Heylin, p. 124. She would have absolutely forbidden the marriage of the clergy, if Cecil had not interposed. Strype's Life of Parker, p. 107, 108, 109. She was an enemy to sermons; and usually said, that she thought two or three preachers were sufficient for a whole county. It was probably for these reasons that one Doring told her to her face from the pulpit, that she was like an untamed heifer, that would not be ruled by God's people, but obstructed his discipline. See Life of Hooker, prefixed to his works.

CHAPTER XL

amuse, and engage the vulgar. She took care to have a law for uniformity strictly enacted: She was empowered by the parliament to add any new ceremonies, which she thought proper: And though she was sparing in the exercise of this prerogative, she continued rigid in exacting an observance of the established laws, and in punishing all nonconformity. The zealots, therefore, who harboured a secret antipathy to the episcopal order and to the whole liturgy, were obliged, in a great measure, to conceal these sentiments, which would have been regarded as highly audacious and criminal; and they confined their avowed objections to the surplice, the confirmation of children, the sign of the cross in baptism, the ring in marriage, kneeling at the sacrament, and bowing at the name of Jesus. So fruitless is it for sovereigns to watch with a rigid care over orthodoxy, and to employ the sword in religious controversy, that the work, perpetually renewed, is perpetually to begin; and a garb, a gesture, nay, a metaphysical or grammatical distinction, when rendered important by the disputes of theologians and the zeal of the magistrate, is sufficient to destroy the unity of the church, and even the peace of society. These controversies had already excited such ferment among the people, that in some places they refused to frequent the churches, where the habits and ceremonies were used; would not salute the conforming clergy; and proceeded so far as to revile them in the streets, to spit in their faces, and to use them with all manner of contumely.[l] And while the sovereign authority checked these excesses, the flame was confined, not extinguished; and burning fiercer from confinement, it burst out in the succeeding reigns to the destruction of the church and monarchy.

All enthusiasts, indulging themselves in rapturous flights, extasies, visions, inspirations, have a natural aversion to episcopal authority, to ceremonies, rites, and forms, which they denominate superstition, or beggarly elements, and which seem to restrain the liberal effusions of their zeal and devotion: But there was another set of opinions adopted by these innovators, which rendered them in a peculiar manner the object of Elizabeth's aversion. The same bold and daring spirit, which accompanied them in their addresses to the divinity, appeared in their political speculations; and the

[l] Strype's Life of Whitgift, p. 460.

principles of civil liberty, which, during some reigns, had been little avowed in the nation, and which were totally incompatible with the present exorbitant prerogative, had been strongly adopted by this new sect. Scarcely any sovereign before Elizabeth, and none after her, carried higher, both in speculation and practice, the authority of the crown; and the puritans (so these sectaries were called, on account of their pretending to a superior purity of worship and discipline) could not recommend themselves worse to her favour, than by inculcating the doctrine of resisting or restraining princes. From all these motives, the queen neglected no opportunity of depressing those zealous innovators; and while they were secretly countenanced by some of her most favoured ministers, Cecil, Leicester, Knolles, Bedford, Walsingham, she never was, to the end of her life, reconciled to their principles and practices.

We have thought proper to insert in this place an account of the rise and the genius of the puritans; because Camden marks the present year, as the period when they began to make themselves considerable in England. We now return to our narration.

1569.
Duke of
Norfolk's
con-
spiracy.
The duke of Norfolk was the only peer, that enjoyed the highest title of nobility; and as there were at present no princes of the blood, the splendor of his family, the opulence of his fortune, and the extent of his influence, had rendered him without comparison the first subject in England. The qualities of his mind corresponded to his high station: Beneficent, affable, generous, he had acquired the affections of the people; prudent, moderate, obsequious, he possessed, without giving her any jealousy, the good graces of his sovereign. His grandfather and father had long been regarded as the leaders of the catholics; and this hereditary attachment, joined to the alliance of blood, had procured him the friendship of the most considerable men of that party: But as he had been educated among the reformers, was sincerely devoted to their principles, and maintained that strict decorum and regularity of life, by which the protestants were at that time distinguished; he thereby enjoyed the rare felicity of being popular even with the most opposite factions. The height of his prosperity alone was the source of his misfortunes, and engaged him in attempts, from which his virtue and prudence would naturally have for ever kept him at a distance.

CHAPTER XL

Norfolk was at this time a widower; and being of a suitable age, his marriage with the queen of Scots had appeared so natural, that it had occurred to several of his friends and those of that princess: But the first person, who, after secretary Lidington, opened the scheme to the duke is said to have been the earl of Murray, before his departure for Scotland.[m] That nobleman set before Norfolk both the advantage of composing the dissentions in Scotland by an alliance, which would be so generally acceptable, and the prospect of reaping the succession of England; and, in order to bind Norfolk's interest the faster with Mary's, he proposed, that the duke's daughter should also espouse the young king of Scotland. The previously obtaining of Elizabeth's consent, was regarded, both by Murray and Norfolk, as a circumstance essential to the success of their project; and all terms being adjusted between them, Murray took care, by means of Sir Robert Melvil, to have the design communicated to the queen of Scots. This princess replied, that the vexations, which she had met with in her two last marriages, had made her more inclined to lead a single life; but she was determined to sacrifice her own inclinations to the public welfare: And therefore, as soon as she should be legally divorced from Bothwel, she would be determined by the opinion of her nobility and people in the choice of another husband.[n]

It is probable, that Murray was not sincere in this proposal. He had two motives to engage him to dissimulation. He knew the danger, which he must run in his return through the north of England, from the power of the earls of Northumberland and Westmoreland, Mary's partizans in that country; and he dreaded an insurrection in Scotland from the duke of Chatelrault, and the earls of Argyle and Huntley, whom she had appointed her lieutenants during her absence. By these feigned appearances of friendship, he both engaged Norfolk to write in his favour to the northern nobleman;[o] and he persuaded the queen of Scots to give her lieutenants permission, and even advice, to conclude a cessation of hostilities with the regent's party.[p]

The duke of Norfolk, though he had agreed, that Elizabeth's consent should be previously obtained, before the completion of

[m] Lesley, p. 36, 37.   [n] Lesley, p. 40, 41.   [o] State Trials, p. 76, 78.
[p] Lesley, p. 41.

his marriage, had reason to apprehend, that he never should prevail with her voluntarily to make that concession. He knew her perpetual and unrelenting jealousy against her heir and rival; he was acquainted with her former reluctance to all proposals of marriage with the queen of Scots; he foresaw, that this princess's espousing a person of his power and character and interest, would give the greatest umbrage; and as it would then become necessary to reinstate her in possession of her throne on some tolerable terms, and even to endeavour the re-establishing of her character, he dreaded, lest Elizabeth, whose politics had now taken a different turn, would never agree to such indulgent and generous conditions. He therefore attempted previously to gain the consent and approbation of several of the most considerable nobility; and he was successful with the earls of Pembroke, Arundel, Derby, Bedford, Shrewsbury, Southampton, Northumberland, Westmoreland, Sussex.[q] Lord Lumley and Sir Nicholas Throgmorton cordially embraced the proposal: Even the earl of Leicester, Elizabeth's declared favourite, who had formerly entertained some views of espousing Mary, willingly resigned all his pretensions, and seemed to enter zealously into Norfolk's interests.[r] There were other motives, besides affection to the duke, which produced this general combination of the nobility.

Sir William Cecil, secretary of state, was the most vigilant, active, and prudent minister ever known in England; and as he was governed by no views but the interests of his sovereign, which he had inflexibly pursued, his authority over her became every day more predominant. Ever cool himself, and uninfluenced by prejudice or affection, he checked those sallies of passion, and sometimes of caprice, to which she was subject; and if he failed of persuading her in the first movement, his perseverance, and remonstrances, and arguments were sure at last to recommend themselves to her sound discernment. The more credit he gained with his mistress, the more was he exposed to the envy of her other counsellors; and as he had been supposed to adopt the interests of the house of Suffolk, whose claim seemed to carry with it no danger to the present establishment, his enemies, in opposition to him, were naturally led to attach themselves to the queen of Scots. Elizabeth saw, without uneasiness, this emulation among her

[q] Lesley, p. 55. Camden, p. 419. Spotswood, p. 230.   [r] Haynes, p. 535.

CHAPTER XL

courtiers, which served to augment her own authority: And though she supported Cecil, whenever matters came to extremities, and dissipated every conspiracy against him, particularly one laid about this time for having him thrown into the Tower on some pretence or other,[s] she never gave him such unlimited confidence as might enable him entirely to crush his adversaries.

Norfolk, sensible of the difficulty, which he must meet with in controuling Cecil's counsels, especially where they concurred with the inclination, as well as interest of the queen, durst not open to her his intentions of marrying the queen of Scots; but proceeded still in the same course, of encreasing his interest in the kingdom, and engaging more of the nobility to take part in his measures. A letter was written to Mary by Leicester, and signed by several of the first rank, recommending Norfolk for her husband, and stipulating conditions for the advantage of both kingdoms; particularly, that she should give sufficient surety to Elizabeth, and the heirs of her body, for the free enjoyment of the crown of England; that a perpetual league, offensive and defensive, should be made between their realms and subjects; that the protestant religion should be established by law in Scotland; and that she should grant an amnesty to her rebels in that kingdom.[t] When Mary returned a favourable answer to this application, Norfolk employed himself with new ardour in the execution of his project; and besides securing the interests of many of the considerable gentry and nobility who resided at court, he wrote letters to such as lived at their country-seats, and possessed the greatest authority in the several counties.[u] The kings of France and Spain, who interested themselves extremely in Mary's cause, were secretly consulted, and expressed their approbation of these measures.[w] And though Elizabeth's consent was always supposed as a previous condition to the finishing of this alliance, it was apparently Norfolk's intention, when he proceeded such lengths without consulting her, to render his party so strong, that it should no longer be in her power to refuse it.[x]

It was impossible, that so extensive a conspiracy could entirely escape the queen's vigilance and that of Cecil. She dropped several intimations to the duke, by which he might learn, that she was

---

[s] Camden, p. 417.   [t] Lesley, p. 50. Camden, p. 420. Haynes, p. 535, 539.
[u] Lesley, p. 62.   [w] Ibid. p. 63.   [x] State Trials, vol. i. p. 82.

acquainted with his designs; and she frequently warned him to beware on what pillow he reposed his head:[y] But he never had the prudence or the courage to open to her his full intentions. Certain intelligence of this dangerous combination was given her first by Leicester, then by Murray,[z] who, if ever he was sincere in promoting Norfolk's marriage, which is much to be doubted, had at least intended, for his own safety and that of his party, that Elizabeth should, in reality as well as in appearance, be entire arbiter of the conditions, and should not have her consent extorted by any confederacy of her own subjects. This information gave great alarm to the court of England; and the more so, as those intrigues were attended with other circumstances, of which, it is probable, Elizabeth was not wholly ignorant.

Among the nobility and gentry, that seemed to enter into Norfolk's views, there were many, who were zealously attached to the catholic religion, who had no other design than that of restoring Mary to her liberty, and who would gladly, by a combination with foreign powers, or even at the expence of a civil war, have placed her on the throne of England. The earls of Northumberland and Westmoreland, who possessed great power in the north, were leaders of this party; and the former nobleman made offer to the queen of Scots, by Leonard Dacres, brother to lord Dacres, that he would free her from confinement, and convey her to Scotland or any other place, to which she should think proper to retire.[a] Sir Thomas and Sir Edward Stanley, sons of the earl of Derby, Sir Thomas Gerrard, Rolstone, and other gentlemen, whose interest lay in the neighbourhood of the place where Mary resided, concurred in the same views; and required, that, in order to facilitate the execution of the scheme, a diversion should, in the mean time, be made from the side of Flanders.[b] Norfolk discouraged, and even in appearance suppressed, these conspiracies; both because his duty to Elizabeth would not allow him to think of effecting his purpose by rebellion, and because he foresaw, that, if the queen of Scots came into the possession of these men, they would rather

[y] Camden, p. 420. Spotswood, p. 231.   [z] Lesley, p. 71. It appears by Haynes, p. 521, 525. that Elizabeth had heard rumours of Norfolk's dealing with Murray; and charged the latter to inform her of the whole truth, which he accordingly did. See also the earl of Murray's letter produced on Norfolk's trial.   [a] Lesley, p. 76.   [b] Ibid. p. 98.

CHAPTER XL

chuse for her husband the king of Spain, or some foreign prince, who had power, as well as inclination, to re-establish the catholic religion.[c]

When men of honour and good principles, like the duke of Norfolk, engage in dangerous enterprizes, they are commonly so unfortunate as to be criminal by halves; and while they balance between the execution of their designs and their remorses, their fear of punishment and their hope of pardon, they render themselves an easy prey to their enemies. The duke, in order to repress the surmises spread against him, spoke contemptuously to Elizabeth of the Scottish alliance; affirmed that his estate in England was more valuable than the revenue of a kingdom wasted by civil wars and factions; and declared, that, when he amused himself in his own tennis-court at Norwich amidst his friends and vassals, he deemed himself at least a petty prince, and was fully satisfied with his condition.[d] Finding, that he did not convince her by these asseverations, and that he was looked on with a jealous eye by the ministers, he retired to his country-seat without taking leave.[e] He soon after repented of this measure, and set out on his return to court, with a view of using every expedient to regain the queen's good graces; but he was met at St. Albans by Fitz-Garret, lieutenant of the band of pensioners, by whom he was conveyed to Burnham, three miles from Windsor, where the court then resided.[f] He was soon after committed to the Tower, under the custody of Sir Henry Nevil.[g] Lesley, bishop of Ross, the queen of Scots' ambassador, was examined and confronted with Norfolk before the council.[h] The earl of Pembroke was confined to his own house: Arundel, Lumley, and Throgmorton were taken into custody. The queen of Scots herself, was removed to Coventry; all access to her was, during some time, more strictly prohibited; and viscount Hereford was joined to the earls of Shrewsbury and Huntingdon, in the office of guarding her.

A rumour had been diffused in the north of an intended rebellion; and the earl of Sussex, president of York, alarmed with the danger, sent for Northumberland and Westmoreland, in order to examine them; but not finding any proof against them, he

Insurrections in the north.

[c] Ibid. p. 77.   [d] Camden, p. 420.   [e] Haynes, p. 528.   [f] Ibid. p. 339.
[g] Camden, p. 421. Haynes, p. 540.   [h] Lesley, p. 80.

allowed them to depart. The report meanwhile gained ground daily; and many appearances of its reality being discovered, orders were dispatched by Elizabeth to these two noblemen, to appear at court, and answer for their conduct.[i] They had already proceeded so far in their criminal designs, that they dared not to trust themselves in her hands: They had prepared measures for a rebellion; had communicated their design to Mary and her ministers;[k] had entered into a correspondence with the duke of Alva, governor of the Low Countries; had obtained his promise of a reinforcement of troops, and of a supply of arms and ammunition; and had prevailed on him to send over to London Chiapino Vitelli, one of his most famous captains, on pretence of adjusting some differences with the queen, but in reality with a view of putting him at the head of the northern rebels. The summons, sent to the two earls, precipitated the rising before they were fully prepared; and Northumberland remained in suspence between opposite dangers, when he was informed, that some of his enemies were on the way with a commission to arrest him. He took horse instantly, and hastened to his associate Westmoreland, whom he found surrounded with his friends and vassals, and deliberating with regard to the measures, which he should follow in the present emergence. They determined to begin the insurrection without delay; and the great credit of these two noblemen, with that zeal for the catholic religion, which still prevailed in the neighbourhood, soon drew together multitudes of the common people. They published a manifesto, in which they declared, that they intended to attempt nothing against the queen, to whom they vowed unshaken allegiance; and that their sole aim was to re-establish the religion of their ancestors, to remove evil counsellors, and to restore the duke of Norfolk and other faithful peers to their liberty and to the queen's favour.[l] The numbers of the malcontents amounted to four thousand foot and sixteen hundred horse; and they expected the concurrence of all the catholics in England.[m]

The queen was not negligent in her own defence, and she had beforehand, from her prudent and wise conduct, acquired the

---

[i] Haynes, p. 552.　[k] Haynes, p. 595. Strype, vol. ii. append. p. 30. MS. in the Advocates' Library from Cott. Lib. Cal. c. 9.　[l] Cabala, p. 169. Strype, vol. i. p. 547.　[m] Stowe, p. 663.

CHAPTER XL

general good will of her people, the best security of a sovereign; insomuch that even the catholics in most counties expressed an affection for her service;[n] and the duke of Norfolk himself, though he had lost her favour, and lay in confinement, was not wanting, as far as his situation permitted, to promote the levies among his friends and retainers. Sussex attended by the earls of Rutland, the lords Hunsdon, Evers, and Willoughby of Parham, marched against the rebels at the head of seven thousand men, and found them already advanced to the bishopric of Durham, of which they had taken possession. They retired before him to Hexham; and hearing that the earl of Warwic and lord Clinton were advancing against them with a greater body, they found no other resource than to disperse themselves without striking a blow. The common people retired to their houses: The leaders fled into Scotland. Northumberland was found skulking in that country, and was confined by Murray in the castle of Lochlevin. Westmoreland received shelter from the chieftains of the Kers and Scots, partizans of Mary; and persuaded them to make an inroad into England, with a view of exciting a quarrel between the two kingdoms. After they had committed great ravages, they retreated to their own country. This sudden and precipitate rebellion was followed soon after by another still more imprudent, raised by Leonard Dacres. Lord Hunsdon, at the head of the garrison of Berwic, was able, without any other assistance, to quell these rebels. Great severity was exercised against such as had taken part in these rash enterprizes. Sixty-six petty constables were hanged;[o] and no less than eight hundred persons are said, on the whole, to have suffered by the hands of the executioner.[p] But the queen was so well pleased with Norfolk's behaviour, that she released him from the Tower: allowed him to live, though under some shew of confinement, in his own house; and only exacted a promise from him not to proceed any farther in his negociations with the queen of Scots.[q]

Elizabeth now found that the detention of Mary was attended with all the ill consequences, which she had foreseen, when she first embraced that measure. This latter princess, recovering, by means of her misfortunes and her own natural good sense, from

[n] Cabala, p. 170. Digges, p. 4.   [o] Camden, p. 423.   [p] Lesley, p. 82.
[q] Ibid. p. 98. Camden, p. 419. Haynes, p. 597.

that delirium, into which she seems to have been thrown during her attachment to Bothwel, had behaved with such modesty, and judgment, and even dignity, that every one, who approached her, was charmed with her demeanor; and her friends were enabled, on some plausible grounds, to deny the reality of all those crimes, which had been imputed to her.[r] Compassion for her situation, and the necessity of procuring her liberty, proved an incitement among all her partizans to be active in promoting her cause; and as her deliverance from captivity, it was thought could no wise be affected but by attempts dangerous to the established government, Elizabeth had reason to expect little tranquillity so long as the Scottish queen remained a prisoner in her hands. But as this inconvenience had been preferred to the danger of allowing that princess to enjoy her liberty, and to seek relief in all the catholic courts of Europe, it behoved the queen to support the measure which she had adopted, and to guard, by every prudent expedient, against the mischiefs, to which it was exposed. She still flattered Mary with hopes of her protection, maintained an ambiguous conduct between that queen and her enemies in Scotland, negociated perpetually concerning the terms of her restoration, made constant professions of friendship to her; and by these artifices endeavoured both to prevent her from making any desperate efforts for her deliverance, and to satisfy the French and Spanish ambassadors, who never intermitted their solicitations, sometimes accompanied with menaces, in her behalf. This deceit was received with the same deceit by the queen of Scots: Professions of confidence were returned by professions equally insincere: And while an appearance of friendship was maintained on both sides, the animosity and jealousy, which had long prevailed between them, became every day more inveterate and incurable. These two princesses, in address, capacity, activity, and spirit, were nearly a match for each other; but unhappily, Mary, besides her present forlorn condition, was always inferior in personal conduct and discretion, as well as in power, to her illustrious rival.

Elizabeth and Mary wrote at the same time letters to the regent. The queen of Scots desired, that her marriage with Bothwel might be examined, and a divorce be legally pronounced between them.

[r] Lesley, p. 232. Haynes, p. 511, 548.

CHAPTER XL

The queen of England gave Murray the choice of three conditions; that Mary should be restored to her dignity on certain terms; that she should be associated with her son, and the administration remain in the regent's hands, till the young prince should come to years of discretion; or that she should be allowed to live at liberty as a private person in Scotland, and have an honourable settlement made in her favour.[s] Murray summoned a convention of states, in order to deliberate on these proposals of the two queens. No answer was made by them to Mary's letter, on pretence that she had there employed the style of a sovereign, addressing herself to her subjects; but in reality, because they saw that her request was calculated to prepare the way for a marriage with Norfolk, or some powerful prince, who could support her cause, and restore her to the throne. They replied to Elizabeth, that the two former conditions were so derogatory to the royal authority of their prince, that they could not so much as deliberate concerning them: The third alone could be the subject of treaty. It was evident, that Elizabeth, in proposing conditions so unequal in their importance, invited the Scots to a refusal of those which were most advantageous to Mary; and as it was difficult, if not impossible, to adjust all the terms of the third, so as to render it secure and eligible to all parties, it was concluded that she was not sincere in any of them.[t]

It is pretended, that Murray had entered into a private negociation with the queen, to get Mary delivered into his hands;[u] and as Elizabeth found the detention of her in England so dangerous, it is probable, that she would have been pleased, on any honourable or safe terms, to rid herself of a prisoner who gave her so much inquietude.[w] But all these projects vanished by the sudden death of the regent, who was assassinated, in revenge of a private injury, by a gentleman of the name of Hamilton. Murray was a person of considerable vigour, abilities, and constancy; but though he was not unsuccessful, during his regency, in composing the dissentions in Scotland, his talents shone out more eminently in the beginning than in the end of his life. His manners were rough and austere; and he possessed not that perfect integrity, which

1570.

23 January. Assassination of the earl of Murray.

[s] MSS. in the Advocates' Library, A. 329, p. 137. from Cott. Lib. catal. c. 1.   [t] Spotswood, p. 230, 231. Lesley, p. 71.   [u] Camden, p. 425. Lesley, p. 83.   [w] See note [N] at the end of the volume.

frequently accompanies, and can alone atone for, that unamiable character.

By the death of the regent, Scotland relapsed into anarchy. Mary's party assembled together, and made themselves masters of Edinburgh. The castle, commanded by Kirkaldy of Grange, seemed to favour her cause; and as many of the principal nobility had embraced that party, it became probable, though the people were in general averse to her, that her authority might again acquire the ascendant. To check its progress, Elizabeth dispatched Sussex, with an army, to the North, under colour of chastizing the ravages committed by the borderers. He entered Scotland, and laid waste the lands of the Kers and Scots, seized the castle of Hume, and committed hostilities on all Mary's partizans, who, he said, had offended his mistress, by harbouring the English rebels. Sir William Drury was afterwards sent with a body of troops, and he threw down the houses of the Hamiltons, who were engaged in the same faction. The English armies were afterwards recalled by agreement with the queen of Scots, who promised, in return, that no French troops should be introduced into Scotland, and that the English rebels should be delivered up to the queen by her partizans.[x]

But though the queen, covering herself with the pretence of revenging her own quarrel, so far contributed to support the party of the young king of Scots, she was cautious not to declare openly against Mary; and she even sent a request, which was equivalent to a command, to the enemies of that princess not to elect, during some time, a regent in the place of Murray.[y] Lenox, the king's grandfather, was, therefore, chosen temporary governor, under the title of Lieutenant. Hearing afterwards that Mary's partizans, instead of delivering up Westmoreland, and the other fugitives, as they had promised, had allowed them to escape into Flanders; she permitted the king's party to give Lenox the title of regent,[z] and she sent Randolph, as her resident, to maintain a correspondence with him. But notwithstanding this step, taken in favour of Mary's enemies, she never laid aside her ambiguous conduct, or quitted the appearance of amity to that princess. Being importuned by the bishop of Ross, and her other agents, as well as by foreign ambassa-

[x] Lesley, p. 91.   [y] Spotswood, p. 240.   [z] Spotswood, p. 241.

dors, she twice procured a suspension of arms between the Scottish factions, and by that means stopped the hands of the regent, who was likely to obtain advantages over the opposite party.[a] By these seeming contrarieties she kept alive the factions in Scotland, encreased their mutual animosity, and rendered the whole country a scene of devastation and of misery.[b] She had no intention to conquer the kingdom, and consequently no interest or design to instigate the parties against each other; but this consequence was an accidental effect of her cautious politics, by which she was engaged, as far as possible, to keep on good terms with the queen of Scots, and never to violate the appearances of friendship with her, at least those of neutrality.[c]

The better to amuse Mary with the prospect of an accommodation, Cecil and Sir Walter Mildmay were sent to her with proposals from Elizabeth. The terms were somewhat rigorous, such as a captive queen might expect from a jealous rival; and they thereby bore the greater appearance of sincerity on the part of the English court. It was required, that the queen of Scots, besides renouncing all title to the crown of England during the life-time of Elizabeth, should make a perpetual league, offensive and defensive, between the kingdoms; that she should marry no Englishman without Elizabeth's consent, nor any other person without the consent of the states of Scotland; that compensation should be made for the late ravages committed in England; that justice should be executed on the murderers of king Henry; that the young prince should be sent into England, to be educated there; and that six hostages, all of them noblemen, should be delivered to the queen of England, with the castle of Hume, and some other fortress, for the security of performance.[d] Such were the conditions upon which Elizabeth promised to contribute her endeavours towards the restoration of the deposed queen. The necessity of Mary's affairs obliged her to consent to them; and the kings of France and Spain, as well as the pope, when consulted by her, approved of her conduct; chiefly on account of the civil wars, by which all Europe was at that time agitated, and which incapacitated the catholic princes from giving her any assistance.[e]

---

[a] Ibid. p. 243.   [b] Crawford, p. 136.   [c] See note [O] at the end of the volume.   [d] Spotswood, p. 245. Lesley, p. 101.   [e] Lesley, p. 109, &c.

Elizabeth's commissioners proposed also to Mary a plan of accommodation with her subjects in Scotland; and after some reasoning on that head, it was agreed, that the queen should require Lenox, the regent, to send commissioners, in order to treat of conditions under her mediation. The partizans of Mary boasted, that all terms were fully settled with the court of England, and that the Scottish rebels would soon be constrained to submit to the authority of their sovereign: But Elizabeth took care that these rumours should meet with no credit, and that the king's party should not be discouraged, nor sink too low in their demands. Cecil wrote to inform the regent, that all the queen of England's proposals, so far from being fixed and irrevocable, were to be discussed anew in the conference; and desired him to send commissioners who should be constant in the king's cause, and cautious not to make concessions which might be prejudicial to their party.[f] Sussex also, in his letters, dropped hints to the same purpose; and Elizabeth herself said to the abbot of Dunfermling, whom Lenox had sent to the court of England, that she would not insist on Mary's restoration, provided the Scots could make the justice of their cause appear to her satisfaction; and that, even if their reasons should fall short of full conviction, she would take effectual care to provide for their future security.[g]

1571.
1st March.
The parliament of Scotland appointed the earl of Morton, and Sir James Macgill, together with the abbot of Dunfermling, to manage the treaty. These commissioners presented memorials, containing reasons for the deposition of their queen; and they seconded their arguments with examples drawn from the Scottish history, with the authority of laws, and with the sentiments of many famous divines. The lofty ideas, which Elizabeth had entertained of the absolute, indefeasable right of sovereigns, made her be shocked with these republican topics; and she told the Scottish commissioners, that she was no-wise satisfied with their reasons for justifying the conduct of their countrymen; and that they might therefore, without attempting any apology, proceed to open the conditions, which they required for their security.[h] They replied, that their commission did not empower them to treat of any terms, which might infringe the title and sovereignty of their young king;

[f] Spotswood, p. 245.   [g] Ibid. p. 247, 248.   [h] Ibid. p. 248, 249.

but they would gladly hear whatever proposals should be made
them by her majesty. The conditions, recommended by the queen,
were not disadvantageous to Mary; but as the commissioners still
insisted, that they were not authorized to treat in any manner,
concerning the restoration of that princess,[i] the conferences were
necessarily at an end; and Elizabeth dismissed the Scottish commissioners with injunctions, that they should return, after having
procured more ample powers from their parliament.[k] The bishop
of Ross openly complained to the English council, that they had
abused his mistress by fair promises and professions; and Mary
herself was no longer at a loss to judge of Elizabeth's insincerity. By
reason of these disappointments, matters came still nearer to extremities between the two princesses; and the queen of Scots, finding all her hopes eluded, was more strongly incited to make, at all
hazards, every possible attempt for her liberty and security.

An incident also happened about this time, which tended to
widen the breach between Mary and Elizabeth, and to encrease the
vigilance and jealousy of the latter princess. Pope Pius V. who had
succeeded Paul, after having endeavoured in vain to conciliate by
gentle means the friendship of Elizabeth, whom his predecessor's
violence had irritated, issued at last a bull of excommunication
against her, deprived her of all title to the crown, and absolved her
subjects from their oaths of allegiance.[l] It seems probable, that
this attack on the queen's authority was made in concert with Mary,
who intended by that means to forward the northern rebellion; a
measure which was at that time in agitation.[m] John Felton affixed
this bull to the gates of the bishop of London's palace; and scorn-
ing either to fly or to deny the fact, he was seized, and condemned,
and received the crown of martyrdom, for which he seems to have
entertained so violent an ambition.[n]

A new parliament, after five years' interval, was assembled at
Westminster; and as the queen, by the rage of the pope against
her, was become still more the head of the ruling party, it might be
expected, both from this incident and from her own prudent and
vigorous conduct, that her authority over the two houses would be

2d of
April.
A par-
liament.

[i] Haynes, p. 623. [k] Spotswood, p. 249, 250, &c. Lesley, p. 133, 136.
Camden, p. 431, 432. [l] Camden, p. 427. [m] Ibid. p. 441. from
Cajetanus's Life of Pius V. [n] Camden, p. 428.

absolutely uncontroulable. It was so in fact; yet is it remarkable, that it prevailed not without some small opposition; and that too arising chiefly from the height of zeal for protestantism; a disposition of the English, which, in general, contributed extremely to encrease the queen's popularity. We shall be somewhat particular in relating the transactions of this session, because they show, as well the extent of the royal power during that age, as the character of Elizabeth and the genius of her government. It will be curious also to observe the faint dawn of the spirit of liberty among the English, the jealousy with which that spirit was repressed by the sovereign, the imperious conduct which was maintained in opposition to it, and the ease with which it was subdued by this arbitrary princess.

The lord keeper, Bacon, after the speaker of the commons was elected, told the parliament, in the queen's name, that she enjoined them not to meddle with any matters of state:[o] Such was his expression; by which he probably meant, the questions of the queen's marriage and the succession, about which they had before given her some uneasiness: For as to the other great points of government, alliances, peace and war, or foreign negociations; no parliament in that age ever presumed to take them under consideration, or question, in these particulars, the conduct of their sovereign, or of his ministers.

In the former parliament, the puritans had introduced seven bills for a farther reformation in religion; but they had not been able to prevail in any one of them.[p] This house of commons had sitten a very few days, when Stricland, a member, revived one of the bills, that for the amendment of the liturgy.[q] The chief objection, which he mentioned, was the sign of the cross in baptism. Another member added, the kneeling at the sacrament; and remarked, that, if a posture of humiliation were requisite in that act of devotion, it were better, that the communicants should throw themselves prostrate on the ground, in order to keep at the widest distance from former superstition.[r]

Religion was a point, of which Elizabeth was, if possible, still more jealous than of matters of state. She pretended, that, in quality of supreme head or governor of the church, she was fully

[o] D'Ewes, p. 141.   [p] D'Ewes, p. 185.   [q] Ibid. p. 156, 157.   [r] Ibid. p. 167.

empowered, by her prerogative alone, to decide all questions, which might arise with regard to doctrine, discipline, or worship; and she never would allow her parliaments so much as to take these points into consideration.[s] The courtiers did not forget to insist on this topic: The treasurer of the household, though he allowed, that any heresy might be repressed by parliament (a concession which seems to have been rash and unguarded; since the act, investing the crown with the supremacy, or rather recognizing that prerogative, gave the sovereign full power to reform all heresies), yet he affirmed, that it belonged to the queen alone, as head of the church, to regulate every question of ceremony in worship.[t] The comptroller seconded this argument; insisted on the extent of the queen's prerogative; and said that the house might, from former examples, have taken warning not to meddle with such matters. One Pistor opposed these remonstrances of the courtiers. He was scandalized, he said, that affairs of such infinite consequence (namely, kneeling and making the sign of the cross) should be passed over so lightly. These questions, he added, concern the salvation of souls, and interest every one more deeply than the monarchy of the whole world. This cause he shewed to be the cause of God; the rest were all but terrene, yea trifles in comparison, call them ever so great: Subsidies, crowns, kingdoms, he knew not what weight they had, when laid in the balance with subjects of such unspeakable importance.[u] Though the zeal of this member seems to have been approved of, the house, overawed by the prerogative, voted upon the question, that a petition should be presented to her majesty, for her licence to proceed farther in this bill; and in the mean time, that they should stop all debate or reasoning concerning it.[w]

Matters would probably have rested here, had not the queen been so highly offended with Stricland's presumption, in moving the bill for reformation of the liturgy, that she summoned him before the council, and prohibited him thenceforth from appearing in the house of commons.[x] This act of power was too violent even for the submissive parliament to endure. Carleton took notice of the matter; complained that the liberties of the house were

[s] Ibid. p. 158. [t] Ibid. p. 166. [u] D'Ewes, p. 166. [w] Ibid. p. 167. [x] Ibid. p. 175.

invaded; observed that Stricland was not a private man, but represented a multitude; and moved, that he might be sent for, and, if
he were guilty of any offence, might answer for it at the bar of the
house, which he insinuated to be the only competent tribunal.[y]
Yelverton enforced the principles of liberty with still greater boldness. He said, that the precedent was dangerous: And though in
this happy time of lenity, among so many good and honourable
personages as were at present invested with authority, nothing of
extremity or injury was to be apprehended; yet the times might
alter; what now is permitted, might hereafter be construed as duty,
and might be enforced even on the ground of the present permission. He added, that all matters not treasonable, or which implied
not *too much* derogation of the imperial crown, might, without
offence, be introduced into parliament; where every question that
concerned the community must be considered, and where even the
right of the crown itself must finally be determined. He remarked,
that men sat not in that house in their private capacities, but as
elected by their country; and though it was proper, that the prince
should retain his prerogative, yet was that prerogative limited by
law: As the sovereign could not of himself make laws, neither could
he break them, merely from his own authority.[z]

These principles were popular, and noble, and generous; but
the open assertion of them was, at this time, somewhat new in
England: And the courtiers were more warranted by present practice, when they advanced a contrary doctrine. The treasurer
warned the house to be cautious in their proceedings; neither to
venture farther than their assured warrant might extend, nor hazard their good opinion with her majesty in any doubtful cause. The
member, he said, whose attendance they required, was not restrained on account of any liberty of speech, but for his exhibiting
a bill in the house against the prerogative of the queen; a temerity
which was not to be tolerated. And he concluded with observing,
that even speeches, made in that house, had been questioned and
examined by the sovereign.[a] Cleere, another member, remarked,
that the sovereign's prerogative is not so much as disputable, and
that the safety of the queen is the safety of the subject. He added,

[y] Ibid.   [z] D'Ewes, p. 175, 176.   [a] Ibid. p. 175.

CHAPTER XL

that, in questions of divinity, every man was for his instruction to repair to his ordinary; and he seems to insinuate, that the bishops themselves, for their instruction, must repair to the queen.[b] Fleetwood observed, that, in his memory, he knew a man, who, in the fifth of the present queen, had been called to account for a speech in the house. But lest this example should be deemed too recent, he would inform them, from the parliament rolls, that, in the reign of Henry V. a bishop was committed to prison by the king's command, on account of his freedom of speech; and the parliament presumed not to go farther than to be humble suitors for him: In the subsequent reign the speaker himself was committed, with another member; and the house found no other remedy than a like submissive application. He advised the house to have recourse to the same expedient; and not to presume either to send for their member, or demand him as of right.[c] During this speech, those members of the privy-council who sat in the house, whispered together; upon which the speaker moved, that the house should make stay of all farther proceedings: A motion, which was immediately complied with. The queen, finding that the experiment, which she had made, was likely to excite a great ferment, saved her honour by this silence of the house; and lest the question might be resumed, she sent next day to Stricland her permission to give his attendance in parliament.[d]

Notwithstanding this rebuke from the throne, the zeal of the commons still engaged them to continue the discussion of those other bills which regarded religion; but they were interrupted by a still more arbitrary proceeding of the queen, in which the lords condescended to be her instruments. This house sent a message to the commons, desiring that a committee might attend them. Some members were appointed for that purpose; and the upper house informed them, that the queen's majesty, being informed of the articles of reformation which they had canvassed, approved of them, intended to publish them, and to make the bishops execute them, by virtue of her royal authority, as supreme head of the church of England: But that she would not permit them to be treated of in parliament.[e] The house, though they did not entirely

[b] D'Ewes, p. 175.   [c] Ibid. p. 176.   [d] Idem ibid.   [e] D'Ewes, p. 180, 185.

stop proceedings on account of this injunction, seem to have been nowise offended at such haughty treatment; and in the issue all the bills came to nothing.

A motion, made by Robert Bell, a puritan, against an exclusive patent granted to a company of merchants in Bristol,[f] gave also occasion to several remarkable incidents. The queen, some days after the motion was made, sent orders by the mouth of the speaker, commanding the house to spend little time in motions, and to avoid long speeches. All the members understood, that she had been offended, because a matter had been moved, which seemed to touch her prerogative.[g] Fleetwood accordingly spoke of this delicate subject. He observed, that the queen had a prerogative of granting patents; that to question the validity of any patent was to invade the royal prerogative; that all foreign trade was entirely subjected to the pleasure of the sovereign; that even the statute, which gave liberty of commerce, admitted of all prohibitions from the crown; and that the prince, when he granted an exclusive patent, only employed the power vested in him, and prohibited all others from dealing in any particular branch of commerce. He quoted the clerk of the parliament's book to prove, that no man might speak in parliament of the statute of wills, unless the king first gave licence: because the royal prerogative in the wards was thereby touched. He shewed likewise the statutes of Edward I. Edward III. and Henry IV. with a saving of the prerogative. And in Edward VI.'s time, the protector was applied to, for his allowance to mention matters of prerogative.[h]

Sir Humphrey Gilbert, the gallant and renowned sea-adventurer, carried these topics still farther. He endeavoured to prove the motion made by Bell to be a vain device, and perilous to be treated of; since it tended to the derogation of the prerogative imperial, which whoever should attempt so much as in fancy, could not, he said, be otherwise accounted than an open enemy. For what difference is there between saying, that the queen is not to use the privilege of the crown, and saying that she is not queen? And though experience has shewn so much clemency in her majesty, as might, perhaps, make subjects forget their duty; it is not good to sport or venture too much with princes. He reminded

[f] Ibid. p. 185.   [g] Ibid. p. 159.   [h] D'Ewes, p. 160.

CHAPTER XL

them of the fable of the hare, who, upon the proclamation, that all
horned beasts should depart the court, immediately fled, lest his
ears should be construed to be horns; and by this apologue he
seems to insinuate, that even those who heard or permitted such
dangerous speeches, would not themselves be entirely free from
danger. He desired them to beware, lest, if they meddled farther
with these matters, the queen might look to her own power; and
finding herself able to suppress their challenged liberty, and to
exert an arbitrary authority, might imitate the example of Lewis
XI. of France, who, as he termed it, delivered the crown from
wardship.[i]

Though this speech gave some disgust, no body, at the time,
replied any thing, but that Sir Humphrey mistook the meaning of
the house, and of the member who made the motion: They never
had any other purpose, than to represent their grievances, in due
and seemly form, unto her majesty. But in a subsequent debate
Peter Wentworth, a man of a superior free spirit, called that speech
an insult on the house; noted Sir Humphrey's disposition to flatter
and fawn on the prince; compared him to the cameleon, which can
change itself into all colours, except white; and recommended to
the house, a due care of liberty of speech; and of the privileges of
parliament.[k] It appears, on the whole, that the motion against the
exclusive patent had no effect. Bell, the member who first introduced it, was sent for by the council, and was severely reprimanded
for his temerity. He returned to the house with such an amazed
countenance, that all the members, well informed of the reason,
were struck with terror; and during some time, no one durst rise
to speak of any matter of importance, for fear of giving offence to
the queen and the council. Even after the fears of the commons
were somewhat abated, the members spoke with extreme precaution; and by employing most of their discourse in preambles
and apologies, they shewed their conscious terror of the rod which
hung over them. Wherever any delicate point was touched, though
ever so gently; nay seemed to be approached, though at ever so
great a distance, the whisper ran about the house, "The queen will
be offended; the council will be extremely displeased." And by
these surmizes men were warned of the danger, to which they

[i] Ibid. p. 168.   [k] D'Ewes, p. 175.

exposed themselves. It is remarkable, that the patent, which the queen defended with such imperious violence, was contrived for the profit of four courtiers, and was attended with the utter ruin of seven or eight thousand of her industrious subjects.[l]

29th May.
Thus, every thing, which passed the two houses, was extremely respectful and submissive; yet did the queen think it incumbent on her, at the conclusion of the session, to check, and that with great severity, those feeble efforts of liberty, which had appeared in the motions and speeches of some members. The lord keeper told the commons, in her majesty's name, that, though the majority of the lower house had shewn themselves in their proceedings, discreet and dutiful, yet a few of them had discovered a contrary character, and had justly merited the reproach of audacious, arrogant, and presumptuous: Contrary to their duty, both as subjects and parliament-men, nay contrary to the express injunctions given them from the throne at the beginning of the session; injunctions, which it might well become them to have better attended to; they had presumed to call in question her majesty's grants and prerogatives. But her majesty warns them, that, since they thus wilfully forget themselves, they are otherwise to be admonished: Some other species of correction must be found for them; since neither the commands of her majesty, nor the example of their wiser brethren, can reclaim their audacious, arrogant, and presumptuous folly, by which they are thus led to meddle with what nowise belongs to them, and what lies beyond the compass of their understanding.[m]

In all these transactions appears clearly the opinion, which Elizabeth had entertained of the duty and authority of parliaments. They were not to convass any matters of state: Still less were they to meddle with the church. Questions of either kind were far above their reach, and were appropriated to the prince alone, or to those councils and ministers, with whom he was pleased to entrust them. What then was the office of parliaments? They might give directions for the due tanning of leather, or milling of cloth; for the preservation of pheasants and partridges; for the reparation of bridges and highways; for the punishment of vagabonds or common beggars. Regulations concerning the police of the country came properly under their inspection; and the laws of

[l] Ibid. p. 242. [m] D'Ewes, p. 151.

CHAPTER XL

this kind which they prescribed, had, if not a greater, yet a more durable authority, than those which were derived solely from the proclamations of the sovereign. Precedents or reports could fix a rule for decisions in private property, or the punishment of crimes; but no alteration or innovation in the municipal law could proceed from any other source than the parliament; nor would the courts of justice be induced to change their established practice by an order of council. But the most acceptable part of parliamentary proceedings was the granting of subsidies; the attainting and punishing of the obnoxious nobility, or any minister of state after his fall; the countenancing of such great efforts of power, as might be deemed somewhat exceptionable, when they proceeded entirely from the sovereign. The redress of grievances was sometimes promised to the people; but seldom could have place, while it was an established rule, that the prerogatives of the crown must not be abridged, or so much as questioned and examined in parliament. Even though monopolies and exclusive companies had already reached an enormous height, and were every day encreasing, to the destruction of all liberty, and extinction of all industry; it was criminal in a member to propose, in the most dutiful and regular manner, a parliamentary application against any of them.

These maxims of government were not kept secret by Elizabeth, or smoothed over by any fair appearances or plausible pretences. They were openly avowed in her speeches and messages to parliament; and were accompanied with all the haughtiness, nay sometimes bitterness, of expression, which the meanest servant could look for from his offended master. Yet notwithstanding this conduct, Elizabeth continued to be the most popular sovereign that ever swayed the scepter of England; because the maxims of her reign were conformable to the principles of the times, and to the opinion, generally entertained with regard to the constitution. The continued encroachments of popular assemblies on Elizabeth's successors have so changed our ideas in these matters, that the passages above mentioned appear to us extremely curious, and even at first surprising; but they were so little remarked, during the time, that neither Camden, though a contemporary writer, nor any other historian, has taken any notice of them. So absolute, indeed, was the authority of the crown, that the precious spark of liberty had been kindled, and was preserved, by the puritans alone; and it was to this sect, whose principles appear so frivolous and habits so ridiculous, that the English owe the whole freedom of their constitution. Actuated by that zeal which belongs to innovators, and by the courage which enthusiasm inspires, they hazarded the utmost indignation of their sovereign; and employing all their industry to be elected into parliament; a matter not difficult, while a seat was rather regarded as a burthen than an advantage;[n] they first acquired a majority in that assembly, and then obtained an ascendant over the church and monarchy.

The following were the principal laws enacted this session. It was declared treason, during the life-time of the queen, to affirm, that she was not the lawful sovereign, or that any other possessed a preferable title, or that she was a heretic, schismatic, or infidel, or that the laws and statutes cannot limit and determine the right of the crown and the successor thereof: To maintain in writing or printing, that any person, except the *natural issue* of her body, is or ought to be the queen's heir or successor, subjected the person and all his abettors, for the first offence, to imprisonment during a year, and to the forfeiture of half their goods: The second offence subjected them to the penalty of a premunire.[o] This law was plainly levelled against the queen of Scots and her partizans; and implied an avowal, that Elizabeth never intended to declare her successor. It may be noted, that the usual phrase of *lawful issue,* which the parliament thought indecent towards the queen, as if she could be supposed to have any other, was changed into that of *natural issue.* But this alteration was the source of pleasantry during the time; and some suspected a deeper design, as if Leicester intended, in case of the queen's demise, to produce some bastard of his own, and affirm that he was her offspring.[p]

It was also enacted, that whosoever by bulls should publish absolutions or other rescripts of the pope, or should, by means of them, reconcile any man to the church of Rome, such offenders, as well as those who were so reconciled, should be guilty of treason. The penalty of a premunire was imposed on every one who imported any *Agnus Dei,* crucifix, or such other implement of super-

[n] It appeared this session, that a bribe of four pounds had been given to a mayor for a seat in parliament. D'Ewes, p. 181. It is probable, that the member had no other view than the privilege of being free from arrests.
[o] 13 Eliz. c. 1. [p] Camden, p. 436.

stition, consecrated by the pope.[q] The former laws against usury, were enforced by a new statute.[r] A supply of one subsidy and two fifteenths was granted by parliament. The queen, as she was determined to yield to them none of her power, was very cautious in asking them for any supply. She endeavoured, either by a rigid frugality to make her ordinary revenues suffice for the necessities of the crown, or she employed her prerogative, and procured money by the granting of patents, monopolies, or by some such ruinous expedient.

Though Elizabeth possessed such uncontrouled authority over her parliaments, and such extensive influence over her people; though during a course of thirteen years, she had maintained the public tranquillity, which was only interrupted by the hasty and ill-concerted insurrection in the north; she was still kept in great anxiety, and felt her throne perpetually totter under her. The violent commotions, excited in France and the Low Countries, as well as in Scotland, seemed in one view to secure her against any disturbance; but they served, on more reflection, to instruct her in the danger of her situation, when she remarked, that England, no less than these neighbouring countries, contained the seeds of intestine discord; the differences of religious opinion, and the furious intolerance and animosity of the opposite sectaries.

The league, formed at Bayonne in 1566 for the extermination of the protestants, had not been concluded so secretly but intelligence of it had reached Condé, Coligni, and the other leaders of the hugonots; and finding, that the measures of the court agreed with their suspicions, they determined to prevent the cruel perfidy of their enemies, and to strike a blow before the catholics were aware of the danger. The hugonots, though dispersed over the whole kingdom, formed a kind of separate empire; and being closely united, as well by their religious zeal, as by the dangers to which they were perpetually exposed, they obeyed with entire submission the orders of their leaders, and were ready on every signal to fly to arms. The king and queen mother were living in great security at Monceaux in Brie; when they found themselves surrounded by protestant troops, which had secretly marched thither from all quarters; and had not a body of Swiss come speed-

Civil wars of France.

---

[q] 13 Eliz. c. 2.   [r] Ibid. c. 8.

ily to their relief, and conducted them with great intrepidity to Paris, they must have fallen, without resistance, into the hands of the malcontents. A battle was afterwards fought in the plains of St. Dennis; where, though the old constable Montmorency, the general of the catholics, was killed combating bravely at the head of his troops, the hugonots were finally defeated. Condé, collecting his broken forces, and receiving a strong reinforcement from the German protestants, appeared again in the field; and laying siege to Chartres, a place of great importance, obliged the court to agree to a new accommodation.

So great was the mutual animosity of those religionists, that even had the leaders on both sides been ever so sincere in their intentions for peace, and reposed ever so much confidence in each other, it would have been difficult to retain the people in tranquillity; much more, where such extreme jealousy prevailed, and where the court employed every pacification as a snare for their enemies. A plan was laid for seizing the person of the prince and admiral; who narrowly escaped to Rochelle, and summoned their partizans to their assistance.[s] The civil wars were renewed with greater fury than ever, and the parties became still more exasperated against each other. The young duke of Anjou, brother to the king, commanded the forces of the catholics; and fought in 1569 a great battle at Jarnac with the hugonots, where the prince of Condé was killed, and his army defeated. This discomfiture, with the loss of so great a leader, reduced not the hugonots to despair. The admiral still supported the cause; and having placed at the head of the protestants the prince of Navarre, then sixteen years of age, and the young prince of Condé, he encouraged the party rather to perish bravely in the field, than ignominiously by the hands of the executioner. He collected such numbers, so determined to endure every extremity, that he was enabled to make head against the duke of Anjou; and being strengthened by a new reinforcement of Germans, he obliged that prince to retreat and to divide his force.

Coligni then laid siege to Poitiers; and as the eyes of all France were fixed on this enterprize, the duke of Guise, emulous of the renown, which his father had acquired by the defence of Metz,

[s] Davila, lib. 4.

CHAPTER XL

threw himself into the place, and so animated the garrison by his valour and conduct, that the admiral was obliged to raise the siege. Such was the commencement of that unrivaled fame and grandeur, afterwards attained by this duke of Guise. The attachment, which all the catholics had borne to his father, was immediately transferred to the son; and men pleased themselves in comparing all the great and shining qualities, which seemed, in a manner, hereditary in that family. Equal in affability, in munificence, in address, in eloquence, and in every quality, which engages the affections of men; equal also in valour, in conduct, in enterprize, in capacity; there seemed only this difference between them, that the son educated in more turbulent times, and finding a greater dissolution of all law and order, exceeded the father in ambition and temerity, and was engaged in enterprizes still more destructive to the authority of his sovereign and to the repose of his native country.

Elizabeth, who kept her attention fixed on the civil commotions of France, was nowise pleased with this new rise of her enemies, the Guises; and being anxious for the fate of the protestants, whose interests were connected with her own,[t] she was engaged, notwithstanding her aversion from all rebellion, and from all opposition to the will of the sovereign, to give them secretly some assistance. Besides employing her authority with the German princes, she lent money to the queen of Navarre, and received some jewels as pledges for the loan. And she permitted Henry Champernon to levy, and transport over into France, a regiment of a hundred gentlemen voluntiers; among whom Walter Raleigh, then a young man, began to distinguish himself, in that great school of military valour.[u] The admiral, constrained by the impatience of his troops, and by the difficulty of subsisting them, fought with the duke of Anjou the battle of Moncontour in Poictou, where he was wounded and defeated. The court of France, notwithstanding their frequent experience of the obstinacy of the hugonots, and the vigour of Coligni, vainly flattered themselves, that the force of the rebels was at last finally annihilated; and they neglected farther preparations against a foe, who, they thought, could never more become dangerous. They were surprized to

[t] Haynes, p. 471.   [u] Camden, p. 423.

hear, that this leader had appeared, without dismay, in another quarter of the kingdom; had encouraged the young princes, whom he governed, to like constancy; had assembled an army; had taken the field; and was even strong enough to threaten Paris. The public finances, diminished by the continued disorders of the kingdom, and wasted by so many fruitless military enterprizes, could no longer bear the charge of a new armament; and the king, notwithstanding his extreme animosity against the hugonots, was obliged, in 1570, to conclude an accommodation with them, to grant them a pardon for all past offences, and to renew the edicts for liberty of conscience.

Though a pacification was seemingly concluded, the mind of Charles was no wise reconciled to his rebellious subjects; and this accommodation, like all the foregoing, was nothing but a snare, by which the perfidious court had projected to destroy at once, without danger, all its formidable enemies. As the two young princes, the admiral, and the other leaders of the hugonots, instructed by past experience, discovered an extreme distrust of the king's intentions, and kept themselves in security, at a distance, all possible artifices were employed to remove their apprehensions, and convince them of the sincerity of the new counsels, which seemed to be embraced. The terms of the peace were religiously observed to them; the toleration was strictly maintained; all attempts, made by the zealous catholics to infringe it, were punished with severity; offices, and favours, and honours were bestowed on the principal nobility among the protestants; and the king and council every where declared, that, tired of civil disorders, and convinced of the impossibility of forcing men's consciences, they were thenceforth determined to allow every one the free exercise of his religion.

Among the other artifices, employed to lull the protestants into a fatal security, Charles affected to enter into close connections with Elizabeth; and as it seemed not the interest of France to forward the union of the two kingdoms of Great Britain, that princess the more easily flattered herself, that the French monarch would prefer her friendship to that of the queen of Scots. The better to deceive her, proposals of marriage were made her with the duke of Anjou; a prince whose youth, beauty, and reputation for valour might naturally be supposed to recommend him to a woman, who had appeared not altogether insensible to these endowments. The queen immediately founded on this offer the project of deceiving the court of France; and being intent on that artifice, she laid herself the more open to be deceived. Negociations were entered into with regard to the marriage; terms of the contract were proposed; difficulties started and removed; and the two courts equally insincere, though not equally culpable, seemed to approach every day nearer to each other in their demands and concessions. The great obstacle seemed to lie in adjusting the difference of religion; because Elizabeth, who recommended toleration to Charles, was determined not to grant it in her own dominions, not even to her husband; and the duke of Anjou seemed unwilling to submit, for the sake of interest, to the dishonour of an apostacy.[w]

The artificial politics of Elizabeth never triumphed so much in any contrivances as in those which were conjoined with her coquetry; and as her character in this particular was generally known, the court of France thought, that they might, without danger of forming any final conclusion, venture the farther in their concessions and offers to her. The queen also had other motives for dissimulation. Besides the advantage of discouraging Mary's partizans by the prospect of an alliance between France and England, her situation with Philip demanded her utmost vigilance and attention; and the violent authority, established in the Low Countries, made her desirous of fortifying herself even with the bare appearance of a new confederacy.

The theological controversies, which had long agitated Europe, had, from the beginning, penetrated into the Low Countries; and as these provinces maintained an extensive commerce, they had early received from every kingdom, with which they corresponded, a tincture of religious innovation. An opinion at that time prevailed, which had been zealously propagated by priests, and implicitly received by sovereigns, that heresy was closely connected with rebellion, and that every great or violent alteration in the church involved a like revolution in the civil government. The forward zeal of the reformers would seldom allow them to wait the consent of the magistrate to their innovations: They became less

Affairs of the Low Countries.

[w] Camden, p. 433. Davila, lib. 5. Digges's Complete Ambassador, p. 84, 110, 111.

dutiful when opposed and punished: And though their pretended spirit of reasoning and enquiry was in reality nothing but a new species of implicit faith, the prince took the alarm; as if no institutions could be secure from the temerity of their researches. The emperor Charles, who purposed to augment his authority under pretence of defending the catholic faith, easily adopted these political principles; and notwithstanding the limited prerogative, which he possessed in the Netherlands, he published the most arbitrary, severe, and tyrannical edicts against the protestants; and he took care that the execution of them should be no less violent and sanguinary. He was neither cruel nor bigotted in his natural disposition; yet an historian, celebrated for moderation and caution, has computed, that, in the several persecutions promoted by that monarch, no less than a hundred thousand persons perished by the hands of the executioner.[x] But these severe remedies, far from answering the purposes intended, had rather served to augment the numbers as well as zeal of the reformers; and the magistrates of the several towns, seeing no end of those barbarous executions, felt their humanity rebel against their principles, and declined any farther persecution of the new doctrines.

When Philip succeeded to his father's dominions, the Flemings were justly alarmed with new apprehensions; lest their prince, observing the lenity of the magistrates, should take the execution of the edicts from such remiss hands, and should establish the inquisition in the Low Countries, accompanied with all the iniquities and barbarities which attended it in Spain. The severe and unrelenting character of the man, his professed attachment to Spanish manners, the inflexible bigotry of his principles; all these circumstances encreased their terror: And when he departed the Netherlands, with a known intention never to return, the disgust of the inhabitants was extremely augmented, and their dread of those tyrannical orders, which their sovereign, surrounded with Spanish ministers, would issue from his cabinet at Madrid. He left the dutchess of Parma, governess of the Low Countries; and the plain good sense and good temper of that princess, had she been entrusted with the sole power, would have preserved the sub-

[x] Grotii Annal. lib. 1. Father Paul, another great authority, computes in a passage above cited, that 50,000 persons were put to death in the Low Countries alone.

CHAPTER XL

mission of those opulent provinces, which were lost from that refinement of treacherous and barbarous politics, on which Philip so highly valued himself. The Flemings found, that the name alone of regent remained with the dutchess; that Cardinal Granville entirely possessed the king's confidence; that attempts were every day made on their liberties; that a resolution was taken never more to assemble the states; that new bishoprics were arbitrarily erected, in order to enforce the execution of the persecuting edicts; and that, on the whole, they must expect to be reduced to the condition of a province under the Spanish monarchy. The discontents of the nobility gave countenance to the complaints of the gentry, which encouraged the mutiny of the populace; and all orders of men showed a strong disposition to revolt. Associations were formed, tumultuary petitions presented, names of distinction assumed, badges of party displayed; and the current of the people, impelled by religious zeal, and irritated by feeble resistance, rose to such a height, that, in several towns, particularly in Antwerp, they made an open invasion on the established worship, pillaged the churches and monasteries, broke the images, and committed the most unwarrantable disorders.

The wiser part of the nobility, particularly the prince of Orange, and the counts Egmont and Horn, were alarmed at these excesses, to which their own discontents had at first given countenance; and seconding the wisdom of the governess, they suppressed the dangerous insurrections, punished the ringleaders, and reduced all the provinces to a state of order and submission. But Philip was not contented with the re-establishment of his ancient authority: He considered, that provinces, so remote from the seat of government, could not be ruled by a limited prerogative; and that a prince, who must entreat rather than command, would necessarily, when he resided not among the people, feel every day a diminution of his power and influence. He determined, therefore, to lay hold of the late popular disorders as a pretence for entirely abolishing the privileges of the Low Country provinces; and for ruling them thenceforth with a military and arbitrary authority.

In the execution of this violent design, he employed a man, who was a proper instrument in the hands of such a tyrant. Ferdinand of Toledo, duke of Alva, had been educated amidst arms; and having attained a consummate knowledge in the military art, his habits led him to transfer into all government the severe discipline of a camp, and to conceive no measures between prince and subject, but those of rigid command and implicit obedience. This general, in 1568, conducted from Italy to the Low Countries a powerful body of veteran Spaniards; and his avowed animosity to the Flemings, with his known character, struck that whole people with terror and consternation. It belongs not to our subject to relate at length those violences, which Alva's natural barbarity, steeled by reflection, and aggravated by insolence, exercised on those flourishing provinces. It suffices to say, that all their privileges, the gift of so many princes, and the inheritance of so many ages, were openly and expressly abolished by edict; arbitrary and sanguinary tribunals erected; the counts Egmont and Horn, in spite of their great merits and past services, brought to the scaffold; multitudes of all ranks thrown into confinement, and thence delivered over to the executioner: And notwithstanding the peaceable submission of all men, nothing was heard of but confiscation, imprisonment, exile, torture, and death.

Elizabeth was equally displeased to see the progress of that scheme, laid for the extermination of the protestants, and to observe the erection of so great a military power, in a state situated in so near a neighbourhood. She gave protection to all the Flemish exiles who took shelter in her dominions; and as many of these were the most industrious inhabitants of the Netherlands, and had rendered that country celebrated for its arts, she reaped the advantage of introducing into England some useful manufactures, which were formerly unknown in that kingdom. Foreseeing that the violent government of Alva could not long subsist without exciting some commotion, she ventured to commit an insult upon him, which she would have been cautious not to hazard against a more established authority. Some Genoese merchants had engaged, by contract with Philip, to transport into Flanders the sum of four hundred thousand crowns; and the vessels, on which this money was embarked, had been attacked in the Channel by some privateers equipped by the French Hugonots, and had taken shelter in Plymouth and Southampton. The commanders of the ships pretended, that the money belonged to the king of Spain; but the queen, finding, upon enquiry, that it was the property of Genoese

CHAPTER XL

merchants, took possession of it as a loan; and by that means deprived the duke of Alva of this resource in the time of his greatest necessity. Alva, in revenge, seized all the English merchants in the Low Countries, threw them into prison, and confiscated their effects. The queen retaliated by a like violence on the Flemish and Spanish merchants; and gave all the English liberty to make reprizals on the subjects of Philip.

These differences were afterwards accommodated by treaty, and mutual reparations were made to the merchants: But nothing could repair the loss, which so well-timed a blow inflicted on the Spanish government in the Low Countries. Alva, in want of money, and dreading the immediate mutiny of his troops, to whom great arrears were due, imposed by his arbitrary will the most ruinous taxes on the people. He not only required the hundredth penny, and the twentieth of all immoveable goods: He also demanded the tenth of all moveable goods on every sale; an absurd tyranny, which would not only have destroyed all arts and commerce, but even have restrained the common intercourse of life. The people refused compliance: The duke had recourse to his usual expedient of the gibbet: And thus matters came still nearer the last extremities between the Flemings and the Spaniards.[y]

All the enemies of Elizabeth, in order to revenge themselves for her insults, had naturally recourse to one policy, the supporting of the cause and pretensions of the queen of Scots; and Alva, whose measures were ever violent, soon opened a secret intercourse with that princess. There was one Rodolphi, a Florentine merchant, who had resided about fifteen years in London, and who, while he conducted his commerce in England, had managed all the correspondence of the court of Rome with the catholic nobility and gentry.[z] He had been thrown into prison at the time when the duke of Norfolk's intrigues with Mary had been discovered; but either no proof was found against him, or the part which he had acted, was not very criminal; and he soon after recovered his liberty. This man, zealous for the catholic faith, had formed a scheme, in concert with the Spanish ambassador, for subverting the government, by a foreign invasion and a domestic insurrection; and when he

New conspiracy of the duke of Norfolk.

[y] Bentivoglio, part I. lib. v. Camden, p. 416.   [z] Lesley, p. 123. State Trials, vol. i. p. 87.

communicated his project, by letter, to Mary, he found, that, as she was now fully convinced of Elizabeth's artifices, and despaired of ever recovering her authority, or even her liberty, by pacific measures, she willingly gave her concurrence. The great number of discontented catholics were the chief source of their hopes on the side of England; and they also observed, that the kingdom was, at that time, full of indigent gentry, chiefly younger brothers, who, having at present, by the late decay of the church, and the yet languishing state of commerce, no prospect of a livelihood suitable to their birth, were ready to throw themselves into any desperate enterprize.[a] But in order to inspire life and courage into all these malcontents, it was requisite, that some great nobleman should put himself at their head; and no one appeared to Rodolphi, and to the bishop of Ross, who entered into all these intrigues, so proper, both on account of his power and his popularity, as the duke of Norfolk.

This nobleman, when released from confinement in the Tower, had given his promise, that he would drop all intercourse with the queen of Scots;[b] but finding that he had lost, and, as he feared, beyond recovery, the confidence and favour of Elizabeth, and being still, in some degree, restrained from his liberty, he was tempted, by impatience and despair, to violate his word, and to open anew his correspondence with the captive princess.[c] A promise of marriage was renewed between them; the duke engaged to enter into all her interests; and as his remorses gradually diminished in the course of these transactions, he was pushed to give his consent to enterprizes still more criminal. Rodolphi's plan was, that the duke of Alva should, on some other pretence, assemble a great quantity of shipping in the Low Countries; should transport a body of six thousand foot, and four thousand horse, into England; should land them at Harwich, where the duke of Norfolk was to join them with all his friends; should thence march directly to London, and oblige the queen to submit to whatever terms the conspirators should please to impose upon her.[d] Norfolk expressed his assent to this plan; and three letters, in consequence of it, were written in his name by Rodolphi, one to Alva, another to

[a] Lesley, p. 123. [b] Haynes, p. 571. [c] State Trials, vol. i. p. 102.
[d] Lesley, p. 155. State Trials, vol. i. p. 86, 87.

the pope, and a third to the king of Spain; but the duke, apprehensive of the danger, refused to sign them.[e] He only sent to the Spanish ambassador a servant and confident, named Barker, as well to notify his concurrence in the plan, as to vouch for the authenticity of these letters; and Rodolphi, having obtained a letter of credence from the ambassador, proceeded on his journey to Brussels and to Rome. The duke of Alva and the pope embraced the scheme with alacrity: Rodolphi informed Norfolk of their intentions:[f] And every thing seemed to concur in forwarding the undertaking.

Norfolk, notwithstanding these criminal enterprizes, had never entirely forgotten his duty to his sovereign, his country, and his religion; and though he had laid the plan both of an invasion and an insurrection, he still flattered himself, that the innocence of his intentions would justify the violence of his measures, and that, as he aimed at nothing but the liberty of the queen of Scots, and the obtaining of Elizabeth's consent to his marriage, he could not justly reproach himself as a rebel and a traitor.[g] It is certain, however, that, considering the queen's vigour and spirit, the scheme, if successful, must finally have ended in dethroning her; and her authority was here exposed to the utmost danger.

The conspiracy hitherto had entirely escaped the vigilance of Elizabeth, and that of secretary Cecil, who now bore the title of lord Burleigh. It was from another attempt of Norfolk's, that they first obtained a hint, which, being diligently traced, led at last to a full discovery. Mary had intended to send a sum of money to lord Herries, and her partizans in Scotland; and Norfolk undertook to have it delivered to Bannister, a servant of his, at that time in the north, who was to find some expedient for conveying it to lord Herries.[h] He entrusted the money to a servant who was not in the secret, and told him, that the bag contained a sum of money in silver, which he was to deliver to Bannister with a letter: But the servant, conjecturing from the weight and size of the bag, that it was full of gold, carried the letter to Burleigh; who immediately ordered Bannister, Barker, and Hicford, the duke's secretary, to

[e] Lesley, p. 159, 161. Camden, p. 432. [f] State Trials, vol. i. p. 93.
[g] Lesley, p. 158. [h] Ibid. p. 169. State Trials, vol. i. p. 87. Camden, p. 434.
Digges, p. 134, 137, 140. Strype, vol. ii. p. 82.

be put under arrest, and to undergo a severe examination. Torture made them confess the whole truth; and as Hicford, though ordered to burn all papers, had carefully kept them concealed under the mats of the duke's chamber, and under the tiles of the house, full evidence now appeared against his master.[i] Norfolk himself, who was entirely ignorant of the discoveries made by his servants, was brought before the council; and though exhorted to atone for his guilt by a full confession, he persisted in denying every crime, with which he was charged. The queen always declared, that, if he had given her this proof of his sincere repentance, she would have pardoned all his former offences;[k] but finding him obstinate, she committed him to the Tower, and ordered him to be brought to his trial. The bishop of Ross had, on some suspicion, been committed to custody before the discovery of Norfolk's guilt; and every expedient was employed to make him reveal his share in the conspiracy. He at first insisted on his privilege; but he was told, that, as his mistress was no longer a sovereign, he would not be regarded as an ambassador, and that, even if that character were allowed, it did not warrant him in conspiring against the sovereign at whose court he resided.[l] As he still refused to answer interrogatories, he was informed of the confession made by Norfolk's servants; after which he no longer scrupled to make a full discovery; and his evidence put the guilt of that nobleman beyond all question. A jury of twenty-five peers unanimously passed sentence upon him. The trial was quite regular, even according to the strict rules observed at present in these matters; except that the witnesses gave not their evidence in court, and were not confronted with the prisoner: A laudable practice, which was not at that time observed in trials for high treason.

1572.

12th Jan. Trial of Norfolk.

The queen still hesitated concerning Norfolk's execution; whether that she was really moved by friendship and compassion towards a peer of that rank and merit, or that, affecting the praise of clemency, she only put on the appearance of these sentiments. Twice she signed a warrant for his execution, and twice revoked the fatal sentence;[m] and though her ministers and counsellors pushed her to rigour, she still appeared irresolute and un-

---

[i] Lesley, p. 173.   [k] Lesley, p. 175.   [l] Ibid. p. 189. Spotswood.   [m] Carte, p. 527. from Fenelon's Dispatches. Digges, p. 166. Strype, vol. ii. p. 83.

determined. After four months hesitation, a parliament was assembled; and the commons addressed her, in strong terms, for the execution of the duke; a sanction, which, when added to the greatness and certainty of his guilt, would, she thought, justify, in the eyes of all mankind, her severity against that nobleman. Norfolk died with calmness and constancy; and though he cleared himself of any disloyal intentions against the queen's authority, he acknowledged the justice of the sentence, by which he suffered.[n] That we may relate together affairs of a similar nature, we shall mention, that the earl of Northumberland, being delivered up to the queen by the regent of Scotland, was also, a few months after, brought to the scaffold for his rebellion.

His execution. 8th May.

2d June.

The queen of Scots was either the occasion or the cause of all these disturbances; but as she was a sovereign princess, and might reasonably, from the harsh treatment which she had met with, think herself entitled to use any expedient for her relief, Elizabeth durst not, as yet, form any resolution of proceeding to extremities against her. She only sent lord Delawar, Sir Ralph Sadler, Sir Thomas Bromley, and Dr. Wilson, to expostulate with her, and to demand satisfaction for all those parts of her conduct, which, from the beginning of her life, had given displeasure to Elizabeth: Her assuming the arms of England, refusing to ratify the treaty of Edinburgh, intending to marry Norfolk without the queen's consent, concurring in the northern rebellion,[o] practising with Rodolphi to engage the king of Spain in an invasion of England,[p] procuring the pope's bull of excommunication, and allowing her friends abroad to give her the title of queen of England. Mary justified herself from the several articles of the charge, either by denying the facts imputed to her, or by throwing the blame on others.[q] But the queen was little satisfied with her apology; and the parliament was so enraged against her, that the commons made a direct application for her immediate trial and execution. They employed some topics derived from practice, and reason, and the laws of nations; but the chief stress was laid on passages and examples from the Old Testament,[r] which, if considered as a general

[n] Camden, p. 440. Strype, vol. ii. App. p. 23. [o] Digges, p. 16, 107. Strype, vol. ii. p. 51, 52. [p] Ibid. p. 194, 208, 209. Strype, vol. ii. p. 40, 51. [q] Camden, p. 442. [r] D'Ewes, p. 207, 208, &c.

rule of conduct (an intention which it is unreasonable to suppose), would lead to consequences destructive of all principles of humanity and morality. Matters were here carried farther than Elizabeth intended; and that princess, satisfied with shewing Mary the disposition of the nation, sent to the house her express commands not to deal any farther at present in the affair of the Scottish queen.[s] Nothing could be a stronger proof, that the puritanical interest prevailed in the house, than the intemperate use of authorities derived from scripture, especially from the Old Testament; and the queen was so little a lover of that sect, that she was not likely to make any concession merely in deference to their solicitation. She shewed, this session, her disapprobation of their schemes in another remarkable instance. The commons had passed two bills, for regulating ecclesiastical ceremonies; but she sent them a like imperious message with her former ones; and by the terror of her prerogative, she stopped all farther proceeding in those matters.[t]

But though Elizabeth would not carry matters to such extremities against Mary, as were recommended by the parliament, she was alarmed at the great interest and the restless spirit of that princess, as well as her close connections with Spain; and she thought it necessary both to encrease the rigour and strictness of her confinement, and to follow maxims, different from those which she had hitherto pursued, in her management of Scotland.[u] That kingdom remained still in a state of anarchy. The castle of Edinburgh, commanded by Kirkaldy of Grange, had declared for Mary; and the lords of that party, encouraged by his countenance, had taken possession of the capital, and carried on a vigorous war against the regent. By a sudden and unexpected inroad, they seized that nobleman at Stirling; but finding that his friends, sallying from the castle, were likely to rescue him, they instantly put him to death. The earl of Marre was chosen regent in his room; and found the same difficulties in the government of that divided country. He was therefore glad to accept of the mediation, offered by the French and English ambassadors; and to conclude on equal terms a truce with the queen's party.[w] He was a man of a free and generous spirit, and scorned to submit to any dependance on Eng-

Scots affairs.

[s] Ibid. p. 219, 241.   [t] Ibid. p. 213, 238.   [u] Digges, p. 152.   [w] Spotswood, p. 263.

CHAPTER XL

land; and for this reason Elizabeth, who had then formed intimate connexions with France, yielded with less reluctance to the
solicitations of that court, still maintained the appearance of neutrality between the parties, and allowed matters to remain on a
balance in Scotland.[x] But affairs soon after took a new turn: Marre
died of melancholy, with which the distracted state of the country
affected him: Morton was chosen regent; and as this nobleman
had secretly taken all his measures with Elizabeth, who no longer
relied on the friendship of the French court, she resolved to exert
herself more effectually for the support of the party, which she
had always favoured. She sent Sir Henry Killegrew ambassador to
Scotland, who found Mary's partizans so discouraged by the discovery and punishment of Norfolk's conspiracy, that they were
glad to submit to the king's authority, and accept of an indemnity
for all past offences.[y] The duke of Chatelrault and the earl of
Huntley, with the most considerable of Mary's friends, laid down
their arms on these conditions. The garrison alone of the castle of
Edinburgh continued refractory. Kirkaldy's fortunes were desperate; and he flattered himself with the hopes of receiving assistance
from the kings of France and Spain, who encouraged his obstinacy, in the view of being able, from that quarter, to give disturbance to England. Elizabeth was alarmed with the danger; she
no more apprehended making an entire breach with the queen of
Scots, who, she found, would not any longer be amused by her
artifices; she had an implicit reliance on Morton; and she saw, that,
by the submission of all the considerable nobility, the pacification
of Scotland would be an easy, as well as a most important undertaking. She ordered, therefore, Sir William Drury, governor of
Berwic, to march with some troops and artillery to Edinburgh, and
to besiege the castle.[z] The garrison surrendered at discretion:
Kirkaldy was delivered into the hands of his countrymen, by whom
he was tried, condemned, and executed: Secretary Lidington, who
had taken part with him, died soon after, a voluntary death, as is
supposed; and Scotland, submitting entirely to the regent, gave
not, during a long time, any farther inquietude to Elizabeth.

The events, which happened in France, were not so agreeable   *French*
to the queen's interests and inclinations. The fallacious pacifi-   *affairs.*

[x] Digges, p. 156, 165, 169.   [y] Spotswood, p. 268.   [z] Camden, p. 449.

cations, which had been so often made with the hugonots, gave them reason to suspect the present intentions of the court; and after all the other leaders of that party were deceived into a dangerous credulity, the sagacious admiral still remained doubtful and uncertain. But his suspicions were at last overcome, partly by the profound dissimulation of Charles, partly by his own earnest desire to end the miseries of France, and return again to the performance of his duty towards his prince and country. He considered besides, that, as the former violent conduct of the court had ever met with such fatal success, it was not unlikely, that a prince, who had newly come to years of discretion, and appeared not to be rivetted in any dangerous animosities or prejudices, would be induced to govern himself by more moderate maxims. And as Charles was young, was of a passionate hasty temper, and addicted to pleasure,[a] such deep perfidy seemed either remote from his character, or difficult and almost impossible to be so uniformly supported by him. Moved by these considerations, the admiral, the queen of Navarre, and all the hugonots began to repose themselves in full security, and gave credit to the treacherous caresses and professions of the French court. Elizabeth herself, notwithstanding her great experience and penetration, entertained not the least distrust of Charles's sincerity, and being pleased to find her enemies of the house of Guise removed from all authority, and to observe an animosity every day growing between the French and Spanish monarchs, she concluded a defensive league with the former,[b] and regarded this alliance as an invincible barrier to her throne. Walsingham, her ambassador, sent her over, by every courier, the most satisfactory accounts of the honour, and plain-dealing, and fidelity of that perfidious prince.

11th April.

The better to blind the jealous hugonots and draw their leaders into the snare prepared for them, Charles offered his sister, Margaret, in marriage to the prince of Navarre; and the admiral, with all the considerable nobility of the party, had come to Paris, in order to assist at the celebration of these nuptials, which, it was hoped, would finally, if not compose the differences, at least appease the bloody animosity of the two religions. The queen of Navarre was poisoned by orders from the court; the admiral was

[a] Digges, p. 8, 39.   [b] Camden, p. 443.

dangerously wounded by an assassin: Yet Charles, redoubling his dissimulation, was still able to retain the hugonots in their security: Till on the evening of St. Bartholomew, a few days after the marriage, the signal was given for a general massacre of those religionists, and the king himself in person led the way to these assassinations. The hatred, long entertained by the Parisians against the protestants, made them second, without any preparation, the fury of the court; and persons of every condition, age, and sex, suspected of any propensity to that religion, were involved in an undistinguished ruin. The admiral, his son-in-law Teligni, Soubize, Rochefoucault, Pardaillon, Piles, Lavardin; men, who, during the late wars, had signalized themselves by the most heroic actions, were miserably butchered without resistance; the streets of Paris flowed with blood; and the people, more enraged than satiated with their cruelty, as if repining that death had saved the victims from farther insult, exercised on their dead bodies all the rage of the most licentious brutality. About five hundred gentlemen and men of rank perished in this massacre; and near ten thousand of inferior condition.[c] Orders were instantly dispatched to all the provinces for a like general execution of the protestants; and in Roüen, Lyons, and many other cities, the people emulated the fury of the capital. Even the murder of the king of Navarre, and prince of Condé, had been proposed by the duke of Guise; but Charles, softened by the amiable manners of the king of Navarre, and hoping that these young princes might easily be converted to the catholic faith, determined to spare their lives, though he obliged them to purchase their safety by a seeming change of their religion.

    Charles, in order to cover this barbarous perfidy, pretended, that a conspiracy of the hugonots to seize his person had been suddenly detected; and that he had been necessitated, for his own defence, to proceed to this severity against them. He sent orders to Fenelon, his ambassador in England, to ask an audience, and to give Elizabeth this account of the late transaction. That minister, a man of probity, abhorred the treachery and cruelty of his court, and even scrupled not to declare, that he was now ashamed to bear the name of Frenchman;[d] yet he was obliged to obey his orders,

24th Aug.

Massacre of Paris.

[c] Davila, lib. v.   [d] Digges, p. 247.

and make use of the apology, which had been prescribed to him. He met with that reception from all the courtiers, which, he knew, the conduct of his master had so well merited. Nothing could be more awful and affecting than the solemnity of his audience. A melancholy sorrow sat on every face: Silence, as in the dead of night, reigned through all the chambers of the royal apartment: The courtiers and ladies, clad in deep mourning, were ranged on each side, and allowed him to pass, without affording him one salute or favourable look; till he was admitted to the queen herself.[e] That princess received him with a more easy, if not a more gracious countenance; and heard his apology, without discovering any visible symptoms of indignation. She then told him, that though, on the first rumour of this dreadful intelligence, she had been astonished, that so many brave men and loyal subjects, who rested secure on the faith of their sovereign, should have been suddenly butchered in so barbarous a manner; she had hitherto suspended her judgment, till farther and more certain information should be brought her: That the account, which he had given, even if founded on no mistake or bad information; though it might alleviate, would by no means remove the blame of the king's counsellors, or justify the strange irregularity of their proceedings: That the same force, which, without resistance, had massacred so many defenceless men, could easily have secured their persons, and have reserved them for a trial, and for punishment by a legal sentence, which would have distinguished the innocent from the guilty: That the admiral in particular, being dangerously wounded, and environed by the guards of the king, on whose protection he seemed entirely to rely, had no means of escape, and might surely, before his death, have been convicted of the crimes imputed to him: That it was more worthy of a sovereign to reserve in his own hands the sword of justice, than to commit it to bloody murderers, who, being the declared and mortal enemies of the persons accused, employed it without mercy and without distinction: That if these sentiments were just, even supposing the conspiracy of the protestants to be real; how much more so, if that crime was a calumny of their enemies, invented for their destruction? That if, upon enquiry, the innocence of these unhappy vic-

[e] Carte, vol. iii. p. 522. from Fenelon's Dispatches.

CHAPTER XL

tims should afterwards appear, it was the king's duty to turn his vengeance on their defamers, who had thus cruelly abused his confidence, had murdered so many of his brave subjects, and had done what in them lay to cover him with everlasting dishonour: And that for her part, she should form her judgment of his intentions by his subsequent conduct; and in the mean time should act as desired by the ambassador, and rather pity than blame his master for the extremities, to which he had been carried.[f]

Elizabeth was fully sensible of the dangerous situation, in which she now stood. In the massacre of Paris, she saw the result of that general conspiracy, formed for the extermination of the protestants; and she knew, that she herself, as the head and protectress of the new religion, was exposed to the utmost fury and resentment of the catholics. The violence and cruelty of the Spaniards in the Low Countries was another branch of the same conspiracy; and as Charles and Philip, two princes nearly allied in perfidy and barbarity, as well as in bigotry, had now laid aside their pretended quarrel, and had avowed the most entire friendship,[g] she had reason, as soon as they had appeased their domestic commotions, to dread the effects of their united counsels. The duke of Guise also and his family, whom Charles, in order to deceive the admiral, had hitherto kept at a distance, had now acquired an open and entire ascendant in the court of France; and she was sensible, that these princes, from personal as well as political reasons, were her declared and implacable enemies. The queen of Scots, their near relation and close confederate, was the pretender to her throne; and though detained in custody, was actuated by a restless spirit, and besides her foreign allies, possessed numerous and zealous partizans in the heart of the kingdom. For these reasons, Elizabeth thought it more prudent not to reject all commerce with the French monarch; but still to listen to the professions of friendship which he made her. She allowed even the negociations to be renewed for her marriage with the duke of Alençon, Charles's third brother:[h] Those with the duke of Anjou had already been broken off. She sent the earl of Worcester to assist in her name at the baptism of a young princess, born to Charles; but before she

[f] Digges, p. 247, 248.   [g] Digges, p. 268, 282.   [h] Ibid. passim. Camden, p. 447.

agreed to give him this last mark of condescension, she thought it becoming her dignity, to renew her expressions of blame and even of detestation against the cruelties, exercised on his protestant subjects.[i] Meanwhile, she prepared herself for that attack, which seemed to threaten her from the combined power and violence of the Romanists: She fortified Portsmouth, put her fleet in order, exercised her militia, cultivated popularity with her subjects, acted with vigour for the farther reduction of Scotland under obedience to the young king, and renewed her alliance with the German princes, who were no less alarmed than herself at these treacherous and sanguinary measures, so universally embraced by the catholics.

But though Elizabeth cautiously avoided coming to extremities with Charles, the greatest security, that she possessed against his violence, was derived from the difficulties, which the obstinate *French affairs.* resistance of the hugonots still created to him. Such of that sect as lived near the frontiers, immediately, on the first news of the massacres, fled into England, Germany, or Switzerland; where *1573.* they excited the compassion and indignation of the protestants, and prepared themselves, with encreased forces and redoubled zeal, to return into France, and avenge the treacherous slaughter of their brethren. Those who lived in the middle of the kingdom, took shelter in the nearest garrisons occupied by the hugonots; and finding, that they could repose no faith in capitulations, and expect no clemency, were determined to defend themselves to the last extremity. The sect, which Charles had hoped at one blow to exterminate, had now an army of eighteen thousand men on foot, and possessed in different parts of the kingdom above a hundred cities, castles, or fortresses;[k] nor could that prince deem himself secure from the invasion threatened him by all the other protestants in Europe. The nobility and gentry of England were rouzed to such a pitch of resentment, that they offered to levy an army of twenty-two thousand foot and four-thousand horse, to transport them into France, and to maintain them six months at their own charge: But Elizabeth, who was cautious in her measures, and who feared to inflame farther the quarrel between the two religions by

[i] Digges, p. 297, 298. Camden, p. 447.   [k] Digges, p. 343.

these dangerous crusades, refused her consent, and moderated the zeal of her subjects.[l] The German princes, less political or more secure from the resentment of France, forwarded the levies made by the protestants; and the young prince of Condé, having escaped from court, put himself at the head of these troops, and prepared to invade the kingdom. The duke of Alençon, the king of Navarre, the family of Montmorenci, and many considerable men even among the catholics, displeased, either on private or public account, with the measures of the court, favoured the progress of the hugonots; and every thing relapsed into confusion. The king, instead of repenting his violent counsels, which had brought matters to such extremities, called aloud for new violences;[m] nor could even the mortal distemper under which he laboured, moderate the rage and animosity, by which he was actuated. He died without male issue, at the age of twenty-five years; a prince, whose character, containing that unusual mixture of dissimulation and ferocity, of quick resentment and unrelenting vengeance, executed the greatest mischiefs, and threatened still worse, both to his native country and to all Europe.

1574.

30th May.

Henry, duke of Anjou, who had, some time before, been elected king of Poland, no sooner heard of his brother's death, than he hastened to take possession of the throne of France; and found the kingdom, not only involved in the greatest present disorders, but exposed to infirmities, for which it was extremely difficult to provide any suitable remedy. The people were divided into two theological factions, furious from their zeal, and mutually enraged from the injuries which they had committed or suffered; and as all faith had been violated and moderation banished, it seemed impracticable to find any terms of composition between them. Each party had devoted itself to leaders, whose commands had more authority than the will of the sovereign; and even the catholics, to whom the king was attached, were entirely conducted by the counsels of Guise and his family. The religious connections had, on both sides, superseded the civil; or rather (for men will always be guided by present interest) two empires being secretly formed in the kingdom, every individual was engaged by new

1575.

[l] Digges, p. 335, 341.   [m] Davila, lib. v.

views of interest to follow those leaders, to whom, during the course of past convulsions, he had been indebted for his honours and preferment.

Henry, observing the low condition of the crown, had laid a scheme for restoring his own authority, by acting as umpire between the parties, by moderating their differences, and by reducing both to a dependance upon himself. He possessed all the talents of dissimulation requisite for the execution of this delicate plan; but being deficient in vigour, application, and sound judgment, instead of acquiring a superiority over both factions, he lost the confidence of both, and taught the partizans of each to adhere still more closely to their particular leaders, whom they found more cordial and sincere in the cause which they espoused. The hugonots were strengthened by the accession of a German army under the prince of Condé and prince Casimir; but much more by the credit and personal virtues of the king of Navarre, who, having fled from court, had placed himself at the head of that formidable party. Henry, in prosecution of his plan, entered into a composition with them; and being desirous of preserving a balance between the sects, he granted them peace on the most advantageous conditions. This was the fifth general peace made with the hugonots; but though it was no more sincere on the part of the court than any of the former, it gave the highest disgust to the catholics; and afforded the duke of Guise the desired pretence of declaiming against the measures, and maxims, and conduct of the king.

That artful and bold leader took thence an occasion of reducing his party into a more formed and regular body; and he laid the first foundations of the famous LEAGUE, which, without paying any regard to the royal authority, aimed at the entire suppression of the hugonots. Such was the unhappy condition of France, from the past severities and violent conduct of its princes, that toleration could no longer be admitted; and a concession for liberty of conscience, which would probably have appeased the reformers, excited the greatest resentment in the catholics. Henry, in order to divert the force of the league from himself, and even to elude its efforts against the hugonots, declared himself the head of that seditious confederacy, and took the field as leader of the Romanists. But his dilatory and feeble measures betrayed his reluc-

1576.

1577.

tance to the undertaking; and after some unsuccessful attempts, he concluded a new peace, which, though less favourable than the former to the protestants, gave no contentment to the catholics. Mutual dissidence still prevailed between the parties; the king's moderation was suspicious to both; each faction continued to fortify itself against that breach, which, they foresaw, must speedily ensue; theological controversy daily whetted the animosity of the sects; and every private injury became the ground of a public quarrel.

The king, hoping, by his artifice and subtlety, to allure the nation into a love of pleasure and repose, was himself caught in the snare; and sinking into a dissolute indolence, wholly lost the esteem, and, in a great measure, the affections of his people. Instead of advancing such men of character and abilities, as were neuters between these dangerous factions, he gave all his confidence to young agreeable favourites, who, unable to prop his falling authority, leaned entirely upon it, and inflamed the general odium against his administration. The public burthens, encreased by his profuse liberality, and felt more heavy on a disordered kingdom, became another ground of complaint; and the uncontrouled animosity of parties, joined to the multiplicity of taxes, rendered peace more calamitous than any open state of foreign or even domestic hostility. The artifices of the king were too refined to succeed, and too frequent to be concealed; and the plain, direct, and avowed conduct of the duke of Guise on one side, and that of the king of Navarre on the other, drew by degrees the generality of the nation to devote themselves without reserve to one or the other of those great leaders.

The civil commotions of France were of too general importance to be overlooked by the other princes of Europe; and Elizabeth's foresight and vigilance, though somewhat restrained by her frugality, led her to take secretly some part in them. Besides employing on all occasions her good offices in favour of the hugonots, she had expended no inconsiderable sums in levying that army of Germans, which the prince of Condé and prince Casimir conducted into France;[n] and notwithstanding her negociations with the court, and her professions of amity, she always considered her

1578.

1579.

[n] Camden, p. 452.

own interests as connected with the prosperity of the French protestants and the depression of the house of Guise. Philip, on the
other hand, had declared himself protector of the league; had
entered into the closest correspondence with Guise; and had employed all his authority in supporting the credit of that factious
leader. This sympathy of religion, which of itself begat a connection of interests, was one considerable inducement; but that
monarch had also in view, the subduing of his rebellious subjects
in the Netherlands; who, as they received great encouragement
from the French protestants, would, he hoped, finally despair
of success, after the entire suppression of their friends and confederates.

Civil wars of the Low Countries. The same political views, which engaged Elizabeth to support
the hugonots, would have led her to assist the distressed prot-
estants in the Low Countries; but the mighty power of Philip, the
tranquillity of all his other dominions, and the great force which he
maintained in these mutinous provinces, kept her in awe, and
obliged her, notwithstanding all temptations and all provocations,
to preserve some terms of amity with that monarch. The Spanish
ambassador represented to her, that many of the Flemish exiles,
who infested the seas, and preyed on his master's subjects, were
received into the harbours of England, and were there allowed to
dispose of their prizes; and by these remonstrances the queen
found herself under a necessity of denying them all entrance into
her dominions. But this measure proved in the issue extremely
prejudicial to the interests of Philip. These desperate exiles, finding no longer any possibility of subsistance, were forced to attempt
the most perilous enterprizes; and they made an assault on the
Brille, a sea-port town in Holland, where they met with success,
and after a short resistance, became masters of the place.[o] The
duke of Alva was alarmed at the danger; and stopping those
bloody executions, which he was making on the defenceless Flemings, he hastened with his army to extinguish the flame, which,
falling on materials so well prepared for combustion, seemed to
menace a general conflagration. His fears soon appeared to be well
grounded. The people in the neighbourhood of the Brille, enraged by that complication of cruelty, oppression, insolence, usur-

[o] Camden, p. 443.

pation, and persecution, under which they and all their countrymen laboured, flew to arms; and in a few days almost the whole
province of Holland and that of Zealand had revolted from the
Spaniards, and had openly declared against the tyranny of Alva.
This event happened in the year 1572.

William, prince of Orange, descended from a sovereign family
of great lustre and antiquity in Germany, inheriting the possessions of a sovereign family in France, had fixed his residence in the
Low Countries; and on account of his noble birth and immense
riches, as well as of his personal merit, was universally regarded as
the greatest subject, that lived in those provinces. He had opposed,
by all regular and dutiful means, the progress of the Spanish
usurpations; and when Alva conducted his army into the Netherlands, and assumed the government, this prince, well acquainted
with the violent character of the man, and the tyrannical spirit of
the court of Madrid, wisely fled from the danger which threatened
him, and retired to his paternal estate and dominions in Germany.
He was cited to appear before Alva's tribunal, was condemned in
absence, was declared a rebel, and his ample possessions in the
Low Countries were confiscated. In revenge, he had levied an
army of protestants in the empire, and had made some attempts to
restore the Flemings to liberty; but was still repulsed with loss by
the vigilance and military conduct of Alva, and by the great bravery as well as discipline of those veteran Spaniards who served
under that general.

The revolt of Holland and Zealand, provinces which the prince
of Orange had formerly commanded, and where he was much
beloved, called him anew from his retreat; and he added conduct,
no less than spirit, to that obstinate resistance, which was here
made to the Spanish dominion. By uniting the revolted cities in a
league, he laid the foundation of that illustrious commonwealth,
the offspring of industry and liberty, whose arms and policy have
long made so signal a figure in every transaction of Europe. He
inflamed the inhabitants by every motive, which religious zeal,
resentment, or love of freedom could inspire. Though the present
greatness of the Spanish monarchy might deprive them of all
courage, he still flattered them with the concurrence of the other
provinces, and with assistance from neighbouring states; and he
exhorted them, in defence of their religion, their liberties, their

lives, to endure the utmost extremities of war. From this spirit proceeded the desperate defence of Harlem; a defence, which nothing but the most consuming famine could overcome, and which the Spaniards revenged by the execution of more than two thousand of the inhabitants.[p] This extreme severity, instead of striking terror into the Hollanders, animated them by despair; and the vigorous resistance made at Alcmaer, where Alva was finally repulsed, showed them that their insolent enemies were not invincible. The duke, finding at last the pernicious effects of his violent councils, solicited to be recalled: Medina-celi, who was appointed his successor, refused to accept the government: Requesens, commendator of Castile, was sent from Italy to replace Alva; and this tyrant departed from the Netherlands in 1574; leaving his name in execration to the inhabitants, and boasting in his turn, that, during the course of five years, he had delivered above eighteen thousand of these rebellious heretics into the hands of the executioner.[q]

Requesens, though a man of milder dispositions, could not appease the violent hatred, which the revolted Hollanders had conceived against the Spanish government; and the war continued as obstinate as ever. In the siege of Leyden, undertaken by the Spaniards, the Dutch opened the dykes and sluices, in order to drive them from the enterprize; and the very peasants were active in ruining their fields by an inundation, rather than fall again under the hated tyranny of Spain. But notwithstanding this repulse, the governor still pursued the war; and the contest seemed too unequal between so mighty a monarchy, and two small provinces, however fortified by nature, and however defended by the desperate resolution of the inhabitants. The prince of Orange, therefore, in 1575, was resolved to sue for foreign succour, and to make applications to one or other of his great neighbours, Henry or Elizabeth. The court of France was not exempt from the same spirit of tyranny and persecution which prevailed among the Spaniards; and that kingdom, torn by domestic dissensions, seemed not to enjoy, at present, either leisure or ability to pay regard to foreign interests. But England, long connected, both by commerce and alliance, with the Netherlands, and now more concerned in the fate of the revolted provinces by sympathy in reli-

[p] Bentivoglio, lib. 7.   [q] Grotius, lib. 2.

CHAPTER XL

gion, seemed naturally interested in their defence; and as Elizabeth had justly entertained great jealousy of Philip, and governed
her kingdom in perfect tranquillity, hopes were entertained, that
her policy, her ambition, or her generosity, would engage her to
support them under their present calamities. They sent, therefore,
a solemn embassy to London, consisting of St. Aldegonde, Douza,
Nivelle, Buys, and Melsen; and after employing the most humble
supplications to the queen, they offered her the possession and
sovereignty of their provinces, if she would exert her power in
their defence.

There were many strong motives which might impel Elizabeth
to accept of so liberal an offer. She was apprized of the injuries
which Philip had done her, by his intrigues with the malcontents
in England and Ireland.[r] She foresaw the danger, which she must
incur from a total prevalence of the catholics in the Low Countries:
And the maritime situation of those provinces, as well as their
command over the great rivers, was an inviting circumstance to a
nation like the English, who were beginning to cultivate commerce
and naval power. But this princess, though magnanimous, had
never entertained the ambition of making conquests, or gaining
new acquisitions; and the whole purpose of her vigilant and active
politics was to maintain, by the most frugal and cautious expedients, the tranquillity of her own dominions. An open war with the
Spanish monarchy was the apparent consequence of her accepting
the dominion of these provinces; and after taking the inhabitants
under her protection, she could never afterwards in honour abandon them, but, however desperate their defence might become,
she must embrace it, even farther than her convenience or interests would permit. For these reasons, she refused, in positive
terms, the sovereignty proffered her; but told the ambassadors,
that, in return for the good-will which the prince of Orange and
the States had shown her, she would endeavour to mediate an
agreement for them, on the most reasonable terms that could be
obtained.[s] She sent accordingly Sir Henry Cobham to Philip; and
represented to him, the danger which he would incur of losing
entirely the Low Countries, if France could obtain the least interval
from her intestine disorders, and find leisure to offer her protec-

[r] Digges, p. 73.   [s] Camden, p. 453, 454.

tion to those mutinous and discontented provinces. Philip seemed to take this remonstrance in good part; but no accord ensued, and war in the Netherlands continued with the same rage and violence as before.

It was an accident that delivered the Hollanders from their present desperate situation. Requesens, the governor, dying suddenly, the Spanish troops, discontented for want of pay, and licentious for want of a proper authority to command them, broke into a furious mutiny; and threw every thing into confusion. They sacked and pillaged the cities of Maestricht and Antwerp, and executed great slaughter on the inhabitants: They threatened the other cities with a like fate: And all the provinces, excepting Luxembourg, united for mutual defence against their violence, and called in the prince of Orange and the Hollanders, as their protectors. A treaty, commonly called the Pacification of Ghent, was formed by common agreement; and the removal of foreign troops, with the restoration of their ancient liberties, was the object which the provinces mutually stipulated to pursue. Don John of Austria, natural brother to Philip, being appointed governor, found, on his arrival at Luxembourg, that the States had so fortified themselves, and that the Spanish troops were so divided by their situation, that there was no possibility of resistance; and he agreed to the terms required of him. The Spaniards evacuated the country; and these provinces seemed at last to breathe a little from their calamities.

But it was not easy to settle entire peace, while the thirst of revenge and dominion governed the king of Spain, and while the Flemings were so strongly agitated with resentment of past, and fear of future injuries. The ambition of Don John, who coveted this great theatre for his military talents, engaged him rather to inflame than appease the quarrel; and as he found the States determined to impose very strict limitations on his authority, he broke all articles, seized Namur, and procured the recal of the Spanish army from Italy. This prince, endowed with a lofty genius, and elated by the prosperous successes of his youth, had opened his mind to vast undertakings; and looking much beyond the conquest of the revolted provinces, had projected to espouse the queen of Scots, and to acquire in her right the dominion of the British kingdoms.[l] Elizabeth was aware of his intentions; and see-

[l] Camden, p. 466, Grotius, lib. iii.

CHAPTER XL

ing now, from the union of all the provinces, a fair prospect of their making a long and vigorous defence against Spain, she no longer scrupled to embrace the protection of their liberties, which seemed so intimately connected with her own safety. After sending them a sum of money, about twenty thousand pounds, for the immediate pay of their troops, she concluded a treaty with them; in which she stipulated to assist them with five thousand foot and a thousand horse, at the charge of the Flemings; and to lend them a hundred thousand pounds, on receiving the bonds of some of the most considerable towns of the Netherlands, for her repayment within the year. It was farther agreed, that the commander of the English army should be admitted into the council of the States; and nothing be determined concerning war or peace, without previously informing the queen or him of it; that they should enter into no league without her consent; that if any discord arose among themselves, it should be referred to her arbitration; and that, if any prince, on an   pretext, should attempt hostilities against her, they should send to her assistance an army equal to that which she had employed in their defence. This alliance was signed on the 7th of January, 1578."

One considerable inducement to the queen for entering into treaty with the States, was to prevent their throwing themselves into the arms of France; and she was desirous to make the king of Spain believe, that it was her sole motive. She represented to him, by her ambassador, Thomas Wilkes, that hitherto she had religiously acted the part of a good neighbour and ally; had refused the sovereignty of Holland and Zealand, when offered her; had advised the prince of Orange to submit to the king; and had even accompanied her counsel with menaces, in case of his refusal. She persevered, she said, in the same friendly intentions; and, as a proof of it, would venture to interpose with her advice for the composure of the present differences: Let Don John, whom she could not but regard as her mortal enemy, be recalled; let some other prince more popular be substituted in his room; let the Spanish armies be withdrawn; let the Flemings be restored to their ancient liberties and privileges: And if, after these concessions, they were still obstinate not to return to their duty, she promised to join her arms with those of the king of Spain, and force them to

" Camden, p. 466.

compliance. Philip dissembled his resentment against the queen; and still continued to supply Don John with money and troops. That prince, though once repulsed at Rimenant, by the valour of the English under Norris, and though opposed, as well by the army of the States as by prince Casimir, who had conducted to the Low Countries a great body of Germans, paid by the queen, gained a great advantage over the Flemings at Gemblours; but was cut off in the midst of his prosperity by poison, given him secretly, as was suspected, by orders from Philip, who dreaded his ambition. The prince of Parma succeeded to the command; who, uniting valour and clemency, negociation and military exploits, made great progress against the revolted Flemings, and advanced the progress of the Spaniards by his arts, as well as by his arms.

During these years, while Europe was almost every where in great commotion, England enjoyed a profound tranquillity; owing chiefly to the prudence and vigour of the queen's administration, and to the wise precautions, which she employed in all her measures. By supporting the zealous protestants in Scotland, she had twice given them the superiority over their antagonists, had closely connected their interests with her own, and had procured herself entire security from that quarter, whence the most dangerous invasions could be made upon her. She saw in France her enemies, the Guises, though extremely powerful, yet counterbalanced by the hugonots, her zealous partizans; and even hated by the king, who was jealous of their restless and exorbitant ambition. The bigotry of Philip gave her just ground of anxiety; but the same bigotry had happily excited the most obstinate opposition among his own subjects, and had created him enemies, whom his arms and policy were not likely soon to subdue. The queen of Scots, her antagonist and rival, and the pretender to her throne, was a prisoner in her hands; and by her impatience and high spirit had been engaged in practices, which afforded the queen a pretence for rendering her confinement more rigorous, and for cutting off her communications with her partizans in England.

Religion was the capital point, on which depended all the political transactions of that age; and the queen's conduct in this particular, making allowance for the prevailing prejudices of the times, could scarcely be accused of severity or imprudence. She established no inquisition into men's bosoms: She imposed no oath of

CHAPTER XL

supremacy, except on those who received trust or emolument from the public: And though the exercise of every religion but the established was prohibited by statute, the violation of this law, by saying mass, and receiving the sacrament, in private houses, was, in many instances, connived at;[w] while, on the other hand, the catholics, in the beginning of her reign, shewed little reluctance against going to church, or frequenting the ordinary duties of public worship. The pope, sensible that this practice would by degrees reconcile all his partizans to the reformed religion, hastened the publication of the bull, which excommunicated the queen, and freed her subjects from their oaths of allegiance; and great pains were taken by the emissaries of Rome, to render the breach between the two religions as wide as possible, and to make the frequenting of protestant churches appear highly criminal in the catholics.[x] These practices, with the rebellion, which ensued, encreased the vigilance and severity of the government; but the Romanists, if their condition were compared with that of the Nonconformists in other countries, and with their own maxims where they domineered, could not justly complain of violence or persecution.

The queen appeared rather more anxious to keep a strict hand over the puritans; who, though their pretensions were not so immediately dangerous to her authority, seemed to be actuated by a more unreasonable obstinacy, and to retain claims, of which, both in civil and ecclestiastical matters, it was, as yet, difficult to discern the full scope and intention. Some secret attempts of that sect to establish a separate congregation and discipline, had been carefully repressed in the beginning of this reign;[y] and when any of the established clergy discovered a tendency to their principles, by omitting the legal habits or ceremonies, the queen had shewn a determined resolution to punish them by fines and deprivation:[z] Though her orders to that purpose had been frequently eluded, by the secret protection which these sectaries received from some of her most considerable courtiers.

But what chiefly tended to gain Elizabeth the hearts of her subjects, was, her frugality, which, though carried sometimes to an

[w] Camden, p. 459.   [x] Walsingham's Letter in Burnet, vol. ii. p. 418. Cabala, p. 406.   [y] Strype's Life of Parker, p. 342. Ibid. Life of Grindal, p. 315.   [z] Heylin, p. 165, 166.

extreme, led her not to amass treasures, but only to prevent impositions upon her people, who were at that time very little accustomed to bear the burthens of government. By means of her rigid economy, she paid all the debts which she found on the crown, with their full interest; though some of these debts had been contracted even during the reign of her father.[a] Some loans, which she had exacted at the commencement of her reign, were repaid by her; a practice in that age somewhat unusual:[b] And she established her credit on such a footing, that no sovereign in Europe could more readily command any sum, which the public exigencies might at any time require.[c] During this peaceable and uniform government, England furnishes few materials for history; and except the small part which Elizabeth took in foreign transactions, there scarcely passed any occurrence, which requires a particular detail.

A parliament.   The most memorable event in this period was a session of parliament, held on the 8th of February, 1576; where debates were started, which may appear somewhat curious and singular. Peter Wentworth, a puritan, who had signalized himself in former parliaments, by his free and undaunted spirit, opened this session with a premeditated harangue, which drew on him the indignation of the house, and gave great offence to the queen and the ministers. As it seems to contain a rude sketch of those principles of liberty, which happily gained afterwards the ascendant in England, it may not be improper to give, in a few words, the substance of it. He premised, that the very name of liberty is sweet; but the thing itself is precious beyond the most inestimable treasure: And that it behoved them to be careful, lest, contenting themselves with the sweetness of the name, they forego the substance, and abandon what of all earthly possessions was of the highest value to the kingdom. He then proceeded to observe, that freedom of speech in that house, a privilege so useful both to sovereign and subject, had been formerly infringed in many essential articles, and was, at present, exposed to the most imminent danger: That it was usual, when any subject of importance was handled, especially if it regarded religion, to surmize, that these topics were disagreeable to the queen, and that the farther proceeding in them would draw

---

[a] D'Ewes, p. 245. Camden, p. 446.   [b] D'Ewes, p. 246.   [c] Ibid. p. 245.

down her indignation upon their temerity: That Solomon had justly affirmed the king's displeasure to be a messenger of death; and it was no wonder if men, even though urged by motives of conscience and duty, should be inclined to stop short, when they found themselves exposed to so severe a penalty: That by the employing of this argument, the house was incapacitated from serving their country, and even from serving the queen herself; whose ears, besieged by pernicious flatterers, were thereby rendered inaccessible to the most salutary truths: That it was a mockery to call an assembly a parliament, yet deny it that privilege, which was so essential to its being, and without which it must degenerate into an abject school of servility and dissimulation: That as the parliament was the great guardian of the laws, they ought to have liberty to discharge their trust, and to maintain that authority, whence even kings themselves derive their being: That a king was constituted such by law, and though he was not dependant on man, yet was he subordinate to God and the law, and was obliged to make their prescriptions, not his own will, the rule of his conduct: That even his commission, as God's vicegerent, enforced, instead of loosening, this obligation; since he was thereby invested with authority to execute on earth the will of God, which is nothing but law and justice: That though these surmizes of displeasing the queen by their proceedings, had impeached, in a very essential point, all freedom of speech, a privilege granted them by a special law; yet was there a more express and more dangerous invasion made on their liberties, by frequent messages from the throne: That it had become a practice, when the house was entering on any question, either ecclesiastical or civil, to bring an order from the queen, inhibiting them absolutely from treating of such matters, and debarring them from all farther discussion of these momentous articles. That the prelates, emboldened by her royal protection, had assumed a decisive power in all questions of religion, and required that every one should implicitly submit his faith to their arbitrary determinations: That the love, which he bore his sovereign, forbade him to be silent under such abuses, or to sacrifice, on this important occasion, his duty to servile flattery and complaisance: And that, as no earthly creature was exempt from fault, so neither was the queen herself; but in imposing this servitude on her faithful commons, had committed a great, and

HISTORY OF ENGLAND

even dangerous, fault against herself and the whole common-wealth.[d]

It is easy to observe, from this speech, that, in this dawn of liberty, the parliamentary style was still crude and unformed; and that the proper decorum of attacking ministers and counsellors, without interesting the honour of the crown, or mentioning the person of the sovereign, was not yet entirely established. The commons expressed great displeasure at this unusual licence: They sequestered Wentworth from the house, and committed him prisoner to the serjeant at arms. They even ordered him to be examined by a committee, consisting of all those members who were also members of the privy-council; and a report to be next day made to the house. This committee met in the star-chamber, and wearing the aspect of that arbitrary court, summoned Wentworth to appear before them, and answer for his behaviour. But though the commons had discovered so little delicacy or precaution, in thus confounding their own authority with that of the star-chamber; Wentworth better understood the principles of liberty, and refused to give these counsellors any account of his conduct in parliament, till he were satisfied, that they acted, not as members of the privy-council, but as a committee of the house.[e] He justified his liberty of speech by pleading the rigour and hardship of the queen's messages; and notwithstanding that the committee shewed him, by instances in other reigns, that the practice of sending such messages was not unprecedented, he would not agree to express any sorrow or repentance. The issue of the affair was, that, after a month's confinement, the queen sent to the commons, informing them, that, from her special grace and favour, she had restored him to his liberty and to his place in the house.[f] By this seeming lenity, she indirectly retained the power, which she had assumed, of imprisoning the members, and obliging them to answer before her for their conduct in parliament. And Sir Walter Mildmay endeavoured to make the house sensible of her Majesty's goodness, in so gently remitting the indignation, which she might justly conceive at the temerity of their member: But he informed them, that they had not the liberty of speaking what and of whom they pleased; and that indiscreet freedoms, used in that house, had,

[d] D'Ewes, p. 236, 237, &c.   [e] D'Ewes, p. 241.   [f] Ibid. p. 244.

CHAPTER XL

both in the present and foregoing ages, met with a proper chastisement. He warned them, therefore, not to abuse farther the
queen's clemency; lest she be constrained, contrary to her inclination, to turn an unsuccessful lenity into a necessary severity.[g]

The behaviour of the two houses was, in every other respect,
equally tame and submissive. Instead of a bill, which was at first
introduced,[h] for the reformation of the church, they were contented to present a petition to her majesty for that purpose: And
when she told them, that she would give orders to her bishops, to
amend all abuses, and if they were negligent, she would herself, by
her supreme power and authority over the church, give such redress as would entirely satisfy the nation; the parliament willingly
acquiesced in this sovereign and peremptory decision.[i]

Though the commons shewed so little spirit in opposing the
authority of the crown, they maintained, this session, their dignity
against an encroachment of the peers, and would not agree to a
conference, which, they thought, was demanded of them in an
irregular manner. They acknowledged, however, with all humbleness, (such is their expression) the superiority of the lords: They
only refused to give that house any reason for their proceedings;
and asserted, that, where they altered a bill sent them by the peers,
it belonged to them to desire a conference, not to the upper house
to require it.[k]

The commons granted an aid of one subsidy and two fifteenths.
Mildmay, in order to satisfy the house concerning the reason-
ableness of this grant, entered into a detail of the queen's past
expences in supporting the government, and of the encreasing
charges of the crown, from the daily encrease in the price of all
commodities. He did not, however, forget to admonish them, that
they were to regard this detail as the pure effect of the queen's
condescension, since she was not bound to give them any account
how she employed her treasure.[l]

[g] D'Ewes, p. 259   [h] Ibid. p. 252.   [i] Ibid. p. 257.   [k] Ibid. p. 263.
[l] D'Ewes, p. 246.

XLI

Affairs of Scotland – Spanish affairs –
Sir Francis Drake – A parliament –
Negociations of marriage with the duke
of Anjou – Affairs of Scotland – Letter
of queen Mary to Elizabeth – Conspiracies in
England – A parliament – The ecclestiastical
commission – Affairs of the Low
Countries – Hostilities with Spain

1580. THE GREATEST and most absolute security, that Elizabeth enjoyed during her whole reign, never exempted her from
vigilance and attention; but the scene began now to be more overcast, and dangers gradually multiplied on her from more than one
quarter.

Affairs of   The earl of Morton had hitherto retained Scotland in strict
Scotland.   alliance with the queen, and had also restored domestic tranquillity
to that kingdom: But it was not to be expected, that the factitious
and legal authority of a regent would long maintain itself in a
country unacquainted with law and order; where even the natural
dominion of hereditary princes so often met with opposition and
controul. The nobility began anew to break into factions: The
people were disgusted with some instances of Morton's avarice:
And the clergy, who complained of farther encroachments on

CHAPTER XLI

their narrow revenue, joined and encreased the discontent of the
other orders. The regent was sensible of his dangerous situation;
and having dropped some peevish expressions, as if he were willing or desirous to resign, the noblemen of the opposite party,
favourites of the young king, laid hold of this concession, and
required that demission which he seemed so frankly to offer them.
James was at this time but eleven years of age; yet Morton, having
secured himself, as he imagined, by a general pardon, resigned his
authority into the hands of the king, who pretended to conduct, in
his own name, the administration of the kingdom. The regent
retired from the government; and seemed to employ himself entirely in the care of his domestic affairs; but either tired with this
tranquillity, which appeared insipid after the agitations of ambition, or thinking it time to throw off dissimulation, he came again
to court; acquired an ascendant in the council; and though he
resumed not the title of regent, governed with the same authority
as before. The opposite party, after holding separate conven-
tions, took to arms, on pretence of delivering their prince from
captivity, and restoring him to the free exercise of his government:
Queen Elizabeth interposed by her ambassador, Sir Robert Bowes,
and mediated an agreement between the factions: Morton kept
possession of the government; but his enemies were numerous
and vigilant, and his authority seemed to become every day more
precarious.

The count d'Aubigney, of the house of Lenox, cousin-german
to the king's father, had been born and educated in France; and
being a young man of good address and a sweet disposition, he
appeared to the duke of Guise a proper instrument for detaching
James from the English interest, and connecting him with his
mother and her relations. He no sooner appeared at Stirling,
where James resided, than he acquired the affections of the young
monarch; and joining his interests with those of James Stuart of
the house of Ochiltree, a man of profligate manners, who had
acquired the king's favour, he employed himself, under the appearance of play and amusement, in instilling into the tender mind
of the prince new sentiments of politics and government. He represented to him the injustice which had been done to Mary in her
deposition, and made him entertain thoughts, either of resigning
the crown into her hands, or of associating her with him in the

administration.^m Elizabeth, alarmed at the danger which might ensue from the prevalence of this interest in Scotland, sent anew Sir Robert Bowes to Stirling; and accusing d'Aubigney, now created earl of Lenox, of an attachment to the French, warned James against entertaining such suspicious and dangerous connexions.ⁿ The king excused himself, by Sir Alexander Hume his ambassador; and Lenox, finding that the queen had openly declared against him, was farther confirmed in his intention of overturning the English interest, and particularly of ruining Morton, who was regarded as the head of it. That nobleman was arrested in council, accused as an accomplice in the late king's murder, committed to prison, brought to trial, and condemned to suffer as a traitor. He confessed, that Bothwel had communicated to him the design, had pleaded Mary's consent, and had desired his concurrence; but he denied, that he himself had ever expressed any approbation of the crime; and in excuse for his concealing it, he alledged the danger of revealing the secret, either to Henry, who had no resolution nor constancy, or to Mary, who appeared to be an accomplice in the murder.^o Sir Thomas Randolph was sent by the queen to intercede in favour of Morton; and that ambassador, not content with discharging this duty of his function, engaged, by his persuasion, the earls of Argyle, Montrose, Angus, Marre, and Glencarne, to enter into a confederacy for protecting, even by force of arms, the life of the prisoner. The more to overawe that nobleman's enemies, Elizabeth ordered forces to be assembled on the borders of England; but this expedient served only to hasten his sentence and execution.^p Morton died with that constancy and resolution, which had attended him through all the various events of his life; and left a reputation, which was less disputed with regard to abilities than probity and virtue. But this conclusion of the scene happened not till the subsequent year.

Spanish affairs.   Elizabeth was, during this period, extremely anxious on account of every revolution in Scotland; both because that country alone, not being separated from England by sea, and bordering on all the catholic and malcontent counties, afforded her enemies a safe and easy method of attacking her; and because she was sensi-

---

^m Digges, p. 412, 428. Melvil, p. 130.   ⁿ Spotswood, p. 309.   ^o Ibid. p. 314. Crawford, p. 333. Moyse's Memoirs, p. 54.   ^p Spotswood, p. 312.

CHAPTER XLI

ble, that Mary, thinking herself abandoned by the French monarch, had been engaged by the Guises to have recourse to the
powerful protection of Philip, who, though he had not yet come to
an open rupture with the queen, was every day, both by the injuries which he committed and suffered, more exasperated against
her. That he might retaliate the assistance, which she gave to his
rebels in the Low Countries, he had sent, under the name of the
pope,[q] a body of seven hundred Spaniards and Italians into Ireland; where the inhabitants, always turbulent, and discontented
with the English government, were now more alienated by religious prejudices, and were ready to join every invader. The Spanish general, San Josepho, built a fort in Kerry; and being there
besieged by the earl of Ormond, president of Munster, who was
soon after joined by lord Gray, the deputy, he made a weak and
cowardly defence. After some assaults, feebly sustained, he surrendered at discretion; and Gray, who commanded but a small force,
finding himself incumbered with so many prisoners, put all the
Spaniards and Italians to the sword without mercy, and hanged
about fifteen hundred of the Irish: A cruelty which gave great
displeasure to Elizabeth.[r]

When the English ambassador made complaints of this invasion, he was answered by like complaints of the piracies committed by Francis Drake, a bold seaman, who had assaulted the
Spaniards in the place where they deemed themselves most secure,
in the new world. This man, sprung from mean parents in the
county of Devon, having acquired considerable riches by depredations made in the isthmus of Panama, and having there gotten
a sight of the Pacific ocean, was so stimulated by ambition and
avarice, that he scrupled not to employ his whole fortune in a new
adventure through those seas, so much unknown at that time to all
the European nations.[s] By means of Sir Christopher Hatton, then
vice-chamberlain, a great favourite of the queen's, he obtained her
consent and approbation; and he set sail from Plymouth in 1577,
with four ships and a pinnace, on board of which were 164 able
sailors.[t] He passed into the South Sea by the Straits of Magellan,
and attacking the Spaniards, who expected no enemy in those

*Sir
Francis
Drake.*

[q] Digges, p. 359, 370.   [r] Camden, p. 475. Cox's history of Ireland, p. 368.
[s] Camden, p. 478. Stowe, p. 689.   [t] Camden, p. 478. Hakluyt's Voyages,
vol. iii. p. 730, 748. Purchas's Pilgrim, vol. i. p. 46.

quarters, he took many rich prizes, and prepared to return with the booty, which he had acquired. Apprehensive of being intercepted by the enemy, if he took the same way homewards, by which he had reached the Pacific ocean, he attempted to find a passage by the north of California; and failing in that enterprize, he set sail for the East Indies, and returned safely this year by the Cape of Good Hope. He was the first Englishman who sailed round the Globe; and the first commander in chief: For Magellan, whose ship executed the same adventure, died in his passage. His name became celebrated on account of so bold and fortunate an attempt; but many, apprehending the resentment of the Spaniards, endeavoured to persuade the queen, that it would be more prudent to disavow the enterprize, to punish Drake, and to restore the treasure. But Elizabeth, who admired valour, and who was allured by the prospect of sharing in the booty, determined to countenance that gallant sailor: She conferred on him the honour of knighthood, and accepted of a banquet from him at Deptford, on board the ship, which had atchieved so memorable a voyage. When Philip's ambassador, Mendoza, exclaimed against Drake's piracies, she told him, that the Spaniards, by arrogating a right to the whole new world, and excluding thence all other European nations, who should sail thither, even with a view of exercising the most lawful commerce, naturally tempted others to make a violent irruption into those countries." To pacify, however, the catholic monarch, she caused part of the booty to be restored to Pedro Sebura, a Spaniard, who pretended to be agent for the merchants, whom Drake had spoiled. Having learned afterwards, that Philip had seized the money, and had employed part of it against herself in Ireland, part of it in the pay of the prince of Parma's troops, she determined to make no more restitutions.

1581.

There was another cause, which induced the queen to take this resolution: She was in such want of money, that she was obliged to assemble a parliament, a measure, which, as she herself openly declared, she never embraced, except when constrained by the

16th Jan.
A parlia-
ment.

necessity of her affairs. The parliament, besides granting her a supply of one subsidy and two fifteenths, enacted some statutes for the security of her government, chiefly against the attempts of the

---

" Camden, p. 480.

CHAPTER XLI

catholics. Whoever, in any way, reconciled any one to the church of Rome, or was himself reconciled, was declared to be guilty of treason; to say mass was subjected to the penalty of a year's imprisonment, and a fine of two hundred marks; the being present was punishable by a year's imprisonment and a fine of a hundred marks: A fine of twenty pounds a-month was imposed on every one who continued, during that time, absent from church.[w] To utter slanderous or seditious words against the queen was punishable, for the first offence, with the pillory and loss of ears; the second offence was declared felony: The writing or printing of such words was felony even on the first offence.[x] The puritans prevailed so far as to have farther applications made for reformation in religion.[y] And Paul Wentworth, brother to the member of that name, who had distinguished himself in the preceding session, moved, that the commons, from their own authority, should appoint a general fast and prayers; a motion, to which the house unwarily assented. For this presumption, they were severely reprimanded by a message from the queen, as encroaching on the royal prerogative and supremacy; and they were obliged to submit, and ask forgiveness.[z]

The queen and parliament were engaged to pass these severe laws against the catholics, by some late discoveries of the treasonable practices of their priests. When the ancient worship was suppressed, and the reformation introduced into the universities, the king of Spain reflected, that, as some species of literature was necessary for supporting these doctrines and controversies, the Romish communion must decay in England, if no means were found to give erudition to the ecclesiastics; and for this reason, he founded a seminary at Doüay, where the catholics sent their children, chiefly such as were intended for the priesthood, in order to receive the rudiments of their education. The cardinal of Lorraine imitated this example, by erecting a like seminary in his diocese of Rheims; and though Rome was somewhat distant, the pope would not neglect to adorn, by a foundation of the same nature, that capital of orthodoxy. These seminaries, founded with so hostile an intention, sent over every year a colony of priests, who maintained

[w] 23 Eliz. cap. 1.   [x] Ibid. cap. 2.   [y] D'Ewes, p. 302.   [z] Ibid. p. 284, 285.

the catholic superstition in its full height of bigotry; and being educated with a view to the crown of martyrdom, were not deterred, either by danger or fatigue, from maintaining and propagating their principles. They infused into all their votaries an extreme hatred against the queen; whom they treated as an usurper, a schismatic, a heretic, a persecutor of the orthodox, and one solemnly and publicly anathematised by the holy father. Sedition, rebellion, sometimes assassination, were the expedients, by which they intended to effect their purposes against her; and the severe restraint, not to say persecution, under which the catholics laboured, made them the more willingly receive, from their ghostly fathers, such violent doctrines.

These seminaries were all of them under the direction of the jesuits, a new order of regular priests erected in Europe, when the court of Rome perceived, that the lazy monks and beggarly friars, who sufficed in times of ignorance, were no longer able to defend the ramparts of the church, assailed on every side, and that the inquisitive spirit of the age required a society more active and more learned, to oppose its dangerous progress. These men, as they stood foremost in the contest against the protestants, drew on them the extreme animosity of that whole sect; and by assuming a superiority over the other more numerous and more ancient orders of their own communion, were even exposed to the envy of their brethren: So that it is no wonder, if the blame, to which their principles and conduct might be exposed, has, in many instances, been much exaggerated. This reproach, however, they must bear from posterity, that, by the very nature of their institution, they were engaged to pervert learning, the only effectual remedy against superstition, into a nourishment of that infirmity; and as their erudition was chiefly of the ecclesiastical and scholastic kind (though a few members have cultivated polite literature), they were only the more enabled, by that acquisition, to refine away the plainest dictates of morality, and to erect a regular system of casuistry, by which prevarication, perjury, and every crime, when it served their ghostly purposes, might be justified and defended.

The jesuits, as devoted servants to the court of Rome, exalted the prerogative of the sovereign pontiff above all earthly power; and by maintaining his authority of deposing kings, set no bounds, either to his spiritual or temporal jurisdiction. This doctrine be-

CHAPTER XLI

came so prevalent among the zealous catholics in England, that the excommunication, fulminated against Elizabeth, excited many scruples of a singular kind, to which it behoved the holy father to provide a remedy. The bull of Pius, in absolving the subjects from their oaths of allegiance, commanded them to resist the queen's usurpation; and many Romanists were apprehensive, that, by this clause, they were obliged in conscience, even though no favourable opportunity offered, to rebel against her, and that no dangers or difficulties could free them from this indispensable duty. But Parsons and Campion, two jesuits, were sent over with a mitigation and explanation of the doctrine; and they taught their disciples, that though the bull was for ever binding on Elizabeth and her partizans, it did not oblige the catholics to obedience, except when the sovereign pontiff should think proper, by a new summons, to require it.[a] Campion was afterwards detected in treasonable practices; and being put to the rack, and confessing his guilt, he was publicly executed. His execution was ordered at the very time when the duke of Anjou was in England, and prosecuted, with the greatest appearance of success, his marriage with the queen; and this severity was probably intended to appease her protestant subjects, and to satisfy them, that, whatever measures she might pursue, she never would depart from the principles of the reformation.

The duke of Alençon, now created duke of Anjou, had never entirely dropped his pretensions to Elizabeth; and that princess, though her suitor was near twenty-five years younger than herself, and had no knowledge of her person, but by pictures or descriptions, was still pleased with the image, which his addresses afforded her, of love and tenderness. The duke, in order to forward his suit, besides employing his brother's ambassador, sent over Simier, an agent of his own; an artful man, of an agreeable conversation, who soon remarking the queen's humour, amused her with gay discourse, and instead of serious political reasonings, which, he found, only awakened her ambition, and hurt his master's interests, he introduced every moment all the topics of passion and of gallantry. The pleasure, which she found in this man's company, soon produced a familiarity between them; and amidst

Negociations of marriage with the duke of Anjou.

[a] Camden, p. 477.

the greatest hurry of business, her most confidential ministers had not such ready access to her, as had Simier, who, on pretence of negociation, entertained her with accounts of the tender attachment borne her by the duke of Anjou. The earl of Leicester, who had never before been alarmed with any courtship payed her, and who always trusted, that her love of dominion would prevail over her inclination to marriage, began to apprehend, that she was at last caught in her own snare, and that the artful encouragement, which she had given to this young suitor, had unawares engaged her affections. To render Simier odious, he availed himself of the credulity of the times, and spread reports, that that minister had gained an ascendant over the queen, not by any natural principles of her constitution, but by incantations and love potions. Simier, in revenge, endeavoured to discredit Leicester with the queen; and he revealed to her a secret, which none of her courtiers dared to disclose, that this nobleman was secretly, without her consent, married to the widow of the earl of Essex; an action which the queen interpreted either to proceed from want of respect to her, or as a violation of their mutual attachment; and which so provoked her, that she threatened to send him to the Tower.[b] The quarrel went so far between Leicester and the French agent, that the former was suspected of having employed one Tudor, a bravo, to take away the life of his enemy; and the queen thought it necessary, by proclamation, to take Simier under her immediate protection. It happened, that, while Elizabeth was rowed in her barge on the Thames, attended by Simier, and some of her courtiers, a shot was fired which wounded one of the bargemen; but the queen finding, upon enquiry, that the piece had been discharged by accident, gave the person his liberty, without farther punishment. So far was she from entertaining any suspicion against her people, that she was often heard to say, "That she would lend credit to nothing against them, which parents would not believe of their own children."[c]

The duke of Anjou, encouraged by the accounts sent him of the queen's prepossessions in his favour, paid her secretly a visit at Greenwich; and after some conference with her, the purport of which is not known, he departed. It appeared, that, though his

[b] Camden, p. 471.   [c] Idem ibid.

CHAPTER XLI

figure was not advantageous, he had lost no ground by being personally known to her; and soon after, she commanded Burleigh, now treasurer, Sussex, Leicester, Bedford, Lincoln, Hatton, and secretary Walsingham, to concert with the French ambassadors the terms of the intended contract of marriage. Henry had sent over on this occasion a splendid embassy, consisting of Francis de Bourbon, prince Dauphin, and many considerable noblemen; and as the queen had in a manner the power of prescribing what terms she pleased, the articles were soon settled with the English commissioners. It was agreed, that the marriage should be celebrated within six weeks after the ratification of the articles; that the duke and his retinue should have the exercise of their religion; that after the marriage he should bear the title of King, but the administration remain solely in the queen; that their children, male or female, should succeed to the crown of England; that if there be two males, the elder, in case of Henry's death without issue, should be king of France, the younger of England; that if there be but one male, and he succeed to the crown of France, he should be obliged to reside in England eight months every two years; that the laws and customs of England should be preserved inviolate; and that no foreigner should be promoted by the duke to any office in England.[d]

These articles, providing for the security of England, in case of its annexation to the crown of France, opened but a dismal prospect to the English; had not the age of Elizabeth, who was now in her forty-ninth year contributed very much to allay their apprehensions of this nature. The queen also, as a proof of her still remaining uncertainty, added a clause, that she was not bound to complete the marriage, till farther articles, which were not specified, should be agreed on between the parties, and till the king of France be certified of this agreement. Soon after, the queen sent over Walsingham, as ambassador to France, in order to form closer connexions with Henry, and enter into a league offensive and defensive against the encreasing power and dangerous usurpations of Spain. The French King, who had been extremely disturbed with the unquiet spirit, the restless ambition, the enterprizing, yet timid and inconstant disposition of Anjou, had already

[d] Camden, p. 484.

sought to free the kingdom from his intrigues, by opening a scene
for his activity in Flanders; and having allowed him to embrace the
protection of the States, had secretly supplied him with men and
money for the undertaking. The prospect of settling him in England was for a like reason very agreeable to that monarch; and he
was desirous to cultivate, by every expedient, the favourable sentiments, which Elizabeth seemed to entertain towards him. But this
princess, though she had gone farther in her amorous[e] dalliance
than could be justified or accounted for by any principles of policy,
was not yet determined to carry matters to a final conclusion; and
she confined Walsingham, in his instructions, to negociating conditions of a mutual alliance between France and England.[f] Henry
with reluctance submitted to hold conferences on that subject; but
no sooner had Walsingham begun to settle the terms of alliance,
than he was informed, that the queen, foreseeing hostility with
Spain to be the result of this confederacy, had declared, that she
would prefer the marriage with the war, before the war without the
marriage.[g] The French court, pleased with this change of resolution, broke off the conferences concerning the league, and opened
a negociation for the marriage.[h] But matters had not long proceeded in this train before the queen again declared for the league
in preference to the marriage, and ordered Walsingham to renew
the conferences for that purpose. Before he had leisure to bring
this point to maturity, he was interrupted by a new change of
resolution;[i] and not only the court of France, but Walsingham
himself, Burleigh, and all the wisest ministers of Elizabeth, were in
amazement, doubtful where this contest between inclination and
reason, love and ambition, would at last terminate.[k]

In the course of this affair, Elizabeth felt another variety of
intentions, from a new contest between her reason and her ruling
passions. The duke of Anjou expected from her some money, by
which he might be enabled to open the campaign in Flanders; and
the queen herself, though her frugality made her long reluctant,
was sensible that this supply was necessary; and she was at last
induced, after much hesitation, to comply with his request.[l] She
sent him a present of a hundred thousand crowns; by which,

[e] Digges, p. 387, 396, 408, 426.   [f] Ibid. p. 352.   [g] Ibid. p. 375, 391.
[h] Digges, p. 392.   [i] Ibid. p. 408.   [k] See note [P] at the end of the volume.
[l] Digges, p. 357, 387, 388, 409, 426, 439. Rymer, xv. p. 793.

CHAPTER XLI

joined to his own demesnes and the assistance of his brother and the queen dowager, he levied an army, and took the field against the prince of Parma. He was successful in raising the siege of Cambray; and being chosen by the States governor of the Netherlands, he put his army into winter quarters, and came over to England, in order to prosecute his suit to the queen. The reception which he met with, made him expect entire success, and gave him hopes, that Elizabeth had surmounted all scruples, and was finally determined to make choice of him for her husband. In the midst of the pomp, which attended the anniversary of her coronation, she was seen; after long and intimate discourse with him, to take a ring from her own finger, and to put it upon his; and all the spectators concluded, that, in this ceremony, she had given him a promise of marriage, and was even desirous of signifying her intentions to all the world. St. Aldegonde, ambassador from the States, dispatched immediately a letter to his masters, informing them of this great event; and the inhabitants of Antwerp, who, as well as the other Flemings, regarded the queen as a kind of tutelar divinity, testified their joy by bonfires and the discharge of their great ordnance." A puritan of Lincoln's-Inn had written a passionate book, which he intituled, "The Gulph in which England will be swallowed by the French Marriage." He was apprehended and prosecuted by order of the queen, and was condemned to lose his right hand as a libeller. Such was the constancy and loyalty of the man, that, immediately after the sentence was executed, he took off his hat with his other hand, and waving it over his head, cried, "God save the queen." *17th Nov.*

But notwithstanding this attachment, which Elizabeth so openly discovered to the duke of Anjou, the combat of her sentiments was not entirely over; and her ambition, as well as prudence, rousing itself by intervals, still filled her breast with doubt and hesitation. Almost all the courtiers, whom she trusted and favoured, Leicester, Hatton, and Walsingham, discovered an extreme aversion to the marriage; and the ladies of her bedchamber made no scruple of opposing her resolution with the most zealous remonstrances." Among other enemies to the match, Sir Philip, son of Sir Henry Sidney, deputy of Ireland, and nephew to Leices-

---

^m Camden, p. 486. Thuan, lib. 74.   ⁿ Camden, p. 486.

ter; a young man the most accomplished of the age; declared himself: And he used the freedom to write her a letter, in which he dissuaded her from her present resolution, with an unusual elegance of expression, as well as force of reasoning. He told her, that the security of her government depended entirely on the affections of her protestant subjects; and she could not, by any measure, more effectually disgust them than by espousing a prince, who was son of the perfidious Catherine, brother to the cruel and perfidious Charles, and who had himself embrued his hands in the blood of the innocent and defenceless protestants: That the catholics were her mortal enemies, and believed either that she had originally usurped the crown, or was now lawfully deposed by the pope's bull of excommunication; and nothing had ever so much elevated their hopes as the prospect of her marriage with the duke of Anjou: That her chief security at present, against the efforts of so numerous, rich, and united a faction, was, that they possessed no head who could conduct their dangerous enterprizes; and she herself was rashly supplying that defect, by giving an interest in the kingdom to a prince, whose education had zealously attached him to that communion: That though he was a stranger to the blood royal of England, the dispositions of men were now such, that they preferred the religious to the civil connections; and were more influenced by sympathy in theological opinions than by the principles of legal and hereditary government: That the duke himself had discovered a very restless and turbulent spirit; and having often violated his loyalty to his elder brother and his sovereign, there remained no hopes that he would passively submit to a woman, whom he might, in quality of husband, think himself intitled to command: That the French nation, so populous, so much abounding in soldiers, so full of nobility, who were devoted to arms, and, for some time, accustomed to serve for plunder, would supply him with partizans, dangerous to a people, unwarlike and defenceless like the generality of her subjects: That the plain and honourable path, which she had followed, of cultivating the affections of her people, had hitherto rendered her reign secure and happy; and however her enemies might seem to multiply upon her, the same invincible rampart was still able to protect and defend her: That so long as the throne of France was filled by Henry or his posterity, it was in vain to hope, that the ties

CHAPTER XLI

of blood would ensure the amity of that kingdom, preferably to the maxims of policy or the prejudices of religion; and if ever the crown devolved on the duke of Anjou, the conjunction of France and England would prove a burthen, rather than a protection, to the latter kingdom: That the example of her sister Mary was sufficient to instruct her in the danger of such connections; and to prove, that the affection and confidence of the English could never be maintained, where they had such reason to apprehend, that their interests would every moment be sacrificed to those of a foreign and hostile nation: That notwithstanding these great inconveniences, discovered by past experience, the house of Burgundy, it must be confessed, was more popular in the nation than the family of France; and, what was of chief moment, Philip was of the same communion with Mary, and was connected with her by this great band of interest and affection: And that however the queen might remain childless, even though old age should grow upon her, the singular felicity and glory of her reign would preserve her from contempt; the affections of her subjects, and those of all the protestants in Europe, would defend her from danger; and her own prudence, without other aid or assistance, would baffle all the efforts of her most malignant enemies.[o]

These reflections kept the queen in great anxiety and irresolution; and she was observed to pass several nights without any sleep or repose. At last her settled habits of prudence and ambition prevailed over her temporary inclination; and having sent for the duke of Anjou, she had a long conference with him in private, where she was supposed to have made him apologies for breaking her former engagements. He expressed great disgust on his leaving her; threw away the ring which she had given him; and uttered many curses on the mutability of women and of islanders.[p] Soon after, he went over to his government of the Netherlands; lost the confidence of the States by a rash and violent attempt on their liberties; was expelled that country; retired into France; and there died. The queen, by timely reflection, saved herself from the numerous mischiefs, which must have attended so imprudent a marriage: And the distracted state of the French monarchy prevented

1582.

---

[o] Letters of the Sydneys, vol. i. p. 287, & seq. Cabala, p. 363.   [p] Camden, p. 486.

her from feeling any effects of that resentment, which she had reason to dread, from the affront so wantonly put upon that royal family.

Affairs of
Scotland.   The anxiety of the queen, from the attempts of the English catholics, never ceased during the whole course of her reign; but the variety of revolutions which happened in all the neighbouring kingdoms, were the source sometimes of her hopes, sometimes of her apprehensions. This year the affairs of Scotland strongly engaged her attention. The influence, which the earl of Lenox, and James Stuart, who now assumed the title of earl of Arran, had acquired over the young king, was but a slender foundation of authority; while the generality of the nobles, and all the preachers, were so much discontented with their administration. The assembly of the church appointed a solemn fast; of which one of the avowed reasons was the danger to which the king was exposed from the company of wicked persons:[q] And on that day, the pulpits resounded with declamations against Lenox, Arran, and all the present counsellors. When the minds of the people were sufficiently prepared by these lectures, a conspiracy of the nobility was formed, probably with the concurrence of Elizabeth, for seiz-
August   ing the person of James at Ruthven, a seat of the earl of Gowry's;
23.   and the design, being kept secret, succeeded without any opposition. The leaders in this enterprize were, the earl of Gowry himself, the earl of Marre, the lords Lindesey and Boyd, the masters of Glamis and Oliphant, the abbots of Dunfermling, Paisley, and Cambuskenneth. The king wept when he found himself detained a prisoner; but the master of Glamis said, "No matter for his tears: Better that boys weep than bearded men." An expression which James could never afterwards forgive.[r] But notwithstanding his resentment, he found it necessary to submit to the present necessity. He pretended an entire acquiescence in the conduct of the associators; acknowledged the detention of his person to be acceptable service; and agreed to summon both an assembly of the church and a convention of estates, in order to ratify that enterprize.

The assembly, though they had established it as an inviolable rule, that the king, on no account and under no pretence, should

[q] Spotswood, p. 319.   [r] Spotswood, p. 320.

ever intermeddle in ecclesiastical matters, made no scruple of taking civil affairs under their cognizance, and of deciding on this occasion, that the attempt of the conspirators was acceptable to all that feared God, or tendered the preservation of the king's person, and prosperous state of the realm. They even enjoined all the clergy to recommend these sentiments from the pulpit; and they threatened with ecclesiastical censures every man, who should oppose the authority of the confederated lords.[s] The convention, being composed chiefly of these lords themselves, added their sanction to these proceedings. Arran was confined a prisoner in his own house: Lenox, though he had power to resist, yet rather than raise a civil war, or be the cause of bloodshed,[t] chose to retire into France, where he soon after died. He persevered to the last in the protestant religion, to which James had converted him, but which the Scottish clergy could never be persuaded that he had sincerely embraced. The king sent for his family, restored his son to his paternal honours and estate, took care to establish the fortunes of all his other children; and to his last moments never forgot the early friendship, which he had borne their father: A strong proof of the good dispositions of that prince.[u]

No sooner was this revolution known in England, than the queen sent Sir Henry Cary and Sir Robert Bowes to James, in order to congratulate him on his deliverance from the pernicious counsels of Lenox and Arran; to exhort him not to resent the seeming violence committed on him by the confederated lords; and to procure from him permission for the return of the earl of Angus, who, ever since Morton's fall, had lived in England. They easily prevailed in procuring the recall of Angus; and as James suspected, that Elizabeth had not been entirely unacquainted with the project of his detention, he thought proper, before the English ambassadors, to dissemble his resentment against the authors of it. Soon after, La Mothe-Fenelon, and Menneville, appeared as ambassadors from France: Their errand was to enquire concerning the situation of the king, make professions of their master's friendship, confirm the ancient league with France, and procure an accommodation between James and the queen of Scots. This last

1583.

---

[s] Ibid. p. 322.   [t] Heylin's Hist. Presbyter. p. 227. Spotswood.   [u] Spotswood, p. 328.

proposal gave great umbrage to the clergy; and the assembly voted the settling of terms between the mother and son to be a most wicked undertaking. The pulpits resounded with declamations against the French ambassadors; particularly Fenelon, whom they called the messenger of the bloody murderer, meaning the duke of Guise: And as that minister, being knight of the Holy Ghost, wore a white cross on his shoulder, they commonly denominated it, in contempt, the badge of Antichrist. The king endeavoured, though in vain, to repress these insolent reflections; but in order to make the ambassadors some compensation, he desired the magistrates of Edinburgh to give a splendid dinner before their departure. To prevent this entertainment, the clergy appointed that very day for a public fast; and finding that their orders were not regarded, they employed their sermons in thundering curses on the magistrates, who, by the king's direction, had put this mark of respect on the ambassadors. They even pursued them afterwards with the censures of the church; and it was with difficulty they were prevented from issuing the sentence of excommunication against them, on account of their submission to royal, preferably to clerical, authority.[w]

What encreased their alarm with regard to an accommodation between James and Mary, was, that the English ambassadors seemed to concur with the French in this proposal; and the clergy were so ignorant as to believe the sincerity of the professions made by the former. The queen of Scots had often made overtures to *Letter of* Elizabeth, which had been entirely neglected; but hearing of *Mary to* James's detention, she wrote a letter in a more pathetic and more *Elizabeth.* spirited strain than usual; craving the assistance of that princess, both for her own and her son's liberty. She said, that the account of the prince's captivity had excited her most tender concern; and the experience, which she herself, during so many years, had of the extreme infelicity attending that situation, had made her the more apprehensive, lest a like fate should pursue her unhappy offspring: That the long train of injustice which she had undergone; the calumnies to which she had been exposed; were so grievous, that, finding no place for right or truth among men, she was reduced to make her last appeal to Heaven, the only competent

[w] Spotswood, p. 324.

CHAPTER XLI

tribunal between princes of equal jurisdiction, degree, and dignity: That after her rebellious subjects, secretly instigated by Elizabeth's ministers, had expelled her the throne, had confined her in
prison, had pursued her with arms, she had voluntarily thrown
herself under the protection of England; fatally allured by those
reiterated professions of amity which had been made her, and by
her confidence in the generosity of a friend, an ally, and a kinswoman: That not content with excluding her from her presence,
with supporting the usurpers of her throne, with contributing to
the destruction of her faithful subjects, Elizabeth had reduced her
to a worse captivity than that from which she had escaped, and had
made her this cruel return for the unlimited confidence, which she
had reposed in her: That though her resentment of such severe
usage had never carried her farther than to use some disappointed
efforts for her deliverance, unhappy for herself, and fatal to others, she found the rigours of confinement daily multiplied upon
her; and at length carried to such a height that it surpassed the
bounds of all human patience any longer to endure them: That she
was cut off from all communication, not only with the rest of
mankind, but with her only son; and her maternal fondness, which
was now more enlivened by their unhappy sympathy in situation,
and was her sole remaining attachment to this world, deprived
even of that melancholy solace, which letters or messages could
give: That the bitterness of her sorrows, still more than her close
confinement, had preyed upon her health, and had added the
insufferable weight of bodily infirmity to all those other calamities,
under which she laboured: That while the daily experience of her
maladies opened to her the comfortable prospect of an approaching deliverance into a region where pain and sorrow are no
more, her enemies envied her that last consolation; and having
secluded her from every joy on earth, had done what in them lay
to debar her from all hopes in her future and eternal existence:
That the exercise of her religion was refused her; the use of those
sacred rites in which she had been educated; the commerce with
those holy ministers, whom Heaven had appointed to receive the
acknowledgment of our transgressions, and to seal our penitence
by a solemn re-admission into heavenly favour and forgiveness:
That it was in vain to complain of the rigours of persecution exercised in other kingdoms; when a queen, and a innocent woman,

was excluded from an indulgence, which never yet, in the most barbarous countries, had been denied to the meanest and most obnoxious malefactor: That could she ever be induced to descend from that royal dignity in which Providence had placed her, or depart from her appeal to Heaven, there was only one other tribunal, to which she would appeal from all her enemies; to the justice and humanity of Elizabeth's own breast, and to that lenity, which, uninfluenced by malignant counsel, she would naturally be induced to exercise towards her: And that she finally intreated her, to resume her natural disposition, and to reflect on the support, as well as comfort, which she might receive from her son and herself, if, joining the obligations of gratitude to the ties of blood, she would deign to raise them from their present melancholy situation, and reinstate them in that liberty and authority, to which they were entitled.[x]

Elizabeth was engaged to obstruct Mary's restoration, chiefly because she foresaw an unhappy alternative attending that event. If this princess recovered any considerable share of authority in Scotland, her resentment, ambition, zeal, and connections, both domestic and foreign, might render her a dangerous neighbour to England, and enable her, after suppressing the protestant party among her subjects, to revive those pretensions, which she had formerly advanced to the crown, and which her partizans in both kingdoms still supported with great industry and assurance. If she were reinstated in power, with such strict limitations as could not be broken, she might be disgusted with her situation; and flying abroad, form more desperate attempts than any sovereign, who had a crown to hazard, would willingly undertake. Mary herself, sensible of these difficulties, and convinced by experience, that Elizabeth would for ever debar her the throne, was now become more humble in her wishes; and as age and infirmities had repressed those sentiments of ambition, by which she had formerly been so much actuated, she was willing to sacrifice all her hopes of grandeur, in order to obtain a little liberty; a blessing to which she naturally aspired with the fondest impatience. She proposed, therefore, that she should be associated with her son in the title to the crown of Scotland, but that the administration should remain

[x] Camden, p. 489.

solely in him: And she was content to live in England, in a private station, and even under a kind of restraint; but with some more liberty, both for exercise and company, than she had enjoyed, since the first discovery of her intrigues with the duke of Norfolk. But Elizabeth, afraid lest such a loose method of guarding her would facilitate her escape into France or Spain, or, at least, would encourage and encrease her partizans, and enable her to conduct those intrigues, to which she had already discovered so strong a propensity, was secretly determined to deny her requests; and though she feigned to assent to them, she well knew how to disappoint the expectations of the unhappy princess. While Lenox maintained his authority in Scotland, she never gave any reply to all the applications made to her by the Scottish queen:[y] At present, when her own creatures had acquired possession of the government, she was resolved to throw the odium of refusal upon them; and pretending, that nothing farther was required to a perfect accommodation, than the concurrence of the council of state in Scotland, she ordered her ambassador, Bowes, to open the negociation for Mary's liberty, and her association with her son in the title to the crown. Though she seemed to make this concession to Mary, she refused her the liberty of sending any ambassador of her own; and that princess could easily conjecture, from this circumstance, what would be the result of the pretended negociation. The privy council of Scotland, instigated by the clergy, rejected all treaty; and James, who was now a captive in their hands, affirmed, that he had never agreed to an association with his mother, and that the matter had never gone farther than some loose proposals for that purpose.[z]

The affairs of Scotland remained not long in the present situation. James, impatient of restraint, made his escape from his keepers; and flying to St. Andrew's, summoned his friends and partizans to attend him. The earls of Argyle, Marshal, Montrose, and Rothes, hastened to pay their duty to their sovereign; and the opposite party found themselves unable to resist so powerful a combination. They were offered a pardon, upon their submission, and an acknowledgment of their fault, in seizing the king's person,

[y] Jebb, vol. ii. p. 540.   [z] MS. in the Advocates' Library, A. 3. 28. p. 401. from the Cott. Lib. Calig. c. 9.

and restraining him from his liberty. Some of them accepted of the terms: The greater number, particularly Angus, Hamilton, Marre, Glamis, left the country; and took shelter in Ireland or England, where they were protected by Elizabeth. The earl of Arran was recalled to court; and the malcontents, who could not brook the authority of Lenox, a man of virtue and moderation, found, that, by their resistance, they had thrown all power into the hands of a person, whose counsels were as violent as his manners were profligate.[a]

Elizabeth wrote a letter to James; in which she quoted a moral sentence from Isocrates, and indirectly reproached him with inconstancy, and a breach of his engagements. James, in his reply, justified his measures; and retaliated, by turning two passages of Isocrates against *her.*[b] She next sent Walsingham in an embassy to him; and her chief purpose in employing that aged minister in an errand, where so little business was to be transacted, was to learn, from a man of so much penetration and experience, the real character of James. This young prince possessed good parts, though not accompanied with that vigour and industry which his station required; and as he excelled in general discourse and conversation, Walsingham entertained a higher idea of his talents than he was afterwards found, when real business was transacted, to have fully merited.[c] The account, which he gave his mistress, induced her to treat James thenceforth with some more regard, than she had hitherto been inclined to pay him.

1584.   The king of Scots, persevering in his present views, summoned a parliament; where it was enacted, that no clergyman should presume, in his sermons, to utter false, untrue, or scandalous speeches against the king, the council, or the public measures, or to meddle, in an improper manner, with the affairs of his majesty and the states.[d] The clergy, finding that the pulpit would be no longer a sanctuary for them, were extremely offended: They said, that the king was become popish in his heart; and they gave their adversaries the epithets of gross libertines, belly gods, and infamous persons.[e] The violent conduct of Arran soon brought over the popularity to their side. The earl of Gowry, though pardoned

[a] Spotswood, p. 325, 326, & seq.   [b] Melvil, p. 140, 141. Strype, vol. iii. p. 165.   [c] Melvil, p. 148. Jebb, vol. ii. p. 530.   [d] Spotswood, p. 333. [e] Ibid. p. 334.

CHAPTER XLI

for the late attempt, was committed to prison, was tried on some new accusations, condemned, and executed. Many innocent persons suffered from the tyranny of this favourite; and the banished lords, being assisted by Elizabeth, now found the time favourable for the recovery of their estates and authority. After they had been foiled in one attempt upon Stirling, they prevailed in another; and being admitted to the king's presence, were pardoned, and restored to his favour.

Arran was degraded from authority; deprived of that estate and title which he had usurped; and the whole country seemed to be composed to tranquillity. Elizabeth, after opposing, during some time, the credit of the favourite, had found it more expedient, before his fall, to compound all differences with him, by means of Davison, a minister whom she sent to Scotland: But having more confidence in the lords, whom she had helped to restore, she was pleased with this alteration of affairs; and maintained a good correspondence with the new court and ministry of James.

These revolutions in Scotland would have been regarded as of small importance to the repose and security of Elizabeth, had her own subjects been entirely united, and had not the zeal of the catholics, excited by constraint more properly than persecution, daily threatened her with some dangerous insurrection. The vigilance of the ministers, particularly of Burleigh and Walsingham, was raised in proportion to the activity of the malcontents; and many arts, which had been blameable in a more peaceful government, were employed, in detecting conspiracies, and even discovering the secret inclinations of men. Counterfeit letters were written in the name of the queen of Scots, or of the English exiles, and privately conveyed to the houses of the catholics: Spies were hired to observe the actions and discourse of suspected persons: Informers were countenanced: And though the sagacity of these two great ministers helped them to distinguish the true from the false intelligence, many calumnies were, no doubt, hearkened to, and all the subjects, particularly the catholics, kept in the utmost anxiety and inquietude. Henry Piercy, earl of Northumberland, brother to the earl beheaded some years before, and Philip Howard, earl of Arundel, son of the unfortunate duke of Norfolk, fell under suspicion; and the latter was, by order of council, confined to his own

Conspir-
acies in
England.

house. Francis Throgmorton, a private gentleman, was committed to custody, on account of a letter which he had written to the queen of Scots, and which was intercepted. Lord Paget and Charles Arundel, who had been engaged with him in treasonable designs, immediately withdrew beyond sea. Throgmorton confessed, that a plan for an invasion and insurrection had been laid; and though, on his trial, he was desirous of retracting this confession, and imputing it to the fear of torture, he was found guilty and executed. Mendoza, the Spanish ambassador, having promoted this conspiracy, was ordered to depart the kingdom; and Wade was sent into Spain, to excuse his dismission, and to desire the king to send another ambassador in his place: But Philip would not so much as admit the English ambassador to his presence. Creighton, a Scottish Jesuit, coming over on board a vessel which was seized, tore some papers, with an intention of throwing them into the sea; but the wind blowing them back upon the ship, they were pieced together, and discovered some dangerous secrets.[f]

Many of these conspiracies were, with great appearance of reason, imputed to the intrigues of the queen of Scots;[g] and as her name was employed in all of them, the council thought, that they could not use too many precautions against the danger of her claims, and the restless activity of her temper. She was removed from under the care of the earl of Shrewsbury, who, though vigilant and faithful in that trust, had also been indulgent to his prisoner, particularly with regard to air and exercise: And she was committed to the custody of Sir Amias Paulet and Sir Drue Drury; men of honour, but inflexible in their care and attention. An association was also set on foot by the earl of Leicester and other courtiers; and as Elizabeth was beloved by the whole nation, except the more zealous catholics, men of all ranks willingly flocked to the subscription of it. The purport of this association was to defend the queen, to revenge her death or any injury committed against her, and to exclude from the throne all claimants, what title soever they might possess, by whose suggestions, or for whose behoof, any violence should be offered to her majesty.[h] The queen of Scots was sensible, that this association was levelled against her; and

[f] Camden, p. 499.   [g] Strype, vol. iii. p. 246.   [h] State Trials, vol. i. p. 122, 123.

CHAPTER XLI

to remove all suspicion from herself, she also desired leave to subscribe it.

Elizabeth, that she might the more discourage malcontents, by shewing them the concurrence of the nation in her favour, summoned a new parliament; and she met with that dutiful attachment, which she expected. The association was confirmed by parliament; and a clause was added, by which the queen was empowered to name commissioners for the trial of any pretender to the crown, who should attempt or imagine any invasion, insurrection, or assassination against her: Upon condemnation, pronounced by these commissioners, the guilty person was excluded from all claim to the succession, and was farther punishable, as her majesty should direct. And for greater security, a council of regency, in case of the queen's violent death, was appointed to govern the kingdom, to settle the succession, and to take vengeance for that act of treason.[i]

A severe law was also enacted against jesuits and popish priests: It was ordained, that they should depart the kingdom within forty days; that those who should remain beyond that time, or should afterwards return, should be guilty of treason; that those who harboured or relieved them should be guilty of felony; that those who were educated in seminaries, if they returned not in six months after notice given, and submitted not themselves to the queen, before a bishop or two justices, should be guilty of treason; and that if any, so submitting themselves, should, within ten years, approach the court, or come within ten miles of it, their submission should be void.[k] By this law, the exercise of the catholic religion, which had formerly been prohibited under lighter penalties, and which was, in many instances, connived at, was totally suppressed. In the subsequent part of the queen's reign, the law was sometimes executed, by the capital punishment of priests; and though the partizans of that princess asserted, that they were punished for their treason, not their religion, the apology must only be understood in this sense, that the law was enacted on account of the treasonable views and attempts of the sect, not that every individual, who suffered the penalty of the law, was convicted of treason.[l]

23d Nov. A parliament.

[i] 27 Eliz. cap. 1.   [k] Ibid. cap. 2.   [l] Some even of those who defend the queen's measures, allow that in ten years fifty priests were executed, and fifty-five banished. Camden, p. 649.

The catholics, therefore, might now with justice complain of a violent persecution; which, we may safely affirm, in spite of the rigid and bigotted maxims of that age, not to be the best method of converting them, or of reconciling them to the established government and religion.

The parliament, besides arming the queen with these powers, granted her a supply of one subsidy and two fifteenths. The only circumstance, in which their proceedings were disagreeable to her, was an application, made by the commons, for a farther reformation in ecclesiastical matters. Yet even in this attempt, which affected her, as well as them, in a delicate point, they discovered how much they were overawed by her authority. The majority of the house were puritans, or inclined to that sect;[m] but the severe reprimands, which they had already, in former sessions, met with from the throne, deterred them from introducing any bill concerning religion; a proceeding which would have been interpreted as an encroachment on the prerogative: They were content to proceed by way of humble petition, and that not addressed to her majesty, which would have given offence, but to the house of lords, or rather the bishops, who had a seat in that house, and from whom alone they were willing to receive all advances towards reformation:[n] A strange departure from what we now apprehend to be the dignity of the commons!

The commons desired in their humble petition, that no bishop should exercise his function of ordination but with the consent and concurrence of six presbyters: But this demand, as it really introduced a change of ecclesiastical government, was firmly rejected by the prelates. They desired, that no clergyman should be instituted into any benefice, without previous notice being given to the parish, that they might examine whether there lay any objection to his life or doctrine: An attempt towards a popular model, which naturally met with the same fate. In another article of the petition,

[m] Besides the petition after mentioned, another proof of the prevalency of the puritans among the commons was their passing a bill for the reverent observance of Sunday, which they termed the Sabbath, and the depriving the people of those amusements, which they were accustomed to take on that day. D'Ewes, p. 335. It was a strong symptom of a contrary spirit in the upper house, that they proposed to add Wednesday to the fast days, and to prohibit entirely the eating of flesh on that day. D'Ewes, p. 373. [n] D'Ewes, p. 357.

CHAPTER XLI

they prayed, that the bishops should not insist upon every ceremony, or deprive incumbents for omitting part of the service: As
if uniformity in public worship had not been established by law; or
as if the prelates had been endowed with a dispensing power. They
complained of abuses, which prevailed, in pronouncing the sentence of excommunication, and they entreated the reverend fathers to think of some law for the remedy of these abuses: Implying, that those matters were too high for the commons of
themselves to attempt.

But the most material article, which the commons touched
upon in their petition, was the court of ecclesiastical commission,
and the oath *ex officio,* as it was called, exacted by that court. This
is a subject of such importance as to merit some explanation.

The first primate after the queen's accession, was Parker; a man
rigid in exacting conformity to the established worship, and in
punishing, by fine or deprivation, all the puritanical clergymen,
who attempted to innovate any thing in the habits, ceremonies, or
liturgy of the church. He died in 1575; and was succeeded by
Grindal, who, as he himself was inclined to the new sect, was with
great difficulty brought to execute the laws against them, or to
punish the nonconforming clergy. He declined obeying the
queen's orders for the suppression of *prophecyings,* or the assemblies of the zealots in private houses, which she apprehended, had
become so many academies of fanaticism; and for this offence, she
had, by an order of the Star Chamber, sequestered him from his
archiepiscopal function, and confined him to his own house. Upon
his death, which happened in 1583, she determined not to fall into
the same error in her next choice; and she named Whitgift, a
zealous churchman, who had already signalized his pen in controversy, and who, having in vain attempted to convince the puritans
by argument, was now resolved to open their eyes by power, and
by the execution of penal statutes. He informed the queen, that all
the spiritual authority, lodged in the prelates, was insignificant
without the sanction of the crown; and as there was no ecclesiastical commission at that time in force, he engaged her to
issue a new one; more arbitrary than any of the former, and conveying more unlimited authority.[a] She appointed forty-four com-

*The ecclesi-
astical
court.*

---

[a] Neal's History of the Puritans, vol. i. p. 410.

missioners, twelve of whom were ecclesiastics; three commissioners made a quorum; the jurisdiction of the court extended over the whole kingdom, and over all orders of men; and every circumstance of its authority, and all its methods of proceeding, were contrary to the clearest principles of law and natural equity. The commissioners were empowered to visit and reform all errors, heresies, schisms, in a word to regulate all opinions as well as to punish all breach of uniformity in the exercise of public worship. They were directed to make enquiry, not only by the legal methods of juries and witnesses, but by all other means and ways, which they could devise; that is, by the rack, by torture, by inquisition, by imprisonment. Where they found reason to suspect any person, they might administer to him an oath, called *ex Officio,* by which he was bound to answer all questions, and might thereby be obliged to accuse himself or his most intimate friend. The fines, which they levied, were discretionary, and often occasioned the total ruin of the offender, contrary to the established laws of the kingdom. The imprisonment, to which they condemned any delinquent, was limited by no rule but their own pleasure. They assumed a power of imposing on the clergy what new articles of subscription, and consequently of faith, they thought proper. Though all other spiritual courts were subject, since the reformation, to inhibitions from the supreme courts of law, the ecclesiastical commissioners were exempted from that legal jurisdiction, and were liable to no controul. And the more to enlarge their authority, they were empowered to punish all incests, adulteries, fornications; all outrages, misbehaviours, and disorders in marriage: And the punishments, which they might inflict, were according to their wisdom, conscience, and discretion. In a word, this court was a real *inquisition*; attended with all the iniquities, as well as cruelties, inseparable from that tribunal. And as the jurisdiction of the ecclesiastical court was destructive of all law, so its erection was deemed by many a mere usurpation of this imperious princess; and had no other foundation than a clause of a statute, restoring the supremacy to the crown, and empowering the sovereign to appoint commissioners for exercising that prerogative. But prerogative in general, especially the supremacy, was supposed in that age to involve powers, which no law, precedent, or reason could limit and determine.

But though the commons, in their humble petition to the prelates, had touched so gently and submissively on the ecclesiastical grievances, the queen, in a speech from the throne at the end of the session, could not forbear taking notice of their presumption, and reproving them for those murmurs, which, for fear of offending her, they had pronounced so low as not directly to reach her royal ears. After giving them some general thanks for their attachment to her, and making professions of affection to her subjects, she told them, that whoever found fault with the church threw a slander upon her, since she was appointed *by God* supreme ruler over it, and no heresies or schisms could prevail in the kingdom but by her permission and negligence: That some abuses must necessarily have place in every thing; but she warned the prelates to be watchful; for if she found them careless of their charge, she was fully determined to depose them: That she was commonly supposed to have employed herself in many studies, particularly philosophical (by which, I suppose, she meant theological) and she would confess, that few, whose leisure had not allowed them to make profession of science, had read or reflected more: That as she could discern the presumption of many, in curiously canvassing the scriptures, and starting innovations, she would no longer endure this licentiousness; but meant to guide her people, by God's rule, in the just mean between the corruptions of Rome and the errors of modern sectaries: And that as the Romanists were the inveterate enemies of her person, so the other innovators were dangerous to all kingly government; and under colour of preaching the word of God, presumed to exercise their private judgment, and to censure the actions of the prince.[p]

From the whole of this transaction, we may observe, that the commons, in making their general application to the prelates, as well as in some particular articles of their petition, showed themselves wholly ignorant, no less than the queen, of the principles of liberty and a legal constitution. And it may not be unworthy of remark, that Elizabeth, so far from yielding to the displeasure of the parliament against the ecclesiastical commission, granted, before the end of her reign, a new commission; in which she enlarged, rather than restrained, the powers of the commissioners.[q]

[p] See note [Q] at the end of the volume.   [q] Rymer, vol. xvi. p. 292, 386, 400.

During this session of parliament, there was discovered a con-spiracy, which much encreased the general animosity against the catholics, and still farther widened the breach between the reli-gious parties. William Parry, a catholic gentleman, had received the queen's pardon for a crime, by which he was exposed to capital punishment; and having obtained permission to travel, he retired to Milan, and made open profession of his religion, which he had concealed while he remained in England. He was here persuaded by Palmio, a jesuit, that he could not perform a more meritorious action, than to take away the life of his sovereign and his bene-factress; the nuncio, Campeggio, when consulted, approved ex-tremely of this pious undertaking; and Parry, though still agitated with doubts, came to Paris, with an intention of passing over to England, and executing his bloody purpose. He was here encour-aged in the design by Thomas Morgan, a gentleman of great credit in the party; and though Watts and some other catholic priests told him, that the enterprise was criminal and impious, he preferred the authority of Raggazzoni, the nuncio at Paris, and determined to persist in his resolution. He here wrote a letter to the pope, which was conveyed to cardinal Como; he communicated his in-tention to the holy father; and craved his absolution and paternal benediction. He received an answer from the cardinal, by which he found that his purpose was extremely applauded; and he came over to England with a full design of carrying it into execution. So deeply are the sentiments of morality engraved in the human breast, that it is difficult even for the prejudices of false religion totally to efface them; and this bigotted assassin resolved, before he came to extremities, to try every other expedient for alleviating the persecutions, under which the catholics at that time laboured. He found means of being introduced to the queen; assured her that many conspiracies were formed against her; and exhorted her, as she tendered her life, to give the Romanists some more indulgence in the exercise of their religion: But lest he should be tempted by the opportunity to assassinate her, he always came to court unprovided with every offensive weapon. He even found means to be elected member of parliament; and having made a vehement harangue against the severe laws enacted this last ses-sion, was committed to custody for his freedom, and sequestered from the house. His failure in these attempts confirmed him the more in his former resolution; and he communicated his intentions to Nevil, who entered zealously into the design, and was determined to have a share in the merits of its execution. A book, newly published by Dr. Allen, afterwards created a cardinal, served farther to efface all their scruples, with regard to the murder of an heretical prince; and having agreed to shoot the queen, while she should be taking the air on horseback, they resolved, if they could not make their escape, to sacrifice their lives, in fulfilling a duty, so agreeable, as they imagined, to the will of God and to true religion. But while they were watching an opportunity for the execution of their purpose, the earl of Westmoreland happened to die in exile; and as Nevil was next heir to that family, he began to entertain hopes, that, by doing some acceptable service to the queen, he might recover the estate and honours, which had been forfeited by the rebellion of the last earl. He betrayed the whole conspiracy to the ministers; and Parry, being thrown into prison, confessed the guilt, both to them, and to the jury who tried him. The letter from cardinal Como, being produced in court, put Parry's narrative beyond all question; and that criminal, having received sentence of death,[r] suffered the punishment, which the law appointed for his treasonable conspiracy.[s]

These bloody designs now appeared every where, as the result of that bigotted spirit by which the two religions, especially the catholic, were at this time actuated. Somerville, a gentleman of the county of Warwic, somewhat disordered in his understanding, had heard so much of the merit attending the assassination of heretics and persecutors, that he came to London with a view of murdering the queen; but having betrayed his design by some extravagances, he was thrown into prison, and there perished by a voluntary death.[t] About the same time, Baltazar Gerard, a Burgundian, undertook, and executed the same design against the prince of Orange; and that great man perished at Delft, by the hands of a desperate assassin, who, with a resolution worthy of a better cause, sacrificed his own life, in order to destroy the famous restorer and protector of religious liberty. The Flemings, who regarded that prince as their father, were filled with great sorrow, as well when

The affairs of the Low Countries.

---

[r] State Trials, vol. i. p. 103, & seq. Strype, vol. iii. p. 255, & seq.   [s] See note [R] at the end of the volume.   [t] Camden, p. 495.

they considered the miserable end of so brave a patriot, as their own forlorn condition, from the loss of so powerful and prudent a leader, and from the rapid progress of the Spanish arms. The prince of Parma had made every year great advances upon them, had reduced several of the provinces to obedience, and had laid close siege to Antwerp, the richest and most populous city of the Netherlands, whose subjection, it was foreseen, would give a mortal blow to the already declining affairs of the revolted provinces. The only hopes, which remained to them, arose from the prospect of foreign succour. Being well acquainted with the cautious and frugal maxims of Elizabeth, they expected better success in France; and in the view of engaging Henry to embrace their defence, they tendered him the sovereignty of their provinces. But the present condition of that monarchy obliged the king to reject so advantageous an offer. The duke of Anjou's death, which, he thought, would have tended to restore public tranquillity, by delivering him from the intrigues of that prince, plunged him into the deepest distress; and the king of Navarre, a professed hugonot, being next heir to the crown, the duke of Guise took thence occasion to revive the catholic league, and to urge Henry, by the most violent expedients, to seek the exclusion of that brave and virtuous prince. Henry himself, though a zealous catholic, yet, because he declined complying with their precipitate measures, became an object of aversion to the league; and as his zeal, in practising all the superstitious observances of the Romish church, was accompanied with a very licentious conduct in private life, the catholic faction, in contradiction to universal experience, embraced thence the pretext of representing his devotion as mere deceit and hyprocrisy. Finding his authority to decline, he was obliged to declare war against the hugonots, and to put arms into the hands of the league, whom, both on account of their dangerous pretensions at home, and their close alliance with Philip, he secretly regarded as his more dangerous enemies. Constrained by the same policy, he dreaded the danger of associating himself with the revolted protestants in the Low Countries, and was obliged to renounce that inviting opportunity of revenging himself for all the hostile intrigues and enterprizes of Philip.

The States, reduced to this extremity, sent over a solemn embassy to London, and made anew an offer to the queen, of ac-

1585.

CHAPTER XLI

knowledging her for their sovereign, on condition of obtaining her protection and assistance. Elizabeth's wisest counsellors were divided in opinion with regard to the conduct, which she should hold in this critical and important emergence. Some advised her to reject the offer of the States, and represented the imminent dangers, as well as injustice, attending the acceptance of it. They said, that the suppression of rebellious subjects was the common cause of all sovereigns, and any encouragement, given to the revolt of the Flemings, might prove the example of a like pernicious licence to the English: That though princes were bound by the laws of the Supreme Being not to oppress their subjects, the people never were entitled to forget all duty to their sovereign, or transfer, from every fancy or disgust, or even from the justest ground of complaint, their obedience to any other master: That the queen, in the succours hitherto afforded the Flemings, had considered them as labouring under oppression, not as entitled to freedom; and had intended only to admonish Philip not to persevere in his tyranny, without any view of ravishing from him these provinces, which he enjoyed by hereditary right from his ancestors: That her situation in Ireland, and even in England, would afford that powerful monarch sufficient opportunity of retaliating upon her; and she must thenceforth expect, that, instead of secretly fomenting faction, he would openly employ his whole force in the protection and defence of the catholics: That the pope would undoubtedly unite his spiritual arms to the temporal ones of Spain: And that the queen would soon repent her making so precarious an acquisition in foreign countries, by exposing her own dominions to the most imminent danger.[u]

Other counsellors of Elizabeth maintained a contrary opinion. They asserted, that the queen had not, even from the beginning of her reign, but certainly had not at present, the choice, whether she would embrace friendship or hostility with Philip: That by the whole tenor of that prince's conduct it appeared, that his sole aims were, the extending of his empire, and the entire subjection of the protestants, under the specious pretence of maintaining the catholic faith: That the provocations, which she had already given him, joined to his general scheme of policy, would for ever render him

[u] Camden, p. 507. Bentivoglio, part 2, lib. iv.

her implacable enemy; and as soon as he had subdued his revolted subjects, he would undoubtedly fall, with the whole force of his united empire, on her defenceless state: That the only question was, whether she would maintain a war abroad, and supported by allies, or wait till the subjection of all the confederates of England should give her enemies leisure to begin their hostilities in the bowels of the kingdom: That the revolted provinces, though in a declining condition, possessed still considerable force; and by the assistance of England, by the advantages of their situation, and by their inveterate antipathy to Philip, might still be enabled, to maintain the contest against the Spanish monarchy: That their maritime power, united to the queen's, would give her entire security on the side from which alone she could be assaulted, and would even enable her to make inroads on Philip's dominions, both in Europe and the Indies: That a war, which was necessary, could never be unjust; and self-defence was concerned, as well in preventing certain dangers at a distance, as in repelling any immediate invasion: And that, since hostility with Spain was the unavoidable consequence of the present interests and situations of the two monarchies, it were better to compensate that danger and loss by the acquisition of such important provinces to the English empire.[w]

Amidst these opposite councils, the queen, apprehensive of the consequences attending each extreme, was inclined to steer a middle course; and though such conduct is seldom prudent, she was not, in this resolution, guided by any prejudice or mistaken affection. She was determined not to permit, without opposition, the total subjection of the revolted provinces, whose interests she deemed so closely connected with her own: But foreseeing that the acceptance of their sovereignty would oblige her to employ her whole force in their defence, would give umbrage to her neighbours, and would expose her to the reproach of ambition and usurpation, imputations which hitherto she had carefully avoided, she immediately rejected this offer. She concluded a league with the States on the following conditions: That she should send over an army to their assistance, of five thousand foot and a thousand horse, and pay them during the war; that the general, and two

[w] Camden, p. 507. Bentivoglio, part 2. lib. iv.

others, whom she should appoint, should be admitted into the council of the States; that neither party should make peace without the consent of the other; that her expences should be refunded after the conclusion of the war; and that the towns of Flushing and the Brille, with the castle of Rammekins, should, in the mean time, be consigned into her hands, by way of security.

The queen knew that this measure would immediately engage her in open hostilities with Philip; yet was not she terrified with the view of the present greatness of that monarch. The continent of Spain was at that time rich and populous; and the late addition of Portugal, besides securing internal tranquillity, had annexed an opulent kingdom to Philip's dominions, had made him master of many settlements in the East-Indies and of the whole commerce of those regions, and had much encreased his naval power, in which he was before chiefly deficient. All the princes of Italy, even the pope and the court of Rome, were reduced to a kind of subjection under him, and seemed to possess their sovereignty on terms somewhat precarious. The Austrian branch in Germany, with their dependant principalities, was closely connected with him, and was ready to supply him with troops for every enterprize. All the treasures of the West-Indies were in his possession; and the present scarcity of the precious metals in every country of Europe, rendered the influence of his riches the more forcible and extensive. The Netherlands seemed on the point of relapsing into servitude; and small hopes were entertained of their withstanding those numerous and veteran armies, which, under the command of the most experienced generals, he employed against them. Even France, which was wont to counterbalance the Austrian greatness, had lost all her force from intestine commotions; and as the catholics, the ruling party, were closely connected with him, he rather expected thence an augmentation, than a diminution, of his power. Upon the whole, such prepossessions were every where entertained concerning the force of the Spanish monarchy, that the king of Sweden, when he heard that Elizabeth had openly embraced the defence of the revolted Flemings, scrupled not to say, that she had now taken the diadem from her head, and had adventured it upon the doubtful chance of war.[x] Yet was this

[x] Camden, p. 508.

princess rather cautious than enterprising in her natural temper: She ever needed more to be impelled by the vigour, than restrained by the prudence of her ministers: But when she saw an evident necessity, she braved danger with magnanimous courage; and trusting to her own consummate wisdom, and to the affections, however divided, of her people, she prepared herself to resist, and even to assault, the whole force of the catholic monarch.

The Earl of Leicester was sent over to Holland, at the head of the English auxiliary forces. He carried with him a splendid retinue; being accompanied by the young earl of Essex, his son-in-law, the lords Audley and North, Sir William Russel, Sir Thomas Shirley, Sir Arthur Basset, Sir Walter Waller, Sir Gervase Clifton, and a select troop of five hundred gentlemen. He was received, on his arrival at Flushing, by his nephew Sir Philip Sidney, the governor; and every town, through which he passed, expressed their joy by acclamations and triumphal arches, as if his presence and the queen's protection had brought them the most certain deliverance. The States, desirous of engaging Elizabeth still farther in their defence, and knowing the interest which Leicester possessed with her, conferred on him the title of governor and captain-general of the United Provinces, appointed a guard to attend him, and treated him, in some respects, as their sovereign. But this step had a contrary effect to what they expected. The queen was displeased with the artifice of the States, and the ambition of Leicester. She severely reprimanded both; and it was with some difficulty, that, after many humble submissions, they were able to appease her.

Hostilities with Spain. America was regarded as the chief source of Philip's power, as well as the most defenceless part of his dominions; and Elizabeth, finding that an open breach with that monarch was unavoidable, resolved not to leave him unmolested in that quarter. The great success of the Spaniards and Portuguese in both Indies had excited a spirit of emulation in England; and as the progress of commerce, still more that of colonies, is slow and gradual, it was happy, that a war, in this critical period, had opened a more flattering prospect to the avarice and ambition of the English, and had tempted them, by the view of sudden and exorbitant profit, to engage in naval enterprizes. A fleet of twenty sail was equipped to attack the Spaniards in the West-Indies: Two thousand three hundred volunteers, besides seamen, engaged on board of it; Sir Francis Drake was

CHAPTER XLI

appointed admiral; Christopher Carlisle commander of the land forces. They took St. Jago, near Cape Verde, by surprize; and found in it plenty of provisions, but no riches. They sailed to Hispaniola; and easily making themselves master of St. Domingo by assault, obliged the inhabitants to ransom their houses by a sum of money. Carthagena fell next into their hands after some more resistance, and was treated in the same manner. They burned St. Anthony and St. Helens, two towns on the coast of Florida. Sailing along the coast of Virginia, they found the small remains of a colony which had been planted there by Sir Walter Raleigh, and which had gone extremely to decay. This was the first attempt of the English to form such settlements; and though they have since surpassed all European nations, both in the situation of their colonies, and in the noble principles of liberty and industry, on which they are founded; they had here been so unsuccessful, that the miserable planters abandoned their settlements, and prevailed on Drake to carry them with him to England. He returned with so much riches as encouraged the volunteers, and with such accounts of the Spanish weakness in those countries as served extremely to enflame the spirits of the nation to future enterprizes. The great mortality, which the climate had produced in his fleet, was, as is usual, but a feeble restraint on the avidity and sanguine hopes of young adventurers.[y] It is thought that Drake's fleet first introduced the use of tobacco into England.

The enterprizes of Leicester were much less successful than those of Drake. This man possessed neither courage nor capacity, equal to the trust reposed in him by the queen; and as he was the only bad choice she made for any considerable employment, men naturally believed, that she had here been influenced by an affection still more partial than that of friendship. He gained at first some advantage in an action against the Spaniards; and threw succours into Grave, by which that place was enabled to make a vigorous defence: But the cowardice of the governor, Van Hemert, rendered all these efforts useless. He capitulated after a feeble resistance; and being tried for his conduct, suffered a capital punishment from the sentence of a court martial. The prince of Parma next undertook the siege of Venlo, which was surrendered to him

1586.
January.

---

[y] Camden, p. 509.

after some resistance. The fate of Nuys was more dismal; being taken by assault, while the garrison was treating of a capitulation. Rhimberg, which was garrisoned by twelve hundred English, under the command of colonel Morgan, was afterwards besieged by the Spaniards; and Leicester, thinking himself too weak to attempt raising the siege, endeavoured to draw off the prince of Parma by forming another enterprize. He first attacked Doesberg, and succeeded: He then sat down before Zutphen, which the Spanish general thought so important a fortress, that he hastened to its relief. He made the marquess of Guasto advance with a convoy, which he intended to throw into the place. They were favoured by a fog; but falling by accident on a body of English cavalry, a furious action ensued, in which the Spaniards were worsted, and the marquess of Gonzaga, an Italian nobleman of great reputation and family, was slain. The pursuit was stopped by the advance of the prince of Parma with the main body of the Spanish army; and the English cavalry, on their return from the field, found their advantage more than compensated by the loss of Sir Philip Sidney, who, being mortally wounded in the action, was carried off by the soldiers, and soon after died. This person is described by the writers of that age as the most perfect model of an accomplished gentleman, that could be formed even by the wanton imagination of poetry or fiction. Virtuous conduct, polite conversation, heroic valour, and elegant erudition, all concurred to render him the ornament and delight of the English court; and as the credit, which he possessed with the queen and the earl of Leicester, was wholly employed in the encouragement of genius and literature, his praises have been transmitted with advantage to posterity. No person was so low as not to become an object of his humanity. After this last action, while he was lying on the field, mangled with wounds, a bottle of water was brought him to relieve his thirst; but observing a soldier near him in a like miserable condition, he said, *This man's necessity is still greater than mine:* And resigned to him the bottle of water. The king of Scots, struck with admiration of Sidney's virtue, celebrated his memory in a copy of Latin verses, which he composed on the death of that young hero.

The English, though a long peace had deprived them of all experience, were strongly possessed of military genius; and the advantages, gained by the prince of Parma, were not attributed to the superior bravery and discipline of the Spaniards, but solely to the want of military abilities in Leicester. The States were much discontented with his management of the war; still more with his arbitrary and imperious conduct; and at the end of the campaign, they applied to him for a redress of all their grievances. But Leicester, without giving them any satisfaction, departed soon after for England.[z]

The queen, while she provoked so powerful an enemy as the king of Spain, was not forgetful to secure herself on the side of Scotland; and she endeavoured both to cultivate the friendship and alliance of her kinsman, James, and to remove all grounds of quarrel between them. An attempt, which she had made some time before, was not well calculated to gain the confidence of that prince. She had dispatched Wotton as her ambassador to Scotland; but though she gave him private instructions with regard to her affairs, she informed James, that, when she had any political business to discuss with him, she would employ another minister; that this man was not fitted for serious negociations; and that her chief purpose in sending him, was to entertain the king with witty and facetious conversation, and to partake without reserve of his pleasures and amusements. Wotton was master of profound dissimulation, and knew how to cover, under the appearance of a careless gaiety, the deepest designs, and most dangerous artifices. When but a youth of twenty, he had been employed by his uncle, Dr. Wotton, ambassador in France during the reign of Mary, to ensnare the constable, Montmorency; and had not his purpose been frustrated by pure accident, his cunning had prevailed over all the caution and experience of that aged minister. It is no wonder, that, after years had improved him in all the arts of deceit, he should gain an ascendant over a young prince, of so open and unguarded a temper as James; especially when the queen's recommendation prepared the way for his reception. He was admitted into all the pleasures of the king; made himself master of his secrets; and had so much the more authority with him in political transactions, as he did not seem to pay the least attention to these matters. The Scottish ministers, who observed the growing interest of this man, endeavoured to acquire his friendship; and scrupled not to sacri-

[z] Camden, p. 512. Bentivoglio, part 2. lib. 4.

fice to his intrigues the most essential interests of their master. Elizabeth's usual jealousies with regard to her heirs began now to be levelled against James; and as that prince had attained the years proper for marriage, she was apprehensive, lest, by being strengthened with children and alliances, he should acquire the greater interest and authority with her English subjects. She directed Wotton to form a secret concert with some Scottish noblemen, and to procure their promise, that James, during three years, should not, on any account, be permitted to marry. In consequence of this view, they endeavoured to embroil him with the king of Denmark, who had sent ambassadors to Scotland, on pretence of demanding restitution of the Orkneys, but really with a view of opening a proposal of marriage between James and his daughter. Wotton is said to have employed his intrigues to purposes still more dangerous. He formed, it is pretended, a conspiracy with some malcontents, to seize the person of the king, and to deliver him into the hands of Elizabeth, who would probably have denied all concurrence in the design, but would have been sure to retain him in perpetual thraldom, if not captivity. The conspiracy was detected, and Wotton fled hastily from Scotland, without taking leave of the king.[a]

James's situation obliged him to dissemble his resentment of this traiterous attempt, and his natural temper inclined him soon to forgive and forget it. The queen found no difficulty in renewing the negociations for a strict alliance between Scotland and England; and the more effectually to gain the prince's friendship, she granted him a pension, equivalent to his claim on the inheritance of his grandmother, the countess of Lenox, lately deceased.[b] A league was formed between Elizabeth and James, for the mutual defence of their dominions, and of their religion, now menaced by the open combination of all the catholic powers of Europe. It was stipulated, that, if Elizabeth were invaded, James should aid her with a body of two thousand horse and five thousand foot; that Elizabeth, in a like case, should send to his assistance three thousand horse and six thousand foot; that the charge of these armies should be defrayed by the prince who demanded assistance; that, if the invasion should be made upon England, within sixty miles of the frontiers of Scotland, this latter kingdom should march its

[a] Melvil.   [b] Spotswood, p. 351.

CHAPTER XLI

whole force to the assistance of the former; and that the present league should supersede all former alliances of either state with any foreign kingdom, so far as religion was concerned.[c]

By this league James secured himself against all attempts from abroad, opened a way for acquiring the confidence and affections of the English, and might entertain some prospect of domestic tranquillity, which, while he lived on bad terms with Elizabeth, he could never expect long to enjoy. Besides the turbulent disposition, and inveterate feuds of the nobility, ancient maladies of the Scottish government, the spirit of fanaticism had introduced a new disorder; so much the more dangerous, as religion, when corrupted by false opinion, is not restrained by any rules of morality, and is even scarcely to be accounted for in its operations, by any principles of ordinary conduct and policy. The insolence of the preachers, who triumphed in their dominion over the populace, had, at this time, reached an extreme height; and they carried their arrogance so far, not only against the king, but against the whole civil power, that they excommunicated the archbishop of St. Andrew's, because he had been active in parliament for promoting a law, which restrained their seditious sermons:[d] Nor could that prelate save himself by any expedient from this terrible sentence, but by renouncing all pretensions to ecclesiastical authority. One Gibson said in the pulpit, that captain James Stuart (meaning the late earl of Arran) and his wife, Jezabel, had been deemed the chief persecutors of the church; but it was now seen, that the king himself was the great offender: And for this crime the preacher denounced against him the curse which fell on Jeroboam, that he should die childless, and be the last of his race.[e]

The secretary, Thirlstone, perceiving the king so much molested with ecclesiastical affairs, and with the refractory disposition of the clergy, advised him to leave them to their own courses: For that in a short time they would become so intolerable, that the people would rise against them, and drive them out of the country. "True," replied the king: "If I purposed to undo the church and religion, your counsel were good: But my intention is to maintain both; therefore cannot I suffer the clergy to follow such a conduct, as will in the end bring religion into contempt and derision."[f]

[c] Ibid. p. 349. Camden, p. 513. Rymer, tom. xv. p. 803.   [d] Spotswood, p. 345, 346.   [e] Ibid. p. 344.   [f] Spotswood, p. 348.

XLII

Zeal of the catholics – Babington's conspiracy –
Mary assents to the conspiracy – The conspirators
seized and executed – Resolution to try the
queen of Scots – The commissioners prevail
on her to submit to the trial – The trial –
Sentence against Mary – Interposition
of king James – Reasons for the execution
of Mary – The execution – Mary's character –
The queen's affected sorrow – Drake destroys
the Spanish fleet at Cadiz – Philip
projects the invasion of England –
The invincible armada – Preparations in
England – The armada arrives in the channel –
Defeated – A parliament – Expedition
against Portugal – Affairs of Scotland

1586.   THE DANGERS, which arose from the character, principles, and
pretensions of the queen of Scots, had very early engaged
Elizabeth to consult, in her treatment of that unfortunate princess,
the dictates of jealousy and politics, rather than of friendship or
generosity: Resentment of this usage had pushed Mary into enterprizes, which had nearly threatened the repose and authority of

CHAPTER XLII

Elizabeth: The rigour and restraint, thence redoubled upon the captive queen,[g] still impelled her to attempt greater extremities; and while her impatience of confinement, her revenge,[h] and her high spirit concurred with religious zeal, and the suggestions of desperate bigots, she was at last engaged in designs, which afforded her enemies, who watched the opportunity, a pretence or reason for effecting her final ruin.

The English seminary at Rheims had wrought themselves up to *Zeal of the* a high pitch of rage and animosity against the queen. The recent *catholics.* persecutions, from which they had escaped; the new rigours, which, they knew, awaited them in the course of their missions; the liberty, which for the present they enjoyed, of declaiming against that princess; and the contagion of that religious fury, which every where surrounded them in France: All these causes had obliterated with them every maxim of common sense, and every principle of morals or humanity. Intoxicated with admiration of the divine power and infallibility of the pope, they revered his bull, by which he excommunicated and deposed the queen; and some of them had gone to that height of extravagance, as to assert, that that performance had been immediately dictated by the Holy Ghost. The assassination of heretical sovereigns, and of that princess in particular, was represented as the most meritorious of all enterprizes; and they taught, that, whoever perished in such pious attempts, enjoyed without dispute the glorious and never-fading crown of martyrdom. By such doctrines, they instigated John Savage, a man of desperate courage, who had served some years in the Low Countries, under the prince of Parma, to attempt the life of Elizabeth; and this assassin, having made a vow to persevere in his design, was sent over to England, and recommended to the confidence of the more zealous catholics.

About the same time, John Ballard, a priest of that seminary, had returned to Paris from his mission in England and Scotland; and as he had observed a spirit of mutiny and rebellion to be very prevalent among the catholic devotees in these countries, he had founded on that disposition the project of dethroning Elizabeth, and of restoring by force of arms the exercise of the ancient religion.[i] The situation of affairs abroad seemed favourable to this

[g] Digges, p. 139. Haynes, p. 607.   [h] See note [S] at the end of the volume.
[i] Murden's State Papers, p. 517.

enterprize: The pope, the Spaniard, the duke of Guise, concurring in interests, had formed a resolution to make some attempt against England: And Mendoza, the Spanish ambassador at Paris, strongly encouraged Ballard to hope for succours from these princes. Charles Paget alone, a zealous catholic and a devoted partizan of the queen of Scots, being well acquainted with the prudence, vigour, and general popularity of Elizabeth, always maintained, that, so long as that princess was allowed to live, it was in vain to expect any success from an enterprize upon England. Ballard, persuaded of this truth, saw more clearly the necessity of executing the design, formed at Rheims: He came over to England in the disguise of a soldier, and assumed the name of captain Fortescue: And he bent his endeavours to effect at once the project of an assassination, an insurrection, and an invasion.[k]

Babing-
ton's con-
spiracy.
The first person, to whom he addressed himself, was Anthony Babington of Dethic in the county of Derby. This young gentleman was of a good family, possessed a plentiful fortune, had discovered an excellent capacity, and was accomplished in literature beyond most of his years or station. Being zealously devoted to the catholic communion, he had secretly made a journey to Paris some time before; and had fallen into intimacy with Thomas Morgan, a bigotted fugitive from England, and with the bishop of Glasgow, Mary's ambassador at the court of France. By continually extolling the amiable accomplishments and heroical virtues of that princess, they impelled the sanguine and unguarded mind of young Babington to make some attempt for her service; and they employed every principle of ambition, gallantry, and religious zeal to give him a contempt of those dangers, which attended any enterprize against the vigilant government of Elizabeth. Finding him well disposed for their purpose, they sent him back to England, and secretly, unknown to himself, recommended him to the queen of Scots, as a person worth engaging in her service. She wrote him a letter, full of friendship and confidence; and Babington, ardent in his temper and zealous in his principles, thought, that these advances now bound him in honour to devote himself entirely to the service of that unfortunate princess. During some time, he had found means of conveying to her all her foreign correspondence;

[k] Camden, p. 515.

CHAPTER XLII

but after she was put under the custody of Sir Amias Paulet, and reduced to a more rigorous confinement, he experienced so much difficulty and danger in rendering her this service, that he had desisted from every attempt of that nature.

When Ballard began to open his intentions to Babington, he found his zeal suspended, not extinguished: His former ardour revived on the mention of any enterprize, which seemed to promise success in the cause of Mary and of the catholic religion. He had entertained sentiments conformable to those of Paget, and represented the folly of all attempts, which, during the life-time of Elizabeth, could be formed against the established religion and government of England. Ballard encouraged by this hint, proceeded to discover to him the design undertaken by Savage;[l] and was well pleased to observe, that, instead of being shocked with the project, Babington only thought it not secure enough, when entrusted to one single hand, and proposed to join five others with Savage in this desperate enterprize.

In prosecution of these views, Babington employed himself in encreasing the number of his associates; and he secretly drew into the conspiracy many catholic gentlemen, discontented with the present government. Barnwel, of a noble family in Ireland, Charnoc, a gentleman of Lancashire, and Abington, whose father had been cofferer to the household, readily undertook the assassination of the queen. Charles Tilney, the heir of an ancient family, and Titchborne of Southampton, when the design was proposed to them, expressed some scruples, which were removed by the arguments of Babington and Ballard. Savage alone refused during some time to share the glory of the enterprize with any others;[m] he challenged the whole to himself; and it was with some difficulty he was induced to depart from this preposterous ambition.

The deliverance of the queen of Scots, at the very same instant, when Elizabeth should be assassinated, was requisite for effecting the purpose of the conspirators; and Babington undertook, with a party of a hundred horse, to attack her guards, while she should be taking the air on horseback. In this enterprize, he engaged Edward Windsor, brother to the lord of that name, Thomas Salisbury, Robert Gage, John Travers, John Jones and Henry Donne; most

[l] Ibid. State Trials, p. 114.   [m] State Trials, vol. i. p. 111.

of them men of family and interest. The conspirators much wanted, but could not find, any nobleman of note, whom they might place at the head of the enterprize; but they trusted, that the great events, of the queen's death and Mary's deliverance, would rouze all the zealous catholics to arms; and that foreign forces, taking advantage of the general confusion, would easily fix the queen of Scots on the throne, and re-establish the ancient religion.

These desperate projects had not escaped the vigilance of Elizabeth's council, particularly of Walsingham, secretary of state. That artful minister had engaged Maud, a catholic priest, whom he retained in pay, to attend Ballard in his journey to France, and had thereby got a hint of the designs, entertained by the fugitives. Polly, another of his spies, had found means to insinuate himself among the conspirators in England: and though not entirely trusted, had obtained some insight into their dangerous secrets. But the bottom of the conspiracy was never fully known, till Gifford, a seminary priest, came over, and made a tender of his services to Walsingham. By his means, the discovery became of the utmost importance, and involved the fate of Mary, as well as of those zealous partizans of that princess.

Babington and his associates, having laid such a plan, as, they thought, promised infallible success, were impatient to communicate the design to the queen of Scots, and to obtain her approbation and concurrence. For this service, they employed Gifford, who immediately applied to Walsingham, that the interest of that minister might forward his secret correspondence with Mary. Walsingham proposed the matter to Paulet, and desired him to connive at Gifford's corrupting one of his servants: But Paulet, averse to the introducing of such a pernicious precedent into his family, desired, that they would rather think of some other expedient. Gifford found a brewer, who supplied the family with ale; and bribed him to convey letters to the captive queen. The letters, by Paulet's connivance, were thrust through a chink in the wall; and answers were returned by the same conveyance.

Ballard and Babington were at first diffident of Gifford's fidelity; and to make trial of him, they gave him only blank papers made up like letters: But finding by the answers, that these had been faithfully delivered, they laid aside all farther scruple, and conveyed by his hands the most criminal and dangerous parts of

CHAPTER XLII

their conspiracy. Babington informed Mary of the design laid for a foreign invasion, the plan of an insurrection at home, the scheme for her deliverance, and the conspiracy for assassinating the usurper, by six noble gentlemen, as he termed them, all of them his private friends; who, from the zeal, which they bore to the catholic cause and her majesty's service, would undertake the *tragical execution*. Mary replied, that she approved highly of the design; that the gentlemen might expect all the rewards, which it should ever be in her power to confer; and that the death of Elizabeth was a necessary circumstance, before any attempts were made, either for her own deliverance or an insurrection." These letters, with others to Mendoza, Charles Paget, the archbishop of Glasgow, and Sir Francis Inglefield, were carried by Gifford to secretary Walsingham; were decyphered by the art of Philips, his clerk; and copies taken of them. Walsingham employed another artifice, in order to obtain full insight into the plot: He subjoined to a letter of Mary's a postscript in the same cypher; in which he made her desire Babington to inform her of the names of the conspirators. The indiscretion of Babington furnished Walsingham with still another means of detection, as well as of defence. That gentleman had caused a picture to be drawn, where he himself was represented standing amidst the six assassins; and a motto was subjoined, expressing that their common perils were the band of their confederacy. A copy of this picture was brought to Elizabeth, that she might know the assassins, and guard herself against their approach to her person.

Mary assents to the conspiracy.

Meanwhile, Babington, anxious to ensure and hasten the foreign succours, resolved to dispatch Ballard into France; and he procured for him, under a feigned name, a licence to travel. In order to remove from himself all suspicion, he applied to Walsingham, pretended great zeal for the queen's service, offered to go abroad, and professed his intentions of employing the confidence, which he had gained among the catholics, to the detection and disappointment of their conspiracies. Walsingham commended his loyal purposes; and promising his own counsel and assistance in the execution of them, still fed him with hopes, and maintained a close correspondence with him. A warrant, mean-

---

" State Trials, vol. i. p. 135. Camden, p. 515.

while, was issued for seizing Ballard; and this incident, joined to the consciousness of guilt, begat in all the conspirators the utmost anxiety and concern. Some advised, that they should immediately make their escape: Others proposed, that Savage and Charnoc should without delay execute their purpose against Elizabeth; and Babington, in prosecution of this scheme, furnished Savage with money, that he might buy good cloaths, and thereby have more easy access to the queen's person. Next day, they began to apprehend, that they had taken the alarm too hastily; and Babington, having renewed his correspondence with Walsingham, was persuaded by that subtle minister, that the seizure of Ballard had proceeded entirely from the usual diligence of informers in the detection of popish and seminary priests. He even consented to take lodgings secretly in Walsingham's house, that they might have more frequent conferences together, before his intended departure for France: But observing, that he was watched and guarded, he made his escape, and gave the alarm to the other conspirators. They all took to flight, covered themselves with several disguises, and lay concealed in woods or barns; but were

The conspirators seized and executed. soon discovered and thrown into prison. In their examinations, they contradicted each other; and the leaders were obliged to make a full confession of the truth. Fourteen were condemned and executed: Of whom, seven acknowledged the crime on their trial; the rest were convicted by evidence.

September. The lesser conspirators being dispatched, measures were taken for the trial and conviction of the queen of Scots; on whose account, and with whose concurrence, these attempts had been made against the life of the queen, and the tranquillity of the kingdom. Some of Elizabeth's counsellors were averse to this procedure; and thought, that the close confinement of a woman, who was become very sickly, and who would probably put a speedy period to their anxiety by her natural death, might give sufficient security to the government, without attempting a measure, of which there scarcely remains any example in history. Leicester advised, that Mary should be secretly dispatched by poison, and he sent a divine to convince Walsingham of the lawfulness of that action: But Walsingham declared his abhorrence of it; and still insisted, in conjunction with the majority of the counsellors, for the open trial of the queen of Scots. The situation of England, and of the English

CHAPTER XLII

ministers, had, indeed, been hitherto not a little dangerous. No successor of the crown was declared; but the heir of blood, to whom the people in general were likely to adhere, was, by education, an enemy to the national religion; was, from multiplied provocations, an enemy to the ministers and principal nobility; and their personal safety, as well as the safety of the public, seemed to depend alone on the queen's life, who was now somewhat advanced in years. No wonder, therefore, that Elizabeth's counsellors, knowing themselves to be so obnoxious to the queen of Scots, endeavoured to push every measure to extremities against her; and were even more anxious than the queen herself, to prevent her from ever mounting the throne of England.

Though all England was acquainted with the detection of Babington's conspiracy, every avenue to the queen of Scots had been so strictly guarded, that she remained in utter ignorance of the matter; and it was a great surprize to her, when Sir Thomas Gorges, by Elizabeth's orders, informed her, that all her accomplices were discovered and arrested. He chose the time for giving her this intelligence, when she was mounted on horseback to go a hunting; and she was not permitted to return to her former place of abode, but was conducted from one gentleman's house to another, till she was lodged in Fotheringay castle in the county of Northampton, which it was determined to make the last stage of her trial and sufferings. Her two secretaries, Nau, a Frenchman, and Curle, a Scot, were immediately arrested: All her papers were seized, and sent up to the council: Above sixty different keys to cyphers were discovered: There were also found many letters from persons beyond sea, and several too from English noblemen, containing expressions of respect and attachment. The queen took no notice of this latter discovery; but the persons themselves, knowing their correspondence to be detected, thought, that they had no other means of making atonement for their imprudence, than by declaring themselves thenceforth the most inveterate enemies of the queen of Scots.[o]

It was resolved to try Mary, not by the common statute of treasons, but by the act which had passed the former year, with a view to this very event; and the queen, in terms of that act, ap-

Resolution to try the queen of Scots.

[o] Camden, p. 518.

pointed a commission, consisting of forty noblemen and privy-counsellors, and empowered them to examine and pass sentence on Mary, whom she denominated the late queen of Scots, and heir to James V. of Scotland. The commissioners came to Fotheringay castle, and sent to her Sir Walter Mildmay, Sir Amias Paulet, and Edward Barker, who delivered her a letter from Elizabeth, informing her of the commission, and of the approaching trial. Mary received the intelligence without emotion or astonishment. She said, however, that it seemed strange to her, that the queen should command her, as a subject, to submit to a trial and examination before subjects: That she was an absolute independant princess, and would yield to nothing, which might derogate either from her royal majesty, from the state of sovereign princes, or from the dignity and rank of her son: That, however oppressed by misfortunes, she was not yet so much broken in spirit, as her enemies flattered themselves; nor would she, on any account; be accessary to her own degradation and dishonour: That she was ignorant of the laws and statutes of England; was utterly destitute of council; and could not conceive who were entitled to be called her peers, or could legally sit as judges on her trial: That though she had lived in England for many years, she had lived in captivity; and not having received the protection of the laws, she could not, merely by her involuntary residence in the country, be supposed to have subjected herself to their jurisdiction: That, notwithstanding the superiority of her rank, she was willing to give an account of her conduct before an English parliament; but could not view these commissioners in any other light, than as men appointed to justify, by some colour of legal proceeding, her condemnation and execution: And that she warned them to look to their conscience and their character, in trying an innocent person; and to reflect, that these transactions would somewhere be subject to revisal, and that the theatre of the whole world was much wider than the kingdom of England.

The commissioners prevail on her to submit to the trial. In return, the commissioners sent a new deputation, informing her, that her plea, either from her royal dignity or from her imprisonment, could not be admitted; and that they were empowered to proceed to her trial, even though she should refuse to answer before them. Burleigh, the treasurer, and Bromley, the chancellor, employed much reasoning to make her submit; but the person, whose arguments had the chief influence, was Sir Christopher Hatton, vice-chamberlain. His speech was to this purpose. "You are accused, Madam," said he, "but not condemned, of having conspired the destruction of our lady and queen anointed. You say, you are a queen: But, in such a crime as this, and such a situation as yours, the royal dignity itself, neither by the civil or canon law, nor by the law of nature or of nations, is exempt from judgment. If you be innocent, you wrong your reputation in avoiding a trial. We have been present at your protestations of innocence: But queen Elizabeth thinks otherwise; and is heartily sorry for the appearances, which lie against you. To examine, therefore, your cause, she has appointed commissioners; honourable persons, prudent and upright men, who are ready to hear you with equity, and even with favour, and will rejoice if you can clear yourself of the imputations, which have been thrown upon you. Believe me, madam, the queen herself will rejoice, who affirmed to me at my departure, that nothing, which ever befel her, had given her so much uneasiness, as that you should be suspected of a concurrence in these criminal enterprizes. Laying aside, therefore, the fruitless claim of privilege from your royal dignity, which can now avail you nothing, trust to the better defence of your innocence, make it appear in open trial, and leave not upon your memory that stain of infamy, which must attend your obstinate silence on this occasion."[p]

By this artful speech, Mary was persuaded to answer before the court; and thereby gave an appearance of legal procedure to the trial, and prevented those difficulties, which the commissioners must have fallen into, had she persevered in maintaining so specious a plea as that of her sovereign and independant character. Her conduct in this particular must be regarded as the more imprudent; because formerly, when Elizabeth's commissioners pretended not to exercise any jurisdiction over her, and only entered into her cause by her own consent and approbation, she declined justifying herself, when her honour, which ought to have been dearer to her than life, seemed absolutely to require it.

On her first appearance before the commissioners, Mary, either sensible of her imprudence, or still unwilling to degrade her- *The trial.*

[p] Camden, p. 523.

self by submitting to a trial, renewed her protestation against the authority of her judges: The chancellor answered her by pleading the supreme authority of the English laws over every one who resided in England: And the commissioners accommodated matters, by ordering both her protestation and his answer to be recorded.

The lawyers of the crown then opened the charge against the queen of Scots. They proved, by intercepted letters, that she had allowed cardinal Allen and others to treat her as queen of England; and that she had kept a correspondence with lord Paget and Charles Paget, in view of engaging the Spaniards to invade the kingdom. Mary seemed not anxious to clear herself from either of these imputations. She only said, that she could not hinder others from using what style they pleased in writing to her; and that she might lawfully try every expedient for the recovery of her liberty.

An intercepted letter of her's to Mendoza was next produced; in which she promised to transfer to Philip her right to the kingdom of England, if her son should refuse to be converted to the catholic faith; an event, she there said, of which there was no expectation, while he remained in the hands of his Scottish subjects.[q] Even this part of the charge, she took no pains to deny, or rather she seemed to acknowledge it. She said, that she had no kingdoms to dispose of; yet was it lawful for her to give at her pleasure what was her own, and she was not accountable to any for her actions. She added, that she had formerly rejected that proposal from Spain; but now, since all her hopes in England were gone, she was fully determined not to refuse foreign assistance. There was also produced evidence to prove, that Allen and Parsons were at that very time negociating by her orders at Rome the conditions of transferring her English crown to the king of Spain, and of disinheriting her heretical son.[r]

It is remarkable, that Mary's prejudices against her son were, at this time, carried so far, that she had even entered into a conspiracy against him, had appointed lord Claud Hamilton regent of Scotland, and had instigated her adherents to seize James's person and deliver him into the hands of the pope or the king of Spain;

[q] State Trials, vol. i. p. 138.   [r] See note [T] at the end of the volume.

CHAPTER XLII

whence he was never to be delivered but on condition of his becoming catholic.^{s}

The only part of the charge, which Mary positively denied, was
her concurrence in the design of assassinating Elizabeth. This
article indeed was the most heavy, and the only one, that could
fully justify the queen in proceeding to extremities against her. In
order to prove the accusation, there were produced the following
evidence: Copies taken in secretary Walsingham's office of the
intercepted letters between her and Babington, in which her approbation of the murder was clearly expressed; the evidence of her
two secretaries, Nau and Curle, who had confessed, without being
put to any torture, both that she received these letters from Babington, and that they had written the answers, by her order; the
confession of Babington, that he had written the letters and received the answers,^{t} and the confession of Ballard and Savage, that
Babington had showed them these letters of Mary written in the
cypher, which had been settled between them.

It is evident, that this complication of evidence, though every
circumstance corroborates the general conclusion, resolves itself
finally into the testimony of the two secretaries, who alone were
certainly acquainted with their mistress's concurrence in Babington's conspiracy, but who knew themselves exposed to all the
rigours of imprisonment, torture, and death, if they refused to
give any evidence, which might be required of them. In the case of
an ordinary criminal, this proof, with all its disadvantages, would
be esteemed legal, and even satisfactory, if not opposed by some
other circumstances, which shake the credit of the witnesses: But
on the present trial, where the absolute power of the prosecutor
concurred with such important interests and such a violent inclination to have the princess condemned; the testimony of two witnesses, even though men of character, ought to be supported by
strong probabilities, in order to remove all suspicion of tyranny
and injustice. The proof against Mary, it must be confessed, is not
destitute of this advantage; and it is difficult, if not impossible, to
account for Babington's receiving an answer, written in her name,
and in the cypher concerted between them, without allowing, that
the matter had been communicated to that princess. Such is the

^{s} See note [U] at the end of the volume. ^{t} State Trials, vol. i. p. 113.

light in which this matter appears, even after time has discovered every thing, which could guide our judgment with regard to it: No wonder, therefore, that the queen of Scots, unassisted by counsel, and confounded by so extraordinary a trial, found herself incapable of making a satisfactory defence before the commissioners. Her reply consisted chiefly in her own denial: Whatever force may be in that denial was much weakened, by her positively affirming, that she never had had any correspondence of any kind with Babington; a fact, however, of which there remains not the least question." She asserted, that, as Nau and Curle had taken an oath of secrecy and fidelity to her, their evidence against her ought not to be credited. She confessed, however, that Nau had been in the service of her uncle, the cardinal of Lorraine, and had been recommended to her by the king of France, as a man in whom she might safely confide. She also acknowledged Curle to be a very honest man, but simple, and easily imposed on by Nau. If these two men had received any letters, or had written any answers, without her knowledge; the imputation, she said, could never lie on her. And she was the more inclined, she added, to entertain this suspicion against them, because Nau had, in other instances, been guilty of a like temerity, and had ventured to transact business in her name, without communicating the matter to her."

The sole circumstance of her defence, which to us may appear to have some force, was her requiring that Nau and Curle should be confronted with her, and her affirming that they never would to her face persist in their evidence. But that demand, however equitable, was not then supported by law in trials of high-treason, and was often refused even in other trials, where the crown was prosecutor. The clause, contained in an act of the 13th of the queen, was a novelty; that the species of treason there enumerated must be proved by two witnesses, confronted with the criminal. But Mary was not tried upon that act; and the ministers and crown lawyers of this reign were always sure to refuse every indulgence beyond what the strict letter of the law and the settled practice of the courts of justice required of them. Not to mention, that these secretaries were not probably at Fotheringay-castle during the

" See note [V] at the end of the volume.   " See note [W] at the end of the volume.

time of the trial, and could not, upon Mary's demand, be produced before the commissioners.[x]

There passed two incidents in this trial, which may be worth observing. A letter between Mary and Babington was read, in which mention was made of the earl of Arundel and his brothers: On hearing their names she broke into a sigh. "Alas," said she, "what has the noble house of the Howards suffered for my sake!" She affirmed, with regard to the same letter, that it was easy to forge the hand-writing and cypher of another; she was afraid, that this was too familiar a practice with Walsingham, who, she also heard, had frequently practised both against her life and her son's. Walsingham, who was one of the commissioners, rose up. He protested, that, in his private capacity, he had never acted any thing against the queen of Scots: In his public capacity, he owned, that his concern for his sovereign's safety had made him very diligent in searching out, by every expedient, all designs against her sacred person or her authority. For attaining that end, he would not only make use of the assistance of Ballard or any other conspirator: He would also reward them for betraying their companions. But if he had tampered in any manner, unbefitting his character and office, why did none of the late criminals, either at their trial or execution, accuse him of such practices? Mary endeavoured to pacify him, by saying that she spoke from information; and she begged him to give thenceforth no more credit to such as slandered her, than she should to such as accused him. The great character indeed, which Sir Francis Walsingham bears for probity and honour, should remove from him all suspicion of such base arts as forgery and subornation; arts, which even the most corrupt ministers, in the most corrupt times, would scruple to employ.

Having finished the trial, the commissioners adjourned from Fotheringay-castle, and met in the Star Chamber at London; where, after taking the oaths of Mary's two secretaries, who, voluntarily, without hope or reward, vouched the authenticity of those

25th Octob.

---

[x] Queen Elizabeth was willing to have allowed Curle and Nau to be produced in the trial, and writes to that purpose, to Burleigh and Walsingham, in her letter of the 7th of October, in Forbes's MS. collections. She only says, that she thinks it needless, though she was willing to agree to it. The not confronting of the witnesses was not the result of design, but the practice of the age.

letters before produced, they pronounced sentence of death upon the queen of Scots, and confirmed it by their seals and sub- *Sentence* scriptions. The same day, a declaration was published by the com- *against* missioners and the judges, "that the sentence did no-wise derogate *Mary.* from the title and honour of James, king of Scotland; but that he was in the same place, degree, and right, as if the sentence had never been pronounced."[y]

The queen had now brought affairs with Mary to that situation, which she had long ardently desired; and had found a plausible reason for executing vengeance on a competitor, whom, from the beginning of her reign, she had ever equally dreaded and hated. But she was restrained from instantly gratifying her resentment, by several important considerations. She foresaw the invidious colours, in which this example of uncommon jurisdiction would be represented by the numerous partizans of Mary, and the reproach, to which she herself might be exposed with all foreign princes, perhaps with all posterity. The rights of hospitality, of kindred, and of royal majesty, seemed, in one signal instance, to be all violated; and this sacrifice of generosity to interest, of clemency to revenge, might appear equally unbecoming a sovereign and a woman. Elizabeth, therefore, who was an excellent hypocrite, pre- tended the utmost reluctance to proceed to the execution of the sentence: affected the most tender sympathy with her prisoner; displayed all her scruples and difficulties; rejected the solicitation of her courtiers and ministers; and affirmed, that, were she not moved by the deepest concern for her people's safety, she would not hesitate a moment in pardoning all the injuries, which she herself had received from the queen of Scots.

29th That the voice of her people might be more audibly heard in *Octob.* the demand of justice upon Mary, she summoned a new parlia- ment; and she knew, both from the usual dispositions of that as- sembly, and from the influence of her ministers over them, that she should not want the most earnest solicitation to consent to that measure, which was so agreeable to her secret inclinations. She did not open this assembly in person, but appointed for that purpose three commissioners, Bromley, the chancellor, Burleigh, the treasurer, and the earl of Derby. The reason assigned for this

[y] Camden, p. 526.

measure, was, that the queen foreseeing that the affair of the queen of Scots would be canvassed in parliament, found her tenderness and delicacy so much hurt by that melancholy incident, that she had not the courage to be present while it was under deliberation, but withdrew her eyes from what she could not behold without the utmost reluctance and uneasiness. She was also willing, that, by this unusual precaution, the people should see the danger, to which her person was hourly exposed; and should thence be more strongly incited to take vengeance on the criminal, whose restless intrigues and bloody conspiracies had so long exposed her to the most imminent perils.[z]

The parliament answered the queen's expectations: The sentence against Mary was unanimously ratified by both houses; and an application was voted to obtain Elizabeth's consent to its publication and execution.[a] She gave an answer ambiguous, embarrassed; full of real artifice, and seeming irresolution. She mentioned the extreme danger to which her life was continually exposed; she declared her willingness to die, did she not foresee the great calamities, which would thence fall upon the nation; she made professions of the greatest tenderness to her people; she displayed the clemency of her temper, and expressed her violent reluctance to execute the sentence against her unhappy kinswoman; she affirmed, that the late law, by which that princess was tried, so far from being made to ensnare her, was only intended to give her warning beforehand, not to engage in such attempts, as might expose her to the penalties, with which she was thus openly menaced; and she begged them to think once again, whether it were possible to find any expedient, besides the death of the queen of Scots, for securing the public tranquillity.[b] The parliament, in obedience to her commands, took the affair again under consideration; but could find no other possible expedient. They reiterated their solicitations, and entreaties, and arguments: They even remonstrated, that mercy to the queen of Scots was cruelty to them, her subjects and children: And they affirmed, that it were injustice to deny execution of the law to any individual; much more to the whole body of the people, now unanimously and earnestly suing for this pledge of her parental care and tenderness.

[z] D'Ewes, p. 375. [a] Ibid. p. 379. [b] Ibid. p. 402, 403.

This second address set the pretended doubts and scruples of Elizabeth anew in agitation: She complained of her own unfortunate situation; expressed her uneasiness from their importunity; renewed the professions of affection to her people; and dismissed the committee of parliament in an uncertainty, what, after all this deliberation, might be her final resolution.[c]

But though the queen affected reluctance to execute the sentence against Mary, she complied with the request of parliament in publishing it by proclamation; and this act seemed to be attended with the unanimous and hearty rejoicings of the people. Lord Buckhurst, and Beale, clerk of the council, were sent to the queen of Scots, and notified to her the sentence pronounced against her, its ratification by parliament, and the earnest applications made for its execution by that assembly, who thought, that their religion could never, while she was alive, attain a full settlement and security. Mary was nowise dismayed at this intelligence: On the contrary, she joyfully laid hold of the last circumstance mentioned to her; and insisted, that, since her death was demanded by the protestants for the establishment of their faith, she was really a martyr to her religion, and was entitled to all the merits attending that glorious character. She added, that the English had often embrued their hands in the blood of their sovereigns: No wonder, they exercised cruelty against her, who derived her descent from these monarchs.[d] Paulet, her keeper, received orders to take down her canopy, and to serve her no longer with the respect due to sovereign princes. He told her, that she was now to be considered as a dead person; and incapable of any dignity.[e] This harsh treatment produced not in her any seeming emotion. She only replied, that she received her royal character from the hands of the Almighty, and no earthly power was ever able to bereave her of it.

The queen of Scots wrote her last letter to Elizabeth; full of dignity, without departing from that spirit of meekness and of charity, which appeared suitable to this concluding scene of her unfortunate life. She preferred no petition for averting the fatal sentence: On the contrary, she expressed her gratitude to Heaven for thus bringing to a speedy period her sad and lamentable pil-

[c] See note [X] at the end of the volume.   [d] Camden, p. 528.   [e] Jebb, vol. ii. p. 293.

CHAPTER XLII

grimage. She requested some favours of Elizabeth, and intreated her, that she might be beholden for them to her own goodness alone, without making applications to those ministers, who had discovered such an extreme malignity against her person and her religion. She desired, that, after her enemies should be satiated with her innocent blood, her body, which, it was determined, should never enjoy rest, while her soul was united to it, might be consigned to her servants, and be conveyed by them into France, there to repose in a catholic land, with the sacred reliques of her mother. In Scotland, she said, the sepulchres of her ancestors were violated, and the churches either demolished or profaned; and in England, where she might be interred among the ancient kings, her own and Elizabeth's progenitors, she could entertain no hopes of being accompanied to the grave with those rites and ceremonies, which her religion required. She requested, that no one might have the power of inflicting a private death upon her, without Elizabeth's knowledge; but that her execution should be public, and attended by her ancient servants, who might bear testimony of her perseverance in the faith, and of her submission to the will of Heaven. She begged, that these servants might afterwards be allowed to depart whithersoever they pleased, and might enjoy those legacies, which she should bequeath them. And she conjured her to grant these favours, by their near kindred; by the soul and memory of Henry VII. the common ancestor of both; and by the royal dignity, of which they equally participated.[f] Elizabeth made no answer to this letter; being unwilling to give Mary a refusal in her present situation, and foreseeing inconveniences from granting some of her requests.

While the queen of Scots thus prepared herself to meet her fate, great efforts were made by foreign powers with Elizabeth to prevent the execution of the sentence, pronounced against her. Besides employing L'Aubespine, the French resident at London, a creature of the house of Guise, Henry sent over Bellievre, with a professed intention of interceding for the life of Mary. The duke of Guise and the league, at that time, threatened very nearly the king's authority; and Elizabeth knew, that though that monarch might, from decency and policy, think himself obliged to interpose

[f] Camden, p. 529. Jebb, vol. ii. p. 295.

publicly in behalf of the queen of Scots, he could not secretly be much displeased with the death of a princess, on whose fortune and elevation his mortal enemies had always founded so many daring and ambitious projects.[g] It is even pretended, that Bellievre had orders, after making public and vehement remonstrances against the execution of Mary, to exhort privately the queen, in his master's name, not to defer an act of justice, so necessary for their common safety.[h] But whether the French king's intercession were sincere or not, it had no weight with the queen; and she still persisted in her former resolution.

Interposition of king James. The interposition of the young king of Scots, though not able to change Elizabeth's determination, seemed, on every account, to merit more regard. As soon as James heard of the trial and condemnation of his mother, he sent Sir William Keith, a gentleman of his bed chamber, to London; and wrote a letter to the queen, in which he remonstrated, in very severe terms, against the indignity of the procedure. He said, that he was astonished to hear of the presumption of English noblemen and counsellors, who had dared to sit in judgment and pass sentence upon a queen of Scotland, descended from the blood royal of England; but he was still more astonished to hear, that thoughts were seriously entertained of putting that sentence in execution: That he entreated Elizabeth to reflect on the dishonour, which she would draw on her name by embruing her hands in the blood of her near kinswoman, a person of the same royal dignity and of the same sex with herself: That, in this unparalleled attempt, she offered an affront to all diadems, and even to her own; and by reducing sovereigns to a level with other men, taught the people to neglect all duty towards those whom Providence had appointed to rule over them: That for his part, he must deem the injury and insult so enormous, as to be incapable of all atonement; nor was it possible for him thenceforward to remain in any terms of correspondence with a person, who, without any pretence of legal authority, had deliberately inflicted an ignominious death upon his parent: And that, even if the sentiments of nature and duty did not inspire him with this purpose of vengeance, his honour required it of him; nor could he ever acquit himself in the eyes of the world, if he did not use every effort, and endure every hazard, to revenge so great an indignity.[i]

[g] Camden, p. 494.   [h] Du Maurier.   [i] Spotswood, p. 351.

CHAPTER XLII

Soon after, James sent the master of Gray and Sir Robert Melvil to enforce the remonstrances of Keith; and to employ with the queen every expedient of argument and menaces. Elizabeth was at first offended with the sharpness of these applications; and she replied in a like strain to the Scottish ambassadors. When she afterwards reflected, that this earnestness was no more than what duty required of James, she was pacified; but still retained her resolution of executing the sentence against Mary.[k] It is believed, that the master of Gray, gained by the enemies of that princess, secretly gave his advice not to spare her, and undertook, in all events, to pacify his master.

The queen also, from many considerations, was induced to pay small attention to the applications of James, and to disregard all the efforts, which he could employ in behalf of his mother. She was well acquainted with his character and interests, the factions which prevailed among his people, and the inveterate hatred, which the zealous protestants, particularly the preachers, bore to the queen of Scots. The present incidents set these dispositions of the clergy in a full light. James, observing the fixed purpose of Elizabeth, ordered prayers to be offered up for Mary in all the churches; and knowing the captious humour of the ecclesiastics, he took care that the form of the petition should be most cautious, as well as humane and charitable: "That it might please God to illuminate Mary with the light of his truth, and save her from the apparent danger, with which she was threatened." But, excepting the king's own chaplains, and one clergyman more, all the preachers refused to pollute their churches by prayers for a papist, and would not so much as prefer a petition for her conversion. James, unwilling or unable to punish this disobedience, and desirous of giving the preachers an opportunity of amending their fault, appointed a new day when prayers should be said for his mother; and that he might at least secure himself from any insult in his own presence, he desired the archbishop of St. Andrew's to officiate before him. In order to disappoint this purpose, the clergy instigated one Couper, a young man, who had not yet received holy orders, to take possession of the pulpit early in the morning, and to exclude the prelate. When the king came to church, and saw the pulpit occupied by Couper, he called to him from his seat, and told him, that the place was

---

[k] Spotswood, p. 353.

destined for another; yet since he was there, if he would obey the charge given, and remember the queen in his prayers, he might proceed to divine service. The preacher replied, that he would do as the Spirit of God should direct him. This answer sufficiently instructed James in his purpose; and he commanded him to leave the pulpit. As Couper seemed not disposed to obey, the captain of the guard went to pull him from his place; upon which the young man cried aloud, That this day would be a witness against the king in the great day of the Lord; and he denounced a woe upon the inhabitants of Edinburgh for permitting him to be treated in that manner.[1] The audience at first appeared desirous to take part with him; but the sermon of the prelate brought them over to a more dutiful and more humane disposition.

Elizabeth, when solicited, either by James or by foreign princes, to pardon the queen of Scots, seemed always determined to execute the sentence against her: But when her ministers urged her to interpose no more delays, her scruples and her hesitation returned; her humanity could not allow her to embrace such violent and sanguinary measures; and she was touched with compassion for the misfortunes, and with respect for the dignity, of the unhappy prisoner. The courtiers, sensible that they could do nothing more acceptable to her, than to employ persuasion on this head, failed not to enforce every motive for the punishment of Mary, and to combat all the objections urged against this act of justice. They said, that the treatment of that princess in England had been, on her first reception, such as sound reason and policy required; and if she had been governed by principles of equity, she would not have refused willingly to acquiesce in it: That the obvious inconveniences, either of allowing her to retire into France, or of restoring her by force to her throne, in opposition to the reformers and the English party in Scotland, had obliged the queen to detain her in England, till time should offer some opportunity of serving her, without danger to the kingdom, or to the protestant religion: That her usage there had been such as became her rank; her own servants, in considerable numbers, had been permitted to attend; her exercise had been allowed her for health, and all access of company for amusement; and these indulgences would, in time,

Reasons for the execution of Mary.

[1] Spotswood, p. 354.

CHAPTER XLII

have been carried farther, if by her subsequent conduct she had appeared worthy of them: That after she had instigated the rebellion of Northumberland, the conspiracy of Norfolk, the bull of excommunication of pope Pius, an invasion from Flanders; after she had reduced the queen's friends, and incited every enemy, foreign and domestic, against her; it became necessary to treat her as a most dangerous rival, and to render her confinement more strict and rigorous: That the queen, notwithstanding these repeated provocations, had, in her favour, rejected the importunity of her parliaments, and the advice of her sagest ministers;[m] and was still, in hopes of her amendment, determined to delay coming to the last extremities against her: That Mary, even in this forlorn condition, retained so high and unconquerable a spirit, that she acted as competitor to the crown, and allowed her partizans every where, and in their very letters, addressed to herself, to treat her as queen of England: That she had carried her animosity so far as to encourage, in repeated instances, the atrocious design of assassinating the queen; and this crime was unquestionably proved upon her, by her own letters, by the evidence of her secretaries, and by the dying confession of her accomplices: That she was but a titular queen, and at present possessed no where any right of sovereignty; much less in England, where, the moment she set foot in the kingdom, she voluntarily became subject to the laws, and to Elizabeth, the only true sovereign: That even allowing her to be still the queen's equal in rank and dignity, self-defence was permitted by a law of nature, which could never be abrogated; and every one, still more a queen, had sufficient jurisdiction over an enemy, who, by open violence, and still more, who, by secret treachery, threatened the utmost danger against her life: That the general combination of the catholics to exterminate the protestants, was no longer a secret; and as the sole resource of the latter persecuted sect lay in Elizabeth, so the chief hope, which the former entertained of final success, consisted in the person, and in the title of the queen of Scots: That this very circumstance brought matters to extremity between these princesses; and rendering the life of one the death of the other, pointed out to Elizabeth the path, which either regard to self-

[m] Digges, p. 276. Strype, vol. ii. p. 48, 135, 136, 139.

preservation, or to the happiness of her people, should direct her to pursue: And that necessity, more powerful than policy, thus demanded of the queen that resolution, which equity would authorise, and which duty prescribed."

When Elizabeth thought, that as many importunities had been used, and as much delay interposed, as decency required, she at last determined to carry the sentence into execution: But even in this final resolution she could not proceed without displaying a new scene of duplicity and artifice. In order to alarm the vulgar, rumours were previously dispersed, that the Spanish fleet was arrived in Milford Haven; that the Scots had made an irruption into England; that the duke of Guise was landed in Sussex with a strong army; that the queen of Scots was escaped from prison, and had raised an army; that the northern counties had begun an insurrection; that there was a new conspiracy on foot to assassinate the queen, and set the city of London of fire; nay, that the queen was actually assassinated.° An attempt of this nature was even imputed to L'Aubespine, the French ambassador; and that minister was obliged to leave the kingdom. The queen, affecting to be in terror and perplexity, was observed to sit much alone, pensive and silent; and sometimes to mutter to herself half sentences, importing the difficulty and distress, to which she was reduced.ᵖ She at last called Davison, a man of parts, but easy to be imposed on, and who had lately, for that very reason, been made secretary, and she ordered him privately to draw a warrant for the execution of the queen of Scots; which, she afterwards said, she intended to keep by her, in case any attempt should be made for the deliverance of that princess. She signed the warrant; and then commanded Davison to carry it to the chancellor, in order to have the great seal appended to it. Next day she sent Killigrew to Davison, enjoining him to forbear, some time, executing her former orders; and when Davison came and told her, that the warrant had already passed the great seal, she seemed to be somewhat moved, and blamed him for his precipitation. Davison, being in perplexity, acquainted the council with this whole transaction; and they endeavoured to persuade him to send off Beale with the warrant: If the queen should be displeased, they promised to justify his con-

" Camden, p. 533.   ° Camden, p. 533.   ᵖ Ibid. p. 534.

duct, and to take on themselves the whole blame of this measure.[q] *1587.*
The secretary, not sufficiently aware of their intention, complied
with the advice; and the warrant was dispatched to the earls of
Shrewsbury and Kent, and some others, ordering them to see the
sentence executed upon the queen of Scots.

The two earls came to Fotheringay-castle, and being intro- *7th Feb.*
duced to Mary, informed her of their commission, and desired her *The ex-*
to prepare for death next morning at eight o'clock. She seemed *ecution.*
no-wise terrified, though somewhat surprised, with the intelligence. She said, with a chearful, and even a smiling countenance,
that she did not think the queen, her sister, would have consented
to her death, or have executed the sentence against a person, not
subject to the laws and jurisdiction of England. "But as such is her
will," said she, "death, which puts an end to all my miseries, shall
be to me most welcome; nor can I esteem that soul worthy the
felicities of heaven, which cannot support the body under the
horrors of the last passage to these blissful mansions."[r] She then
requested the two noblemen, that they would permit some of her
servants, and particularly her confessor, to attend her: But they
told her, that compliance with this last demand was contrary to
their conscience,[s] and that Dr. Fletcher, dean of Peterborow, a
man of great learning, should be present, to instruct her in the
principles of true religion. Her refusal to have any conference with
this divine inflamed the zeal of the earl of Kent; and he bluntly told
her, that her death would be the life of their religion; as, on the
contrary, her life would have been the death of it. Mention being
made of Babington, she constantly denied his conspiracy to have
been at all known to her; and the revenge of her wrongs, she
resigned into the hands of the Almighty.

When the earls had left her, she ordered supper to be hastened,
that she might have the more leisure, after it, to finish the few
affairs which remained to her in this world, and to prepare for her

---

[q] It appears by some letters published by Strype, vol. iii. book ii c. i. that
Elizabeth had not expressly communicated her intention to any of her
ministers, not even to Burleigh: They were such experienced courtiers, that
they knew they could not gratify her more than by serving her without
waiting till she desired them.   [r] Camden, p. 534. Jebb, vol. ii. p. 301. MS.
in the Advocates' Library, p. 2. from the Cott. Lib. Cal. c. 9.   [s] Jebb, vol.
ii. p. 302.

passage to another. It was necessary for her, she said, to take some sustenance, lest a failure of her bodily strength should depress her spirits on the morrow, and lest her behaviour should thereby betray a weakness unworthy of herself.[t] She supped sparingly, as her manner usually was; and her wonted chearfulness did not even desert her on this occasion. She comforted her servants under the affliction which overwhelmed them, and which was too violent for them to conceal it from her. Turning to Burgoin, her physician, she asked him, Whether he did not remark the great and invincible force of truth? "They pretend," said she, "that I must die, because I conspired against their queen's life: But the earl of Kent avowed, that there was no other cause of my death, than the apprehensions, which, if I should live, they entertain for their religion. My constancy in the faith is my real crime: The rest is only a colour, invented by interested and designing men." Towards the end of supper, she called in all her servants, and drank to them: They pledged her, in order, on their knees; and craved her pardon for any past neglect of their duty: She deigned, in return, to ask their pardon for her offences towards them; and a plentiful effusion of tears attended this last solemn farewel, and exchange of mutual forgiveness.[u]

Mary's care of her servants was the sole remaining affair, which employed her concern. She perused her will, in which she had provided for them by legacies: She ordered the inventory of her goods, cloaths, and jewels to be brought her; and she wrote down the names of those to whom she bequeathed each particular: To some she distributed money with her own hands; and she adapted the recompence to their different degrees of rank and merit. She wrote also letters of recommendation for her servants to the French king, and to her cousin, the duke of Guise, whom she made the chief executor of her testament. At her wonted time she went to bed; slept some hours; and then rising, spent the rest of the night in prayer. Having foreseen the difficulty of exercising the rites of her religion, she had had the precaution to obtain a consecrated hoste from the hands of pope Pius; and she had reserved the use of it for this last period of her life. By this expedient she

---

[t] Jebb, vol. ii. p. 489.   [u] Jebb, vol. ii. p. 302, 626. Camden, p. 534.

CHAPTER XLII

supplied, as much as she could, the want of a priest and confessor, who was refused her.[w]

Towards the morning she dressed herself in a rich habit of silk and velvet, the only one which she had reserved to herself. She told her maids, that she would willingly have left them this dress rather than the plain garb which she wore the day before: But it was necessary for her to appear at the ensuing solemnity in a decent habit.

Thomas Andrews, sheriff of the county, entered the room, and informed her, that the hour was come, and that he must attend her to the place of execution. She replied, That she was ready; and bidding adieu to her servants, she leaned on two of Sir Amias Paulet's guards, because of an infirmity in her limbs; and she followed the sheriff with a serene and composed countenance. In passing through a hall adjoining to her chamber, she was met by the earls of Shrewsbury and Kent, Sir Amias Paulet, Sir Drue Drury, and many other gentlemen of distinction. Here she also found Sir Andrew Melvil, her steward, who flung himself on his knees before her; and, wringing his hands, cried aloud, "Ah, Madam! unhappy me! what man was ever before the messenger of such heavy tidings as I must carry, when I shall return to my native country, and shall report, that I saw my gracious queen and mistress beheaded in England?" His tears prevented farther speech; and Mary too felt herself moved, more from sympathy than affliction. "Cease, my good servant," said she, "cease to lament: Thou hast cause rather to rejoice than to mourn: For now shalt thou see the troubles of Mary Stuart receive their long expected period and completion. Know," continued she, "good servant, that all the world at best is vanity, and subject still to more sorrow than a whole ocean of tears is able to bewail. But I pray thee, carry this message from me, that I die a true woman to my religion, and unalterable in my affections to Scotland and to France. Heaven forgive them, that have long desired my end, and have thirsted for my blood as the hart panteth after the water brooks." "O God," added she, "thou that art the author of truth, and truth itself, thou knowest the inmost recesses of my heart: Thou knowest that I was ever

[w] Jebb, vol. ii. p. 489.

desirous to preserve an entire union between Scotland and England, and to obviate the source of all these fatal discords. But recommend me, Melvil, to my son, and tell him, that, notwithstanding all my distresses, I have done nothing prejudicial to the state and kingdom of Scotland." After these words, reclining herself, with weeping eyes, and face bedewed with tears, she kissed him. "And so," said she, "good Melvil, farewel: Once again, farewel, good Melvil; and grant the assistance of thy prayers to thy queen and mistress."[x]

She next turned to the noblemen who attended her, and made a petition in behalf of her servants, that they might be well treated, be allowed to enjoy the presents which she had made them, and be sent safely into their own country. Having received a favourable answer, she preferred another request, that they might be permitted to attend her at her death: In order, said she, that their eyes may behold, and their hearts bear witness, how patiently their queen and mistress can submit to her execution, and how constantly she perseveres in her attachment to her religion. The earl of Kent opposed this desire, and told her, that they would be apt, by their speeches and cries, to disturb both herself and the spectators: He was also apprehensive, lest they should practise some superstition, not meet for him to suffer; such as dipping their handkerchiefs in her blood: For that was the instance which he made use of. "My lord," said the queen of Scots, "I will give my word (although it be but dead) that they shall not incur any blame in any of the actions which you have named. But alas! poor souls! it would be a great consolation to them to bid their mistress farewel. And I hope," added she, "that your mistress, being a maiden queen, would vouchsafe, in regard of womanhood, that I should have some of my own people about me at my death. I know, that her majesty hath not given you any such strict command, but that you might grant me a request of far greater courtesy, even though I were a woman of inferior rank to that which I bear." Finding that the earl of Kent persisted still in his refusal, her mind, which had fortified itself against the terrors of death, was affected by this indignity, for which she was not prepared. "I am cousin to your queen," cried she, "and descended from the blood-royal of Henry

[x] MS. p. 4. Jeb, vol. ii. p. 634. Strype, vol. iii. p. 384.

CHAPTER XLII

VII. and a married queen of France, and an anointed queen of Scotland." The commissioners, perceiving how invidious their obstinacy would appear, conferred a little together, and agreed, that she might carry a few of her servants along with her. She made choice of four men, and two maid-servants, for that purpose.

She then passed into another hall, where was erected the scaffold, covered with black; and she saw, with an undismayed countenance, the executioners, and all the preparations of death. The room was crowded with spectators; and no one was so steeled against all sentiments of humanity, as not to be moved, when he reflected on her royal dignity; considered the surprising train of her misfortunes, beheld her mild but inflexible constancy, recalled her amiable accomplishments, or surveyed her beauties, which, though faded by years, and yet more by her afflictions, still discovered themselves in this fatal moment. Here the warrant for her execution was read to her; and during this ceremony she was silent, but shewed, in her behaviour, an indifference and unconcern, as if the business had no wise regarded her. Before the executioners performed their office, the dean of Peterborow stepped forth; and though the queen frequently told him, that he needed not concern himself about her, that she was settled in the ancient catholic and Roman religion, and that she meant to lay down her life in defence of that faith; he still thought it his duty to persist in his lectures and exhortations, and to endeavour her conversion. The terms, which he employed, were, under colour of pious instructions, cruel insults on her unfortunate situation; and besides their own absurdity, may be regarded as the most mortifying indignities, to which she had ever yet been exposed. He told her, that the queen of England had on this occasion shewn a tender care of her; and notwithstanding the punishment justly to be inflicted on her, for her manifold trespasses, was determined to use every expedient for saving her soul from that destruction, with which it was so nearly threatened: That she was now standing upon the brink of eternity, and had no other means of escaping endless perdition, than by repenting her former wickedness, by justifying the sentence pronounced against her, by acknowledging the queen's favours, and by exerting a true and lively faith in Christ Jesus: That the scriptures were the only rule of doctrine, the merits of Christ the only means of salvation; and if she trusted in the inventions or devices of men, she must expect in an instant to fall into utter darkness, into a place where shall be weeping, howling, and gnashing of teeth: That the hand of death was upon her, the ax was laid to the root of the tree, the throne of the great judge of heaven was erected, the book of her life was spread wide, and the particular sentence and judgment was ready to be pronounced upon her: And that it was now, during this important moment, in her choice, either to rise to the resurrection of life, and hear that joyful salutation, *Come, ye blessed of my Father,* or to share the resurrection of condemnation, replete with sorrow and anguish; and to suffer that dreadful denunciation, *Go, ye cursed, into everlasting fire.*[y]

During this discourse Mary could not sometimes forbear betraying her impatience, by interrupting the preacher; and the dean, finding that he had profited nothing by his lecture, at last bade her change her opinion, repent her of her former wickedness, and settle her faith upon this ground, that only in Christ Jesus could she hope to be saved. She answered, again and again, with great earnestness: "Trouble not yourself any more about the matter: For I was born in this religion; I have lived in this religion; and in this religion I am resolved to die." Even the two earls perceived, that it was fruitless to harass her any farther with theological disputes; and they ordered the dean to desist from his unseasonable exhortations, and to pray for her conversion. During the dean's prayer, she employed herself in private devotion from the office of the Virgin; and after he had finished, she pronounced aloud some petitions in English, for the afflicted church, for an end of her own troubles, for her son, and for queen Elizabeth; and prayed God, that that princess might long prosper, and be employed in his service. The earl of Kent, observing, that, in her devotions, she made frequent use of the crucifix, could not forbear reproving her for her attachment to that popish trumpery, as he termed it; and he exhorted her to have Christ in her heart, not in her hand.[z] She replied with presence of mind, that it was difficult to hold such an object in her hand, without feeling her heart touched with some compunction.[a]

She now began, with the aid of her two women, to disrobe

[y] MS. p. 8, 9, 10, 11. Strype, vol. iii. p. 385.   [z] MS. p. 15. Jebb, vol. ii. p. 307, 491, 637.   [a] Jebb, ibid.

CHAPTER XLII

herself; and the executioner also lent his hand, to assist them. She smiled, and said, That she was not accustomed to undress herself before so large a company, nor to be served by such valets. Her servants, seeing her in this condition, ready to lay her head upon the block, burst into tears and lamentations: She turned about to them; put her finger upon her lips, as a sign of imposing silence upon them;[b] and having given them her blessing, desired them to pray for her. One of her maids, whom she had appointed for that purpose, covered her eyes with a handkerchief; she laid herself down, without any sign of fear or trepidation; and her head was severed from her body at two strokes by the executioner. He instantly held it up to the spectators, streaming with blood and agitated with the convulsions of death: The dean of Peterborow alone exclaimed, "So perish all queen Elizabeth's enemies:" The earl of Kent alone replied "Amen:" The attention of all the other spectators was fixed on the melancholy scene before them; and zeal and flattery alike gave place to present pity and admiration of the expiring princess.

Thus perished, in the forty-fifth year of her age, and nineteenth of her captivity in England, Mary queen of Scots; a woman of great accomplishments both of body and mind, natural as well as acquired; but unfortunate in her life, and during one period, very unhappy in her conduct. The beauties of her person and graces of her air combined to make her the most amiable of women; and the charms of her address and conversation aided the impression, which her lovely figure made on the hearts of all beholders. Ambitious and active in her temper, yet inclined to chearfulness and society; of a lofty spirit, constant and even vehement in her purpose, yet polite, and gentle, and affable in her demeanour; she seemed to partake only so much of the male virtues as to render her estimable, without relinquishing those soft graces, which compose the proper ornament of her sex. In order to form a just idea of her character, we must set aside one part of her conduct, while she abandoned herself to the guidance of a profligate man; and must consider these faults, whether we admit them to be imprudences or crimes, as the result of an inexplicable, though not uncommon, inconstancy in the human mind, of the

Mary's character.

[b] Jebb, p. 307, 492.

frailty of our nature, of the violence of passion, and of the influence, which situations, and sometimes momentary incidents, have on persons, whose principles are not thoroughly confirmed by experience and reflection. Enraged by the ungrateful conduct of her husband, seduced by the treacherous counsels of one in whom she reposed confidence, transported by the violence of her own temper, which never lay sufficiently under the guidance of discretion; she was betrayed into actions, which may, with some difficulty, be accounted for, but which admit of no apology, nor even of alleviation. An enumeration of her qualities might carry the appearance of a panegyric; an account of her conduct must, in some parts, wear the aspect of severe satire and invective.

Her numerous misfortunes, the solitude of her long and tedious captivity, and the persecutions, to which she had been exposed on account of her religion, had wrought her up to a degree of bigotry during her later years; and such were the prevalent spirit and principles of the age, that it is the less wonder, if her zeal, her resentment, and her interest uniting, induced her to give consent to a design, which conspirators, actuated only by the first of these motives, had formed against the life of Elizabeth.

The queen's affected sorrow.

When the queen was informed of Mary's execution, she affected the utmost surprize and indignation. Her countenance changed; her speech faltered and failed her; for a long time, her sorrow was so deep that she could not express it, but stood fixed, like a statue, in silence and mute astonishment. After her grief was able to find vent, it burst out in loud wailings and lamentations; she put herself in deep mourning for this deplorable event; and she was seen perpetually bathed in tears, and surrounded only by her maids and women. None of her ministers or counsellors dared to approach her; or if any had such temerity, she chased them from her, with the most violent expressions of rage and resentment: They had all of them been guilty of an unpardonable crime, in putting to death her dear sister and kinswoman, contrary to her fixed purpose,[c] of which they were sufficiently apprized and acquainted.

No sooner was her sorrow so much abated as to leave room for reflection, than she wrote a letter of apology to the king of Scots,

[c] Camden, p. 536. Strype, vol. iii. Appendix, p. 145. Jebb, vol. ii. p. 608.

CHAPTER XLII

and sent it by Sir Robert Cary, son of lord Hunsdon. She there told him, that she wished he knew, but not felt, the unutterable grief which she experienced, on account of that lamentable accident, which, without her knowledge, much less concurrence, had happened in England: That as her pen trembled, when she attempted to write it, she found herself obliged to commit the relation of it to the messenger, her kinsman; who would likewise inform his majesty of every circumstance, attending this dismal and unlooked for misfortune: That she appealed to the supreme Judge of heaven and earth for her innocence; and was also so happy, amidst her other afflictions, as to find, that many persons in her court could bear witness to her veracity in this protestation: That she abhorred dissimulation; deemed nothing more worthy of a prince than a sincere and open conduct; and could never surely be esteemed so base and poor-spirited, as that, if she had really given orders for this fatal execution, she could, on any consideration, be induced to deny them: That, though sensible of the justice of the sentence pronounced against the unhappy prisoner, she determined from clemency never to carry it into execution; and could not but resent the temerity of those, who on this occasion had disappointed her intention: And that as no one loved him more dearly than herself, or bore a more anxious concern for his welfare; she hoped, that he would consider every one as his enemy, who endeavoured, on account of the present incident, to excite any animosity between them.[d]

In order the better to appease James, she committed Davison to prison, and ordered him to be tried in the Star-Chamber for his misdemeanour. The secretary was confounded; and being sensible of the danger, which must attend his entering into a contest with the queen, he expressed penitence for his error, and submitted very patiently to be railed at by those very counsellors, whose persuasion had induced him to incur the guilt, and who had promised to countenance and protect him. He was condemned to imprisonment during the queen's pleasure, and to pay a fine of ten thousand pounds. He remained a long time in custody; and the fine, though it reduced him to beggary, was rigorously levied upon him. All the favour, which he could obtain from the queen, was

[d] Camden, p. 536. Spotswood, p. 358.

sending him small supplies from time to time, to keep him from perishing in necessity.[e] He privately wrote an apology to his friend Walsingham, which contains many curious particulars. The French and Scotch ambassadors, he said, had been remonstrating with the queen in Mary's behalf; and immediately after their departure, she commanded him, of her own accord, to deliver her the warrant for the execution of that princess. She signed it readily, and ordered it to be sealed with the great seal of England. She appeared in such good humour on the occasion, that she said to him in a jocular manner, "Go tell all this to Walsingham, who is now sick: Though I fear he will die of sorrow, when he hears of it." She added, that, though she had so long delayed the execution, lest she should seem to be actuated by malice or cruelty, she was all along sensible of the necessity of it. In the same conversation, she blamed Drury and Paulet, that they had not before eased her of this trouble; and she expressed her desire, that Walsingham would bring them to compliance in that particular. She was so bent on this purpose, that, some time after, she asked Davison, Whether any letter had come from Paulet with regard to the service expected of him? Davison showed her Paulet's letter; in which that gentleman positively refused to act any thing inconsistent with the principles of honour and justice. The queen fell into a passion; and accused Paulet, as well as Drury, of perjury; because, having taken the oath of association, in which they had bound themselves to avenge her wrongs, they had yet refused to lend their hand on this occasion. "But others," she said, "will be found less scrupulous." Davison adds, that nothing but the consent and exhortations of the whole council could have engaged him to send off the warrant: He was well aware of his danger; and remembered, that the queen, after having ordered the execution of the duke of Norfolk, had endeavoured, in a like manner, to throw the whole blame and odium of that action upon lord Burleigh.[f]

Elizabeth's dissimulation was so gross, that it could deceive no body, who was not previously resolved to be blinded; but as James's concern for his mother was certainly more sincere and cordial, he discovered the highest resentment, and refused to admit Cary into

[e] Camden, p. 538.   [f] Camden, p. 538. Strype, vol. iii. p. 375, 376. MS. in the Advocates' Library, A. 3. 28. p. 17. from the Cott. Lib. Calig. c. 9. Biogr. Brit. p. 1625, 1627.

his presence. He recalled his ambassadors from England; and seemed to breathe nothing but war and vengeance. The States of Scotland, being assembled, took part in his anger; and professed, that they were ready to spend their lives and fortunes in revenge of his mother's death, and in defence of his title to the crown of England. Many of his nobility instigated him to take arms: Lord Sinclair, when the courtiers appeared in deep mourning, presented himself to the king arrayed in complete armour, and said, that this was the proper mourning for the queen. The catholics took the opportunity of exhorting James to make an alliance with the king of Spain, to lay immediate claim to the crown of England, and to prevent the ruin, which, from his mother's example, he might conclude, would certainly, if Elizabeth's power prevailed, overwhelm his person and his kingdom. The queen was sensible of the danger attending these counsels; and after allowing James some decent interval to vent his grief and anger, she employed her emissaries to pacify him, and to set before him every motive of hope or fear, which might induce him to live in amity with her.

Walsingham wrote to lord Thirlstone, James's secretary, a judicious letter to the same purpose. He said, that he was much surprized to hear of the violent resolutions taken in Scotland, and of the passion discovered by a prince of so much judgment and temper as James: That a war, founded merely on the principle of revenge, and that too on account of an act of justice which necessity had extorted, would for ever be exposed to censure, and could not be excused by any principles of equity or reason: That if these views were deemed less momentous among princes, policy and interest ought certainly to be attended to; and these motives did still more evidently oppose all thoughts of a rupture with Elizabeth, and all revival of exploded claims to the English throne: That the inequality between the two kingdoms deprived James of any hopes of success, if he trusted merely to the force of his own state, and had no recourse to foreign powers for assistance: That the objections, attending the introduction of succours from a more potent monarch, appeared so evident from all the transactions of history, that they could not escape a person of the King's extensive knowledge; but there were, in the present case, several peculiar circumstances, which ought for ever to deter him from having recourse to so dangerous an expedient: That the French monarch,

4th March.

the ancient ally of Scotland, might willingly use the assistance of
that kingdom against England; but would be displeased to see the
union of these two kingdoms in the person of James; a union,
which would ever after exclude him from practising that policy,
formerly so useful to the French, and so pernicious to the Scottish,
nation: That Henry besides, infested with faction and domestic
war, was not in a condition of supporting distant allies; much less
would he expose himself to any hazard or expence, in order to
aggrandize a near kinsman of the house of Guise, the most determined enemies of his repose and authority: That the extensive
power and exorbitant ambition of the Spanish monarch rendered
him a still more dangerous ally to Scotland; and as he evidently
aspired to an universal monarchy in the west, and had in particular
advanced some claims to England, as if he were descended from
the house of Lancaster, he was at the same time the common
enemy of all princes, who wished to maintain their independence;
and the immediate rival and competitor of the king of Scots: That
the queen, by her own naval power, and her alliance with the
Hollanders, would probably intercept all succours which might be
sent to James from abroad, and be enabled to decide the controversy in this island with the superior forces of her own kingdom,
opposed to those of Scotland: That if the king revived his mother's
pretensions to the crown of England, he must also embrace her
religion, by which alone they could be justified; and must thereby
undergo the infamy of abandoning those principles, in which he
had been strictly educated, and to which he had hitherto religiously adhered: That as he would, by such an apostacy, totally
alienate all the protestants in Scotland and England, he could
never gain the confidence of the catholics, who would still entertain reasonable doubts of his sincerity: That by advancing a
present claim to the crown, he forfeited the certain prospect of his
succession; and revived that national animosity, which the late
peace and alliance between the kingdoms had happily extinguished: That the whole gentry and nobility of England had
openly declared themselves for the execution of the queen of
Scots; and if James showed such violent resentment against that act
of justice, they would be obliged, for their own security, to prevent
for ever so implacable a prince from ruling over them: And that,
however some persons might represent his honour as engaged to

CHAPTER XLII

seek vengeance for the present affront and injury, the true honour of a prince consisted in wisdom and moderation and justice, not in following the dictates of blind passion, or in pursuing revenge at the expence of every motive and every interest.[g] These considerations, joined to the peaceable, unambitious temper of the young prince, prevailed over his resentment; and he fell gradually into a good correspondence with the court of England. It is probable, that the queen's chief object in her dissimulation with regard to the execution of Mary, was, that she might thereby afford James a decent pretence for renewing his amity with her, on which their mutual interests so much depended.

While Elizabeth ensured tranquillity from the attempts of her nearest neighbour, she was not negligent of more distant dangers. Hearing that Philip, though he seemed to dissemble the daily insults and injuries, which he received from the English, was secretly preparing a great navy to attack her; she sent Sir Francis Drake with a fleet to intercept his supplies, to pillage his coast, and to destroy his shipping. Drake carried out four capital ships of the queen's, and twenty-six, great and small, with which the London merchants, in hopes of sharing in the plunder, had supplied him. Having learned from two Dutch ships, which he met with in his passage, that a Spanish fleet, richly laden, was lying at Cadiz, ready *Drake* to set sail for Lisbon, the rendezvous of the intended Armada; he *destroys* bent his course to the former harbour, and boldly, as well as fortu- *the fleet* nately, made an attack on the enemy. He obliged six gallies, which *at Cadiz.* made head against him, to take shelter under the forts; he burned about a hundred vessels, laden with ammunition and naval stores; and he destroyed a great ship of the marquess of Santa Croce. Thence, he set sail for Cape St. Vincent, and took by assault the castle situated on that promontory, with three other fortresses. He next insulted Lisbon; and finding, that the merchants, who had engaged entirely in expectation of profit, were discontented at these military enterprizes, he set sail for the Terceras, with an intention of lying in wait for a rich Carrack, which was expected in those parts. He was so fortunate as to meet with his prize; and by this short expedition, in which the public bore so small a share, the adventurers were encouraged to attempt farther enterprizes, the

[g] Strype, vol. iii. p. 377. Spotswood.

English seamen learned to despise the great unwieldy ships of the enemy, the naval preparations of Spain were destroyed, the intended expedition against England was retarded a twelvemonth, and the queen thereby had leisure to take more secure measures against that formidable invasion.[h]

This year Thomas Cavendish, a gentleman of Devonshire, who had dissipated a good estate by living at court, being resolved to repair his fortune at the expence of the Spaniards, fitted out three ships at Plymouth, one of a hundred and twenty tons, another of sixty, and a third of forty; and with these small vessels he ventured into the South Sea, and committed great depredations on the Spaniards. He took nineteen vessels, some of which were richly laden; and returning by the Cape of Good Hope, he came to London, and entered the river in a kind of triumph. His mariners and soldiers were cloathed in silk, his sails were of damask, his top-sail cloth of gold; and his prizes were esteemed the richest that ever had been brought into England.[i]

The land enterprizes of the English were not, during this campaign, so advantageous or honourable to the nation. The important place of Deventer was intrusted by Leicester to William Stanley, with a garrison of twelve hundred English; and this gentleman, being a catholic, was alarmed at the discovery of Babington's conspiracy, and became apprehensive, lest every one of his religion should thenceforth be treated with distrust in England. He entered into a correspondence with the Spaniards, betrayed the city to them for a sum of money, and engaged the whole garrison to desert with him to the Spanish service. Roland York, who commanded a fort near Zutphen, imitated his example; and the Hollanders, formerly disgusted with Leicester, and suspicious of the English, broke out into loud complaints against the improvidence, if not the treachery, of his administration. Soon after, he himself arrived in the Low Countries; but his conduct was no-wise calculated to give them satisfaction, or to remove the suspicions, which they had entertained against him. The prince of Parma having besieged Sluys, Leicester attempted to relieve the place, first by sea, then by land; but failed in both enterprizes; and

---

[h] Camden, p. 540. Sir William Monson's Naval Tracts in Churchill's Voyages, vol. iii. p. 156.   [i] Birch's Memoirs, vol. i. p. 57.

CHAPTER XLII

as he ascribed his bad success, to the ill behaviour of the Hollanders, they were equally free in reflections upon his conduct. The breach between them became wider every day: They slighted his authority, opposed his measures, and neglected his counsels; while he endeavoured, by an imperious behaviour, and by violence, to recover that influence, which he had lost by his imprudent and ill-concerted measures. He was even suspected by the Dutch of a design to usurp upon their liberties; and the jealousy, entertained against him, began to extend towards the queen herself. That princess had made some advances towards a peace with Spain: A congress had been opened at Bourbourg, a village near Graveline: And though the two courts, especially that of Spain, had no other intention than to amuse each of them its enemy by negociation, and mutually relax the preparations for defence or attack, the Dutch, who were determined, on no terms, to return under the Spanish yoke, became apprehensive lest their liberty should be sacrificed to the political interests of England.[k] But the queen, who knew the importance of her alliance with the States during the present conjuncture, was resolved to give them entire satisfaction by recalling Leicester, and commanding him to resign his government. Maurice, son of the late prince of Orange, a youth of twenty years of age, was elected by the States governor in his place; and Peregrine lord Willoughby was appointed by the queen commander of the English forces. The measures of these two generals were much embarrassed by the malignity of Leicester, who had left a faction behind him, and who still attempted, by means of his emissaries, to disturb all the operations of the States. As soon as Elizabeth received intelligence of these disorders, she took care to redress them; and she obliged all the partizans of England to fall into unanimity with prince Maurice.[l] But though her good sense so far prevailed over her partiality to Leicester, she never could be made fully sensible of his vices and incapacity: The submissions, which he made her, restored him to her wonted favour; and Lord Buckhurst, who had accused him of misconduct in Holland, lost her confidence, for some time, and was even committed to custody.

[k] Bentivoglio, part ii. lib. 4. Strype, vol. iv. No. 246.   [l] Rymer, tom. xv. p. 66.

Sir Christopher Hatton was another favourite, who at this time, received some marks of her partiality. Though he had never followed the profession of the law, he was made chancellor in the place of Bromley, deceased; but notwithstanding all the expectations and perhaps wishes of the lawyers, he behaved in a manner not unworthy of that high station: His good natural capacity supplied the place of experience and study; and his decisions were not found deficient either in point of equity or judgment. His enemies had contributed to this promotion, in hopes that his absence from court, while he attended the business of chancery, would gradually estrange the queen from him, and give them an opportunity of undermining him in her favour.

1588.

These little intrigues and cabals of the court were silenced by the account which came from all quarters, of the vast preparations made by the Spaniards for the invasion of England, and for the entire conquest of that kingdom. Philip, though he had not yet declared war, on account of the hostilities, which Elizabeth every where committed upon him, had long harboured a secret and violent desire of revenge against her. His ambition also and the hopes of extending his empire were much encouraged by the present prosperous state of his affairs; by the conquest of Portugal, the acquisition of the East-Indian commerce and settlements, and the yearly importation of vast treasures from America. The point, on which he rested his highest glory, the perpetual object of his policy, was to support orthodoxy and exterminate heresy; and as the power and credit of Elizabeth were the chief bulwark of the protestants, he hoped, if he could subdue that princess, to acquire the eternal renown, of re-uniting the whole christian world in the catholic communion. Above all, his indignation against his revolted subjects in the Netherlands instigated him to attack the English, who had encouraged that insurrection, and who, by their vicinity, were so well enabled to support the Hollanders, that he could never hope to reduce these rebels, while the power of that kingdom remained entire and unbroken. To subdue England seemed a necessary preparative to the re-establishment of his authority in the Netherlands; and notwithstanding appearances, the former was in itself, as a more important, so a more easy undertaking than the latter. That kingdom lay nearer Spain than the Low Countries, and was more exposed to invasions from that quar-

Philip projects the invasion of England.

CHAPTER XLII

ter; after an enemy had once obtained entrance, the difficulty seemed to be over, as it was neither fortified by art or nature; a long peace had deprived it of all military discipline and experience; and the catholics, in which it still abounded, would be ready, it was hoped, to join any invader, who should free them from those persecutions, under which they laboured, and should revenge the death of the queen of Scots, on whom they had fixed all their affections. The fate of England must be decided in one battle at sea, and another at land; and what comparison between the English and Spaniards, either in point of naval force, or in the numbers, reputation, and veteran bravery of their armies? Besides the acquisition of so great a kingdom, success against England ensured the immediate subjection of the Hollanders, who, attacked on every hand, and deprived of all support, must yield their stubborn necks to that yoke, which they had so long resisted. Happily this conquest, as it was of the utmost importance to the grandeur of Spain, would not at present be opposed by the jealousy of other powers, naturally so much interested to prevent the success of the enterprize. A truce was lately concluded with the Turks; the Empire was in the hands of a friend and near ally; and France, the perpetual rival of Spain, was so torn with intestine commotions, that she had no leisure to pay attention to her foreign interests. This favourable opportunity, therefore, which might never again present itself, must be seized; and one bold effort made for acquiring that ascendant in Europe, to which the present greatness and prosperity of the Spaniards seemed so fully to entitle them.[m]

These hopes and motives engaged Philip, notwithstanding his cautious temper, to undertake this hazardous enterprize; and though the prince, now created by the pope, duke of Parma, when consulted, opposed the attempt, at least represented the necessity of previously getting possession of some sea-port town in the Netherlands, which might afford a retreat to the Spanish navy,[n] it was determined by the catholic monarch to proceed immediately to the execution of his ambitious project. During some time he had been secretly making preparations; but as soon as the resolution was fully taken, every part of his vast empire resounded with the noise of armaments, and all his ministers, generals, and admirals, were

[m] Camden. Strype, vol. iii. p. 512.   [n] Bentivoglio, part 2. lib. 4.

The Invincible Armada.

employed in forwarding the design. The marquess of Santa Croce, a sea-officer of great reputation and experience, was destined to command the fleet; and by his counsels were the naval equipments conducted. In all the ports of Sicily, Naples, Spain, and Portugal, artizans were employed in building vessels of uncommon size and force; naval stores were bought at a great expence; provisions amassed; armies levied and quartered in the maritime towns of Spain; and plans laid for fitting out such a fleet and embarkation as had never before had its equal in Europe. The military preparations in Flanders were no less formidable. Troops from all quarters were every moment assembling, to reinforce the duke of Parma. Capizuchi and Spinelli, conducted forces from Italy: The marquess of Borgaut, a prince of the house of Austria, levied troops in Germany: The Walloon and Burgundian regiments were completed or augmented: The Spanish infantry was supplied with recruits; and an army of thirty-four thousand men was assembled in the Netherlands, and kept in readiness to be transported into England. The duke of Parma employed all the carpenters whom he could procure, either in Flanders or in Lower Germany, and the coasts of the Baltic; and he built at Dunkirk, and Newport, but especially at Antwerp, a great number of boats and flat-bottomed vessels, for the transporting of his infantry and cavalry. The most renowned nobility and princes of Italy and Spain were ambitious of sharing in the honour of this great enterprize. Don Amadaeus of Savoy, Don John of Medicis, Vespasian Gonzaga, duke of Sabionetta, and the duke of Pastrana, hastened to join the army under the duke of Parma. About two thousand volunteers in Spain, many of them men of family, had enlisted in the service. No doubts were entertained, but such vast preparations, conducted by officers of such consummate skill, must finally be successful. And the Spaniards, ostentatious of their power, and elated with vain hopes, had already denominated their navy the *Invincible Armada*.

Preparations in England.

News of these extraordinary preparations soon reached the court of London; and notwithstanding the secrecy of the Spanish council, and their pretending to employ this force in the Indies, it was easily concluded, that they meant to make some effort against England. The queen had foreseen the invasion; and finding that she must now contend for her crown with the whole force of Spain, she made preparations for resistance; nor was she dismayed with that power, by which, all Europe apprehended, she must of necessity be overwhelmed. Her force indeed seemed very unequal to resist so potent an enemy. All the sailors in England amounted at that time to about fourteen thousand men.[o] The size of the English shipping was, in general, so small, that, except a few of the queen's ships of war, there were not four vessels belonging to the merchants which exceeded four hundred tons.[p] The royal navy consisted only of twenty-eight sail,[q] many of which were of small size; none of them exceeded the bulk of our largest frigates, and most of them deserved rather the name of pinnaces than of ships. The only advantage of the English fleet consisted in the dexterity and courage of the seamen, who, being accustomed to sail in tempestuous seas, and expose themselves to all dangers, as much exceeded in this particular the Spanish mariners, as their vessels were inferior in size and force to those of that nation.[r] All the commercial towns of England were required to furnish ships for reinforcing this small navy; and they discovered, on the present occasion, great alacrity in defending their liberty and religion against those imminent perils, with which they were menaced. The citizens of London, in order to shew their zeal in the common cause, instead of fifteen vessels, which they were commanded to equip, voluntarily fitted out double the number.[s] The gentry and nobility hired, and armed, and manned, forty-three ships at their own charge;[t] and all the loans of money, which the queen demanded, were frankly granted by the persons applied to. Lord Howard of Effingham, a man of courage and capacity, was admiral, and took on him the command of the navy: Drake, Hawkins, and Frobisher, the most renowned seamen in Europe, served under him. The principal fleet was stationed at Plymouth. A smaller squadron, consisting of forty vessels, English and Flemish, was commanded by lord Seymour, second son of protector Somerset; and lay off Dunkirk, in order to intercept the duke of Parma.

The land forces of England, compared to those of Spain, possessed contrary qualities to its naval power: They were more numerous than the enemy, but much inferior in discipline, reputation, and experience. An army of twenty thousand men was

---

[o] Monson, p. 256.   [p] Ibid. p. 268.   [q] Ibid. p. 157.   [r] Ibid. p. 321.
[s] Monson, p. 267.   [t] Lives of the Admirals, vol. i. p. 451.

disposed in different bodies along the south coast; and orders were given them, if they could not prevent the landing of the Spaniards, to retire backwards, to waste the country around, and to wait for reinforcement from the neighbouring counties, before they approached the enemy. A body of twenty-two thousand foot, and a thousand horse, under the command of the earl of Leicester, was stationed at Tilbury, in order to defend the capital. The principal army consisted of thirty-four thousand foot, and two thousand horse, and was commanded by lord Hunsdon. These forces were reserved for guarding the queen's person; and were appointed to march whithersoever the enemy should appear. The fate of England, if all the Spanish armies should be able to land, seemed to depend on the issue of a single battle; and men of reflection entertained the most dismal apprehensions, when they considered the force of fifty thousand veteran Spaniards, commanded by experienced officers, under the duke of Parma, the most consummate general of the age; and compared this formidable armament with the military power, which England, not enervated by peace, but long disused to war, could muster up against it.

The chief support of the kingdom seemed to consist in the vigour and prudence of the queen's conduct; who, undismayed by the present dangers, issued all her orders with tranquillity, animated her people to a steady resistance, and employed every resource, which either her domestic situation or her foreign alliances could afford her. She sent Sir Robert Sydney into Scotland; and exhorted the king to remain attached to her, and to consider the danger, which at present menaced his sovereignty no less than her own, from the ambition of the Spanish tyrant:[u] The ambassador found James well disposed to cultivate a union with England, and that prince even kept himself prepared to march with the force of his whole kingdom to the assistance of Elizabeth. Her authority with the king of Denmark, and the tie of their common religion, engaged this monarch, upon her application, to seize a squadron of ships, which Philip had bought or hired in the Danish harbours:[w] The Hanse Towns, though not at that time on good terms

[u] She made him some promises which she never fulfilled, to give him a dukedom in England, with suitable lands and revenue, to settle 5000 l. a-year on him, and pay him a guard, for the safety of his person. From a MS. of lord Royston's.   [w] Strype, vol. iii. p. 524.

CHAPTER XLII

with Elizabeth, were induced, by the same motives, to retard so long the equipment of some vessels in their ports, that they became useless to the purpose of invading England. All the protestants throughout Europe regarded this enterprize as the critical event, which was to decide for ever the fate of their religion; and though unable, by reason of their distance, to join their force to that of Elizabeth, they kept their eyes fixed on her conduct and fortune, and beheld with anxiety, mixed with admiration, the intrepid countenance, with which she encountered that dreadful tempest, which was every moment advancing towards her.

The queen also was sensible, that, next to the general popularity, which she enjoyed, and the confidence, which her subjects reposed in her prudent government, the firmest support of her throne consisted in the general zeal of the people for the protestant religion, and the strong prejudices which they had imbibed against popery. She took care, on the present occasion, to revive in the nation this attachment to their own sect, and this abhorrence of the opposite. The English were reminded of their former danger from the tyranny of Spain: All the barbarities, exercised by Mary against the protestants, were ascribed to the counsels of that bigotted and imperious nation: The bloody massacres in the Indies, the unrelenting executions in the Low Countries, the horrid cruelties and iniquities of the inquisition, were set before men's eyes: A list and description was published, and pictures dispersed, of the several instruments of torture, with which, it was pretended, the Spanish Armada was loaded: And every artifice, as well as reason, was employed, to animate the people to a vigorous defence of their religion, their laws, and their liberties.

But while the queen, in this critical emergence, rouzed the animosity of the nation against popery, she treated the partizans of that sect with moderation, and gave not way to an undistinguishing fury against them. Though she knew, that Sixtus Quintus, the present pope, famous for his capacity and his tyranny, had fulminated a new bull of excommunication against her, had deposed her, had absolved her subjects from their oaths of allegiance, had published a crusade against England, and had granted plenary indulgences to every one engaged in the present invasion; she would not believe, that all her catholic subjects could be so blinded, as to sacrifice to bigotry their duty to their sovereign, and the liberty and independence of their native country. She rejected all violent counsels, .by which she was urged to seek pretences for dispatching the leaders of that party: She would not even confine any considerable number of them: And the catholics, sensible of this good usage, generally expressed great zeal for the public service. Some gentlemen of that sect, conscious that they could not justly expect any trust or authority, entered themselves as volunteers in the fleet or army:[x] Some equipped ships at their own charge, and gave the command of them to protestants: Others were active in animating their tenants, and vassals, and neighbours, to the defence of their country: And every rank of men, burying for the present all party distinctions, seemed to prepare themselves, with order as well as vigour, to resist the violence of these invaders.

The more to excite the martial spirit of the nation, the queen appeared on horseback in the camp at Tilbury; and riding through the lines, discovered a chearful and animated countenance, exhorted the soldiers to remember their duty to their country and their religion, and professed her intention, though a woman, to lead them herself into the field against the enemy, and rather to perish in battle than survive the ruin and slavery of her people.[y] By this spirited behaviour she revived the tenderness and admiration of the soldiery: An attachment to her person became a kind of enthusiasm among them: And they asked one another, Whether it were possible, that Englishmen could abandon this glorious cause, could display less fortitude than appeared in the female sex, or could ever, by any dangers, be induced to relinquish the defence of their heroic princess?

The Spanish Armada was ready in the beginning of May; but the moment it was preparing to sail, the marquess of Santa Croce, the admiral, was seized with a fever, of which he soon after died. The vice-admiral, the duke of Paliano, by a strange concurrence of accidents, at the very same time, suffered the same fate; and the king appointed for admiral the duke of Medina Sidonia, a nobleman of great family, but unexperienced in action, and entirely unacquainted with sea affairs. Alcarede was appointed vice-admiral. This misfortune, besides the loss of so great an officer as

[x] Stowe, p. 747.   [y] See note [Y] at the end of the volume.

CHAPTER XLII

Santa Croce, retarded the sailing of the Armada, and gave the English more time for their preparations to oppose them. At last, the Spanish fleet, full of hopes and alacrity, set sail from Lisbon; but next day met with a violent tempest, which scattered the ships, *29th May.* sunk some of the smallest, and forced the rest to take shelter in the Groine, where they waited till they could be refitted. When news of this event was carried to England, the queen concluded, that the design of an invasion was disappointed for this summer; and being always ready to lay hold on every pretence for saving money, she made Walsingham write to the admiral, directing him to lay up some of the larger ships, and to discharge the seamen: But lord Effingham, who was not so sanguine in his hopes, used the freedom to disobey these orders; and he begged leave to retain all the ships in service; though it should be at his own expence.[z] He took advantage of a north wind, and sailed towards the coast of Spain, with an intention of attacking the enemy in their harbours; but the wind changing to the south, he became apprehensive, lest they might have set sail, and by passing him at sea, invade England, now exposed by the absence of the fleet. He returned, therefore, with the utmost expedition to Plymouth, and lay at anchor in that harbour.

Meanwhile, all the damages of the Armada were repaired; and the Spaniards with fresh hopes set out again to sea, in prosecution of their enterprize. The fleet consisted of a hundred and thirty vessels, of which near a hundred were galleons, and were of greater size than any ever before used in Europe. It carried on board nineteen thousand two hundred and ninety-five soldiers, eight thousand four hundred and fifty-six mariners, two thousand and eighty-eight galley-slaves, and two thousand six hundred and thirty great pieces of brass ordnance. It was victualled for six months; and was attended by twenty lesser ships, called caravals, and ten salves with six oars apiece.[a]

The plan formed by the king of Spain was, that the Armada should sail to the coast opposite to Dunkirk and Newport; and having chased away all English or Flemish vessels, which might obstruct the passage, (for it was never supposed they could make opposition) should join themselves with the duke of Parma, should

[z] Camden, p. 545. [a] Strype, vol. iii. Append. p. 221.

thence make sail to the Thames, and having landed the whole Spanish army, thus complete at one blow the entire conquest of England. In prosecution of this scheme, Philip gave orders to the duke of Medina, that, in passing along the channel, he should sail as near the coast of France as he could with safety; that he should by this policy avoid meeting with the English fleet; and keeping in view the main enterprize, should neglect all smaller successes, which might prove an obstacle, or even interpose a delay, to the acquisition of a kingdom.[b] After the Armada was under sail, they took a fisherman, who informed them, that the English admiral had been lately at sea, had heard of the tempest which scattered the Armada, had retired back into Plymouth, and no longer expecting an invasion this season, had laid up his ships, and discharged most of the seamen. From this false intelligence the duke of Medina conceived the great facility of attacking and destroying the English ships in harbour; and he was tempted, by the prospect of so decisive an advantage, to break his orders, and make sail directly for Plymouth: A resolution which proved the safety of England. The Lizard was the first land made by the Armada, about sun-set; and as the Spaniards took it for the Ram-head near Plymouth, they bore out to sea with an intention of returning next day, and attacking the English navy. They were descried by Fleming, a Scottish pirate, who was roving in those seas, and who immediately set sail, to inform the English admiral of their approach:[c] Another fortunate event, which contributed extremely to the safety of the fleet. Effingham had just time to get out of port, when he saw the Spanish Armada coming full sail towards him, disposed in the form of a crescent, and stretching the distance of seven miles from the extremity of one division to that of the other.

19th July. The Armada arrives in the Channel.

The writers of that age raise their stile by a pompous description of this spectacle; the most magnificent that had ever appeared upon the ocean, infusing equal terror and admiration into the minds of all beholders. The lofty masts, the swelling sails, and the towering prows of the Spanish galleons, seem impossible to be justly painted, but by assuming the colours of poetry; and an eloquent historian of Italy, in imitation of Camden, has asserted, that the Armada, though the ships bore every sail, yet advanced

[b] Monson, p. 157.   [c] Monson, p. 158.

CHAPTER XLII

with a slow motion; as if the ocean groaned with supporting, and the winds were tired with impelling, so enormous a weight.[d] The truth, however, is, that the largest of the Spanish vessels would scarcely pass for third rates in the present navy of England; yet were they so ill framed, or so ill governed, that they were quite unwieldy, and could not sail upon a wind, nor tack on occasion, nor be managed in stormy weather by the seamen. Neither the mechanics of ship-building, nor the experience of mariners, had attained so great perfection as could serve for the security and government of such bulky vessels; and the English, who had already had experience how unserviceable they commonly were, beheld without dismay their tremendous appearance.

Effingham gave orders not to come to close fight with the Spaniards; where the size of the ships, he suspected, and the numbers of the soldiers, would be a disadvantage to the English; but to cannonade them at a distance, and to wait the opportunity, which winds, currents, or various accidents must afford him, of intercepting some scattered vessels of the enemy. Nor was it long before the event answered expectation. A great ship of Biscay, on board of which was a considerable part of the Spanish money, took fire by accident; and while all hands were employed in extinguishing the flames, she fell behind the rest of the Armada: The great galleon of Andaluzia was detained by the springing of her mast: And both these vessels were taken, after some resistance, by Sir Francis Drake. As the Armada advanced up the channel, the English hung upon its rear, and still infested it with skirmishes. Each trial abated the confidence of the Spaniards, and added courage to the English; and the latter soon found, that even in close fight the size of the Spanish ships was no advantage to them. Their bulk exposed them the more to the fire of the enemy; while their cannon, placed too high, shot over the heads of the English. The alarm having now reached the coast of England, the nobility and gentry hastened out with their vessels from every harbour, and reinforced the admiral. The earls of Oxford, Northumberland, and Cumberland, Sir Thomas Cecil, Sir Robert Cecil, Sir Walter Raleigh, Sir Thomas Vavasor, Sir Thomas Gerrard, Sir Charles Blount, with many others, distinguished themselves by this gener-

---

[d] Bentivoglio, part ii. lib. 4.

ous and disinterested service of their country. The English fleet, after the conjunction of those ships, amounted to a hundred and forty sail.

The Armada had now reached Calais, and cast anchor before that place; in expectation, that the duke of Parma, who had gotten intelligence of their approach, would put to sea, and join his forces to them. The English admiral practised here a successful stratagem upon the Spaniards. He took eight of his smaller ships, and filling them with all combustible materials, sent them, one after another, into the midst of the enemy. The Spaniards fancied, that they were fireships of the same contrivance with a famous vessel, which had lately done so much execution in the Schelde near Antwerp; and they immediately cut their cables, and took to flight with the greatest disorder and precipitation. The English fell upon them next morning, while in confusion; and besides doing great damage to other ships, they took or destroyed about twelve of the enemy.

By this time, it was become apparent, that the intention, for which these preparations were made by the Spaniards, was entirely frustrated. The vessels, provided by the duke of Parma, were made for transporting soldiers, not for fighting; and that general, when urged to leave the harbour, positively refused to expose his flourishing army to such apparent hazard; while the English, not only were able to keep the sea, but seemed even to triumph over their enemy. The Spanish admiral found, in many rencounters, that, while he lost so considerable a part of his own navy, he had destroyed only one small vessel of the English; and he foresaw, that by continuing so unequal a combat, he must draw inevitable destruction on all the remainder. He prepared therefore to return homewards; but as the wind was contrary to his passage through the channel, he resolved to sail northwards, and making the tour of the island reach the Spanish harbours by the ocean. The English fleet followed him during some time; and had not their ammunition fallen short, by the negligence of the offices in supplying them, they had obliged the whole Armada to surrender at discretion. The duke of Medina had once taken that resolution; but was diverted from it by the advice of his confessor. This conclusion of the enterprize would have been more glorious to the English; *Defeated.* but the event proved almost equally fatal to the Spaniards. A violent tempest overtook the Armada after it passed the Orkneys:

CHAPTER XLII

The ships had already lost their anchors, and were obliged to keep to sea: The mariners, unaccustomed to such hardships, and not able to govern such unwieldly vessels, yielded to the fury of the storm, and allowed their ships to drive either on the western isles of Scotland, or on the coast of Ireland, where they were miserably wrecked. Not a half of the navy returned to Spain; and the seamen, as well as soldiers, who remained, were so overcome with hardships and fatigue, and so dispirited by their discomfiture, that they filled all Spain with accounts of the desperate valour of the English, and of the tempestuous violence of that ocean which surrounds them.

Such was the miserable and dishonourable conclusion of an enterprize which had been preparing for three years, which had exhausted the revenue and force of Spain, and which had long filled all Europe with anxiety or expectation. Philip, who was a slave to his ambition, but had an entire command over his countenance, no sooner heard of the mortifying event, which blasted all his hopes, than he fell on his knees, and rendering thanks for that gracious dispensation of Providence, expressed his joy, that the calamity was not greater. The Spanish priests, who had so often blest this holy crusade, and foretold its infallible success, were somewhat at a loss to account for the victory gained over the catholic monarch by excommunicated heretics and an execrable usurper: But they at last discovered, that all the calamities of the Spaniards had proceeded from their allowing the infidel Moors to live among them.[e]

Soon after the defeat and dispersion of the Spanish Armada, the queen summoned a new parliament; and received from them a supply of two subsidies and four fifteenths payable in four years. This is the first instance that subsidies were doubled in one supply; and so unusual a concession was probably obtained from the joy of the present success, and from the general sense of the queen's necessities. Some members objected to this heavy charge, on account of the great burthen of loans, which had lately been imposed upon the nation.[f]

Elizabeth foresaw, that this house of commons, like all the fore-

1589.
4th Feb.

A parliament.

[e] See note [Z] at the end of the volume. [f] See note [AA] at the end of the volume.

going, would be governed by the puritans; and therefore, to obviate their enterprizes, she renewed, at the beginning of the session,
her usual injunction, that the parliament should not, on any account, presume to treat of matters ecclesiastical. Notwithstanding
this strict inhibition, the zeal of one Damport moved him to
present a bill to the commons for remedying spiritual grievances,
and for restraining the tyranny of the ecclesiastical commission,
which were certainly great: But when Mr. Secretary Woley reminded the house of her majesty's commands, no one durst second
the motion; the bill was not so much as read; and the speaker
returned it to Damport, without taking the least notice of it.[g] Some
members of the house, notwithstanding the general submission,
were even committed to custody on account of this attempt.[h]

The imperious conduct of Elizabeth appeared still more clearly
in another parliamentary transaction. The right of purveyance was
an ancient prerogative, by which the officers of the crown could at
pleasure take provisions for the household from all the neighbouring counties, and could make use of the carts and carriages of
the farmers; and the price of these commodities and services was
fixed and stated. The payment of the money was often distant and
uncertain; and the rates, being fixed before the discovery of the
West-Indies, were much inferior to the present market price; so
that purveyance, besides the slavery of it, was always regarded as
a great burthen, and being arbitrary and casual, was liable to great
abuses: We may fairly presume, that the hungry courtiers of Elizabeth, supported by her unlimited power, would be sure to render
this prerogative very oppressive to the people; and the commons
had, last session, found it necessary to pass a bill for regulating
these exactions: But the bill was lost in the house of peers.[i] The
continuance of the abuses begat a new attempt for redress; and the
same bill was now revived again, and sent up to the house of peers,
together with a bill for some new regulations in the court of exchequer. Soon after the commons received a message from the
upper house, desiring them to appoint a committee for a conference. At this conference, the peers informed them, that the queen,
by a message, delivered by lord Burleigh, had expressed her dis-

[g] D'Ewes, p. 438.   [h] Strype's Life of Whitgift, p. 280. Neal, vol. i. p. 500.
[i] D'Ewes, p. 434.

CHAPTER XLII

pleasure, that the commons should presume to touch on her prerogative. If there were any abuses, she said, either in imposing
purveyance, or in the practice of the court of exchequer, her majesty was both able and willing to provide due reformation; but
would not permit the parliament to intermeddle in these matters.[k]
The commons alarmed at this intelligence, appointed another
committee to attend the queen, and endeavour to satisfy her of
their humble and dutiful intentions. Elizabeth gave a gracious
reception to the committee: She expressed her great *inestimable
loving care* towards her loving subjects; which, she said, was greater
than of her own self, or even than any of them could have of
themselves. She told them, that she had already given orders for an
enquiry into the abuses attending purveyance, but the dangers of
the Spanish invasion had retarded the progress of the design; that
she had as much skill, will, and power to rule her household as any
subjects whatsoever to govern theirs, and needed as little the assistance of her neighbours; that the exchequer was her chamber,
consequently more near to her than even her household, and
therefore the less proper for them to intermeddle with; and that
she would of herself, with advice of her council and the judges,
redress every grievance in these matters, but would not permit the
commons, by laws moved without her privity, to bereave her of the
honour attending these regulations.[l] The issue of this matter was
the same that attended all contests between Elizabeth and her
parliament.[m] She seems even to have been more imperious, in this
particular, than her predecessors; at least, her more remote ones:
For they often permitted the abuses of purveyance[n] to be re-
dressed by law.[o] Edward III., a very arbitrary prince, allowed ten
several statutes to be enacted for that purpose.

In so great awe did the commons stand of every courtier, as well
as of the crown, that they durst use no freedom of speech, which,
they thought, would give the least offence to any of them. Sir
Edward Hobby shewed in the house his extreme grief, that, by
some great personage, not a member of the house, he had been
sharply rebuked for speeches delivered in parliament: He craved
the favour of the house, and desired that some of the members

---

[k] D'Ewes, p. 440.   [l] Ibid. p. 444.   [m] *Si rixa est, ubi tu pulsas, ego vapulo
tantum.* Juven.   [n] See note [BB] at the end of the volume.   [o] See the
statutes under this head of purveyance.

might inform that great personage of his true meaning and intention in these speeches.[p] The commons, to obviate these inconveniencies, passed a vote, that no one should reveal the secrets of the house.[q]

The discomfiture of the Armada had begotten in the nation a kind of enthusiastic passion for enterprizes against Spain; and nothing seemed now impossible to be atchieved by the valour and fortune of the English. Don Antonio, prior of Crato, a natural son of the royal family of Portugal, trusting to the aversion of his countrymen against the Castilians, had advanced a claim to the crown; and flying first to France, thence to England, had been encouraged both by Henry and Elizabeth in his pretensions. A

Expedition against Portugal.

design was formed by the people, not the court, of England to conquer the kingdom of Don Antonio: Sir Francis Drake and Sir John Norris were the leaders in this romantic enterprize: Near twenty thousand volunteers[r] enlisted themselves in the service: And ships were hired, as well as arms provided, at the charge of the adventurers. The queen's frugality kept her from contributing more than sixty thousand pounds to the expence; and she only allowed six of her ships of war to attend the expedition.[s] There was more spirit and bravery, than foresight or prudence, in the conduct of this enterprize. The small stock of the adventurers did not enable them to buy either provisions or ammunition sufficient for such an undertaking: They even wanted vessels to stow the numerous volunteers, who crowded to them; and they were obliged to seize by force some ships of the Hanse Towns, which they met with at sea: An expedient, which set them somewhat more at ease in point of room for their men, but remedied not the deficiency of their provisions.[t] Had they sailed directly to Portugal, it is believed, that the good will of the people, joined to the defenceless state of the country, might have ensured them of success: But hearing, that great preparations were making at the Groine, for the in-

[p] D'Ewes, p. 432, 433.　[q] An act was passed this session, enforcing the former statute, which imposed twenty pounds a month on every one absent from public worship: But the penalty was restricted to two thirds of the income of the recusant. 29 Eliz. cap. 6.　[r] Birch's Memoirs of queen Elizabeth, vol. i. p. 61. Monson, p. 267, says, that there were only fourteen thousand soldiers and four thousand seamen in the whole on this expedition: But the account contained in Dr. Birch, is given by one of the most considerable of the adventurers.　[s] Monson, p. 267.　[t] Ibid. p. 159.

CHAPTER XLII

vasion of England, they were induced to go thither, and destroy this new armament of Spain. They broke into the harbour; burned some ships of war, particularly one commanded by Recalde, vice-admiral of Spain; they defeated an army of four or five thousand men, which was assembled to oppose them; they assaulted the Groine, and took the lower town, which they pillaged; and they would have taken the higher, though well fortified, had they not found their ammunition and provisions beginning to fail them. The young earl of Essex, a nobleman of promising hopes, who, fired with the thirst of military honour, had secretly, unknown to the queen, stolen from England, here joined the adventurers; and it was then agreed by common consent to make sail for Portugal, the main object of their enterprize.

The English landed at Paniche, a sea-port town, twelve leagues from Lisbon; and Norris led the army to that capital, while Drake undertook to sail up the river, and attack the city with united forces. By this time the court of Spain had gotten leisure to prepare against the invasion. Forces were thrown into Lisbon: The Portuguese were disarmed: All suspected persons were taken into custody: And thus, though the inhabitants bore great affection to Don Antonio, none of them durst declare in favour of the invaders. The English army, however, made themselves masters of the suburbs, which abounded with riches of all kinds; but as they desired to conciliate the affections of the Portuguese, and were more intent on honour than profit, they observed a strict discipline, and abstained from all plunder. Meanwhile, they found their ammunition and provisions much exhausted; they had not a single cannon to make a breach in the walls; the admiral had not been able to pass some fortresses, which guarded the river; there was no appearance of an insurrection in their favour; sickness, from fatigue, hunger, and intemperance in wine and fruits, had seized the army: So that it was found necessary to make all possible haste to reimbark. They were not pursued by the enemy; and finding, at the mouth of the river, sixty ships laden with naval stores, they seized them as lawful prize; though they belonged to the Hanse Towns, a neutral power. They sailed thence to Vigo, which they took and burned; and having ravaged the country around, they set sail and arrived in England. Above half of these gallant adventurers perished by sickness, famine, fatigue, and the sword;" and England reaped more honour than profit from this extraordinary enterprize. It is computed, that eleven hundred gentlemen embarked on board the fleet, and that only three hundred and fifty survived those multiplied disasters.""

When these ships were on their voyage homewards, they met with the earl of Cumberland, who was outward bound, with a fleet of seven sail, all equipped at his own charge, except one ship of war, which the queen had lent him. That nobleman supplied Sir Francis Drake with some provisions; a generosity which saved the lives of many of Drake's men, but for which the others afterwards suffered severely. Cumberland sailed towards the Terceras, and took several prizes from the enemy; but the richest, valued at a hundred thousand pounds, perished in her return, with all her cargo, near St. Michael's Mount in Cornwal. Many of these adventurers were killed in a rash attempt at the Terceras: A great mortality seized the rest: And it was with difficulty that the few hands, which remained, were able to steer the ships back into harbour."

Affairs of Scotland. Though the signal advantages, gained over the Spaniards, and the spirit thence infused into the English, gave Elizabeth great security during the rest of her reign, she could not forbear keeping an anxious eye on Scotland, whose situation rendered its revolutions always of importance to her. It might have been expected, that this high-spirited princess, who knew so well to brave danger, would not have retained that malignant jealousy towards her heir, with which, during the life-time of Mary, she had been so much agitated. James had indeed succeeded to all the claims of his mother; but he had not succeeded to the favour of the catholics, which could alone render these claims dangerous:" And as the queen was now well advanced in years, and enjoyed an uncontrouled authority over her subjects, it was not likely, that the king of Scots, who was of an indolent unambitious temper, would ever give her any disturbance in her possession of the throne. Yet all these circumstances could not remove her timorous suspicions: And so far from satisfying the nation by a settlement of the succession, or a declaration of James's title, she was as anxious to prevent every incident, which might anywise raise his credit, or procure him the regard of the English, as if he had been her immediate rival and competitor. Most of his ministers and favourites were her

" Birch's Memoirs, vol. i. p. 61.   " Birch's Memoirs, vol. i. p. 61.
ˣ Monson, p. 161.   ʸ Winwood, vol. i. p. 41.

pensioners; and as she was desirous to hinder him from marrying and having children, she obliged them to throw obstacles in the way of every alliance, even the most reasonable, which could be offered him; and during some years, she succeeded in this malignant policy.[z] He had fixed on the elder daughter of the king of Denmark, who, being a remote prince and not powerful, could give her no umbrage; yet did she so artfully cross this negociation, that the Danish monarch, impatient of delay, married his daughter to the duke of Brunswick. James then renewed his suit to the younger princess; and still found obstacles from the intrigues of Elizabeth, who, merely with a view of interposing delay, proposed to him the sister of the king of Navarre, a princess much older than himself, and entirely destitute of fortune. The young king, besides the desire of securing himself, by the prospect of issue, from those traiterous attempts, too frequent among his subjects, had been so watched by the rigid austerity of the ecclesiastics, that he had another inducement to marry, which is not so usual with monarchs. His impatience therefore broke through all the politics of Elizabeth: The articles of marriage were settled: The ceremony was performed by proxy: And the princess embarked for Scotland; but was driven by a storm into a port of Norway. This tempest, and some others, which happened near the same time, were universally believed in Scotland and Denmark to have proceeded from a combination of the Scottish and Danish witches; and the dying confession of the criminals was supposed to put the accusation beyond all controversy.[a] James, however, though a great believer in sorcery, was not deterred by this incident from taking a voyage, in order to conduct his bride home: He arrived in Norway; carried the queen thence to Copenhagen; and having passed the winter in that city, he brought her next spring to Scotland, where they were joyfully received by the people. The clergy alone, who never neglected an opportunity of vexing their prince, made opposition to the queen's coronation, on account of the ceremony of anointing her, which, they alledged, was either a Jewish or a popish rite; and therefore utterly antichristian and unlawful. But James was as much bent on the ceremony, as they were averse to it; and after much controversy and many intrigues, his authority, which had not often happened, at last prevailed over their opposition.[b]

---

[z] Melvil, p. 166, 177.   [a] Melvil, p. 180.   [b] Spotswood, p. 381.

XLIII

French affairs –
Murder of the duke of Guise – Murder
of Henry III. – Progress of Henry IV. –
Naval enterprizes against Spain –
A Parliament – Henry IV. embraces the
catholic religion – Scotch affairs –
Naval enterprizes – A parliament –
Peace of Vervins –
The earl of Essex

1590.
AFTER A STATE OF GREAT ANXIETY and many difficulties, Elizabeth had at length reached a situation, where, though her affairs still required attention, and found employment for her active spirit, she was removed from all danger of any immediate revolution, and might regard the efforts of her enemies with some degree of confidence and security. Her successful and prudent administration had gained her, together with the admiration of foreigners, the affections of her own subjects; and after the death of the queen of Scots, even the catholics, however discontented, pretended not to dispute her title, or adhere to any other person as her competitor. James, curbed by his factious nobility and ecclesiastics, possessed at home very little authority; and was solicitous to remain on good terms with Elizabeth and the English nation, in hopes that time, aided by his patient tranquillity, would

CHAPTER XLIII

secure him that rich succession, to which his birth entitled him. The Hollanders, though overmatched in their contest with Spain, still made an obstinate resistance; and such was their unconquerable antipathy to their old masters, and such the prudent conduct of young Maurice, their governor, that the subduing of that small territory, if at all possible, must be the work of years, and the result of many and great successes. Philip, who, in his powerful effort against England, had been transported by resentment and ambition beyond his usual cautious maxims, was now disabled, and still more discouraged, from adventuring again on such hazardous enterprizes. The situation also of affairs in France began chiefly to employ his attention; but notwithstanding all his artifice, and force, and expence, the events in that kingdom proved every day more contrary to his expectations, and more favourable to the friends and confederates of England.

The violence of the league having constrained Henry to declare war against the Hugonots, these religionists seemed exposed *French affairs.* to the utmost danger; and Elizabeth, sensible of the intimate connection between her own interests and those of that party, had supported the king of Navarre by her negociations in Germany, and by large sums of money, which she remitted for levying forces in that country. This great prince, not discouraged by the superiority of his enemies, took the field; and in the year 1587 gained at Coutras, a complete victory over the army of the French king; but as his allies, the Germans, were at the same time discomfited by the army of the league, under the duke of Guise, his situation, notwithstanding his victory, seemed still as desperate as ever. The chief advantage, which he reaped by this diversity of success, arose from the dissentions, which, by that means, took place among his enemies. The inhabitants of Paris, intoxicated with admiration of Guise, and strongly prejudiced against their king, whose intentions had become suspicious to them, took to arms, and obliged Henry to fly for his safety. That prince, dissembling his resentment, entered into a negociation with the league; and having conferred many high offices on Guise and his partizans, summoned an assembly of the states at Blois, on pretence of finding expedients to support the intended war against the Hugonots. The various scenes of perfidy and cruelty, which had been exhibited in France, had justly begotten à mutual dissidence among all parties; yet

Guise, trusting more to the timidity than honour of the king, rashly put himself into the hands of that monarch, and expected, by the ascendant of his own genius, to make him submit to all his exorbitant pretensions. Henry, though of an easy disposition, not steady to his resolutions, or even to his promises, wanted neither courage nor capacity; and finding all his subtilties eluded by the vigour of Guise, and even his throne exposed to the most imminent danger, he embraced more violent counsels than were natural to him, and ordered that prince and his brother, the cardinal of Guise, to be assassinated in his palace.

Murder of the duke of Guise.

This cruel execution, which the necessity of it alone could excuse, had nearly proved fatal to the author, and seemed at first to plunge him into greater dangers than those which he sought to avoid, by taking vengeance on his enemy. The partizans of the league were enflamed with the utmost rage against him: The populace every where, particularly at Paris, renounced allegiance to him: The ecclesiastics and the preachers filled all places with execrations against his name: And the most powerful cities and most opulent provinces appeared to combine in a resolution, either of renouncing monarchy, or of changing their monarch, Henry, finding slender resources among his catholic subjects, was constrained to enter into a confederacy with the Hugonots and the king of Navarre: He enlisted large bodies of Swiss infantry and German cavalry: And being still supported by his chief nobility, he assembled, by all these means, an army of near forty thousand men, and advanced to the gates of Paris, ready to crush the league, and subdue all his enemies. The desperate resolution of one man diverted the course of these great events. Jaques Clement, a Dominican fryar, inflamed by that bloody spirit of bigotry, which distinguishes this century and a great part of the following beyond all ages of the world, embraced the resolution of sacrificing his own life, in order to save the church from the persecutions of a heretical tyrant; and being admitted, under some pretext, to the king's presence, he gave that prince a mortal wound, and was immediately put to death by the courtiers, who hastily revenged the murder of their sovereign. This memorable incident happened on the first of August, 1589.

Murder of Henry the third.

The king of Navarre, next heir to the crown, assumed the government, by the title of Henry IV. but succeeded to much

CHAPTER XLIII

greater difficulties than those which surrounded his predecessor. The prejudices, entertained against his religion, made a great part of the nobility immediately desert him; and it was only by his promise of hearkening to conferences and instruction, that he could engage any of the catholics to adhere to his undoubted title. The league, governed by the duke of Mayenne, brother to Guise, gathered new force; and the king of Spain entertained views, either of dismembering the French monarchy, or of annexing the whole to his own dominions. In these distressful circumstances, Henry addressed himself to Elizabeth, and found her well disposed to contribute to his assistance, and to oppose the progress of the catholic league, and of Philip her inveterate and dangerous enemies. To prevent the desertion of his Swiss and German auxiliaries, she made him a present of twenty-two thousand pounds; a greater sum than, as he declared, he had ever seen before: And sent him a reinforcement of four thousand men, under lord Willoughby, an officer of reputation, who joined the French at Dieppe. Strengthened by these supplies, Henry marched directly to Paris; and having taken the suburbs, sword in hand, he abandoned them to be pillaged by his soldiers. He employed this body of English in many other enterprizes; and still found reason to praise their courage and fidelity. The time of their service being elapsed, he dismissed them with many high commendations. Sir William Drury, Sir Thomas Baskerville, and Sir John Boroughs acquired reputation this campaign, and revived in France the ancient fame of English valour.

The army, which Henry next campaign led into the field, was much inferior to that of the league; but as it was composed of the chief nobility of France, he feared not to encounter his enemies in a pitched battle at Yvrée, and he gained a complete victory over them. This success enabled him to blockade Paris, and he reduced that capital to the last extremity of famine: When the duke of Parma, in consequence of orders from Philip, marched to the relief of the league, and obliged Henry to raise the blockade. Having performed this important service, he retreated to the Low Countries; and by his consummate skill in the art of war, performed these long marches in the face of the enemy, without affording the French monarch that opportunity which he sought, of giving him battle, or so much as once putting his army in disorder. The only

Progress of Henry the fourth.

loss, which he sustained, was in the Low Countries; where prince Maurice took advantage of his absence, and recovered some places, which the duke of Parma had formerly conquered from the States.[c]

1591. The situation of Henry's affairs, though promising, was not so well advanced or established as to make the queen discontinue her succours; and she was still more confirmed in the resolution of supporting him, by some advantages gained by the king of Spain. The duke of Mercoeur, governor of Britanny, a prince of the house of Lorraine, had declared for the league; and finding himself hard pressed by Henry's forces, he had been obliged, in order to secure himself, to introduce some Spanish troops into the seaport towns of that province. Elizabeth was alarmed at the danger; and foresaw, that the Spaniards, besides infesting the English commerce by privateers, might employ these harbours as the seat of their naval preparations, and might more easily, from that vicinity, than from Spain or Portugal, project an invasion of England. She concluded, therefore, a new treaty with Henry, in which she engaged to send over three thousand men, to be employed in the reduction of Britanny, and she stipulated that her charges should, in a twelvemonth, or as soon as the enemy was expelled, be refunded her.[d] These forces were commanded by Sir John Norris; and under him by his brother Henry, and by Anthony Shirley. Sir Roger Williams was at the head of a small body which garrisoned Dieppe: And a squadron of ships, under the command of Sir Henry Palmer, lay upon the coast of France, and intercepted all the vessels belonging to the Spaniards or the leaguers.

The operations of war can very little be regulated beforehand by any treaty or agreement; and Henry, who found it necessary to lay aside the projected enterprize against Britanny, persuaded the English commanders to join his army, and to take a share in the hostilities, which he carried into Picardy.[e] Notwithstanding the disgust, which Elizabeth received from this disappointment, he laid before her a plan for expelling the leaguers from Normandy, and persuaded her to send over a new body of four thousand men, to assist him in that enterprize. The earl of Essex was appointed

[c] See note [CC] at the end of the volume.   [d] Camden, p. 561.   [e] Rymer, tom. xiv. p. 116.

CHAPTER XLIII

general of these forces; a young nobleman, who, by many exterior accomplishments, and still more real merit, was daily advancing in favour with Elizabeth, and seemed to occupy that place in her affections, which Leicester, now deceased, had so long enjoyed. Essex, impatient for military fame, was extremely uneasy to lie some time at Dieppe unemployed; and had not the orders, which he received from his mistress, been so positive, he would gladly have accepted of Henry's invitation, and have marched to join the French army now in Champagne. This plan of operations was also proposed to Elizabeth by the French ambassador; but she rejected it with great displeasure; and she threatened immediately to recall her troops, if Henry should persevere any longer in his present practice, of breaking all concert with her, and attending to nothing but his own interests.[f] Urged by these motives, the French king, at last, led his army into Normandy, and laid siege to Roüen, which he reduced to great difficulties. But the league, unable of themselves to take the field against him, had again recourse to the duke of Parma, who received orders to march to their relief. He executed this enterprize with his usual abilities and success; and, for the present, frustrated all the projects of Henry and Elizabeth. This princess, who kept still in view the interests of her own kingdom in all her foreign transactions, was impatient, under these disappointments, blamed Henry for his negligence in the execution of treaties, and complained, that the English forces were thrust foremost in every hazardous enterprize.[g] It is probable, however, that their own ardent courage, and their desire of distinguishing themselves in so celebrated a theatre of war, were the causes why they so often enjoyed this perilous honour.

Notwithstanding the indifferent success of former enterprizes, the queen was sensible how necessary it was to support Henry against the league and the Spaniards; and she formed a new treaty with him, in which they agreed never to make peace with Philip, but by common consent; *she* promised to send him a new supply of four thousand men; and *he* stipulated to repay her charges in a twelvemonth, to employ these forces, joined to a body of French troops, in an expedition against Britanny, and to consign into her

[f] Birch's Negociations, p. 5. Rymer, tom. xiv. p. 123, 140.　[g] Camden, p. 562.

hands a sea-port town of that province, for a retreat to the Eng-. lish.[h] Henry knew the impossibility of executing some of these articles, and the imprudence of fulfilling others; but finding them rigidly insisted on by Elizabeth, he accepted of her succours, and trusted that he might easily, on some pretence, be able to excuse his failure in executing his part of the treaty. This campaign was the least successful of all those which he had yet carried on against the league.

Naval enter-prizes against Spain.
    During these military operations in France, Elizabeth employed her naval power against Philip, and endeavoured to intercept his West-Indian treasures, the source of that greatness, which rendered him so formidable to all his neighbours. She sent a squadron of seven ships, under the command of lord Thomas Howard, for this service; but the king of Spain, informed of her purpose, fitted out a great force, of fifty-five sail, and dispatched them to escort the Indian fleet. They fell in with the English squadron; and by the courageous obstinacy of Sir Richard Greenville, the vice-admiral, who refused to make his escape by flight, they took one vessel, the first English ship of war that had yet fallen into the hands of the Spaniards.[i] The rest of the squadron returned safely into England; frustrated of their expectations, but pleasing themselves with the idea that their attempt had not been altogether fruitless in hurting the enemy. The Indian fleet had been so long detained in the Havanna, from the fear of the English, that they were obliged at last to set sail in an improper season, and most of them perished by shipwreck, ere they reached the Spanish harbours.[k] The earl of Cumberland made a like unsuccessful enterprize against the Spanish trade. He carried out one ship of the queen's, and seven others, equipped at his own expence; but the prizes, which he made, did not compensate the charges.[l]
    The spirit of these expensive and hazardous adventures was very prevalent in England. Sir Walter Raleigh, who had enjoyed great favour with the queen, finding his interest to decline, determined to recover her good graces by some important undertaking; and as his reputation was high among his countrymen, he persuaded great numbers to engage with him as volunteers, in an

[h] Rymer, vol. xvi. p. 151, 168, 171, 173.   [i] See note [DD] at the end of the volume.   [k] Monson, p. 163.   [l] Ibid. p. 169.

CHAPTER XLIII

attempt on the West-Indies. The fleet was detained so long in the Channel by contrary winds, that the season was lost: Raleigh was recalled by the queen: Sir Martin Frobisher succeeded to the command, and made a privateering voyage against the Spaniards. He took one rich Carrack near the Island of Flores, and destroyed another.[m] About the same time, Thomas White, a Londoner, took two Spanish ships, which, besides fourteen hundred chests of quicksilver, contained above two millions of bulls for indulgences; a commodity useless to the English, but which had cost the king of Spain three hundred thousand florins, and would have been sold by him in the Indies for five millions.

1592.

This war did great damage to Spain; but it was attended with considerable expence to England; and Elizabeth's ministers computed, that since the commencement of it, she had spent in Flanders and France, and on her naval expeditions, above one million two hundred thousand pounds;[n] a charge which, notwithstanding her extreme frugality, was too burthensome for her narrow revenues to support. She summoned, therefore, a parliament, in order to obtain supply: But she either thought her authority so established, that she needed to make them no concessions in return, or she rated her power and prerogative above money: For there never was any parliament, whom she treated in a more haughty manner, whom she made more sensible of their own weakness, or whose privileges she more openly violated. When the speaker, Sir Edward Coke, made the three usual requests, of freedom from arrests, of access to her person, and of liberty of speech; she replied to him, by the mouth of Puckering, lord keeper, that liberty of speech was granted to the commons, but they must know what liberty they were entitled to; not a liberty for every one to speak what he listeth, or what cometh in his brain to utter; their privilege extended no farther than a liberty of Aye or No: That she enjoined the speaker, if he perceived any idle heads so negligent of their own safety, as to attempt reforming the church, or innovating in the commonwealth, that he should refuse the bills exhibited for that purpose, till they were examined by such as were fitter to consider of these things, and could better judge of them: That she would not impeach the freedom of their persons; but they

1593.
Feb. 19.
A parlia-
ment.

---

[m] Ibid. p. 165. Camden, p. 569.   [n] Strype, vol. iii.

must beware, lest, under colour of this privilege, they imagined, that any neglect of their duty could be covered or protected: And that she would not refuse them access to her person; provided it were upon urgent and weighty causes, and at times convenient, and when she might have leisure from other important affairs of the realm.[o]

Notwithstanding the menacing and contemptuous air of this speech, the intrepid and indefatigable Peter Wentworth, not discouraged by his former ill success, ventured to transgress the imperial orders of Elizabeth. He presented to the lord keeper a petition, in which he desired the upper house to join with the lower in a supplication to her majesty, for entailing the succession of the crown; and he declared, that he had a bill ready prepared for that purpose. This method of proceeding was sufficiently respectful and cautious; but the subject was always extremely disagreeable to the queen, and what she had expressly prohibited any one from meddling with: She sent Wentworth immediately to the Tower; committed Sir Thomas Bromley, who had seconded him, to the Fleet prison, together with Stevens, and Welsh, two members, to whom Sir Thomas had communicated his intention.[p] About a fortnight after, a motion was made in the house, to petition the queen, for the release of these members; but it was answered by all the privy counsellors there present, that her majesty had committed them for causes best known to herself, and that to press her on that head would only tend to the prejudice of the gentlemen, whom they meant to serve: She would release them whenever she thought proper, and would be better pleased to do it of her own proper motion, than from their suggestion.[q] The house willingly acquiesced in this reasoning.

So arbitrary an act, at the commencement of the session, might well repress all farther attempts for freedom: But the religious zeal of the puritans, was not so easily restrained; and it inspired a courage, which no human motive was able to surmount. Morrice, chancellor of the dutchy, and attorney of the court of wards, made a motion for redressing the abuses in the bishops' courts, but above all, in the high commission; where subscriptions, he said, were

<hr>

[o] D'Ewes, p. 460, 469. Townsend, p. 37. [p] D'Ewes, p. 470. Townsend, p. 54. [q] D'Ewes, p. 497.

CHAPTER XLIII

exacted to articles at the pleasure of the prelates; where oaths were imposed, obliging persons to answer to all questions without distinction, even though they should tend to their own condemnation; and where every one, who refused entire satisfaction to the commissioners, was imprisoned, without relief or remedy.[r] This motion was seconded by some members; but the ministers and privy counsellors opposed it; and foretold the consequences which ensued. The queen sent for the speaker; and after requiring him to deliver to her Morrice's bill, she told him, that it was in her power to call parliaments, in her power to dissolve them, in her power to give assent or dissent to any determination, which they should form: That her purpose in summoning this parliament was twofold, to have laws enacted for the farther enforcement of uniformity in religion, and to provide for the defence of the nation, against the exorbitant power of Spain: That these two points ought, therefore, to be the object of their deliberations: She had enjoined them already, by the mouth of the lord keeper, to meddle neither with matters of state nor of religion; and she wondered how any one could be so assuming, as to attempt a subject so expressly contrary to her prohibition: That she was highly offended with this presumption; and took the present opportunity to reiterate the commands given by the keeper, and to require, that no bill, regarding either state affairs, or reformation in causes ecclesiastical, be exhibited in the house: And that in particular she charged the speaker upon his allegiance, if any such bills were offered, absolutely to refuse them a reading, and not so much as permit them to be debated by the members.[s] This command from the queen was submitted to, without farther question. Morrice was seized in the house itself by a serjeant at arms, discharged from his office of chancellor of the dutchy, incapacitated from any practice in his profession as a common lawyer, and kept some years prisoner in Tilbury castle.[t]

The queen having thus expressly pointed out, both what the house should and should not do, the commons were as obsequious to the one as to the other of her injunctions. They passed a law against recusants; such a law as was suited to the severe character

[r] D'Ewes, p. 474. Townsend, p. 60. [s] D'Ewes, p. 474, 478. Townsend, p. 68. [t] Heylin's History of the Presbyterians, p. 320.

of Elizabeth and to the persecuting spirit of the age. It was intitled, *An act to retain her majesty's subjects in their due obedience;* and was meant, as the preamble declares, to obviate such inconveniences and perils as might grow from the wicked practices of seditious sectaries and disloyal persons: For these two species of criminals were always, at that time, confounded together, as equally danger-ous to the peace of society. It was enacted, that any person, above sixteen years of age, who obstinately refused, during the space of a month, to attend public worship, should be committed to prison; that, if, after being condemned for this offence, he persist three months in his refusal, he must abjure the realm; and that, if he either refuse this condition, or return after banishment, he should suffer capitally as a felon, without benefit of clergy.[u] This law bore equally hard upon the puritans and upon the catholics; and had it not been imposed by the queen's authority, was certainly, in that respect, much contrary to the private sentiments and inclinations of the majority in the house of commons. Very little opposition, however, appears there to have been openly made to it.[w]

The expences of the war with Spain, having reduced the queen to great difficulties, the grant of subsidies seems to have been the most important business of this parliament; and it was a signal proof of the high spirit of Elizabeth, that, while conscious of a present dependance on the commons, she opened the session with the most haughty treatment of them, and covered her weakness under such a lofty appearance of superiority. The commons readily voted two subsidies and four fifteenths; but this sum not appearing sufficient to the court, an unusual expedient was fallen upon to induce them to make an enlargement in their concessions. The peers informed the commons in a conference, that they could not give their assent to the supply voted, thinking it too small for the queen's occasions: They therefore proposed a grant of three subsidies and six fifteenths, and desired a farther conference, in order to persuade the commons to agree to this measure. The commons, who had acquired the privilege of beginning bills of subsidy, took offence at this procedure of the lords, and at first

[u] 35 Eliz. c. 1. [w] After enacting this statute, the clergy, in order to remove the odium from themselves, often took care that recusants should be tried by the civil judges at the assizes, rather than by the ecclesiastical commis-sioners. Strype's Ann. vol. iv. p. 264.

absolutely rejected the proposal: But being afraid, on reflection, that they had, by this refusal, given offence to their superiors, they both agreed to the conference, and afterwards voted the additional subsidy.[x]

The queen, notwithstanding this unusual concession of the commons, ended the session with a speech, containing some reprimands to them, and full of the same high pretensions, which she had assumed at the opening of the parliament. She took notice, by the mouth of the keeper, that certain members spent more time than was necessary, by indulging themselves in harangues and reasonings: And she expressed her displeasure on account of their not paying due reverence to privy counsellors, "who," she told them, "were not to be accounted as common knights and burgesses of the house, who are counsellors but during the parliament: Whereas the others are standing counsellors, and for their wisdom and great service are called to the council of the state."[y] The queen also, in her own person, made the parliament a spirited harangue; in which she spoke of the justice and moderation of her government, expressed the small ambition she had ever entertained of making conquests, displayed the just grounds of her quarrel with the king of Spain, and discovered how little she apprehended the power of that monarch, even though he should make a greater effort against her than that of his Invincible Armada. "But I am informed," added she, "that when he attempted this last invasion, some upon the sea-coast forsook their towns, fled up higher into the country, and left all naked and exposed to his entrance: But I swear unto you, by God, if I knew those persons, or may know of any that shall do so hereafter, I will make them feel what it is to be so fearful in so urgent a cause."[z] By this menace, she probably gave the people to understand, that she would execute martial law upon such cowards: For there was no statute, by which a man could be punished for changing his place of abode.

The king of France, though he had hitherto made war on the league with great bravery and reputation, though he had this campaign gained considerable advantages over them, and though he was assisted by a considerable body of English under Norris,

---

[x] D'Ewes, p. 483, 487, 488. Townsend, p. 66.   [y] D'Ewes, p. 466. Townsend, p. 47.   [z] D'Ewes, p. 466. Townsend, p. 48.

who carried hostilities into the heart of Britanny; was become sensible, that he never could, by force of arms alone, render himself master of his kingdom. The nearer he seemed by his military successes to approach to a full possession of the throne, the more discontent and jealousy arose among those Romanists who adhered to him; and a party was formed in his own court to elect some catholic monarch of the royal blood, if Henry should any longer refuse to satisfy them by declaring his conversion. This excellent prince was far from being a bigot to his sect; and as he deemed these theological disputes entirely subordinate to the public good, he had secretly determined, from the beginning, to come, some time or other, to the resolution required of him. He had found, on the death of his predecessor, that the hugonots, who formed the bravest and most faithful part of his army, were such determined zealots, that, if he had, at that time, abjured their faith, they would instantly have abandoned him to the pretensions and usurpations of the catholics. The more bigotted catholics, he knew, particularly those of the league, had entertained such an unsurmountable prejudice against his person, and diffidence of his sincerity, that even his abjuration would not reconcile them to his title; and he must either expect to be entirely excluded from the throne, or be admitted to it on such terms as would leave him little more than the mere shadow of royalty. In this delicate situation he had resolved to temporize; to retain the hugonots by continuing in the profession of their religion; to gain the moderate catholics by giving them hopes of his conversion; to attach both to his person by conduct and success; and he hoped, either that the animosity, arising from war against the league, would make them drop gradually the question of religion, or that he might, in time, after some victories over his enemies and some conferences with divines, make finally, with more decency and dignity, that abjuration, which must have appeared, at first, mean, as well as suspicious to both parties.

Henry IV. embraces the catholic religion.　　When the people are attached to any theological tenets, merely from a general persuasion or prepossession, they are easily induced, by any motive or authority, to change their faith in these mysterious subjects; as appears from the example of the English, who, during some reigns, usually embraced, without scruple, the still varying religion of their sovereigns. But the French nation, where principles had so long been displayed as the badges of faction, and where each party had fortified its belief by an animosity against the other, were not found so pliable or inconstant; and Henry was at last convinced, that the catholics of his party would entirely abandon him, if he gave them not immediate satisfaction in this particular. The hugonots also, taught by experience, clearly saw, that his desertion of them was become absolutely necessary for the public settlement; and so general was this persuasion among them, that, as the duke of Sully pretends, even the divines of that party purposely allowed themselves to be worsted in the disputes and conferences; that the king might more readily be convinced of the weakness of their cause, and might more cordially and sincerely, at least more decently, embrace the religion, which it was so much his interest to believe. If this self-denial, in so tender a point, should appear incredible and supernatural in theologians, it will, at least, be thought very natural, that a prince, so little instructed in these matters as Henry, and desirous to preserve his sincerity, should insensibly bend his opinion to the necessity of his affairs, and should believe that party to have the best arguments, who could alone put him in possession of a kingdom. All circumstances, therefore, being prepared for this great event, that monarch renounced the protestant religion, and was solemnly received, by the French prelates of his party, into the bosom of the church.

Elizabeth, who was, herself, attached to the protestants, chiefly by her interests and the circumstances of her birth, and who seems to have entertained some propensity, during her whole life, to the catholic superstition, at least to the ancient ceremonies, yet pretended, to be extremely displeased with this abjuration of Henry; and she wrote him an angry letter, reproaching him with this interested change of his religion. Sensible, however, that the league and the king of Spain were still their common enemies, she hearkened to his apologies; continued her succours both of men and money; and formed a new treaty, in which they mutually stipulated never to make peace but by common agreement.

The intrigues of Spain were not limited to France and England: *Scotch* By means of the never failing pretence of religion, joined to the *affairs.* influence of money, Philip excited new disorders in Scotland, and gave fresh alarms to Elizabeth. George Ker, brother to lord Newbottle, had been taken, while he was passing secretly into Spain; and papers were found about him, by which a dangerous conspiracy of some catholic noblemen with Philip was discovered. The earls of Angus, Errol, and Huntley, the heads of three potent families, had entered into a confederacy with the Spanish monarch: And had stipulated to raise all their forces; to join them to a body of Spanish troops, which Philip promised to send into Scotland; and after re-establishing the catholic religion in that kingdom, to march with their united power, in order to effect the same purpose in England.[a] Graham of Fintry, who had also entered into this conspiracy, was taken, and arraigned, and executed. Elizabeth sent lord Borough ambassador into Scotland, and exhorted the king to exercise the same severity on the three earls, to confiscate their estates, and by annexing them to the crown, both encrease his own demesnes, and set an example to all his subjects of the dangers attending treason and rebellion. The advice was certainly rational, but not easy to be executed by the small revenue and limited authority of James. He desired, therefore, some supply from her of men and money; but though she had reason to deem the prosecution of the three popish earls a common cause, she never could be prevailed on to grant him the least assistance. The tenth part of the expence, which she bestowed in supporting the French king, and the States, would have sufficed to execute this purpose, more immediately essential to her security:[b] But she seems ever to have borne some degree of malignity to James, whom she hated, both as her heir, and as the son of Mary, her hated rival and competitor.

So far from giving James assistance to prosecute the catholic conspirators, the queen rather contributed to encrease his inquietude, by countenancing the turbulent disposition of the earl of Bothwel,[c] a nobleman descended from a natural son of James V. Bothwel more than once attempted to render himself master of the king's person; and being expelled the kingdom for these traiterous enterprizes, he took shelter in England, was secretly protected by the queen, and lurked near the borders, where his power lay, with a view of still committing some new violence. He succeeded at last in an attempt on the king; and by the mediation of the English

[a] Spotswood, p. 391. Rymer, tom. xvi. p. 190.   [b] Spotswood, p. 393. Rymer, tom. xvi. p. 235.   [c] Spotswood, p. 257, 258.

ambassador, imposed dishonourable terms upon that prince: But James, by the authority of the convention of States, annulled this agreement as extorted by violence; again expelled Bothwel; and obliged him to take shelter in England. Elizabeth, pretending ignorance of the place of his retreat, never executed the treaties, by which she was bound to deliver up all rebels and fugitives to the king of Scotland. During these disorders, encreased by the refractory disposition of the ecclesiastics, the prosecution of the catholic earls remained in suspence; but at last the parliament passed an act of attainder against them, and the king prepared himself to execute it by force of arms. The noblemen, though they obtained a victory over the earl of Argyle, who acted by the king's commission, found themselves hard pressed by James himself, and agreed, on certain terms, to leave the kingdom. Bothwel, being detected in a confederacy with them, forfeited the favour of Elizabeth; and was obliged to take shelter, first in France, then in Italy, where he died, some years after, in great poverty. *1594.*

The established authority of the queen secured her from all such attempts as James was exposed to from the mutinous disposition of his subjects; and her enemies found no other means of giving her domestic disturbance than by such traiterous and perfidious machinations, as ended in their own disgrace, and in the ruin of their criminal instruments. Roderigo Lopez, a Jew, domestic physician to the queen, being imprisoned on suspicion, confessed, that he had received a bribe to poison her from Fuentes and Ibarra, who had succeeded Parma lately deceased, in the government of the Netherlands; but he maintained, that he had no other intention than to cheat Philip of his money, and never meant to fulfil his engagement. He was, however, executed for the conspiracy; and the queen complained to Philip of these dishonourable attempts of his ministers, but could obtain no satisfaction.[d] York and Williams, two English traitors, were afterwards executed for a conspiracy with Ibarra, equally atrocious.[e]

Instead of avenging herself, by retaliating in a like manner, Elizabeth sought a more honourable vengeance, by supporting the king of France, and assisting him in finally breaking the force of

---

[d] Camden, p. 577. Birch's Negot. p. 15. Bacon, vol. iv. p. 381.   [e] Camden, p. 582.

the league, which, after the conversion of that monarch, went daily to decay, and was threatened with speedy ruin and dissolution. Norris commanded the English forces in Britanny, and assisted at the taking of Morlaix, Quimpercorentin, and Brest, towns garrisoned by Spanish forces. In every action, the English, though they had so long enjoyed domestic peace, discovered a strong military disposition; and the queen, though herself a heroine, found more frequent occasion to reprove her generals for encouraging their temerity, than for countenancing their fear or caution:[f] Sir Martin Frobisher, her brave admiral, perished, with many others, before Brest. Morlaix had been promised to the English for a place of retreat; but the duke d'Aumont, the French general, eluded this promise, by making it be inserted in the capitulation, that none but catholics should be admitted into that city.

1595.   Next campaign, the French king, who had long carried on hostilities with Philip, was at last provoked, by the taking of Chatelet and Dourlens, and the attack of Cambray, to declare war against that monarch. Elizabeth being threatened with a new invasion in England, and with an insurrection in Ireland, recalled most of her forces, and sent Norris to command in this latter kingdom. Finding also, that the French league was almost entirely dissolved, and that the most considerable leaders had made an accommodation with their prince, she thought, that he could well support himself by his own force and valour; and she began to be more sparing, in his cause, of the blood and treasure of her subjects.

1596.   Some disgusts, which she had received from the States, joined to the remonstrances of her frugal minister Burleigh, made her also inclined to diminish her charges on that side; and she even demanded, by her ambassador, Sir Thomas Bodley, to be reimbursed all the money, which she had expended in supporting them. The States, besides alledging the conditions of the treaty, by which they were not bound to repay her, till the conclusion of a peace, pleaded their present poverty and distress, the great superiority of the Spaniards, and the difficulty in supporting the war; much more in saving money to discharge their incumbrances. After much negociation, a new treaty was formed; by which the

[f] Camden, p. 578.

CHAPTER XLIII

States engaged to free the queen immediately from the charge of the English auxiliaries, computed at forty thousand pounds a-year; to pay her annually twenty thousand pounds for some years; to assist her with a certain number of ships; and to conclude no peace or treaty without her consent. They also bound themselves, on finishing a peace with Spain, to pay her annually the sum of a hundred thousand pounds for four years; but on this condition; that the payment should be in lieu of all demands, and that they should be supplied, though at their own charge, with a body of four thousand auxiliaries from England.[g]

The queen still retained in her hands the cautionary towns, which were a great check on the rising power of the States; and she committed the important trust of Flushing to Sir Francis Vere, a brave officer, who had distinguished himself by his valour in the Low Countries. She gave him the preference to Essex, who expected so honourable a command; and though this nobleman was daily rising both in reputation with the people, and favour with herself, the queen, who was commonly reserved in the advancement of her courtiers, thought proper, on this occasion, to give him a refusal. Sir Thomas Baskerville was sent over to France at the head of two thousand English, with which Elizabeth, by a new treaty concluded with Henry, engaged to supply that prince. Some stipulations for mutual assistance were formed by the treaty; and all former engagements were renewed.

This body of English were maintained at the expence of the French king; yet did Henry esteem the supply of considerable advantage, on account of the great reputation acquired by the English, in so many fortunate enterprizes, undertaken against the common enemy. In the great battle of Tournholt, gained this campaign by prince Maurice, the English auxiliaries, under Sir Francis Vere and Sir Robert Sydney, had acquired honour; and the success of that day was universally ascribed to their discipline and valour.

1597.

Though Elizabeth, at a considerable expence of blood and treasure, made war against Philip in France and the Low Countries, the most severe blows, which she gave him, were by those naval enterprizes, which either she or her subjects scarcely ever

Naval enterprizes.

[g] Camden, p. 586.

intermitted during one season. In 1594, Richard Hawkins, son of Sir John, the famous navigator, procured the queen's commission, and sailed with three ships to the South Sea by the straits of Magellan: But his voyage proved unfortunate, and he himself was taken prisoner on the coast of Chili. James Lancaster was supplied the same year with three ships and a pinnace by the merchants of London; and was more fortunate in his adventure. He took thirty nine ships of the enemy; and not content with this success, he made an attack on Fernambouc in Brazil, where, he knew, great treasures were at that time lodged. As he approached the shore, he saw it lined with great numbers of the enemy; but no-wise daunted at this appearance, he placed the stoutest of his men in boats, and ordered them to row with such violence, on the landing place, as to split them in pieces. By this bold action, he both deprived his men of all resource but in victory, and terrified the enemy, who fled after a short resistance. He returned home with the treasure, which he had so bravely acquired. In 1595, Sir Walter Raleigh, who had anew forfeited the queen's friendship by an intrigue with a maid of honour, and who had been thrown into prison for this misdemeanor, no sooner recovered his liberty, than he was pushed, by his active and enterprizing genius, to attempt some great action. The success of the first Spanish adventurers against Mexico and Peru had begotten an extreme avidity in Europe; and a prepossession universally took place, that, in the inland parts of South America, called Guiana, a country as yet undiscovered, there were mines and treasures far exceeding any which Cortes or Pizzaro had met with. Raleigh, whose turn of mind was somewhat romantic and extravagant, undertook at his own charge the discovery of this wonderful country. Having taken the small town of St. Joseph in the isle of Trinidado, where he found no riches, he left his ship, and sailed up the river Oroonoko in pinnaces, but without meeting any thing to answer his expectations. On his return, he published an account of the country, full of the grossest and most palpable lies, that were ever attempted to be imposed on the credulity of mankind.[h]

The same year, Sir Francis Drake and Sir John Hawkins undertook a more important expedition against the Spanish settlements

[h] Camden, p. 584.

CHAPTER XLIII

in America; and they carried with them six ships of the queen's and twenty more, which either were fitted out at their own charge, or were furnished them by private adventurers. Sir Thomas Baskerville was appointed commander of the land forces, which they carried on board. Their first design was to attempt Porto Rico, where, they knew, a rich carrack was at that time stationed; but as they had not preserved the requisite secresy, a pinnace, having strayed from the fleet, was taken by the Spaniards, and betrayed the intentions of the English. Preparations were made in that island for their reception; and the English fleet, notwithstanding the brave assault, which they made on the enemy, was repulsed with loss. Hawkins soon after died; and Drake pursued his voyage to Nombre di Dios, on the isthmus of Darien; where, having landed his men, he attempted to pass forward to Panama, with a view of plundering that place, or, if he found such a scheme practicable, of keeping and fortifying it. But he met not with the same facility, which had attended his first enterprizes in those parts. The Spaniards, taught by experience, had every where fortified the passes, and had stationed troops in the woods; who so infested the English by continual alarms and skirmishes, that they were obliged to return, without being able to effect any thing. Drake himself, from the intemperance of the climate, the fatigues of his journey, and the vexation of his disappointment, was seized with a distemper, of which he soon after died. Sir Thomas Baskerville took the command of the fleet, which was in a weak condition; and after having fought a battle near Cuba with a Spanish fleet, of which the event was not decisive, he returned to England. The Spaniards suffered some loss from this enterprize; but the English reaped no profit.[i]

The bad success of this enterprize in the Indies made the English rather attempt the Spanish dominions in Europe, where, they heard, Philip was making great preparations for a new invasion of England. A powerful fleet was equipped at Plymouth consisting of a hundred and seventy vessels, seventeen of which were capital ships of war; the rest tenders and small vessels: Twenty ships were added by the Hollanders. In this fleet there were computed to be embarked six thousand three hundred and sixty soldiers, a thousand volunteers, and six thousand seven hundred and seventy-two

[i] Monson, p. 167.

seamen, beside the Dutch. The land forces were commanded by the earl of Essex: The navy by lord Effingham, high admiral. Both these commanders had expended great sums of their own in the armament: For such was the spirit of Elizabeth's reign. Lord Thomas Howard, Sir Walter Raleigh, Sir Francis Vere, Sir George Carew, and Sir Coniers Clifford had commands in this expedition, and were appointed council to the general and admiral.[k]

The fleet set sail on the first of June 1596; and meeting with a fair wind, bent its course to Cadiz, at which place, by sealed orders delivered to all the captains, the general rendezvous was ap-pointed. They sent before them some armed tenders, which inter-cepted every ship, that could carry intelligence to the enemy; and they themselves were so fortunate when they came near Cadiz, as to take an Irish vessel, by which they learned, that that port was full of merchant ships of great value, and that the Spaniards lived in perfect security, without any apprehensions of an enemy. This intelligence much encouraged the English fleet, and gave them the prospect of a fortunate issue to the enterprize.

After a fruitless attempt to land at St. Sebastian's on the western side of the island of Cadiz; it was, upon deliberation, resolved by the council of war to attack the ships and gallies in the bay. This attempt was deemed rash; and the admiral himself, who was cau-tious in his temper, had entertained great scruples with regard to it: But Essex strenuously recommended the enterprize; and when he found the resolution at last taken, he threw his hat into the sea, and gave symptoms of the most extravagant joy. He felt, however, a great mortification, when Effingham informed him, that the queen, anxious for his safety, and dreading the effects of his youthful ardour, had secretly given orders, that he should not be permitted to command the van in the attack.[l] That duty was performed by Sir Walter Raleigh and lord Thomas Howard; but Essex no sooner came within reach of the enemy, than he forgot the promise, which the admiral had exacted from him, to keep in the midst of the fleet; he broke through and pressed forward into the thickest of the fire. Emulation for glory, avidity of plun-der, animosity against the Spaniards, proved incentives to every one; and the enemy was soon obliged to slip anchor, and retreat

[k] Camden, p. 591.   [l] Monson, p. 196.

CHAPTER XLIII

farther into the bay, where they ran many of their ships aground. Essex then landed his men at the fort of Puntal; and immediately marched to the attack of Cadiz, which the impetuous valour of the English soon carried sword in hand. The generosity of Essex, not inferior to his valour, made him stop the slaughter, and treat his prisoners with the greatest humanity, and even affability and kindness. The English made rich plunder in the city; but missed of a much richer by the resolution, which the duke of Medina, the Spanish admiral, took of setting fire to the ships, in order to prevent their falling into the hands of the enemy. It was computed, that the loss, which the Spaniards sustained in this enterprize, amounted to twenty millions of ducats;[m] besides the indignity, which that proud and ambitious people suffered from the sacking of one of their chief cities, and destroying in their harbour a fleet of such force and value.

Essex, all on fire for glory, regarded this great success only as a step to future atchievements: He insisted on keeping possession of Cadiz; and he undertook with four hundred men and three months provisions, to defend the place, till succours should arrive from England: But all the other seamen and soldiers were satisfied with the honour, which they had acquired; and were impatient to return home, in order to secure their plunder. Every other proposal of Essex to annoy the enemy met with a like reception; his scheme for intercepting the carracks at the Azores, for assaulting the Groine, for taking St. Andero, and St. Sebastian: And the English, finding it so difficult to drag the impatient warrior from the enemy, at last left him on the Spanish coast, attended by very few ships. He complained much to the queen, of their want of spirit in this enterprize; nor was she pleased, that they had returned without attempting to intercept the Indian fleet;[n] but the great success, in the enterprize on Cadiz, had covered all their miscarriages: And that princess, though she admired the lofty genius of Essex, could not forbear expressing an esteem for the other officers.[o] The admiral was created earl of Nottingham; and his promotion gave great disgust to Essex.[p] In the preamble of the patent it was said, that the new dignity was conferred on him on

[m] Birch's Memoirs, vol. ii. p. 97.   [n] Birch's Memoirs, vol. ii. p. 121.
[o] Camden, p. 593.   [p] Sidney Papers, vol. ii. p. 77.

account of his good services in taking Cadiz, and destroying the Spanish ships; a merit which Essex pretended to belong solely to himself: And he offered to maintain this plea by single combat against the earl of Nottingham, or his sons, or any of his kindred.

The atchievements in the subsequent year proved not so fortunate; but as the Indian fleet very narrowly escaped the English, Philip had still reason to see the great hazard and disadvantage of that war in which he was engaged, and the superiority which the English, by their naval power and their situation, had acquired over him. The queen, having received intelligence, that the Spaniards, though their fleets were so much shattered and destroyed, by the expedition to Cadiz, were preparing a squadron at Ferrol and the Groine, and were marching troops thither, with a view of making a descent in Ireland, was resolved to prevent their enterprize, and to destroy the shipping in these harbours. She prepared a large fleet of a hundred and twenty sail, of which seventeen were her own ships, forty-three were smaller vessels, and the rest tenders and victuallers: She embarked on board this fleet five thousand new-levied soldiers, and added a thousand veteran troops, whom Sir Francis Vere brought from the Netherlands. The earl of Essex, commander in chief, both of the land and sea forces, was at the head of one squadron: Lord Thomas Howard was appointed vice-admiral of another; Sir Walter Raleigh of the third: Lord Mountjoy commanded the land forces under Essex: Vere was appointed marshal: Sir George Carew lieutenant of the ordnance, and Sir Christopher Blount first colonel. The earls of Rutland and Southampton, the lords Grey, Cromwell, and Rich, with several other persons of distinction, embarked as volunteers. Essex declared his resolution either to destroy the new Armada, which threatened England, or to perish in the attempt.

9th July.   This powerful fleet set sail from Plymouth; but were no sooner out of harbour than they met with a furious storm, which shattered and dispersed them; and before they could be refitted, Essex found, that their provisions were so far spent, that it would not be safe to carry so numerous an army along with him. He dismissed, therefore, all the soldiers, except the thousand veterans under Vere; and laying aside all thoughts of attacking Ferrol or the Groine, he confined the object of his expedition to the intercepting of the Indian fleet; which had at first been considered only as the second enterprize which he was to attempt.

The Indian fleet, in that age, by reason of the imperfection of navigation, had a stated course, as well as season, both in their going out, and in their return; and there were certain islands, at which, as at fixed stages, they always touched, and where they took in water and provisions. The Azores, being one of these places, where, about this time, the fleet was expected, Essex bent his course thither; and he informed Raleigh, that he, on his arrival, intended to attack Fayal, one of these islands. By some accident the squadrons were separated; and Raleigh arriving first before Fayal, thought it more prudent, after waiting some time for the general, to begin the attack alone, lest the inhabitants should, by farther delay, have leisure to make preparations for their defence. He succeeded in the enterprize; but Essex, jealous of Raleigh, expressed great displeasure at his conduct, and construed it as an intention of robbing the general of the glory which attended that action: He cashiered, therefore, Sydney, Bret, Berry, and others, who had concurred in the attempt; and would have proceeded to inflict the same punishment on Raleigh himself, had not lord Thomas Howard interposed with his good offices, and persuaded Raleigh, though high-spirited, to make submissions to the general. Essex, who was placable, as well as hasty and passionate, was soon appeased, and both received Raleigh into favour, and restored the other officers to their commands.[q] This incident, however, though the quarrel was seemingly accommodated, laid the first foundation of that violent animosity, which afterwards took place between these two gallant commanders.

Essex made next a disposition proper for intercepting the Indian galleons; and Sir William Monson, whose station was the most remote of the fleet, having fallen in with them, made the signals which had been agreed on. That able officer, in his Memoirs, ascribes Essex's failure, when he was so near attaining so mighty an advantage, to his want of experience in seamanship; and the account which he gives of the errors committed by that nobleman, appears very reasonable as well as candid.[r] The Spanish fleet,

[q] Monson, p. 173.   [r] Monson, p. 174.

finding that the enemy was upon them, made all the sail possible to the Terceras, and got into the safe and well fortified harbour of Angra, before the English fleet could overtake them. Essex intercepted only three ships; which, however, were so rich as to repay all the charges of the expedition.

The causes of the miscarriage in this enterprize were much canvassed in England, upon the return of the fleet; and though the courtiers took part differently, as they affected either Essex or Raleigh, the people, in general, who bore an extreme regard to the gallantry, spirit, and generosity of the former, were inclined to justify every circumstance of his conduct. The queen, who loved the one as much as she esteemed the other, maintained a kind of neutrality, and endeavoured to share her favours with an impartial hand between the parties. Sir Robert Cecil, second son of lord Burleigh, was a courtier of promising hopes, much connected with Raleigh; and she made him secretary of state, preferably to Sir Thomas Bodley, whom Essex recommended for that office. But not to disgust Essex, she promoted him to the dignity of earl Marshal of England; an office which had been vacant since the death of the earl of Shrewsbury. Essex might perceive from this conduct, that she never intended to give him the entire ascendant over his rivals, and might thence learn the necessity of moderation and caution. But his temper was too high for submission; his behaviour too open and candid to practice the arts of a court; and his free sallies, while they rendered him but more amiable in the eyes of good judges, gave his enemies many advantages against him.

24th Oct. The war with Spain, though successful, having exhausted the queen's exchequer, she was obliged to assemble a parliament; where Yelverton, a lawyer, was chosen speaker of the house of commons.ˢ Elizabeth took care, by the mouth of Sir Thomas Egerton, lord keeper, to inform this assembly of the necessity of a supply. She said, that the wars, formerly waged in Europe, had commonly been conducted by the parties without farther view than to gain a few towns, or at most a province, from each other; but the object of the present hostilities, on the part of Spain, was no other than utterly to bereave England of her religion, her liberty, and her independance: That these blessings, however, she

ˢ See note [EE] at the end of the volume.

herself had hitherto been able to preserve, in spite of the devil, the pope, and the Spanish tyrant, and all the mischievous designs of all her enemies: That in this contest she had disbursed a sum triple to all the parliamentary supplies granted her; and besides expending her ordinary revenues, had been obliged to sell many of the crown lands: And that she could not doubt, but her subjects, in a cause where their own honour and interest were so deeply concerned, would willingly contribute to such moderate taxations as should be found necessary for the common defence.' The parliament granted her three subsidies and six fifteenths; the same supply which had been given four years before, but which had then appeared so unusual, that they had voted it should never afterwards be regarded as a precedent.

The commons, this session, ventured to engage in two controversies about forms with the house of peers; a prelude to those encroachments, which, as they assumed more courage, they afterwards made upon the prerogatives of the crown. They complained, that the lords failed in civility to them, by receiving their messages sitting with their hats on; and that the keeper returned an answer in the same negligent posture: But the upper house proved, to their full satisfaction, that they were not entitled, by custom, and the usage of parliament, to any more respect." Some amendments had been made by the lords, to a bill sent up by the commons; and these amendments were written on parchment, and returned with the bill to the commons. The lower house took umbrage at the novelty: They pretended, that these amendments ought to have been written on paper, not on parchment; and they complained of this innovation to the peers. The peers replied, that they expected not such a frivolous objection from the gravity of the house; and that it was not material, whether the amendments were written on parchment or on paper, nor whether the paper were white, black, or brown. The commons were offended at this reply, which seemed to contain a mockery of them; and they complained of it, though without obtaining any satisfaction.ᵂ

An application was made by way of petition to the queen, from the lower house, against monopolies; an abuse which had risen to

---

' D'Ewes, p. 525, 527. Townsend, p. 79. " D'Ewes, p. 539, 540, 580, 585. Townsend, p. 93, 94, 95. ᵂ D'Ewes, p. 576, 577.

an enormous height; and they received a gracious, though a general answer; for which they returned their thankful acknowledgments:[x] But not to give them too much encouragement in such applications, she told them, in the speech which she delivered at their dissolution, "That with regard to these patents, she hoped, that her dutiful and loving subjects would not take away her prerogative, which is the chief flower in her garden, and the principal and head pearl in her crown and diadem; but that they would rather leave these matters to her disposal."[y] The commons also took notice, this session, of some transactions in the court of high commission; but not till they had previously obtained permission from her majesty to that purpose.[z]

1598.   Elizabeth had reason to foresee, that parliamentary supplies would now become more necessary to her than ever; and that the chief burthen of the war with Spain would thenceforth lie upon England. Henry had received an overture for peace with Philip; but before he would proceed to a negociation, he gave intelligence of it to his allies, the queen and the States; that, if possible, a general pacification might be made by common agreement. These two powers sent ambassadors to France, in order to remonstrate against peace; the queen, Sir Robert Cecil, and Henry Herbert; the States, Justin Nassau, and John Barnevelt. Henry said to these ministers, that his early education had been amidst war and danger, and he had passed the whole course of his life either in arms or in military preparations: That after the proofs, which he had given of his alacrity in the field, no one could doubt, but he would willingly, for his part, have continued in a course of life, to which he was now habituated, till the common enemy were reduced to such a condition as no longer to give umbrage either to him or to his allies: That no private interests of his own, not even those of his people, nothing but the most invincible necessity, could ever induce him to think of a separate peace with Philip, or make him embrace measures not entirely conformable to the wishes of all his confederates: That his kingdom, torne with the convulsions and civil wars of near half a century, required some interval of repose, ere it could reach a condition, in which it might sustain itself, much more support its allies: That after the minds of his subjects were

---

[x] Ibid. p. 570, 573.   [y] D'Ewes, p. 547.   [z] Ibid. p. 557, 558.

composed to tranquillity and accustomed to obedience, after his finances were brought into order, and after agriculture and the arts were restored, France, instead of being a burthen, as at present, to her confederates, would be able to lend them effectual succour, and amply to repay them all the assistance, which she had received during her calamities: And that, if the ambition of Spain would not at present grant them such terms as they should think reasonable, he hoped, that, in a little time, he should attain such a situation as would enable him to mediate more effectually, and with more decisive authority, in their behalf.

The ambassadors were sensible, that these reasons were not feigned; and they therefore remonstrated with the less vehemence against the measures, which, they saw, Henry was determined to pursue. The States knew, that that monarch was interested never to permit their final ruin; and having received private assurances, that he would still, notwithstanding the peace, give them assistance both of men and money, they were well pleased to remain on terms of amity with him. His greatest concern was to give satisfaction to Elizabeth for this breach of treaty. He had a cordial esteem for that princess, a sympathy of manners, and a gratitude for the extraordinary favours, which he had received from her, during his greatest difficulties: And he used every expedient to apologize and atone for that measure, which necessity extorted from him. But as Spain refused to treat with the Dutch as a free state, and Elizabeth would not negociate without her ally, Henry found himself obliged to conclude at Vervins, a separate peace, by which he recovered *Peace of* possession of all the places seized by Spain during the course of the *Vervins.* civil wars, and procured to himself leisure to pursue the domestic settlement of his kingdom. His capacity for the arts of peace was not inferior to his military talents; and, in a little time, by his frugality, order, and wise government, he raised France, from the desolation and misery, in which she was involved, to a more flourishing condition than she had ever before enjoyed.

The queen knew, that she could also, whenever she pleased, finish the war on equitable terms; and that Philip, having no claims upon her, would be glad to free himself from an enemy, who had foiled him in every contes , and who still had it so much in her power to make him feel the weight of her arms. Some of her wisest counsellors, particularly the treasurer, advised her to embrace pacific measures; and set before her the advantages of tranquillity, security, and frugality, as more considerable than any success, which could attend the greatest victories. But this high-spirited princess, though at first averse to war, seemed now to have attained such an ascendant over the enemy, that she was unwilling to stop the course of her prosperous fortune. She considered, that her situation and her past victories had given her entire security against any dangerous invasion; and the war must thenceforth be conducted by sudden enterprizes and naval expeditions, in which she possessed an undoubted superiority: That the weak condition of Philip in the Indies, opened to her the view of the most durable advantages; and the yearly return of his treasure by sea afforded a continual prospect of important, though more temporary, successes: That, after his peace with France, if she also should consent to an accommodation, he would be able to turn his whole force against the revolted provinces of the Netherlands, which, though they had surprisingly encreased their power by commerce and good government, were still unable, if not supported by their confederates, to maintain war against so potent a monarch: And that as her defence of that commonwealth was the original ground of the quarrel, it was unsafe, as well as dishonourable, to abandon its cause, till she had placed it in a state of greater security.

These reasons were frequently inculcated on her by the earl of Essex, whose passion for glory, as well as his military talents, made him earnestly desire the continuance of war, from which he ex-

The earl of Essex. pected to reap so much advantage and distinction. The rivalship between this nobleman and lord Burleigh made each of them insist the more strenuously on his own counsel; but as Essex's person was agreeable to the queen, as well as his advice conformable to her inclinations, the favourite seemed daily to acquire an ascendant over the minister. Had he been endowed with caution and self-command, equal to his shining qualities, he would have so rivetted himself in the queen's confidence, that none of his enemies had ever been able to impeach his credit: But his lofty spirit could ill submit to that implicit deference, which her temper required, and which she had ever been accustomed to receive from all her subjects. Being once engaged in a dispute with her about the choice of a governor for Ireland, he was so heated in the argument, that he entirely forgot the rules both of duty and civility; and turned his back upon her in a contemptuous manner. Her anger, naturally prompt and violent, rose at this provocation; and she instantly gave him a box on the ear; adding a passionate expression, suited to his impertinence. Instead of recollecting himself, and making the submissions due to her sex and station, he clapped his hand to his sword, and swore, that he would not bear such usage, were it from Henry VIII. himself; and he immediately withdrew from court. Egerton, the chancellor, who loved Essex, exhorted him to repair his indiscretion by proper acknowledgments; and entreated him not to give that triumph to his enemies, that affliction to his friends, which must ensue from his supporting a contest with his sovereign, and deserting the service of his country: But Essex was deeply stung with the dishonour, which he had received; and seemed to think, that an insult, which might be pardoned in a woman, was become a mortal affront when it came from his sovereign. "If the vilest of all indignities," said he, "is done me, does religion enforce me to sue for pardon? Doth God require it? Is it impiety not to do it? Why? Cannot princes err? Cannot subjects receive wrong? Is an earthly power infinite? Pardon me, my lord, I can never subscribe to these principles. Let Solomon's fool laugh when he is stricken; let those that mean to make their profit of princes, shew no sense of princes' injuries: Let *them* acknowledge an infinite absoluteness on earth, that do not believe an absolute infiniteness in heaven:" (alluding, probably, to the character and conduct of Sir Walter Raleigh, who lay under the reproach of impiety) "As for me," continued he, "I have received wrong, I feel it: My cause is good, I know it; and whatsoever happens, all the powers on earth can never exert more strength and constancy in oppressing, than I can shew in suffering every thing that can or shall be imposed upon me. Your lordship, in the beginning of your letter, makes me a player, and yourself a looker on: And me a player of my own game, so you may see more than I: But give me leave to tell you, that since you do but see, and I do suffer, I must of necessity feel more than you."[a]

This spirited letter was shown by Essex to his friends; and they were so imprudent as to disperse copies of it: Yet notwithstanding this additional provocation, the queen's partiality was so prevalent,

[a] See note [FF] at the end of the volume.

that she reinstated him in his former favour; and her kindness to him appeared rather to have acquired new force from this short interval of anger and resentment. The death of Burleigh, his an-

4th Aug. tagonist, which happened about the same time, seemed to ensure him constant possession of the queen's confidence; and nothing indeed but his own indiscretion could thenceforth have shaken his well-established credit. Lord Burleigh died in an advanced age; and by a rare fortune, was equally regretted by his sovereign and the people. He had risen gradually, from small beginnings, by the mere force of merit; and though his authority was never entirely absolute, or uncontrouled with the queen, he was still, during the course of near forty years, regarded as her principal minister. None of her other inclinations or affections could ever overcome her confidence in so useful a counsellor; and as he had had the generosity or good sense to pay assiduous court to her, during her sister's reign, when it was dangerous to appear her friend, she thought herself bound in gratitude, when she mounted the throne, to persevere in her attachments to him. He seems not to have possessed any shining talents of address, eloquence, or imagination; and was chiefly distinguished by solidity of understanding, probity of manners, and indefatigable application in business: Virtues, which, if they do not always enable a man to attain high stations, do certainly qualify him best for filling them. Of all the queen's ministers he alone left a considerable fortune to his posterity; a fortune not acquired by rapine or oppression, but gained by the regular profits of his offices, and preserved by frugality.

8th Aug. The last act of this able minister was the concluding of a new treaty with the Dutch; who, after being, in some measure, deserted by the king of France, were glad to preserve the queen's alliance, by submitting to any terms which she pleased to require of them. The debt, which they owed her, was now settled as eight hundred thousand pounds: Of this sum they agreed to pay, during the war, thirty thousand pounds a-year; and these payments were to continue till four hundred thousand pounds of the debt should be extinguished. They engaged also, during the time that England should continue the war with Spain, to pay the garrisons of the cautionary towns. They stipulated, that, if Spain should invade England, or the Isle of Wight, or Jersey, or Scilly, they should assist her with a body of five thousand foot, and five hundred horse; and that in case she undertook any naval armament against Spain, they should join an equal number of ships to hers.[b] By this treaty the queen was eased of an annual charge of a hundred and twenty thousand pounds.

Soon after the death of Burleigh, the queen, who regretted extremely the loss of so wise and faithful a minister, was informed of the death of her capital enemy, Philip II. who, after languishing under many infirmities, expired in an advanced age at Madrid. This haughty prince, desirous of an accommodation with his re-volted subjects in the Netherlands, but disdaining to make in his own name the concessions necessary for that purpose, had trans-ferred to his daughter, married to archduke Albert, the title to the Low Country provinces; but as it was not expected, that this prin-cess could have posterity, and as the reversion, on failure of her issue, was still reserved to the crown of Spain, the States considered this deed only as the change of a name, and they persisted with equal obstinacy in their resistance to the Spanish arms. The other powers also of Europe made no distinction between the courts of Brussels and Madrid; and the secret opposition of France, as well as of the avowed efforts of England, continued to operate against the progress of Albert, as it had done against that of Philip.

[b] Rymer, vol. xvi. p. 340.

XLIV

State of Ireland – Tyrone's
rebellion – Essex sent over to Ireland –
His ill success – Returns to England –
Is disgraced – His intrigues –
His insurrection – His trial
and execution – French affairs –
Mountjoy's success in Ireland –
Defeat of the Spaniards and Irish –
A parliament – Tyrone's submission –
Queen's sickness – And death –
And character

THOUGH the dominion of the English over Ireland had been
seemingly established above four centuries, it may safely be
affirmed, that their authority had hitherto been little more than
nominal. The Irish princes and nobles, divided among themselves,
readily paid the exterior marks of obeisance to a power which they
were not able to resist; but, as no durable force was ever keeped on
foot to retain them in their duty, they relapsed still into their
former state of independance. Too weak to introduce order and
obedience among the rude inhabitants, the English authority was
yet sufficient to check the growth of any enterprizing genius
among the natives: And though it could bestow no true form of

CHAPTER XLIV

civil government, it was able to prevent the rise of any such form, from the internal combination or policy of the Irish.[e]

Most of the English institutions likewise, by which that island was governed, were to the last degree absurd, and such as no state before had ever thought of, for preserving dominion over its conquered provinces.

The English nation, all on fire for the project of subduing France, a project, whose success was the most improbable, and would to them have proved the most pernicious; neglected all other enterprizes, to which their situation so strongly invited them, and which, in time, would have brought them an accession of riches, grandeur, and security. The small army, which they maintained in Ireland, they never supplied regularly with pay; and as no money could be levied on the island, which possessed none, they gave their soldiers the privilege of free quarter upon the natives. Rapine and insolence inflamed the hatred, which prevailed between the conquerors and the conquered: Want of security among the Irish, introducing despair, nourished still more the sloth, natural to that uncultivated people.

But the English carried farther their ill-judged tyranny. Instead of inviting the Irish to adopt the more civilized customs of their conquerors, they even refused, though earnestly solicited, to communicate to them the privilege of their laws, and every where marked them out as aliens and as enemies. Thrown out of the protection of justice, the natives could find no security but in force; and flying the neighbourhood of cities, which they could not approach with safety, they sheltered themselves in their marshes and forests from the insolence of their inhuman masters. Being treated like wild beasts, they became such; and joining the ardor of revenge to their yet untamed barbarity, they grew every day more intractable and more dangerous.[d]

As the English princes deemed the conquest of the dispersed Irish to be more the object of time and patience than the source of military glory, they willingly delegated that office to private adventurers, who, inlisting soldiers at their own charge, reduced provinces of that island, which they converted to their own profit. Separate jurisdictions and principalities were established by these

[e] Sir J. Davies, p. 5, 6, 7, &c.   [d] Sir J. Davies, p. 102, 103, &c.

lordly conquerors: The power of peace and war was assumed: Military law was exercised over the Irish, whom they subdued, and, by degrees, over the English, by whose assistance they conquered: And, after their authority had once taken root, deeming the English institutions less favourable to barbarous dominion, they degenerated into mere Irish, and abandoned the garb, language, manners, and laws of their mother country.[e]

By all this imprudent conduct of England, the natives of its dependant state remained still in that abject condition, into which the northern and western parts of Europe were sunk, before they received civility and slavery from the refined policy and irresistible bravery of Rome. Even at the end of the sixteenth century, when every christian nation was cultivating with ardour every civil art of life, that island, lying in a temperate climate, enjoying a fertile soil, accessible in its situation, possessed of innumerable harbours, was still, notwithstanding these advantages, inhabited by a people, whose customs and manners approached nearer those of savages than of barbarians.[f]

As the rudeness and ignorance of the Irish were extreme, they were sunk below the reach of that curiosity and love of novelty, by which every other people in Europe had been seized at the beginning of that century, and which had engaged them in innovations and religious disputes, with which they were still so violently agitated. The ancient superstition, the practices and observances of their fathers, mingled and polluted with many wild opinions, still maintained an unshaken empire over them; and the example alone of the English was sufficient to render the reformation odious to the prejudiced and discontented Irish. The old opposition of manners, laws, and interest was now inflamed by religious antipathy; and the subduing and civilizing of that country seemed to become every day more difficult and more impracticable.

The animosity against the English was carried so far by the Irish, that, in an insurrection, raised by two sons of the earl of Clanricarde, they put to the sword all the inhabitants of the town of Athenry, though Irish; because they began to conform themselves to English customs, and had embraced a more civilized form of life, than had been practiced by their ancestors.[g]

[e] Sir J. Davies, p. 133, 134, &c.   [f] See Spencer's account of Ireland, throughout.   [g] Camden, p. 457.

CHAPTER XLIV

The usual revenue of Ireland amounted only to six thousand pounds a-year:[h] The queen, though with much repining,[i] commonly added twenty thousand more, which she remitted from England: And with this small revenue, a body of a thousand men was supported, which, on extraordinary emergencies, was augmented to two thousand.[k] No wonder that a force, so disproportioned to the object, instead of subduing a mutinous kingdom, served rather to provoke the natives, and to excite those frequent insurrections, which still farther inflamed the animosity between the two nations, and encreased the disorders, to which the Irish were naturally subject.

In 1560, Shan O'Neale, or the great O'Neale, as the Irish called him, because head of that potent clan, raised a rebellion in Ulster; but after some skirmishes, he was received into favour, upon his submission, and his promise of a more dutiful behaviour for the future.[l] This impunity tempted him to undertake a new insurrection in 1567; but being pushed by Sir Henry Sidney, lord deputy, he retreated into Clandeboy, and rather than submit to the English, he put himself into the hands of some Scottish islanders, who commonly infested those parts by their incursions. The Scots, who retained a quarrel against him on account of former injuries, violated the laws of hospitality, and murdered him at a festival, to which they had invited him. He was a man equally noted for his pride, his violence, his debaucheries, and his hatred of the English nation. He is said to have put some of his followers to death, because they endeavoured to introduce the use of bread after the English fashion.[m] Though so violent an enemy to luxury, he was extremely addicted to riot; and was accustomed, after his intemperance had thrown him into a fever, to plunge his body into mire, that he might allay the flame, which he had raised by former excesses.[n] Such was the life led by this haughty barbarian, who scorned the title of the earl of Tyrone, which Elizabeth intended to have restored to him, and who assumed the rank and appellation of king of Ulster. He used also to say, that, though the queen was his sovereign lady, he never made peace with her but at her seeking.[o]

[h] Memoirs of the Sidneys, vol. i. p. 86.   [i] Cox, p. 342. Sidney, vol. i. p. 85, 200.   [k] Camden, p. 542. Sidney, vol. i. p. 65, 109, 183, 184.   [l] Camden, p. 385, 391.   [m] Camden, p. 409.   [n] Ibid. p. 409. Cox, p. 324.   [o] Ibid. p. 321.

Sir Henry Sidney was one of the wisest and most active governors that Ireland had enjoyed for several reigns;[p] and he possessed
his authority eleven years; during which, he struggled with many
difficulties, and made some progress in repressing those disorders,
which had become inveterate among the people. The earl of Desmond, in 1569, gave him disturbance, from the hereditary animosity, which prevailed between that nobleman and the earl of
Ormond, descended from the only family, established in Ireland,
that had steddily maintained its loyalty to the English crown.[q] The
earl of Thomond, in 1570, attempted a rebellion in Connaught,
but was obliged to fly into France, before his designs were ripe for
execution. Stukely, another fugitive, found such credit with the
pope, Gregory the XIIIth, that he flattered that pontiff with the
prospect of making his nephew, Buon Compagno, king of Ireland;
and as if this project had already taken effect, he accepted the title
of marquiss of Leinster from the new sovereign.[r] He passed next
into Spain; and after having received much encouragement and
great rewards from Philip, who intended to employ him as an
instrument in disturbing Elizabeth, he was found to possess too
little interest for executing those high promises, which he had
made to that monarch: He retired into Portugal; and following the
fortunes of Don Sebastian, he perished with that gallant prince in
his bold but unfortunate expedition against the Moors.

Lord Gray, after some interval, succeeded to the government of
Ireland; and, in 1579, suppressed a new rebellion of the earl of
Desmond, though supported by a body of Spaniards and Italians.
The rebellion of the Bourks followed a few years after; occasioned
by the strict and equitable administration of Sir Richard Bingham,
governor of Connaught, who endeavoured to repress the tyranny
of the chieftains over their vassals.[s] The queen, finding Ireland so
burthensome to her, tried several expedients for reducing it to a
state of greater order and submission. She encouraged the earl of
Essex, father to that nobleman, who was afterwards her favourite,
to attempt the subduing and planting of Clandeboy, Ferny, and
other territories, part of some late forfeitures: But that enterprize
proved unfortunate; and Essex died of a distemper, occasioned, as

[p] Cox, p. 350.   [q] Camden, p. 424.   [r] Ibid. p. 430. Cox, p. 354.   [s] Stowe,
p. 720.

is supposed, by the vexation, which he had conceived, from his disappointments. An university was founded in Dublin with a view of introducing arts and learning into that kingdom, and civilizing the uncultivated manners of the inhabitants.[1] But the most unhappy expedient, employed in the government of Ireland, was that made use of in 1585, by Sir John Perrot, at that time lord deputy: He put arms into the hands of the Irish inhabitants of Ulster, in order to enable them, without the assistance of the government, to repress the incursions of the Scottish islanders, by which these parts were much infested.[2] At the same time, the invitations of Philip, joined to their zeal for the catholic religion, engaged many of the gentry to serve in the Low Country wars; and thus Ireland, being provided with officers and soldiers, with discipline and arms, became formidable to the English, and was thenceforth able to maintain a more regular war against her ancient masters.

Hugh O'Neale, nephew to Shan O'Neale, had been raised by the queen to the dignity of earl of Tyrone; but having murdered his cousin, son of that rebel, and being acknowledged head of his clan, he preferred the pride of barbarous licence and dominion to the pleasures of opulence and tranquillity, and he fomented all those disorders, by which he hoped to weaken or overturn the English government. He was noted for the vices of perfidy and cruelty, so common among uncultivated nations; and was also eminent for courage, a virtue, which their disorderly course of life requires, and which notwithstanding, being less supported by the principle of honour, is commonly more precarious among them, than among a civilized people. Tyrone, actuated by this spirit, secretly fomented the discontents of the Maguires, Odonnels, O'Rourks, Macmahons, and other rebels; yet trusting to the influence of his deceitful oaths and professions, he put himself into the hands of Sir William Russel, who, in the year 1594, was sent over deputy to Ireland. Contrary to the advice and protestation of Sir Henry Bagnal, marshal of the army, he was dismissed; and returning to his own country, he embraced the resolution of raising an open rebellion, and of relying no longer on the lenity or inexperience of the English government. He entered into a correspon-

Tyrone's rebellion.

[1] Camden, p. 566.　[2] Nanton's Fragmenta Regalia, p. 203.

dence with Spain: He procured thence a supply of arms and
ammunition: And having united all the Irish chieftains in a dependance upon himself, he began to be regarded as a formidable enemy.

The native Irish were so poor, that their country afforded few
other commodities than cattle and oatmeal, which were easily concealed or driven away on the approach of the enemy; and as Elizabeth was averse to the expence requisite for supporting her
armies, the English found much difficulty in pushing their advantages, and in pursuing the rebels into the bogs, woods, and other
fastnesses, to which they retreated. These motives rendered Sir
John Norris, who commanded the English army, the more willing
to hearken to any proposals of truce or accommodation made him
by Tyrone; and after the war was spun out by these artifices for
some years, that gallant Englishman, finding that he had been
deceived by treacherous promises, and that he had performed
nothing worthy of his ancient reputation, was seized with a languishing distemper, and died of vexation and discontent. Sir
Henry Bagnal, who succeeded him in the command, was still more
unfortunate. As he advanced to relieve the fort of Black-water,
besieged by the rebels, he was surrounded in disadvantageous
ground; his soldiers, discouraged by part of their powder's acci-
dentally taking fire, were put to flight; and, though the pursuit was
stopped by Montacute, who commanded the English horse, fifteen
hundred men, together with the general himself, were left dead
upon the spot. This victory, so unusual to the Irish, rouzed their
courage, supplied them with arms and ammunition, and raised the
reputation of Tyrone, who assumed the character of the deliverer
of his country, and patron of Irish liberty.[w]

The English council were now sensible, that the rebellion of
Ireland was come to a dangerous head, and that the former tempo-
rizing arts, of granting truces and pacifications to the rebels, and
of allowing them to purchase pardons by resigning part of the
plunder, acquired during their insurrection, served only to encourage the spirit of mutiny and disorder among them. It was
therefore resolved to push the war by more vigorous measures;
and the queen cast her eye on Charles Blount, lord Mountjoy, as

[w] Cox, p. 415.

CHAPTER XLIV

a man, who, though hitherto less accustomed to arms than to books and literature, was endowed, she thought, with talents equal to the undertaking. But the young earl of Essex, ambitious of fame, and desirous of obtaining this government for himself, opposed the choice of Mountjoy; and represented the necessity of appointing, for that important employment, some person more experienced in war than this nobleman, more practised in business, and of higher quality and reputation. By this description, he was understood to mean himself;[x] and no sooner was his desire known, than his enemies, even more zealously than his friends, conspired to gratify his wishes. Many of his friends thought, that he never ought to consent, except for a short time, to accept of any employment, which must remove him from court, and prevent him from cultivating that personal inclination, which the queen so visibly bore him.[y] His enemies hoped, that if, by his absence, she had once leisure to forget the charms of his person and conversation, his impatient and lofty demeanor would soon disgust a princess, who usually exacted such profound submission and implicit obedience from all her servants. But Essex was incapable of entering into such cautious views; and even Elizabeth, who was extremely desirous of subduing the Irish rebels, and who was much prepossessed in favour of Essex's genius, readily agreed to appoint him governor of Ireland, by the title of lord lieutenant. The more to encourage him in his undertaking, she granted him by his patent more extensive authority than had ever before been conferred on any lieutenant; the power of carrying on or finishing the war as he pleased, of pardoning the rebels, and of filling all the most considerable employments of the kingdom.[z] And to ensure him of success, she levied a numerous army of sixteen thousand foot and thirteen hundred horse, which she afterwards augmented to twenty thousand foot and two thousand horse: A force, which, it was apprehended, would be able, in one campaign, to overwhelm the rebels, and make an entire conquest of Ireland. Nor did Essex's enemies, the earl of Nottingham, Sir Robert Cecil, Sir Walter Raleigh, and lord Cobham, throw any obstacles in the way of these preparations; but hoped that the higher the queen's expectations of success were raised, the more difficult it would be for the event

Essex sent over to Ireland.

[x] Bacon, vol. iv. p. 512.   [y] Cabala, p. 79.   [z] Rymer, tom. xvi. p. 366.

to correspond to them. In a like view, they rather seconded than opposed, those exalted encomiums, which Essex's numerous and sanguine friends dispersed, of his high genius, of his elegant endowments, his heroic courage, his unbounded generosity, and his noble birth; nor were they displeased to observe that passionate fondness, which the people every where expressed for this nobleman. These artful politicians had studied his character; and finding, that his open and undaunted spirit, if taught temper and reserve from opposition, must become invincible, they resolved rather to give full breath to those sails, which were already too much expanded, and to push him upon dangers, of which he seemed to make such small account.[a] And the better to make advantage of his indiscretions, spies were set upon all his actions and even expressions; and his vehement spirit, which, while he was in the midst of the court and environed by his rivals, was unacquainted with disguise, could not fail, after he thought himself surrounded by none but friends, to give a pretence for malignant suspicions and constructions.

Essex left London in the month of March, attended with the acclamations of the populace; and what did him more honour, accompanied by a numerous train of nobility and gentry, who, from affection to his person, had attached themselves to his fortunes, and sought fame and military experience under so renowned a commander. The first act of authority, which he exercised, after his arrival in Ireland, was an indiscretion, but of the generous kind; and in both these respects, suitable to his character. He appointed his intimate friend, the earl of Southampton, general of the horse; a nobleman, who had incurred the queen's displeasure, by secretly marrying without her consent, and whom she had therefore enjoined Essex not to employ in any command under him. She no sooner heard of this instance of disobedience than she reprimanded him, and ordered him to recal his commission to Southampton. But Essex, who had imagined, that some reasons, which he opposed to her first injunctions, had satisfied her, had the imprudence to remonstrate against these second orders;[b] and it was not till she reiterated her commands, that he could be prevailed on to displace his friend.

[a] Camden. Osborne, p. 371.   [b] Birch's Memoirs, vol. ii. p. 421, 451.

CHAPTER XLIV

Essex, on his landing at Dublin, deliberated with the Irish coun-   *His ill*
cil, concerning the proper methods of carrying on the war against   *success.*
the rebels; and here he was guilty of a capital error, which was the
ruin of his enterprize. He had always, while in England, blamed
the conduct of former commanders, who artfully protracted the
war, who harassed their troops in small enterprizes, and who, by
agreeing to truces and temporary pacifications with the rebels, had
given them leisure to recruit their broken forces.[c] In conformity to
these views, he had ever insisted upon leading his forces immediately into Ulster against Tyrone, the chief enemy; and his instructions had been drawn agreeably to these his declared resolutions. But the Irish counsellors persuaded him, that the season was
too early for the enterprize, and that, as the morasses, in which the
northern Irish usually sheltered themselves, would not, as yet, be
passable to the English forces, it would be better to employ the
present time in an expedition into Munster. Their secret reason
for this advice was, that many of them possessed estates in
that province, and were desirous to have the enemy dislodged
from their neighbourhood:[d] But the same selfish spirit, which
had induced them to give this counsel, made them soon after disown it, when they found the bad consequences, with which it was
attended.[e]

Essex obliged all the rebels of Munster either to submit or to fly
into the neighbouring provinces: But as the Irish, from the greatness of the queen's preparations, had concluded, that she intended
to reduce them to total subjection, or even utterly to exterminate
them, they considered their defence as a common cause; and the
English forces were no sooner withdrawn, than the inhabitants of
Munster relapsed into rebellion, and renewed their confederacy
with their other countrymen. The army, meanwhile, by the fatigue
of long and tedious marches, and by the influence of the climate,
was become sickly; and on its return to Dublin, about the middle
of July, was surprizingly diminished in number. The courage of
the soldiers was even much abated: For though they had prevailed
in some lesser enterprizes, against lord Cahir and others; yet had
they sometimes met with more stout resistance than they expected

[c] Ibid. p. 431. Bacon, vol. iv. p. 512.   [d] Birch's Memoirs, vol. ii. p. 448.
[e] Winwood, vol. i. p. 140.

from the Irish, whom they were wont to despise; and as they were raw troops and unexperienced, a considerable body of them had been put to flight at the Glins, by an inferior number of the enemy. Essex was so enraged at this misbehaviour, that he cashiered all the officers, and decimated the private men.[f] But this act of severity, though necessary, had intimidated the soldiers, and encreased their aversion to the service.

The queen was extremely disgusted, when she heard, that so considerable a part of the season was consumed in these frivolous enterprizes; and was still more surprized, that Essex persevered in the same practice, which he had so much condemned in others, and which he knew to be so much contrary to her purpose and intention. That nobleman, in order to give his troops leisure to recruit from their sickness and fatigue, left the main army in quarters, and marched with a small body, of fifteen hundred men, into the county of Ophelie against the O'Connors and O'Mores, whom he forced to a submission: But, on his return to Dublin, he found the army so much diminished, that he wrote to the English council an account of its condition, and informed them, that, if he did not immediately receive a reinforcement of two thousand men, it would be impossible for him this season to attempt any thing against Tyrone. That there might be no pretence for farther inactivity, the queen immediately sent over the number demanded;[g] and Essex began at last to assemble his forces for the expedition into Ulster. The army was so averse to this enterprize, and so terrified with the reputation of Tyrone, that many of them counterfeited sickness, many of them deserted;[h] and Essex found, that, after leaving the necessary garrisons, he could scarcely lead four thousand men against the rebels. He marched, however, with this small army; but was soon sensible, that, in so advanced a season, it would be impossible for him to effect any thing against an enemy, who, though superior in number, was determined to avoid every decisive action. He hearkened therefore, to a message sent him by Tyrone, who desired a conference; and a place, near the two camps, was appointed for that purpose. The generals met without any of their attendants, and a river ran between them, into which

[f] Cox, p. 421.   [g] Birch's Memoirs, vol. ii. p. 430. Cox, p. 421.   [h] Sydney's Letters, vol. ii. p. 112, 113.

CHAPTER XLIV

Tyrone entered to the depth of his saddle: But Essex stood on the opposite bank. After half an hour's conference, where Tyrone behaved with great submission to the lord lieutenant, a cessation of arms was concluded to the first of May, renewable from six weeks to six weeks; but which might be broken off by either party upon a fortnight's warning.[i] Essex also received from Tyrone proposals for a peace, in which that rebel had inserted many unreasonable and exorbitant conditions: And there appeared afterwards some reason to suspect, that he had here commenced a very unjustifiable correspondence with the enemy.[k]

So unexpected an issue of an enterprize, the greatest and most expensive that Elizabeth had ever undertaken, provoked her extremely against Essex; and this disgust was much augmented by other circumstances of that nobleman's conduct. He wrote many letters to the queen and council, full of peevish and impatient expressions; complaining of his enemies, lamenting that their calumnies should be believed against him, and discovering symptoms of a mind, equally haughty and discontented. She took care to inform him of her dissatisfaction; but commanded him to remain in Ireland till farther orders.

Essex heard at once of Elizabeth's anger, and of the promotion of his enemy, Sir Robert Cecil, to the office of master of the wards, an office to which he himself aspired: And dreading, that, if he remained any longer absent, the queen would be totally alienated from him, he hastily embraced a resolution, which, he knew, had once succeeded with the earl of Leicester, the former favourite of Elizabeth. Leicester, being informed, while in the Low Countries, that his mistress was extremely displeased with his conduct, disobeyed her orders by coming over to England; and having pacified her by his presence, by his apologies, and by his flattery and insinuation, disappointed all the expectations of his enemies.[l] Essex, therefore, weighing more the similarity of circumstances than the difference of character between himself and Leicester, immediately set out for England; and making speedy journeys, he arrived at court before any one was in the least apprized of his intentions.[m] Though besmeared with dirt and sweat, he hastened up stairs to

Returns to England.

[i] Ibid. p. 125.   [k] Winwood, vol. i. p. 307. State Trials. Bacon, vol. iv. p. 514, 535, 537.   [l] Birch's Memoirs, vol. ii. p. 453.   [m] Winwood, vol. i. p. 118.

the presence chamber, thence to the privy chamber; nor stopped till he was in the queen's bed-chamber, who was newly risen, and was sitting with her hair about her face. He threw himself on his knees, kissed her hand, and had some private conference with her; where he was so graciously received, that, on his departure, he was heard to express great satisfaction, and to thank God, that, though he had suffered much trouble and many storms abroad, he found a sweet calm at home."

But this placability of Elizabeth was merely the result of her surprise, and of the momentary satisfaction, which she felt on the sudden and unexpected appearance of her favourite: After she had leisure for recollection, all his faults recurred to her; and she thought it necessary, by some severe discipline, to subdue that haughty imperious spirit, who, presuming on her partiality, had pretended to domineer in her councils, to engross all her favour, and to act, in the most important affairs, without regard to her orders and instructions. When Essex waited on her in the afternoon, he found her extremely altered in her carriage towards him: She ordered him to be confined to his chamber; to be twice examined by the council; and though his answers were calm and submissive, she committed him to the custody of lord keeper Egerton, and held him sequestered from all company, even from that of his countess, nor was so much as the intercourse of letters permitted between them. Essex dropped many expressions of humiliation and sorrow, none of resentment: He professed an entire submission to the queen's will: Declared his intention of retiring into the country, and of leading thenceforth a private life, remote from courts and business: But though he affected to be so entirely cured of his aspiring ambition, the vexation of this disappointment, and of the triumph gained by his enemies, preyed upon his haughty spirit, and he fell into a distemper, which seemed to put his life in danger.

Is disgraced.

The queen had always declared to all the world, and even to the earl himself, that the purpose of her severity was to correct, not to ruin him;" and when she heard of his sickness, she was not a little alarmed with his situation. She ordered eight physicians of the best

---

" Sydney's Letters, vol. ii. p. 127.   " Birch's Memoirs, p. 444, 445. Sydney's Letters, vol. ii. p. 196.

CHAPTER XLIV

reputation and experience to consult of his case; and being informed, that the issue was much to be apprehended, she sent Dr. James to him with some broth, and desired that physician to deliver him a message, which she probably deemed of still greater virtue; that, if she thought such a step consistent with her honour, she would herself pay him a visit. The bystanders, who carefully observed her countenance, remarked, that, in pronouncing these words, her eyes were suffused with tears.[p]

When these symptoms of the queen's returning affection towards Essex were known, they gave a sensible alarm to the faction, which had declared their opposition to him. Sir Walter Raleigh, in particular, the most violent as well as the most ambitious of his enemies, was so affected with the appearance of this sudden revolution, that he was seized with sickness in his turn; and the queen was obliged to apply the same salve to his wound, and to send him a favourable message, expressing her desire of his recovery.[q]

The medicine, which the queen administered to these aspiring rivals, was successful with both; and Essex, being now allowed the company of his countess, and having entertained more promising hopes of his future fortunes, was so much restored in his health, as to be thought past danger. A belief was instilled into Elizabeth, that his distemper had been entirely counterfeit, in order to move her compassion;[r] and she relapsed into her former rigour against him. He wrote her a letter, and sent her a rich present on New-Year's day; as was usual with the courtiers at that time: She read the letter, but rejected the present.[s] After some interval, however, of severity, she allowed him to retire to his own house: And though he remained still under custody, and was sequestered from all company, he was so grateful for this mark of lenity, that he sent her a letter of thanks on the occasion. "This farther degree of goodness," said he, "doth sound in my ears, as if your majesty spake these words, *Die not, Essex; for though I punish thine offence, and humble thee for thy good, yet will I one day be served again by thee.* My prostrate soul makes this answer: *I hope for that blessed day.* And in expectation of it, all my afflictions of body and mind are humbly, patiently, and chearfully borne by me."[t] The countess of Essex,

1600.

---

[p] Sydney's Letters, vol. ii. p. 151.   [q] Ibid. p. 139.   [r] Sydney's Letters, vol. ii. p. 153.   [s] Ibid. p. 155, 156.   [t] Birch's Memoirs, p. 444.

daughter of Sir Francis Walsingham, possessed, as well as her husband, a refined taste in literature; and the chief consolation which Essex enjoyed, during this period of anxiety and expectation, consisted in her company, and in reading with her those instructive and entertaining authors, which, even during the time of his greatest prosperity, he had never entirely neglected.

There were several incidents, which kept alive the queen's anger against Essex. Every account which she received from Ireland, convinced her more and more of his misconduct in that government, and of the insignificant purposes, to which he had employed so much force and treasure. Tyrone, so far from being quelled, had thought proper, in less than three months, to break the truce; and joining with O'Donel, and other rebels, had over-run almost the whole kingdom. He boasted, that he was certain of receiving a supply of men, money, and arms from Spain: He pretended to be champion of the catholic religion: And he openly exulted in the present of a phoenix plume, which the pope, Clement VIII. in order to encourage him in the prosecution of so good a cause, had consecrated, and had conferred upon him." The queen, that she might check his progress, returned to her former intention, of appointing Mountjoy lord-deputy; and though that nobleman, who was an intimate friend of Essex, and desired his return to the government of Ireland, did at first very earnestly excuse himself, on account of his bad state of health, she obliged him to accept of the employment. Mountjoy found the island almost in a desperate condition; but being a man of capacity and vigour, he was so little discouraged, that he immediately advanced against Tyrone in Ulster. He penetrated into the heart of that country, the chief seat of the rebels: He fortified Derry and Mount-Norris, in order to bridle the Irish: He chaced them from the field, and obliged them to take shelter in the woods and morasses: He employed, with equal success, Sir George Carew in Munster: And by these promising enterprizes, he gave new life to the queen's authority in that island.

As the comparison of Mountjoy's administration with that of Essex, contributed to alienate Elizabeth from her favourite, she received additional disgust from the partiality of the people, who, prepossessed with an extravagant idea of Essex's merit, com-

" Camden, p. 617.

plained of the injustice done him by his removal from court, and by his confinement. Libels were secretly dispersed against Cecil and Raleigh, and all his enemies: And his popularity, which was always great, seemed rather to be encreased than diminished by his misfortunes. Elizabeth, in order to justify to the public her conduct with regard to him, had often expressed her intentions of having him tried in the Star-chamber for his offences: But her tenderness for him prevailed at last over her severity; and she was contented to have him only examined by the privy-council. The attorney-general, Coke, opened the cause against him, and treated him with the cruelty and insolence, which that great lawyer usually exercised against the unfortunate. He displayed in the strongest colours, all the faults committed by Essex in his administration of Ireland: His making Southampton general of the horse, contrary to the queen's injunctions; his deserting the enterprize against Tyrone, and marching to Leinster and Munster; his conferring knighthood on too many persons; his secret conference with Tyrone; and his sudden return from Ireland, in contempt of her majesty's commands. He also exaggerated the indignity of the conditions, which Tyrone had been allowed to propose; odious and abominable conditions, said he; a public toleration of an idolatrous religion, pardon for himself and every traitor in Ireland, and full restitution of lands and possessions to all of them.[w] The solicitor-general, Fleming, insisted upon the wretched situation, in which the earl had left that kingdom; and Francis, son of Sir Nicholas Bacon, who had been lord-keeper in the beginning of the present reign, closed the charge with displaying the undutiful expressions contained in some letters written by the earl.

Essex, when he came to plead in his own defence, renounced, with great submission and humility, all pretensions to an apology;[x] and declared his resolution never, on this or any other occasion, to have any contest with his sovereign. He said, that, having severed himself from the world, and abjured all sentiments of ambition, he had no scruple to confess every failing or error, into which his youth, folly, or manifold infirmities might have betrayed him; that his inward sorrow for his offences against her majesty was so profound, that it exceeded all his outward crosses and afflictions, nor

[w] Birch's Memoirs, vol. ii. p. 449.   [x] Sydney's Letters, vol. ii. p. 200.

had he any scruple of submitting to a public confession of whatever she had been pleased to impute to him; that, in his acknowledgments, he retained only one reserve, which he never would relinquish but with his life, the assertion of a loyal and unpolluted heart, of an unfeigned affection, of an earnest desire ever to perform to her majesty the best service which his poor abilities would permit; and that, if this sentiment were allowed by the council, he willingly acquiesced in any condemnation or sentence which they could pronounce against him. This submission was uttered with so much eloquence, and in so pathetic a manner, that it drew tears from many of the audience.[y] All the privy-counsellors, in giving their judgment, made no scruple of doing the earl justice, with regard to the loyalty of his intentions. Even Cecil, whom he believed his capital enemy, treated him with regard and humanity. And the sentence pronounced by the Lord keeper, (to which the council assented) was in these words. "If this cause," said he, "had been heard in the Star-Chamber, my sentence must have been for as great a fine as ever was set upon any man's head in that court, together with perpetual confinement in that prison, which belongeth to a man of his quality, the Tower. But since we are now in another place, and in a course of favour, my censure is, that the earl of Essex is not to execute the office of a counsellor, nor that of earl marshal of England, nor of master of the ordnance; and to return to his own house, there to continue a prisoner, till it shall please her majesty to release this and all the rest of his sentence."[z] The earl of Cumberland made a slight opposition to this sentence; and said, that, if he thought it would stand, he would have required a little more time to deliberate; that he deemed it somewhat severe; and that any commander in chief might easily incur a like penalty. But, however, added he, in confidence of her majesty's mercy, I agree with the rest. The earl of Worcester delivered his opinion in a couple of Latin verses; importing, that, where the Gods are offended, even misfortunes ought to be imputed as crimes, and that accident is no excuse for transgressions against the Divinity.

Bacon, so much distinguished afterwards by his high offices, and still more by his profound genius for the sciences, was nearly

[y] Sydney's Letters, vol. ii. p. 200, 201.   [z] Birch's Memoirs, vol. ii. p. 454. Camden, p. 626, 627.

CHAPTER XLIV

allied to the Cecil family, being nephew to lord Burleigh, and cousin-german to the secretary: But notwithstanding his extraordinary talents, he had met with so little protection from his powerful relations, that he had not yet obtained any preferment in the law, which was his profession. But Essex, who could distinguish merit, and who passionately loved it, had entered into an intimate friendship with Bacon; had zealously attempted, though without success, to procure him the office of solicitor-general; and in order to comfort his friend under the disappointment, had conferred on him a present of land to the value of eighteen hundred pounds.[a] The public could ill excuse Bacon's appearance before the council, against so munificent a benefactor; though he acted in obedience to the queen's commands: But she was so well pleased with his behaviour, that she imposed on him a new task, of drawing a narrative of that day's proceedings, in order to satisfy the public of the justice and lenity of her conduct. Bacon, who wanted firmness of character, more than humanity, gave to the whole transaction the most favourable turn for Essex; and, in particular, painted out, in elaborate expression, the dutiful submission, which that nobleman discovered in the defence that he made for his conduct. When he read the paper to her, she smiled at that passage, and observed to Bacon, that old love, she saw, could not easily be forgotten. He replied, that he hoped she meant that of herself.[b]

All the world, indeed, expected, that Essex would soon be reinstated in his former credit;[c] perhaps, as is usual in reconcilements founded on inclination, would acquire an additional ascendant over the queen, and after all his disgraces, would again appear more a favourite than ever. They were confirmed in this hope, when they saw, that, though he was still prohibited from appearing at court,[d] he was continued in his office of master of horse, and was restored to his liberty, and that all his friends had access to him. Essex himself seemed determined to persevere in that conduct, which had hitherto been so successful, and which the queen, by all this discipline, had endeavoured to render habitual to him: He wrote to her, that he kissed her majesty's hands, and the rod with which she had corrected him; but that he could never

[a] Cabala, p. 78. [b] Cabala, p. 83. [c] Winwood, vol. i. p. 254. [d] Birch's Memoirs, vol. ii. p. 462.

recover his wonted chearfulness, till she deigned to admit him to
that presence, which had ever been the chief source of his happiness and enjoyment: And that he had now resolved to make
amends for his past errors, to retire into a country solitude, and say
with Nebuchadnezzar, "Let my dwelling be with the beasts of the
field; let me eat grass as an ox, and be wet with the dew of heaven;
till it shall please the queen to restore me to my understanding."
The queen was much pleased with these sentiments, and replied,
that she heartily wished his actions might correspond with his
expressions; that he had tried her patience a long time, and it was
but fitting she should now make some experiment of his submission; that her father would never have pardoned so much
obstinacy; but that, if the furnace of affliction produced such good
effects, she should ever after have the better opinion of her
chemistry.[e]

The earl of Essex possessed a monopoly of sweet wines; and as
his patent was near expiring, he patiently expected that the queen
would renew it, and he considered this event as the critical circumstance of his life, which would determine whether he could ever
hope to be reinstated in credit and authority.[f] But Elizabeth,
though gracious in her deportment, was of a temper somewhat
haughty and severe; and being continually surrounded with Essex's enemies, means were found to persuade her, that his lofty
spirit was not yet sufficiently subdued, and that he must undergo
this farther trial, before he could again be safely received into
favour. She therefore denied his request; and even added, in a
contemptuous stile, that an ungovernable beast must be stinted in
his provender.[g]

His in-
trigues.
This rigour, pushed one step too far, proved the final ruin of
this young nobleman, and was the source of infinite sorrow and
vexation to the queen herself. Essex, who had with great difficulty
so long subdued his proud spirit, and whose patience was now
exhausted, imagining that the queen was entirely inexorable, burst
at once all restraints of submission and of prudence, and determined to seek relief, by proceeding to the utmost extremities
against his enemies. Even during his greatest favour he had ever
been accustomed to carry matters with a high hand towards his

[e] Camden, p. 628. [f] Birch's Memoirs, vol. ii. p. 472. [g] Camden, p. 628.

CHAPTER XLIV

sovereign; and as this practice gratified his own temper, and was sometimes successful, he had imprudently imagined, that it was the only proper method of managing her:[h] But being now reduced to despair, he gave entire reins to his violent disposition, and threw off all appearance of duty and respect. Intoxicated with the public favour, which he already possessed, he practised anew every art of popularity; and endeavoured to encrease the general good-will by a hospitable manner of life, little suited to his situation and circumstances. His former employments had given him great connections with men of the military profession; and he now entertained, by additional caresses and civilities, a friendship with all desperate adventurers, whose attachment, he hoped, might, in his present views, prove serviceable to him. He secretly courted the confidence of the catholics; but his chief trust lay in the puritans, whom he openly caressed, and whose manners he seemed to have entirely adopted. He engaged the most celebrated preachers of that sect to resort to Essex-house; he had daily prayers and sermons in his family; and he invited all the zealots in London to attend those pious exercises. Such was the disposition now beginning to prevail among the English, that, instead of feasting and public spectacles, the methods anciently practised to gain the populace, nothing so effectually ingratiated an ambitious leader with the public, as these fanatical entertainments. And as the puritanical preachers frequently inculcated in their sermons the doctrine of resistance to the civil magistrate, they prepared the minds of their hearers for those seditious projects, which Essex was secretly meditating.[i]

But the greatest imprudence of this nobleman proceeded from the openness of his temper, by which he was ill qualified to succeed in such difficult and dangerous enterprizes. He indulged himself in great liberties of speech, and was even heard to say of the queen, that she was now grown an old woman, and was become as crooked in her mind as in her body.[k] Some court ladies, whose favours Essex had formerly neglected, carried her these stories, and incensed her to a high degree against him. Elizabeth was ever remarkably jealous on this head; and though she was now approaching to her seventieth year, she allowed her courtiers[l] and

[h] Cabala, p. 79.   [i] Birch's Memoirs, vol. ii. p. 463. Camden, p. 630.
[k] Camden, p. 629. Osborne, p. 397. Sir Walter Raleigh's Prerogative of parliament, p. 43.   [l] Birch's Memoirs, vol. ii. p. 442, 443.

even foreign ambassadors,[m] to compliment her upon her beauty; nor had all her good sense been able to cure her of this preposterous vanity.[n]

There was also an expedient employed by Essex, which, if possible, was more provoking to the queen than those sarcasms on her age and deformity; and that was, his secret applications to the king of Scots, her heir and successor. That prince had this year very narrowly escaped a dangerous, though ill formed, conspiracy of the earl of Gowry; and even his deliverance was attended with this disagreeable circumstance, that the obstinate ecclesiastics persisted, in spite of the most incontestible evidence, to maintain to his face, that there had been no such conspiracy. James, harassed with his turbulent and factious subjects, cast a wishful eye to the succession of England; and in proportion as the queen advanced in years, his desire encreased of mounting that throne, on which, besides acquiring a great addition of power and splendor, he hoped to govern a people, so much more tractable and submissive. He negociated with all the courts of Europe, in order to ensure himself friends and partizans: He even neglected not the court of Rome and that of Spain; and though he engaged himself in no positive promise, he flattered the catholics with hopes, that, in the event of his succession, they might expect some more liberty than was at present indulged them. Elizabeth was the only sovereign in Europe to whom he never dared to mention his right of succession: He knew, that, though her advanced age might now invite her to think of fixing an heir to the crown, she never could bear the prospect of her own death without horror, and was determined still to retain him, and all other competitors, in an entire dependance upon her.

Essex was descended by females from the royal family; and some of his sanguine partizans had been so imprudent as to mention his name among those of other pretenders to the crown; but the earl took care, by means of Henry Lee, whom he secretly sent into Scotland, to assure James, that, so far from entertaining such ambitious views, he was determined to use every expedient for extorting an immediate declaration in favour of that monarch's

[m] Sydney's Letters, vol. ii. p. 171.   [n] See note [GG] at the end of the volume.

CHAPTER XLIV

right of succession. James willingly hearkened to this proposal; but did not approve of the violent methods which Essex intended to employ. Essex had communicated his scheme to Mountjoy, deputy of Ireland; and as no man ever commanded more the cordial affection and attachment of his friends, he had even engaged a person of that virtue and prudence to entertain thoughts of bringing over part of his army into England, and of forcing the queen to declare the king of Scots her successor.[o] And such was Essex's impatient ardour, that, though James declined this dangerous expedient, he still endeavoured to persuade Mountjoy not to desist from the project: But the deputy, who thought that such violence, though it might be prudent, and even justifiable, when supported by a sovereign prince, next heir to the crown, would be rash and criminal, if attempted by subjects, absolutely refused his concurrence. The correspondence, however, between Essex and the court of Scotland was still conducted with great secrecy and cordiality; and that nobleman, besides conciliating the favour of James, represented all his own adversaries as enemies to that prince's succession, and as men entirely devoted to the interests of Spain, and partizans of the chimerical title of the Infanta.

The Infanta and the archduke, Albert, had made some advances to the queen for peace; and Boulogne, as a neutral town, was chosen for the place of conference. Sir Henry Nevil, the English resident in France, Herbert, Edmondes, and Beale, were sent thither as ambassadors from England; and negociated with Zuniga, Carillo, Richardot, and Verheiken, ministers of Spain and the archduke: But the conferences were soon broken off, by disputes with regard to the ceremonial. Among the European states England had ever been allowed the precedency above Castile, Arragon, Portugal, and the other kingdoms, of which the Spanish monarchy was composed; and Elizabeth insisted, that this ancient right was not lost on account of the junction of these states, and that that monarchy, in its present situation, though it surpassed the English in extent, as well as in power, could not be compared with it in point of antiquity, the only durable and regular foundation of precedency among kingdoms as well as noble families. That she might shew, however, a pacific disposition, she was content to

16th May.

[o] Birch's Memoirs, vol. ii. p. 471.

yield to an equality; but the Spanish ministers, as their nation had always disputed precedency even with France, to which England yielded, would proceed no farther in the conference, till their superiority of rank were acknowledged.[p] During the preparations for this abortive negociation, the earl of Nottingham, the admiral, lord Buckhurst, treasurer, and secretary Cecil, had discovered their inclination to peace; but as the English nation, flushed with success, and sanguine in their hopes of plunder and conquest, were in general averse to that measure, it was easy for a person so popular as Essex, to infuse into the multitude an opinion, that these ministers had sacrificed the interests of their country to Spain, and would even make no scruple of receiving a sovereign from that hostile nation.

1601.

But Essex, not content with these arts for decrying his adversaries, proceeded to concert more violent methods of ruining them; chiefly instigated by Cuffe, his secretary, a man of a bold and arrogant spirit, who had acquired a great ascendant over his patron. A select council of malcontents was formed, who commonly met at Drury-house, and were composed of Sir Charles Davers, to whom the house belonged, the earl of Southampton, Sir Ferdinando Gorges, Sir Christopher Blount, Sir John Davies, and John Littleton; and Essex, who boasted, that he had a hundred and twenty barons, knights, and gentlemen of note, at his devotion, and who trusted still more to his authority with the populace, communicated to his associates those secret designs with which his confidence in so powerful a party had inspired him. Among other criminal projects, the result of blind rage and despair, he deliberated with them concerning the method of taking arms; and asked their opinion whether he had best begin with seizing the palace or the Tower, or set out with making himself master at once of both places. The first enterprize being preferred, a method was concerted for executing it. It was agreed, that Sir Christopher Blount, with a choice detachment, should possess himself of the palace

His insur-
rections.

gates; that Davies should seize the hall, Davers, the guard-chamber, and presence-chamber; and that Essex should rush in from the Meuse, attended by a body of his partizans; should entreat the queen, with all demonstrations of humility, to remove his enemies;

[p] Winwood's Memorials, vol. i. p. 186–226.

CHAPTER XLIV

should oblige her to assemble a parliament; and should with common consent settle a new plan of government.[q]

While these desperate projects were in agitation, many reasons of suspicion were carried to the queen; and she sent Robert Sacville, son of the treasurer, to Essex-house, on pretence of a visit, but, in reality, with a view of discovering whether there were in that place any unusual concourse of people, or any extraordinary preparations, which might threaten an insurrection. Soon after, Essex received a summons to attend the council, which met at the treasurer's house; and while he was musing on this circumstance, and comparing it with the late unexpected visit from Sacville, a private note was conveyed to him, by which he was warned to provide for his own safety. He concluded, that all his conspiracy was discovered, at least suspected; and that the easiest punishment which he had reason to apprehend, was a new and more severe confinement: He therefore excused himself to the council on pretence of an indisposition; and he immediately dispatched messages to his more intimate confederates, requesting their advice and assistance in the present critical situation of his affairs. They deliberated, whether they should abandon all their projects, and fly the kingdom; or instantly seize the palace with the force which they could assemble; or rely upon the affections of the citizens, who were generally known to have a great attachment to the earl. Essex declared against the first expedient, and professed himself determined to undergo any fate rather than submit to live the life of a fugitive. To seize the palace seemed impracticable without more preparations; especially as the queen seemed now aware of their projects, and, as they heard, had used the precaution of doubling her ordinary guards. There remained, therefore, no expedient but that of betaking themselves to the city; and while the prudence and feasibility of this resolution was under debate, a person arrived, who, as if he had received a commission for the purpose, gave them assurance of the affections of the Londoners, and affirmed, that they might securely rest any project on that foundation. The popularity of Essex had chiefly buoyed him up in all his vain undertakings; and he fondly imagined, that, with no other assis-

7th Feb.

[q] Camden, p. 630. Birch's Memoirs, vol. ii. p. 464. State Trials. Bacon, vol. iv. p. 542, 543.

tance than the good will of the multitude, he might overturn Elizabeth's government, confirmed by time, revered for wisdom, supported by vigour, and concurring with the general sentiments of the nation. The wild project of raising the city was immediately resolved on; the execution of it was delayed till next day; and emissaries were dispatched to all Essex's friends, informing them that Cobham and Raleigh had laid schemes against his life, and entreating their presence and assistance.

8th Feb. Next day, there appeared at Essex-house the earls of Southampton and Rutland, the lords Sandy and Monteagle, with about three hundred gentlemen of good quality and fortune; and Essex informed them of the danger, to which, he pretended, the machinations of his enemies exposed him. To some, he said, that he would throw himself at the queen's feet, and crave her justice and protection: To others, he boasted of his interest in the city, and affirmed, that, whatever might happen, this resource could never fail him. The queen was informed of these designs, by means of intelligence, conveyed, as is supposed, to Raleigh, by Sir Ferdinando Gorges; and having ordered the magistrates of London to keep the citizens in readiness; she sent Egerton, lord keeper, to Essex-house, with the earl of Worcester, Sir William Knollys, controller, and Popham, chief justice, in order to learn the cause of these unusual commotions. They were with difficulty admitted through a wicket; but all their servants were excluded, except the purse-bearer. After some altercation, in which they charged Essex's retainers, upon their allegiance, to lay down their arms, and were menaced in their turn by the angry multitude, who surrounded them, the earl, who found, that matters were past recal, resolved to leave them prisoners in his house, and to proceed to the execution of his former project. He sallied forth with about two hundred attendants, armed only with walking swords; and in his passage to the city was joined by the earl of Bedford and lord Cromwel. He cried aloud, *For the queen! for the queen! a plot is laid for my life;* and then proceeded to the house of Smith the sheriff, on whose aid he had great reliance. The citizens flocked about him in amazement; but though he told them, that England was sold to the Infanta, and exhorted them to arm instantly, otherwise they could not do him any service, no one showed a disposition to join him. The sheriff, on the earl's approach to his house, stole out at the back door, and made the best of his way to the mayor. Essex, meanwhile, observing the coldness of the citizens, and hearing, that he was proclaimed a traitor by the earl of Cumberland and lord Burleigh, began to despair of success, and thought of retreating to his own house. He found the streets in his passage barricadoed and guarded by the citizens under the command of Sir John Levison. In his attempt to force his way, Tracy, a young gentleman, to whom he bore great friendship, was killed, with two or three of the Londoners; and the earl himself, attended by a few of his partizans (for the greater part began secretly to withdraw themselves) retired towards the river, and taking boat, arrived at Essex-house. He there found, that Gorges, whom he had sent before to capitulate with the lord keeper and the other counsellors, had given all of them their liberty, and had gone to court with them. He was now reduced to despair; and appeared determined, in prosecution of lord Sandys' advice, to defend himself to the last extremity, and rather to perish, like a brave man, with his sword in his hand, than basely by the hands of the executioner: But after some parley, and after demanding in vain, first hostages, then conditions, from the besiegers, he surrendered at discretion; requesting only civil treatment, and a fair and impartial hearing.[r]

The queen, who, during all this commotion, had behaved with as great tranquillity and security, as if there had only passed a fray in the streets, in which she was nowise concerned,[s] soon gave orders for the trial of the most considerable of the criminals. The earls of Essex and Southampton were arraigned before a jury of twenty-five peers, where Buckhurst acted as lord steward. The guilt of the prisoners was too apparent to admit of any doubt; and, besides the insurrection known to every body, the treasonable conferences at Drury-house were proved by undoubted evidence. Sir Ferdinando Gorges was produced in court: The confessions of the earl of Rutland, of the lords Cromwel, Sandys, and Monteagle, of Davers, Blount, and Davies, were only read to the peers, according to the practice of that age. Essex's best friends were scandalized at his assurance in insisting so positively on his innocence, and the goodness of his intentions; and still more at his vindictive disposition, in accusing, without any appearance of reason, secretary

19th Feb.
His trial.

[r] Camden, p. 632.   [s] Birch's Memoirs, vol. ii. p. 469.

Cecil as a partizan of the Infanta's title. The secretary, who had expected this charge, stepped into the court, and challenged Essex to produce his authority, which, on examination, was found extremely weak and frivolous.' When sentence was pronounced, Essex spoke like a man who expected nothing but death: But he added, that he should be sorry, if he were represented to the queen as a person that despised her clemency; though he should not, he believed, make any cringing submissions to obtain it. Southampton's behaviour was more mild and submissive: He entreated the good offices of the peers in so modest and becoming a manner, as excited compassion in every one.

The most remarkable circumstance in Essex's trial was Bacon's appearance against him. He was none of the crown lawyers; so was not obliged by his office to assist at this trial: Yet did he not scruple, in order to obtain the queen's favour, to be active in bereaving of life his friend and patron, whose generosity he had often experienced. He compared Essex's conduct, in pretending to fear the attempts of his adversaries, to that of Pisistratus, the Athenian, who cut and wounded his own body; and making the people believe, that his enemies had committed the violence, obtained a guard for his person, by whose assistance he afterwards subdued the liberties of his country.

After Essex had passed some days in the solitude and reflections of a prison, his proud heart was at last subdued, not by the fear of death, but by the sentiments of religion; a principle, which he had before attempted to make the instrument of his ambition, but which now took a more firm hold of his mind, and prevailed over every other motive and consideration. His spiritual directors persuaded him, that he never could obtain the pardon of Heaven, unless he made a full confession of his disloyalty; and he gave in to the council an account of all his criminal designs, as well as of his correspondence with the king of Scots. He spared not even his most intimate friends, such as lord Mountjoy, whom he had engaged in these conspiracies; and he sought to pacify his present remorse, by making such atonements, as, in any other period of his life, he would have deemed more blameable than those attempts themselves, which were the objects of his penitence." Sir Harry

' Bacon, vol. iv. p. 530.   " Winwood, vol. i. p. 300.

CHAPTER XLIV

Nevil, in particular, a man of merit, he accused of a correspondence with the conspirators; though it appears, that this gentleman had never assented to the proposals made him, and was no
farther criminal than in not revealing the earl's treason; an office
to which every man of honour naturally bears the strongest reluctance.[w] Nevil was thrown into prison, and underwent a severe
persecution: But as the queen found Mountjoy an able and successful commander, she continued him in his government, and
sacrificed her resentment to the public service.

Elizabeth affected extremely the praise of clemency; and in
every great example, which she had made during her reign, she
had always appeared full of reluctance and hesitation: But the
present situation of Essex called forth all her tender affections, and
kept her in the most real agitation and irresolution. She felt a
perpetual combat between resentment and inclination, pride and
compassion, the care of her own safety and concern for her favourite; and her situation, during this interval, was perhaps more an
object of pity, than that to which Essex himself was reduced. She
signed the warrant for his execution; she countermanded it; she
again resolved on his death; she felt a new return of tenderness.
Essex's enemies told her, that he himself desired to die, and had
assured her, that she could never be in safety while he lived: It is
likely, that this proof of penitence and of concern for her would
produce a contrary effect to what they intended, and would revive
all the fond affection, which she had so long indulged towards the
unhappy prisoner. But what chiefly hardened her heart against
him was his supposed obstinacy, in never making, as she hourly
expected, any application to her for mercy; and she finally gave
her consent to his execution. He discovered at his death symptoms
rather of penitence and piety than of fear; and willingly acknowledged the justice of the sentence by which he suffered. The execution was private in the Tower, agreeably to his own request. He
was apprehensive, he said, lest the favour and compassion of the
people would too much raise his heart in those moments, when
humiliation under the afflicting hand of Heaven was the only
proper sentiment, which he could indulge.[x] And the queen, no

*25th Feb.
And exe-
cution.*

___

[w] Ibid. vol. i. p. 302.   [x] Dr. Barlow's sermon on Essex's execution. Bacon,
vol. iv. p. 534.

doubt, thought that prudence required the removing of so melancholy a spectacle from the public eye. Sir Walter Raleigh, who came to the Tower on purpose, and who beheld Essex's execution from a window, encreased much by this action the general hatred, under which he already laboured: It was thought, that his sole intention was to feast his eyes with the death of an enemy; and no apology, which he could make for so ungenerous a conduct, could be accepted by the public. The cruelty and animosity, with which he urged on Essex's fate, even when Cecil relented,[y] were still regarded as the principles of this unmanly behaviour.

The earl of Essex was but thirty-four years of age, when his rashness, imprudence, and violence brought him to this untimely end. We must here, as in many other instances, lament the inconstancy of human nature, that a person endowed with so many noble virtues, generosity, sincerity, friendship, valour, eloquence, and industry, should, in the later period of his life, have given reins to his ungovernable passions, and involved, not only himself, but many of his friends, in utter ruin. The queen's tenderness and passion for him, as it was the cause of those premature honours, which he attained, seems on the whole, the chief circumstance, which brought on his unhappy fate. Confident of her partiality towards him, as well as of his own merit, he treated her with a haughtiness, which neither her love nor her dignity could bear; and as her amorous inclinations, in so advanced an age, would naturally make her appear ridiculous, if not odious, in his eyes, he was engaged, by an imprudent openness, of which he made profession, to discover too easily those sentiments to her. The many reconciliations and returns of affection, of which he had still made advantage, induced him to venture on new provocations, till he pushed her beyond all bounds of patience; and he forgot, that though the sentiments of the woman were ever strong in her, those of the sovereign had still in the end appeared predominant.

Some of Essex's associates, Cuffe, Davers, Blount, Meric, and Davis, were tried and condemned, and all of these, except Davis, were executed. The queen pardoned the rest; being persuaded that they were drawn in merely from their friendship to that nobleman, and their care of his safety; and were ignorant of the more

[y] Murdin, p. 811.

CHAPTER XLIV

criminal part of his intentions. Southampton's life was saved with great difficulty; but he was detained in prison during the remainder of this reign.

The king of Scots, apprehensive lest his correspondence with Essex might have been discovered, and have given offence to Elizabeth, sent the earl of Marre and lord Kinloss as ambassadors to England, in order to congratulate the queen on her escape from the late insurrection and conspiracy. They were also ordered to make secret enquiry, whether any measures had been taken by her for excluding him from the succession, as well as to discover the inclinations of the chief nobility and counsellors, in case of the queen's demise.[z] They found the dispositions of men as favourable as they could wish; and they even entered into a correspondence with secretary Cecil, whose influence, after the fall of Essex, was now uncontrouled,[a] and who was resolved, by this policy, to acquire, in time, the confidence of the successor. He knew how jealous Elizabeth ever was of her authority, and he therefore carefully concealed from her his attachment to James: But he afterwards asserted, that nothing could be more advantageous to her, than this correspondence; because the king of Scots, secure of mounting the throne by his undoubted title, aided by those connections with the English ministry, was the less likely to give any disturbance to the present sovereign. He also persuaded that prince to remain in quiet, and patiently to expect, that time should open to him the inheritance of the crown, without pushing his friends on desperate enterprizes, which would totally incapacitate them from serving him. James's equity, as well as his natural facility of disposition, easily inclined him to embrace that resolution;[b] and in this manner the minds of the English were silently, but universally disposed to admit, without opposition, the succession of the Scottish line: The death of Essex, by putting an end to faction, had been rather favourable than prejudicial to that great event.

The French king, who was little prepossessed in favour of James, and who, for obvious reasons, was averse to the union of England and Scotland,[c] made his ambassador drop some hints to

---

[z] Birch's Memoirs, vol. ii. p. 510.   [a] Osborne, p. 615.   [b] Spotswood, p. 471, 472.   [c] Winwood, vol. i. p. 352.

Cecil of Henry's willingness to concur in any measure for disappointing the hopes of the Scottish monarch; but as Cecil showed an entire disapprobation of such schemes, the court of France took no farther steps in that matter; and thus, the only foreign power, which could give much disturbance to James's succession, was in- *French affairs.* duced to acquiesce in it.[d] Henry made a journey this summer to Calais; and the queen, hearing of his intentions, went to Dover, in hopes of having a personal interview with a monarch, whom, of all others, she most loved and most respected. The king of France, who felt the same sentiments towards her, would gladly have accepted of the proposal; but as many difficulties occurred, it appeared necessary to lay aside, by common consent, the project of an interview. Elizabeth, however, wrote successively two letters to Henry, one by Edmondes, another by Sir Robert Sydney; in which she expressed a desire of conferring, about a business of importance, with some minister in whom that prince reposed entire confidence. The marquess of Rosni, the king's favourite and prime minister, came to Dover in disguise; and the Memoirs of that able statesman contain a full account of his conference with Elizabeth. This princess had formed a scheme for establishing, in conjunction with Henry, a new system in Europe, and of fixing a durable balance of power, by the erection of new states on the ruins of the house of Austria. She had even the prudence to foresee the perils, which might ensue from the aggrandizement of her ally; and she purposed to unite all the seventeen provinces of the Low Countries in one republic, in order to form a perpetual barrier against the dangerous encrease of the French, as well as of the Spanish, monarchy. Henry had himself long meditated such a project against the Austrian family; and Rosni could not forbear expressing his astonishment, when he found that Elizabeth and his master, though they had never communicated their sentiments on this subject, not only had entered into same general views, but had also formed the same plan for their execution. The affairs, however, of France were not yet brought to a situation, which might enable Henry to begin that great enterprize; and Rosni satisfied the queen, that it would be necessary to postpone for some years their united attack on the house of Austria. He departed, filled with just

[d] Spotswood, p. 471.

admiration at the solidity of Elizabeth's judgment, and the greatness of her mind; and he owns, that she was entirely worthy of that high reputation, which she enjoyed in Europe.

The queen's magnanimity in forming such extensive projects was the more remarkable, as, besides her having fallen so far into the decline of life, the affairs of Ireland, though conducted with abilities and success, were still in disorder, and made a great diversion of her forces. The expence, incurred by this war, lay heavy upon her narrow revenues; and her ministers, taking advantage of her disposition to frugality, proposed to her an expedient of saving, which, though she at first disapproved of it, she was at last induced to embrace. It was represented to her, that the great sums of money, remitted to Ireland for the pay of the English forces, came, by the necessary course of circulation, into the hands of the rebels, and enabled them to buy abroad all necessary supplies of arms and ammunition, which, from the extreme poverty of that kingdom and its want of every useful commodity, they could not otherwise find means to purchase. It was therefore recommended to her, that she should pay her forces in base money; and it was asserted, that, besides the great saving to the revenue, this species of coin could never be exported with advantage, and would not pass in any foreign market. Some of her wiser counsellors maintained, that, if the pay of the soldiers were raised in proportion, the Irish rebels would necessarily reap the same benefit from the base money, which would always be taken at a rate suitable to its value; if the pay were not raised, there would be danger of a mutiny among the troops, who, whatever names might be affixed to the pieces of metal, would soon find from experience, that they were defrauded in their income.[e] But Elizabeth, though she justly valued herself, on fixing the standard of the English coin, much debased by her predecessors, and had innovated very little in that delicate article, was seduced by the specious arguments employed by the treasurer on this occasion; and she coined a great quantity of base money, which he made use of in the pay of her forces in Ireland.[f]

Mountjoy, the deputy, was a man of abilities; and foreseeing the danger of mutiny among the troops, he led them instantly into

Mountjoy's success in Ireland.

[e] Camden, p. 643.   [f] Rymer, tom. xvi. p. 414.

the field, and resolved, by means of strict discipline, and by keeping them employed against the enemy, to obviate those inconveniences, which were justly to be apprehended. He made military
roads, and built a fortress at Moghery; he drove the Mac-Genises
out of Lecale; he harassed Tyrone in Ulster with inroads and lesser
expeditions; and by destroying, every where, and during all seasons, the provisions of the Irish, he reduced them to perish by
famine in the woods and morasses, to which they were obliged to
retreat. At the same time, Sir Henry Docwray, who commanded
another body of troops, took the castle of Derry, and put garrisons
into Newton and Aihogh; and having seized the monastery of
Donnegal near Balishannon, he threw troops into it, and defended
it against the assaults of O'Donnel and the Irish. Nor was Sir
George Carew idle in the province of Munster. He seized the
titular earl of Desmond, and sent him over, with Florence Macarty,
another chieftain, prisoner to England. He arrested many suspected persons, and took hostages from others. And having got a
reinforcement of two thousand men from England, he threw himself into Corke, which he supplied with arms and provisions; and
he put every thing in a condition for resisting the Spanish invasion,
which was daily expected. The deputy, informed of the danger, to
which the southern provinces were exposed, left the prosecution
of the war against Tyrone, who was reduced to great extremities;
and he marched with his army into Munster.

23d Sept.   At last, the Spaniards, under Don John d'Aquila, arrived at
Kinsale; and Sir Richard Piercy, who commanded in the town with
a small garrison of a hundred and fifty men, found himself obliged
to abandon it on their appearance. These invaders amounted to
four thousand men, and the Irish discovered a strong propensity
to join them, in order to free themselves from the English government, with which they were extremely discontented. One chief
ground of their complaint, was the introduction of trials by jury;[g]
an institution, abhorred by that people, though nothing con-
tributes more to the support of that equity and liberty, for which
the English laws are so justly celebrated. The Irish also bore a great
favour to the Spaniards, having entertained the opinion that they
themselves were descended from that nation; and their attach-

[g] Camden, p. 644.

CHAPTER XLIV

ment to the catholic religion proved a new cause of affection to the invaders. D'Aquila assumed the title of general *in the holy war for the preservation of the faith* in Ireland; and he endeavoured to persuade the people, that Elizabeth was, by several bulls of the pope, deprived of her crown; that her subjects were absolved from their oath of allegiance; and that the Spaniards were come to deliver the Irish from the dominion of the devil.[h] Mountjoy found it necessary to act with vigour, in order to prevent a total insurrection of the Irish; and having collected his forces, he formed the siege of Kinsale by land; while Sir Richard Levison, with a small squadron, blockaded it by sea. He had no sooner begun his operations than he heard of the arrival of another body of two thousand Spaniards under the command of Alphonso Ocampo, who had taken possession of Baltimore and Berehaven; and he was obliged to detach Sir George Carew to oppose their progress. Tyrone, meanwhile, with Randal, Mac-Surley, Tirel baron of Kelley, and other chieftains of the Irish, had joined Ocampo with all their forces, and were marching to the relief of Kinsale. The deputy, informed of their design by intercepted letters, made preparations to receive them; and being re-inforced by Levison with six hundred marines, he posted his troops on an advantageous ground, which lay on the passage of the enemy, leaving some cavalry to prevent a sally from d'Aquila and the Spanish garrison. When Tyrone, with a detachment of Irish and Spaniards, approached, he was surprized to find the English so well posted, and ranged in good order; and he immediately sounded a retreat: But the deputy gave orders to pursue him; and having thrown these advanced troops into disorder, he followed them to the main body, whom he also attacked, and put to flight, with the slaughter of twelve hundred men.[i] Ocampo was taken prisoner; Tyrone fled into Ulster; Odonnel made his escape into Spain; and d'Aquila, finding himself reduced to the greatest difficulties, was obliged to capitulate upon such terms as the deputy prescribed to him: He surrendered Kinsale and Baltimore, and agreed to evacuate the kingdom. This great blow, joined to other successes, gained by Wilmot, governor of Kerry, and by Roger and Gavin Harvey, threw the rebels into dismay, and gave a prospect of the final reduction of Ireland.

[h] Camden, p. 645. [i] Winwood, vol. i. p. 369.

The Irish war, though successful, was extremely burthensome on the queen's revenue; and besides the supplies granted by parliament, which were indeed very small, but which they ever regarded as mighty concessions, she had been obliged, notwithstanding her great frugality, to employ other expedients, such as selling the royal demesnes and crown jewels,[k] and exacting loans from the people;[l] in order to support this cause, so essential to the honour and interests of England. The necessity of her affairs obliged her again to summon a parliament; and it here appeared, that, though old age was advancing fast upon her, though she had lost much of her popularity by the unfortunate execution of Essex, insomuch that, when she appeared in public, she was not attended with the usual acclamations,[m] yet the powers of her prerogative, supported by her vigour, still remained as high and uncontroulable as ever.

October 27.
A parlia-
ment.

The active reign of Elizabeth had enabled many persons to distinguish themselves in civil and military employments; and the queen, who was not able, from her revenue, to give them any rewards proportioned to their services, had made use of an expedient, which had been employed by her predecessors, but which had never been carried to such an extreme as under her administration. She granted her servants and courtiers patents for monopolies; and these patents they sold to others, who were thereby enabled to raise commodities to what price they pleased, and who put invincible restraints upon all commerce, industry, and emulation in the arts. It is astonishing to consider the number and importance of those commodities, which were thus assigned over to patentees. Currants, salt, iron, powder, cards, calf-skins, fells, pouldavies, ox-shin-bones, train oil, lists of cloth, pot-ashes, anniseeds, vinegar, sea-coals, steel, aquavitae, brushes, pots, bottles, saltpetre, lead, accidences, oil, calamine stone, oil of blubber, glasses, paper, starch, tin, sulphur, new drapery, dried pilchards, transportation of Iron ordnance, of beer, of horn, of leather, importation of Spanish wool, of Irish yarn: These are but a part of the commodities, which had been appropriated to monopolists.[n] When this list was read in the house, a member cried, *Is not bread in the number? Bread,* said every one with astonishment: *Yes, I assure*

---

[k] D'Ewes, p. 629. [l] Ibid. [m] Ibid. p. 602. Osborne, p. 604. [n] D'Ewes, p. 648, 650, 652.

CHAPTER XLIV

you, replied he, *if affairs go on at this rate, we shall have bread reduced to a monopoly before next parliament.* [o] These monopolists were so exorbitant in their demands, that in some places they raised the price of salt, from sixteen-pence a bushel, to fourteen or fifteen shillings.[p] Such high profits naturally begat intruders upon their commerce; and in order to secure themselves against en-croachments, the patentees were armed with high and arbitrary powers from the council, by which they were enabled to oppress the people at pleasure, and to exact money from such as they thought proper to accuse of interfering with their patent.[q] The patentees of salt-petre, having the power of entering into every house, and of committing what havock they pleased in stables, cellars, or wherever they suspected salt-petre might be gathered, commonly extorted money from those who desired to free them-selves from this damage or trouble.[r] And while all domestic intercourse was thus restrained, lest any scope should remain for industry, almost every species of foreign commerce was confined to exclusive companies, who bought and sold at any price, that they themselves thought proper to offer or exact.

These grievances, the most intolerable for the present, and the most pernicious in their consequences, that ever were known in any age or under any government, had been mentioned in that last parliament, and a petition had even been presented to the queen, complaining of the patents; but she still persisted in defending her monopolists against her people. A bill was now introduced into the lower house, abolishing all these monopolies; and as the former application had been unsuccessful, a law was insisted on as the only certain expedient for correcting these abuses. The courtiers, on the other hand, maintained, that this matter regarded the prerog-ative, and that the commons could never hope for success, if they did not make application, in the most humble and respectful man-ner, to the queen's goodness and beneficence. The topics, which were advanced in the house, and which came equally from the courtiers and the country gentlemen, and were admitted by both, will appear the most extraordinary to such as are prepossessed with an idea of the privileges enjoyed by the people during that

[o] Ibid. p. 648.   [p] Ibid. p. 647.   [q] D'Ewes, p. 644, 646, 652.   [r] Ibid. p. 653.

age, and of the liberty possessed under the administration of Elizabeth. It was asserted, that the queen inherited both an enlarging
and a restraining power; by her prerogative she might set at liberty
what was restrained by statute or otherwise, and by her prerogative
she might restrain what was otherwise at liberty:[s] That the royal
prerogative was not to be canvassed nor disputed nor examined;[t]
and did not even admit of any limitation.[u] That absolute princes,
such as the sovereigns of England, were a species of divinity.[w] That
it was in vain to attempt tying the queen's hands by laws or statutes;
since, by means of her dispensing power, she could loosen herself
at pleasure:[x] And that even if a clause should be annexed to a
statute, excluding her dispensing power, she could first dispense
with that clause, and then with the statute.[y] After all this discourse,
more worthy of a Turkish divan than of an English house of
commons, according to our present idea of this assembly, the
queen, who perceived how odious monopolies had become, and
what heats were likely to arise, sent for the speaker, and desired
him to acquaint the house, that she would immediately cancel the
most grievous and oppressive of these patents.[z]

The house was struck with astonishment, and admiration, and
gratitude at this extraordinary instance of the queen's goodness
and condescension. A member said, with tears in his eyes, that, if
a sentence of everlasting happiness had been pronounced in his
favour, he could not have felt more joy than that with which he was
at present overwhelmed.[a] Another observed, that this message
from the sacred person of the queen, was a kind of gospel or
glad-tidings, and ought to be received as such, and be written in
the tablets of their hearts.[b] And it was farther remarked, that, in
the same manner as the Deity would not give his glory to another,
so the queen herself was the only agent in their present prosperity
and happiness.[c] The house voted, that the speaker, with a committee, should ask permission to wait on her majesty, and return
thanks to her for her gracious concessions to her people.

When the speaker, with the other members, was introduced to
the queen, they all flung themselves on their knees; and remained

---

[s] D'Ewes, p. 644, 675.　[t] Ibid. p. 644, 649.　[u] Ibid. p. 646, 654.　[w] Ibid.
p. 649.　[x] Ibid.　[y] Ibid. p. 640, 646.　[z] See note [HH] at the end of the
volume.　[a] D'Ewes, p. 654.　[b] Ibid. p. 656.　[c] D'Ewes, p. 657.

in that posture a considerable time, till she thought proper to express her desire, that they should rise.[d] The speaker displayed the gratitude of the commons; because her sacred ears were ever open to hear them, and her blessed hands ever stretched out to relieve them. They acknowledged, he said, in all duty and thankfulness acknowledged, that, before they called, her *preventing grace* and *all-deserving goodness* watched over them for their good; more ready to give than they could desire, much less deserve. He remarked, that the attribute which was most proper to God, to perform all he promiseth, appertained also to her; and that she was all truth, all constancy, and all goodness. And he concluded with these expressions, "Neither do we present our thanks in words or any outward sign, which can be no sufficient retribution for so great goodness; but in all duty and thankfulness, prostrate at your feet, we present our most loyal and thankful hearts, even the last drop of blood in our hearts, and the last spirit of breath in our nostrils, to be poured out, to be breathed up, for your safety."[e] The queen heard very patiently this speech, in which she was flattered in phrases appropriated to the Supreme Being; and she returned an answer, full of such expressions of tenderness towards her people, as ought to have appeared fulsome after the late instances of rigour, which she had employed, and from which nothing but necessity had made her depart. Thus was this critical affair happily terminated; and Elizabeth, by prudently receding, in time, from part of her prerogative, maintained her dignity, and preserved the affections of her people.

The commons granted her a supply quite unprecedented, of four subsidies and eight fifteenths; and they were so dutiful as to vote this supply before they received any satisfaction in the business of monopolies, which they justly considered as of the utmost importance to the interest and happiness of the nation. Had they

[d] We learn from Hentzner's Travels, that no one spoke to queen Elizabeth without kneeling; though now and then she raised some with waving her hand. Nay, wherever she turned her eye, every one fell on his knees. Her successor first allowed his courtiers to omit this ceremony; and as he exerted not the power, so he relinquished the appearance of despotism. Even when queen Elizabeth was absent, those who covered her table, though persons of quality, neither approached it nor retired from it without kneeling, and that often three times.   [e] D'Ewes, p. 658, 659.

attempted to extort that concession by keeping the supply in suspence; so haughty was the queen's disposition, that this appearance of constraint and jealousy had been sufficient to have produced a denial of all their requests, and to have forced her into
some acts of authority still more violent and arbitrary.

1602.   The remaining events of this reign are neither numerous nor
important. The queen, finding that the Spaniards had involved
her in so much trouble, by fomenting and assisting the Irish
rebellion, resolved to give them employment at home; and she
fitted out a squadron of nine ships, under Sir Richard Levison,
admiral, and Sir William Monson, vice-admiral, whom she sent on
an expedition to the coast of Spain. The admiral, with part of the
squadron, met the galleons loaded with treasure; but was not
strong enough to attack them. The vice-admiral also fell in with
some rich ships; but they escaped for a like reason: And these two
brave officers, that their expedition might not prove entirely fruitless, resolved to attack the harbour of Cerimbra in Portugal;
where, they received intelligence, a very rich carrack had taken
shelter. The harbour was guarded by a castle: There were eleven
gallies stationed in it: And the militia of the country, to the number, as was believed, of twenty thousand men, appeared in arms on
the shore: Yet, notwithstanding these obstacles, and others derived from the winds and tides, the English squadron broke into
the harbour, dismounted the guns of the castle, sunk, or burnt, or
put to flight, the gallies, and obliged the carrack to surrender.[f]
They brought her home to England, and she was valued at a
million of ducats.[g] A sensible loss to the Spaniards; and a supply
still more important to Elizabeth.[h]

The affairs of Ireland, after the defeat of Tyrone, and the
expulsion of the Spaniards, hastened to a settlement. Lord Mountjoy divided his army into small parties, and harassed the rebels on
every side: He built Charlemont, and many other small forts,
which were impregnable to the Irish, and guarded all the important passes of the country: The activity of Sir Henry Docwray

[f] Monson, p. 181.   [g] Camden, p. 647.   [h] This year the Spaniards began
the siege of Ostend, which was bravely defended for five months by Sir
Francis Vere. The states then relieved him, by sending him a new governor;
and on the whole the siege lasted three years, and is computed to have cost
the lives of a hundred thousand men.

and Sir Arthur Chichester permitted no repose or security to the rebels: And many of the chieftains, after skulking, during some time, in woods and morasses, submitted to mercy, and received such conditions as the deputy was pleased to impose upon them. Tyrone himself made application by Arthur Mac-Baron, his brother, to be received upon terms; but Mountjoy would not admit him, except he made an absolute surrender of his life and fortunes to the queen's mercy. He appeared before the deputy at Millefont, in a habit and posture suitable to his present fortune; and after acknowledging his offence in the most humble terms, he was committed to custody by Mountjoy; who intended to bring him over captive into England, to be disposed of at the queen's pleasure.

1603.

Tyrone's submission.

But Elizabeth was now incapable of receiving any satisfaction from this fortunate event: She had fallen into a profound melancholy; which all the advantages of her high fortune, all the glories of her prosperous reign, were unable, in any degree, to alleviate or assuage. Some ascribed this depression of mind to her repentance of granting a pardon to Tyrone, whom she had always resolved to bring to condign punishment for his treasons, but who had made such interest with the ministers, as to extort a remission from her. Others, with more likelihood, accounted for her dejection, by a discovery, which she had made, of the correspondence maintained in her court with her successor the king of Scots, and by the neglect, to which, on account of her old age and infirmities, she imagined herself to be exposed. But there is another cause assigned for her melancholy, which has long been rejected by historians as romantic, but which late discoveries seem to have confirmed:[i] Some incidents happened, which revived her tenderness for Essex, and filled her with the deepest sorrow for the consent, which she had unwarily given to his execution.

Queen's sickness.

The earl of Essex, after his return from the fortunate expedition against Cadiz, observing the encrease of the queen's fond attachment towards him, took occasion to regret, that the necessity of her service required him often to be absent from her person, and exposed him to all those ill offices, which his enemies, more assiduous in their attendance, could employ against him. She was

---

[i] See the proofs of this remarkable fact collected in Birch's Negociations, p. 206. And Memoirs, vol. ii. p. 481, 505, 506, &c.

moved with this tender jealousy; and making him the present of a ring, desired him to keep that pledge of her affection, and assured him, that, into whatever disgrace he should fall, whatever prejudices she might be induced to entertain against him, yet, if he sent her that ring, she would immediately, upon the sight of it, recall her former tenderness, would afford him a patient hearing, and would lend a favourable ear to his apology. Essex, notwithstanding all his misfortunes, reserved this precious gift to the last extremity; but after his trial and condemnation, he resolved to try the experiment, and he committed the ring to the countess of Nottingham, whom he desired to deliver it to the queen. The countess was prevailed on by her husband, the mortal enemy of Essex, not to execute the commission; and Elizabeth, who still expected, that her favourite would make this last appeal to her tenderness, and who ascribed the neglect of it to his invincible obstinacy, was, after much delay, and many internal combats, pushed by resentment and policy to sign the warrant for his execution. The countess of Nottingham, falling into sickness, and affected with the near approach of death, was seized with remorse for her conduct; and having obtained a visit from the queen, she craved her pardon, and revealed to her the fatal secret. The queen, astonished with this incident, burst into a furious passion: She shook the dying countess in her bed; and crying to her, *That God might pardon her, but she never could,* she broke from her, and thenceforth resigned herself over to the deepest and most incurable melancholy. She rejected all consolation: She even refused food and sustenance: And throwing herself on the floor, she remained sullen and immoveable, feeding her thoughts on her afflictions, and declaring life and existence an insufferable burthen to her. Few words she uttered; and they were all expressive of some inward grief, which she cared not to reveal: But sighs and groans were the chief vent, which she gave to her despondency, and which, though they discovered her sorrows, were never able to ease or assuage them. Ten days and nights she lay upon the carpet, leaning on cushions which her maids brought her; and her physicians could not persuade her to allow herself to be put to bed, much less to make trial of any remedies, which they prescribed to her.[k] Her anxious mind, at last,

[k] Strype, vol. iv. No. 276.

had so long preyed on her frail body, that her end was visibly approaching; and the council, being assembled, sent the keeper, admiral, and secretary, to know her will with regard to her successor. She answered with a faint voice, that, as she had held a regal scepter, she desired no other than a royal successor. Cecil requesting her to explain herself more particularly, she subjoined, that she would have a king to succeed her; and who should that be but her nearest kinsman, the king of Scots? Being then advised by the archbishop of Canterbury to fix her thoughts upon God, she replied, that she did so, nor did her mind in the least wander from him. Her voice soon after left her; her senses failed; she fell into a lethargic slumber, which continued some hours; and she expired gently, without farther struggle or convulsion, in the seventieth year of her age, and forty-fifth of her reign.

And death.
24th March.

So dark a cloud overcast the evening of that day, which had shone out with a mighty lustre in the eyes of all Europe. There are few great personages in history, who have been more exposed to the calumny of enemies, and the adulation of friends, than queen Elizabeth; and yet there scarcely is any, whose reputation has been more certainly determined, by the unanimous consent of posterity. The unusual length of her administration, and the strong features of her character, were able to overcome all prejudices; and obliging her detractors to abate much of their invectives, and her admirers somewhat of their panegyrics, have at last, in spite of political factions, and what is more, of religious animosities, produced a uniform judgment with regard to her conduct. Her vigour, her constancy, her magnanimity, her penetration, vigilance, address, are allowed to merit the highest praises, and appear not to have been surpassed by any person that ever filled a throne: A conduct less rigorous, less imperious, more sincere, more indulgent to her people, would have been requisite to form a perfect character. By the force of her mind, she controuled all her more active and stronger qualities, and prevented them from running into excess: Her heroism was exempt from temerity, her frugality from avarice, her friendship from partiality, her active temper from turbulency and a vain ambition: She guarded not herself with equal care or equal success from lesser infirmities; the rivalship of beauty, the desire of admiration, the jealousy of love, and the sallies of anger.

And
character.

Her singular talents for government were founded equally on her temper and on her capacity. Endowed with a great command over herself, she soon obtained an uncontrouled ascendant over her people; and while she merited all their esteem by her real virtues, she also engaged their affections by her pretended ones. Few sovereigns of England succeeded to the throne in more difficult circumstances; and none ever conducted the government with such uniform success and felicity. Though unacquainted with the practice of toleration, the true secret for managing religious factions, she preserved her people, by her superior prudence, from those confusions, in which theological controversy had involved all the neighbouring nations: And though her enemies were the most powerful princes of Europe, the most active, the most enterprising, the least scrupulous, she was able by her vigour to make deep impressions on their states: Her own greatness, meanwhile, remained untouched and unimpaired.

The wise ministers and brave warriors, who flourished under her reign, share the praise of her success; but instead of lessening the applause due to her, they make great addition to it. They owed, all of them, their advancement to her choice; they were supported by her constancy; and with all their abilities, they were never able to acquire any undue ascendant over her. In her family, in her court, in her kingdom, she remained equally mistress: The force of the tender passions was great over her, but the force of her mind was still superior; and the combat, which her victory visibly cost her, serves only to display the firmness of her resolution, and the loftiness of her ambitious sentiments.

The fame of this princess, though it has surmounted the prejudices both of faction and bigotry, yet lies still exposed to another prejudice, which is more durable because more natural, and which, according to the different views in which we survey her, is capable either of exalting beyond measure, or diminishing the lustre of her character. This prejudice is founded on the consideration of her sex. When we contemplate her as a woman, we are apt to be struck with the highest admiration of her great qualities and extensive capacity; but we are also apt to require some more softness of disposition, some greater lenity of temper, some of those amiable weaknesses by which her sex is distinguished. But the true method of estimating her merit, is to lay aside all these

CHAPTER XLIV

considerations, and consider her merely as a rational being, placed in authority, and entrusted with the government of mankind. We may find it difficult to reconcile our fancy to her as a wife or a mistress; but her qualities as a sovereign, though with some considerable exceptions, are the object of undisputed applause and approbation.

APPENDIX III

Government of England –
Revenues – Commerce – Military force –
Manners – Learning

Govern-
ment of
England. THE PARTY AMONG US, who have distinguished themselves by
their adhering to liberty and a popular government, have
long indulged their prejudices against the succeeding race of
princes, by bestowing unbounded panegyrics on the virtue and
wisdom of Elizabeth. They have even been so extremely ignorant
of the transactions of this reign, as to extol her for a quality, which,
of all others, she was the least possessed of; a tender regard for the
constitution, and a concern for the liberties and privileges of her
people. But as it is scarcely possible for the prepossessions of party
to throw a veil much longer over facts so palpable and undeniable,
there is danger lest the public should run into the opposite extreme, and should entertain an aversion to the memory of a princess, who exercised the royal authority in a manner so contrary to
all the ideas, which we at present entertain of a legal constitution.
But Elizabeth only supported the prerogatives, transmitted to her
by her predecessors: She believed that her subjects were entitled to
no more liberty than their ancestors had enjoyed: She found that
they entirely acquiesced in her arbitrary administration: And it was
not natural for her to find fault with a form of government, by
which she herself was invested with such unlimited authority. In
the particular exertions of power, the question ought never to be
forgotten, *What is best?* But in the general distribution of power
among the several members of a constitution, there can seldom be
admitted any other question, than *What is established?* Few examples occur of princes, who have willingly resigned their power:
None of those who have, without struggle and reluctance, allowed

it to be extorted from them. If any other rule than established practice be followed, factions and dissentions must multiply without end: And though many constitutions, and none more than the British, have been improved even by violent innovations, the praise, bestowed on those patriots, to whom the nation has been indebted for its privileges, ought to be given with some reserve, and surely without the least rancour against those who adhered to the ancient constitution.[l]

In order to understand the ancient constitution of England, there is not a period which deserves more to be studied than the reign of Elizabeth. The prerogatives of this princess were scarcely ever disputed, and she therefore employed them without scruple: Her imperious temper, a circumstance in which she went far beyond her successors, rendered her exertions of power violent and frequent, and discovered the full extent of her authority: The great popularity, which she enjoyed, proves, that she did not infringe any *established* liberties of the people: There remains evidence sufficient to ascertain the most noted acts of her administration: And though that evidence must be drawn from a source wide of the ordinary historians, it becomes only the more authentic on that account, and serves as a stronger proof, that her particular exertions of power were conceived to be nothing but the ordinary course of administration, since they were not thought remarkable enough to be recorded even by contemporary writers. If there was any difference in this particular, the people, in former reigns, seem rather to have been more submissive than even during the age of Elizabeth:[m] It may not here be improper to recount some of

[l] By the ancient constitution, is here meant that which prevailed before the settlement of our present plan of liberty. There was a more ancient constitution, where, though the people had perhaps less liberty than under the Tudors, yet the king had also less authority: The power of the barons was a great check upon him, and exercised great tyranny over them. But there was still a more ancient constitution, viz. that before the signing of the charters, when neither the people nor the barons had any regular privileges; and the power of the government, during the reign of an able prince, was almost wholly in the king. The English constitution, like all others, has been in a state of continual fluctuation. [m] In a memorial of the state of the realm, drawn by secretary Cecil, in 1569, there is this passage: "Then followeth the decay of obedience in civil policy, which being compared with the fearfulness and reverence of all inferior estates to their superiors in

the ancient prerogatives of the crown, and lay open the sources of that great power, which the English monarchs formerly enjoyed.

One of the most ancient and most established instruments of power was the court of Star-chamber, which possessed an unlimited discretionary authority of fining, imprisoning, and inflicting corporal punishment, and whose jurisdiction extended to all sorts of offences, contempts, and disorders, that lay not within reach of the common law. The members of this court consisted of the privy council and the judges; men, who all of them enjoyed their offices during pleasure: And when the prince himself was present, he was the sole judge, and all the others could only interpose with their advice. There needed but this one court in any government, to put an end to all regular, legal, and exact plans of liberty. For who durst set himself in opposition to the crown and ministry, or aspire to the character of being a patron of freedom, while exposed to so arbitrary a jurisdiction? I much question, whether any of the absolute monarchies in Europe contain, at present, so illegal and despotic a tribunal.

The court of High Commission was another jurisdiction still more terrible; both because the crime of heresy, of which it took cognizance, was more undefinable than any civil offence, and because its methods of inquisition and of administering oaths, were more contrary to all the most simple ideas of justice and equity. The fines and imprisonments imposed by this court were frequent: The deprivations and suspensions of the clergy for non-conformity were also numerous, and comprehended at one time the third of all the ecclesiastics of England." The queen, in a letter to the archbishop of Canterbury, said expressly, that she was resolved, "That no man should be suffered to decline either on the left or on the right hand, from the drawn line limited by authority, and by her laws and injunctions."[o]

But Martial Law went beyond even these two courts in a prompt and arbitrary and violent method of decision. Whenever there was any insurrection or public disorder, the crown employed martial law; and it was, during that time, exercised not only over

---

times past, will astonish any wise and considerate person, to behold the desperation of reformation." Haynes, p. 586. Again, p. 588.   " Neal, vol. i. p. 479.   [o] Murden, p. 183.

the soldiers, but over the whole people: Any one might be punished as a rebel, or an aider and abettor of rebellion, whom the provost-martial, or lieutenant of a county, or their deputies, pleased to suspect. Lord Bacon says, that the trial at common law granted to the earl of Essex, and his fellow conspirators, was a favour: For that the case would have born and required the severity of martial law.[p] We have seen instances of its being employed by queen Mary in defence of orthodoxy. There remains a letter of queen Elizabeth's to the earl of Sussex, after the suppression of the northern rebellion, in which she sharply reproves him, because she had not heard of his having executed any criminals by martial law;[q] though it is probable, that near eight hundred persons suffered, one way or other, on account of that slight insurrection. But the kings of England did not always limit the exercise of this law to times of civil war and disorder. In 1552, when there was no rebellion, or insurrection, king Edward granted a commission of martial law; and empowered the commissioners to execute it, *as should be thought by their discretions most necessary.*[r] Queen Elizabeth too was not sparing in the use of this law. In 1573, one Peter Burchet a puritan, being persuaded that it was meritorious to kill such as opposed the truth of the gospel, ran into the streets, and wounded Hawkins, the famous sea-captain, whom he took for Hatton, the queen's favourite. The queen was so incensed, that she ordered him to be punished instantly by martial law; but upon the remonstrance of some prudent counsellors, who told her, that this law was usually confined to turbulent times, she recalled her order, and delivered over Burchet to the common law.[s] But she continued not always so reserved in exerting this authority. There remains a proclamation of hers, in which she orders martial law to be used against all such as import bulls, or even forbidden books and pamphlets from abroad;[t] and prohibits the questioning of the lieutenants or their deputies for their arbitrary punishment of such offenders, *any law or statute to the contrary in any wise notwithstanding.* We have another act of hers still more extraordinary. The streets of London were much infested with idle vagabonds and riotous persons: The lord mayor had endeavoured to repress this

[p] Vol. iv. p. 510.   [q] MS. of Lord Royston's from the Paper Office.   [r] Strype's Eccles. Memoirs, vol. ii. p. 373, 458, 9.   [s] Camden, p. 446. Strype, vol. ii. p. 288.   [t] Strype, vol. iii. p. 570.

disorder: The Star-chamber had exerted its authority, and inflicted punishments on these rioters: But the queen, finding those remedies ineffectual, revived martial law, and gave Sir Thomas Wilford a commission of provost-martial: "Granting him authority, and commanding him, upon signification given by the Justices of peace in London or the neighbouring counties, of such offenders, worthy to be speedily executed by martial law, to attach and take the same persons, and in the presence of the said justices, according to justice of martial law, to execute them upon the gallows or gibbet openly, or near to such place where the said rebellious and incorrigible offenders shall be found to have committed the said great offences."[u] I suppose it would be difficult to produce an instance of such an act of authority in any place nearer than Muscovy. The patent of High Constable, granted to Earl Rivers by Edward IV., proves the nature of the office. The powers are unlimited, perpetual, and remain in force, during peace, as well as during war and rebellion. The parliament, in Edward VIth's reign, acknowledged the jurisdiction of the Constable and Martial's-court to be part of the law of the land.[w]

The Star-chamber, and High Commission, and Court-martial, though arbitrary jurisdictions, had still some pretence of a trial, at least of a sentence; but there was a grievous punishment very generally inflicted in that age, without any other authority than the warrant of a secretary of state, or of the privy-council;[x] and that was, imprisonment in any jail, and during any time that the ministers should think proper. In suspicious times, all the jails were full of prisoners of state; and these unhappy victims of public jealousy were sometimes thrown into dungeons, and loaded with irons, and treated in the most cruel manner, without their being able to obtain any remedy from law.

This practice was an indirect way of employing torture: But the rack itself, though not admitted in the ordinary execution of justice,[y] was frequently used, upon any suspicion, by authority of a warrant from a secretary or the privy-council. Even the council in the marches of Wales was empowered, by their very commission,

[u] Rymer, vol. xvi. p. 279.   [w] 7 Edw. VI. cap. 20. See Sir John Davis's question concerning impositions, p. 9.   [x] In 1588, the lord mayor committed several citizens to prison, because they refused to pay the loan demanded of them. Murden, p. 632.   [y] Harrison, book ii. chap. 11.

to make use of torture, whenever they thought proper.[z] There cannot be a stronger proof how lightly the rack was employed, than the following story, told by lord Bacon. We shall give it in his own words: "The queen was mightily incensed against Haywarde, on account of a book he dedicated to lord Essex, being a story of the first year of Henry IV. thinking it a seditious prelude to put into the people's heads boldness and faction:[a] She said, she had an opinion that there was treason in it, and asked me, If I could not find any places in it, that might be drawn within the case of treason? Whereto I answered, For treason, sure I found none; but for felony, very many: And when her majesty hastily asked me, Wherein? I told her, the author had committed very apparent theft: For he had taken most of the sentences of Cornelius Tacitus, and translated them into English, and put them into his text. And another time, when the queen could not be persuaded, that it was his writing whose name was to it, but that it had some more mischievous author, and said with great indignation, that she would have him racked to produce his author; I replied, Nay, madam, he is a doctor, never rack his person, but rack his style: Let him have pen, ink, and paper, and help of books, and be enjoined to continue the story where it breaketh off, and I will undertake, by collating the styles, to judge whether he were the author or no."[b] Thus, had it not been for Bacon's humanity, or rather his wit, this author, a man of letters, had been put to the rack, for a most innocent performance. His real offence was, his dedicating a book to that munificent patron of the learned, the earl of Essex, at a time when this nobleman lay under her majesty's displeasure.

The queen's menace, of trying and punishing Haywarde for treason, could easily have been executed, let his book have been ever so innocent. While so many terrors hung over the people, no jury durst have acquitted a man, when the court was resolved to have him condemned. The practice also, of not confronting witnesses with the prisoner, gave the crown lawyers all imaginable advantage against him. And, indeed, there scarcely occurs an in-

[z] Haynes, p. 196. See farther la Boderie, vol. i. p. 211.   [a] To our apprehension, Haywarde's book seems rather to have a contrary tendency. For he has there preserved the famous speech of the bishop of Carlisle, which contains, in the most express terms, the doctrine of passive obedience. But queen Elizabeth was very difficult to please on this head.   [b] Cabala, p. 81.

stance, during all these reigns, that the sovereign, or the ministers, were ever disappointed in the issue of a prosecution. Timid juries, and judges who held their offices during pleasure, never failed to second all the views of the crown. And as the practice was anciently common of fining, imprisoning, or otherwise punishing the jurors, merely at the discretion of the court, for finding a verdict contrary to the direction of these dependant judges; it is obvious, that juries were then no manner of security to the liberty of the subject.

The power of pressing, both for sea and land service, and obliging any person to accept of any office, however mean or unfit for him, was another prerogative totally incompatible with freedom. Osborne gives the following account of Elizabeth's method of employing this prerogative. "In case she found any likely to interrupt her occasions," says he, "she did seasonably prevent him by a chargeable employment abroad, or putting him upon some service at home, which she knew least grateful to the people: Contrary to a false maxim, since practised with far worse success, by such princes as thought it better husbandry to buy off enemies than reward friends."[c] The practice with which Osborne reproaches the two immediate successors of Elizabeth, proceeded partly from the extreme difficulty of their situation, partly from the greater lenity of their disposition. The power of pressing, as may naturally be imagined, was often abused, in other respects, by men of inferior rank; and officers often exacted money for freeing persons from the service.[d]

The government of England during that age, however different in other particulars, bore, in this respect, some resemblance to that of Turkey at present: The sovereign possessed every power, except that of imposing taxes: And in both countries this limitation, unsupported by other privileges, appears rather prejudicial to the people. In Turkey, it obliges the Sultan to permit the extortion of the bashas and governors of provinces, from whom he afterwards squeezes presents or takes forfeitures: In England, it engaged the queen to erect monopolies, and grant patents for exclusive trade: An invention so pernicious, that, had she gone on, during a track of years, at her own rate, England, the seat of riches,

[c] Page 392. [d] Murden, p. 181.

APPENDIX III

and arts, and commerce, would have contained at present as little industry as Morocco, or the coast of Barbary.

We may farther observe, that this valuable privilege, valuable only because it proved afterwards the means by which the parliament extorted all their other privileges, was very much encroached on, in an indirect manner, during the reign of Elizabeth as well as of her predecessors. She often exacted loans from her people; an arbitrary and unequal kind of imposition, and which individuals felt severely: For though the money had been regularly repayed, which was seldom the case,[e] it lay in the prince's hands without interest, which was a sensible loss to the persons from whom the money was borrowed.[f]

There remains a proposal made by lord Burleigh, for levying a general loan on the people, equivalent to a subsidy;[g] a scheme which would have laid the burthen more equally, but which was, in different words, a taxation, imposed without consent of parliament. It is remarkable, that the scheme, thus proposed, without any visible necessity, by that wise minister, is the very same which Henry VIII. executed, and which Charles I. enraged by ill usage from his parliament, and reduced to the greatest difficulties, put afterwards in practice, to the great discontent of the nation.

The demand of benevolence was another invention of that age for taxing the people. This practice was so little conceived to be irregular, that the commons, in 1585, offered the queen a benevolence; which she very generously refused, as having no occasion, at that time, for money.[h] Queen Mary also, by an order of council, encreased the customs in some branches; and her sister imitated the example.[i] There was a species of ship money imposed at the time of the Spanish invasion: The several ports were required to equip a certain number of vessels at their own charge; and such was the alacrity of the people for the public defence, that some of

[e] Bacon, vol. iv. p. 362.   [f] In the second of Richard II. it was enacted that in loans, which the king shall require of his subjects, upon letters of Privy Seal, such as have *reasonable* excuse of not lending, may there be received without further summons, travel, or grief. See Cotton's Abridg. p. 170. By this law, the king's prerogative of exacting loans was ratified; and what ought to be deemed a *reasonable* excuse was still left in his own breast, to determine.   [g] Haynes, p. 518, 519.   [h] D'Ewes, p. 494.   [i] Bacon, vol. iv. p. 362.

the ports, particularly London, sent double the number demanded of them.[k] When any levies were made for Ireland, France, or the Low Countries, the queen obliged the counties to levy the soldiers, to arm and cloath them, and carry them to the sea-ports at their own charge. New-year's gifts were, at that time, expected from the nobility, and from the more considerable gentry.[l]

Purveyance and pre-emption were also methods of taxation, unequal, arbitrary, and oppressive. The whole kingdom sensibly felt the burthen of those impositions; and it was regarded as a great privilege conferred on Oxford and Cambridge, to prohibit the purveyors from taking any commodities within five miles of these universities. The queen victualled her navy by means of this prerogative, during the first years of her reign.[m]

Wardship was the most regular and legal of all these imposi-tions by prerogative: Yet was it a great badge of slavery, and op-pressive to all the considerable families. When an estate devolved to a female, the sovereign obliged her to marry any one he pleased: Whether the heir were male or female, the crown enjoyed the whole profit of the estate during the minority. The giving of a rich wardship was a usual method of rewarding a courtier or favourite.

The inventions were endless, which arbitrary power might em-ploy for the extorting of money, while the people imagined, that their property was secured by the crown's being debarred from imposing taxes. Strype has preserved a speech of lord Burleigh to the queen and council, in which are contained some particulars not a little extraordinary.[n] Burleigh proposes, that she should erect a court for the correction of all abuses, and should confer on the commissioners a general inquisitorial power over the whole king-dom. He sets before her the example of her wise grandfather, Henry VII. who, by such methods, extremely augmented his reve-nue; and he recommends, that this new court should proceed, "as well by the direction and ordinary course of the laws, as by virtue of her majesty's supreme regiment and *absolute power, from whence law proceeded.* " In a word he expects from this institution, greater accession to the royal treasure, than Henry VIII. derived from the abolition of the abbeys, and all the forfeitures of ecclesiastical

[k] Monson, p. 267.   [l] Strype's Memoirs, vol. i. p. 137.   [m] Camden, p. 388.
[n] Annals, vol. iv. p. 234, & seq.

revenues. This project of lord Burleigh's needs not, I think, any comment. A form of government must be very arbitrary indeed, where a wise and good minister could make such a proposal to the sovereign.

Embargoes on merchandize was another engine of royal power, by which the English princes were able to extort money from the people. We have seen instances in the reign of Mary. Elizabeth, before her coronation, issued an order to the custom house, prohibiting the sale of all crimson silks, which should be imported, till the court were first supplied.[o] She expected, no doubt, a good penny-worth from the merchants, while they lay under this restraint.

The parliament pretended to the right of enacting laws, as well as of granting subsidies; but this privilege was, during that age, still more insignificant than the other. Queen Elizabeth expressly prohibited them from meddling either with state matters or ecclesiastical causes; and she openly sent the members to prison, who dared to transgress her imperial edict in these particulars. There passed few sessions of parliament, during her reign, where there occur not instances of this arbitrary conduct.

But the legislative power of the parliament was a mere fallacy; while the sovereign was universally acknowledged to possess a dispensing power, by which all the laws could be invalidated, and rendered of no effect. The exercise of this power was also an indirect method practised for erecting monopolies. Where the statutes laid any branch of manufacture under restrictions, the sovereign, by exempting one person from the laws, gave him in effect the monopoly of that commodity.[p] There was no grievance, at that time, more universally complained of, than the frequent dispensing with the penal laws.[q]

But in reality, the crown possessed the full legislative power, by means of proclamations, which might affect any matter, even of the greatest importance, and which the Star-chamber took care to see more rigorously executed than the laws themselves. The motives for these proclamations were sometimes frivolous and even ridiculous. Queen Elizabeth had taken offence at the smell of

[o] Strype, vol. i. p. 27.   [p] Rymer, tom. xv. p. 756. D'Ewes, p. 645.
[q] Murden, p. 325.

woad; and she issued an edict prohibiting any one from cultivating that useful plant.[r] She was also pleased to take offence at the long swords and high ruffs then in fashion: She sent about her officers, to break every man's sword, and clip every man's ruff, which was beyond a certain dimension.[s] This practice resembles the method employed by the great Czar Peter, to make his subjects change their garb.

The queen's prohibition of the *prophesyings,* or the assemblies, instituted for fanatical prayers and conferences, was founded on a better reason; but shews still the unlimited extent of her prerogative. Any number of persons could not meet together, in order to read the scriptures, and confer about religion, though in ever so orthodox a manner, without her permission.

There were many other branches of prerogative incompatible with an exact or regular enjoyment of liberty. None of the nobility could marry without permission from the sovereign. The queen detained the earl of Southampton long in prison, because he privately married the earl of Essex's cousin.[t] No man could travel without the consent of the prince. Sir William Evers underwent a severe persecution, because he had presumed to pay a private visit to the king of Scots.[u] The sovereign even assumed a supreme and uncontrouled authority over all foreign trade; and neither allowed any person to enter or depart the kingdom, nor any commodity to be imported or exported, without his consent.[w]

The parliament, in the thirteenth of the queen, praised her for not imitating the practice, usual among her predecessors, of stopping the course of justice by particular warrants.[x] There could not possibly be a greater abuse, nor a stronger mark of arbitrary power; and the queen, in refraining from it, was very laudable. But she was by no means constant in this reserve. There remain in the public records some warrants of her's for exempting particular persons from all lawsuits and prosecutions;[y] and these warrants, she says, she grants from her royal prerogative, which she will not allow to be disputed.

---

[r] Townsend's Journals, p. 250. Stow's Annals.   [s] Townsend's Journals, p. 250. Stow's Annals. Strype, vol. ii. p. 603.   [t] Birch's Memoirs, vol. ii. p. 422.   [u] Ibid. p. 511.   [w] Sir John Davis's question concerning impositions, passim.   [x] D'Ewes, p. 141.   [y] Rymer, tom. xv. p. 652, 708, 777.

APPENDIX III

It was very usual in queen Elizabeth's reign, and probably in all the preceding reigns, for noblemen or privy-counsellors to commit to prison any one, who had happened to displease them by suing for his just debts; and the unhappy person, though he gained his cause in the courts of justice, was commonly obliged to relinquish his property in order to obtain his liberty. Some likewise, who had been delivered from prison by the judges, were again committed to custody in secret places, without any possibility of obtaining relief; and even the officers and serjeants of the courts of law were punished for executing the writs in favour of these persons. Nay, it was usual to send for people by pursuivants, a kind of harpies, who then attended the orders of the council and high commission; and they were brought up to London, and constrained by imprisonment, not only to withdraw their lawful suits, but also to pay the pursuivants great sums of money. The judges, in the 34th of the queen, complain to her majesty of the frequency of this practice. It is probable, that so egregious a tyranny was carried no farther down than the reign of Elizabeth; since the parliament, who presented the petition of right, found no later instances of it.[z] And even these very judges of Elizabeth, who thus protect the people against the tyranny of the great, expressly allow, that a person, committed by special command of the queen, is not bailable.

It is easy to imagine, that, in such a government, no justice could, by course of law, be obtained of the sovereign, unless he were willing to allow it. In the naval expedition, undertaken by Raleigh and Frobisher against the Spaniards, in the year 1592, a very rich carrack was taken, worth two hundred thousand pounds. The queen's share in the adventure was only a tenth; but as the prize was so great, and exceeded so much the expectation of all the adventurers, she was determined not to rest contented with her share. Raleigh humbly and earnestly begged her to accept of a hundred thousand pounds, in lieu of all demands, or rather extortions; and says, that the present, which the proprietors were willing to make her, of eighty thousand pounds, was the greatest that ever prince received from a subject.[a]

[z] Rushworth, vol. i. p. 511. Franklyn's Annals, p. 250, 251.   [a] Strype, vol. iv. p. 128, 129.

But it is no wonder the queen, in her administration, should pay so little regard to liberty; while the parliament itself, in enacting laws, was entirely negligent of it. The persecuting statutes, which they passed against papists and puritans, are extremely contrary to the genius of freedom; and by exposing such multitudes to the tyranny of priests and bigots, accustomed the people to the most disgraceful subjection. Their conferring an unlimited supremacy on the queen, or what is worse, acknowledging her inherent right to it, was another proof of their voluntary servitude.

The law of the 23rd of her reign, making seditious words against the queen capital, is also a very tyrannical statute; and a use, no less tyrannical, was sometimes made of it. The case of Udal, a puritanical clergyman, seems singular, even in those arbitrary times. This man had published a book, called a demonstration of discipline, in which he inveighed against the government of bishops; and though he had carefully endeavoured to conceal his name, he was thrown into prison upon suspicion, and brought to a trial for this offence. It was pretended, that the bishops were part of the queen's political body; and to speak against them, was really to attack her, and was therefore felony by the statute. This was not the only iniquity to which Udal was exposed. The judges would not allow the jury to determine any thing but the fact, whether Udal had written the book or not, without examining his intention, or the import of the words. In order to prove the fact, the crown lawyers did not produce a single witness to the court: They only read the testimony of two persons absent, one of whom said, that Udal had told him he was the author; another, that a friend of Udal's had said so. They would not allow Udal to produce any exculpatory evidence; which, they said, was never to be permitted against the crown.[b] And they tendered him an oath, by which he was required to depose, that he was not author of the book; and his refusal to make that deposition was employed as the strongest proof of his guilt. It is almost needless to add, that notwithstanding these multiplied iniquities, a verdict of death was given by the jury against Udal: For as the queen was extremely bent upon his pros-

[b] It was never fully established, that the prisoner could legally produce evidence against the crown, till after the revolution. See Blackstone's Commentaries, vol. iv. p. 352.

ecution, it was impossible he could escape.[c] He died in prison, before execution of the sentence.

The case of Penry was, if possible, still harder. This man was a zealous puritan, or rather a Brownist, a small sect, which afterwards encreased, and received the name of Independants. He had written against the hierarchy several tracts, such as Martin Marprelate, *Theses Martinianae,* and other compositions, full of low scurrility and petulant satire. After concealing himself for some years, he was seized; and as the statute against seditious words required, that the criminal should be tried within a year after committing the offence, he could not be indicted for his printed books. He was therefore tried for some papers found in his pocket, as if he had thereby scattered sedition.[d] It was also imputed to him, by the lord keeper, Puckering, that, in some of these papers, "he had only acknowledged her majesty's royal power to *establish* laws, ecclesiastical and civil; but had avoided the *usual* terms of *making, enacting, decreeing, and ordaining* laws: Which imply," says the lord keeper, "a most absolute authority."[e] Penry for these offences was condemned and executed.

Thus we have seen, that *the most absolute* authority of the sovereign, to make use of the lord keeper's expression, was established on above twenty branches of prerogative, which are now abolished, and which were, every one of them, totally incompatible with the liberty of the subject. But what ensured more effectually the slavery of the people, than even these branches of prerogative, was, the established principles of the times, which attributed to the prince such an unlimited and indefeizable power, as was supposed to be the origin of all law, and could be circumscribed by none. The homilies, published for the use of the clergy, and which they were enjoined to read every Sunday in all the churches, inculcate every where a blind and unlimited passive-obedience to the prince, which, on no account, and under no pretence, is it ever lawful for subjects, in the smallest article, to depart from or infringe. Much noise has been made, because some court chaplains, during the succeeding reigns, were permitted to preach such doctrines; but

[c] State Trials, vol. i. p. 144. Strype, vol. iv. p. 21. Id. Life of Whitgift, p. 343.
[d] Strype's Life of Whitgift, book iv. chap. 11. Neal, vol. i. p. 564. [e] Strype's annals, vol. iv. p. 177.

there is a great difference between these sermons, and discourses published by authority, avowed by the prince and council, and promulgated to the whole nation.*f* So thoroughly were these principles imbibed by the people, during the reigns of Elizabeth and her predecessors, that opposition to them was regarded as the most flagrant sedition, and was not even rewarded by that public praise and approbation, which can alone support men under such dangers and difficulties, as attend the resistance of tyrannical authority.*g* It was only during the next generation that the noble principles of liberty took root, and spreading themselves, under the shelter of puritanical absurdities, became fashionable among the people.

It is worth remarking, that the advantage, usually ascribed to absolute monarchy, a greater regularity of police and a more strict execution of the laws, did not attend the former English government, though in many respects it fell under that denomination. A demonstration of this truth is contained in a judicious paper, which is preserved by Strype,*h* and which was written by an eminent justice of peace of Somersetshire, in the year 1596, near the end of the queen's reign; when the authority of that princess may be supposed to be fully corroborated by time, and her maxims of government improved by long practice. This paper contains an account of the disorders which then prevailed in the county of Somerset. The author says, that forty persons had there been executed in a year for robberies, thefts, and other felonies; thirty-five burnt in the hand, thirty-seven whipped, one hundred and eighty-three discharged: That those who were discharged were most wicked and desperate persons, who never could come to any

f Gifford, a clergyman, was suspended in the year 1584, for preaching up a limited obedience to the civil magistrate, Neal, vol. i. p. 435.   *g* It is remarkable, that in all the historical plays of Shakespear, where the manners and characters, and even the transactions of the several reigns are so exactly copied, there is scarcely any mention of *civil Liberty*; which some pretended historians have imagined to be the object of all the ancient quarrels, insurrections, and civil wars. In the elaborate panegyric of England, contained in the tragedy of Richard II. and the detail of its advantages, not a word of its civil constitution, as anywise different from or superior to that of other European kingdoms: An omission, which cannot be supposed in any English author that wrote since the Restoration, at least since the Revolution.   *h* Annals, vol. iv. p. 290.

good, because they would not work, and none would take them
into service: That notwithstanding this great number of indict-
ments, the fifth part of the felonies committed in the county were
not brought to a trial; the greater number escaped censure, either
from the superior cunning of the felons, the remissness of the
magistrates, or the foolish lenity of the people: That the rapines
committed by the infinite number of wicked, wandering, idle people, were intolerable to the poor countrymen, and obliged them to
keep a perpetual watch over their sheep-folds, their pastures, their
woods, and their corn-fields: That the other counties of England
were in no better condition than Somersetshire; and many of them
were even in a worse: That there were at least three or four hundred able-bodied vagabonds in every county, who lived by theft
and rapine; and who sometimes met in troops to the number of
sixty, and committed spoil on the inhabitants: That if all the felons
of this kind were assembled, they would be able, if reduced to good
subjection, to give the greatest enemy her majesty has a *strong
battle:* And that the magistrates themselves were intimidated from
executing the laws upon them; and there were instances of justices
of peace, who, after giving sentence against rogues, had interposed to stop the execution of their own sentence, on account of
the danger, which hung over them from the confederates of these
felons.

In the year 1575, the queen complained in parliament of the
bad execution of the laws; and threatened, that, if the magistrates
were not, for the future, more vigilant, she would entrust authority
to indigent and needy persons, who would find an interest in a
more exact administration of justice.[i] It appears, that she was as
good as her word. For in the year 1601, there were great complaints made in parliament of the rapine of justices of peace; and
a member said, that this magistrate was an animal, who, for half a
dozen of chickens, would dispense with a dozen of penal statutes.[k]
It is not easy to account for this relaxation of government, and
neglect of police, during a reign of so much vigour as that of
Elizabeth. The small revenue of the crown is the most likely cause
that can be assigned. The queen had it not in her power to interest
a great number in assisting her to execute the laws.[l]

[i] D'Ewes, p. 234. [k] D'Ewes, p. 661–664. [l] See note [II] at the end of the
volume.

On the whole, the English have no reason, from the example of their ancestors, to be in love with the picture of absolute monarchy; or to prefer the unlimited authority of the prince and his unbounded prerogatives, to that noble liberty, that sweet equality, and that happy security, by which they are at present distinguished above all nations in the universe. The utmost that can be said in favour of the government of that age (and perhaps it may be said with truth) is, that the power of the prince, though really unlimited, was exercised after the European manner, and entered not into every part of the administration; that the instances of a high exerted prerogative were not so frequent as to render property sensibly insecure, or reduce the people to a total servitude; that the freedom from faction, the quickness of execution, and the promptitude of those measures, which could be taken for offence or defence, made some compensation for the want of a legal and determinate liberty; that as the prince commanded no mercenary army, there was a tacit check on him, which maintained the government in that medium, to which the people had been accustomed; and that this situation of England, though seemingly it approached nearer, was in reality more remote from a despotic and eastern monarchy, than the present government of that kingdom, where the people, though guarded by multiplied laws, are totally naked, defenceless, and disarmed, and besides, are not secured by any middle power, or independant powerful nobility, interposed between them and the monarch.

We shall close the present Appendix with a brief account of the revenues, the military force, the commerce, the arts, and the learning of England during this period.

Revenues.   Queen Elizabeth's economy was remarkable; and in some instances seemed to border on avarice. The smallest expence, if it could possibly be spared, appeared considerable in her eyes; and even the charge of an express, during the most delicate transactions, was not below her notice.[m] She was also attentive to every profit; and embraced opportunities of gain, which may appear somewhat extraordinary. She kept, for instance, the see of Ely vacant nineteen years, in order to retain the revenue;[n] and it was usual with her, when she promoted a bishop, to take the opportu-

---

[m] Birch's Negot. p. 21.   [n] Strype, vol. iv. p. 351.

nity of pillaging the see of some of its manors.[o] But that in reality there was little or no avarice in the queen's temper appears from this circumstance, that she never amassed any treasure; and even refused subsidies from the parliament, when she had no present occasion for them. Yet we must not conclude from this circumstance, that her economy proceeded from a tender concern for her people: She loaded them with monopolies and exclusive patents, which are much more oppressive than the most heavy taxes, levied in an equal and regular manner. The real source of her frugal conduct was derived from her desire of independency, and her care to preserve her dignity, which would have been endangered, had she reduced herself to the necessity of having frequent recourse to parliamentary supplies. In consequence of this motive, the queen, though engaged in successful and necessary wars, thought it more prudent to make a continual dilapidation of the royal demesnes,[p] than demand the most moderate supplies from the commons. As she lived unmarried and had no posterity, she was content to serve her present turn, though at the expence of her successors; who, by reason of this policy, joined to other circumstances, found themselves, on a sudden, reduced to the most extreme indigence.

The splendor of a court was, during this age, a great part of the public charge; and as Elizabeth was a single woman, and expensive in no kind of magnificence, except cloaths, this circumstance enabled her to perform great things by her narrow revenue. She is said to have paid four millions of debt, left on the crown by her father, brother, and sister; an incredible sum for that age.[q] The

[o] Ibid. p. 215. There is a curious letter of the queen's, writ to a bishop of Ely, and preserved in the register of that see. It is in these words: *Proud prelate, I understand you are backward in complying with your agreement: But I would have you know, that I, who made you what you are, can unmake you; and if you do not forthwith fulfil your engagement, by God, I will immediately unfrock you. Yours, as you demean yourself, Elizabeth.* The bishop, it seems, had promised to exchange some part of the land belonging to the see for a pretended equivalent; and did so, but it was in consequence of the above letter. Annual Register, 1761. p. 15. [p] Rymer, tom. xvi. p. 141. D'Ewes, p. 151, 457, 525, 629. Bacon, vol. iv. p. 363. [q] D'Ewes, p. 473. I think it impossible to reconcile this account of the public debts with that given by Strype, Eccles. Mem. vol. ii. p. 344. that in the year 1553, the crown owed but 300,000 pounds. I own, that this last sum appears a great deal more likely. The whole revenue of queen Elizabeth would not in ten years have paid four millions.

States, at the time of her death, owed her about eight hundred thousand pounds: And the king of France four hundred and fifty thousand.[r] Though that prince was extremely frugal, and after the peace of Vervins, was continually amassing treasure, the queen never could, by the most pressing importunities, prevail on him to make payment of those sums, which she had so generously advanced him, during his greatest distresses. One payment of twenty thousand crowns, and another of fifty thousand, were all she could obtain, by the strongest representations she could make of the difficulties, to which the rebellion in Ireland had reduced her.[s] The queen expended on the wars with Spain, between the years 1589 and 1593, the sum of one million three hundred thousand pounds, beside the pittance of a double subsidy, amounting to two hundred and eighty thousand pounds, granted her by parliament.[t] In the year 1599, she spent six hundred thousand pounds in six months on the service of Ireland.[u] Sir Robert Cecil affirmed, that, in ten years, Ireland cost her three millions four hundred thousand pounds.[w] She gave the earl of Essex a present of thirty thousand pounds upon his departure for the government of that kingdom.[x] Lord Burleigh computed, that the value of the gifts, conferred on that favourite, amounted to three hundred thousand pounds; a sum, which, though probably exaggerated, is a proof of her strong affection towards him! It was a common saying during this reign; *The queen pays bountifully, though she rewards sparingly.*[y]

It is difficult to compute exactly the queen's ordinary revenue, but it certainly fell much short of five hundred thousand pounds a-year.[z] In the year 1590, she raised the customs from fourteen thousand pounds a-year to fifty thousand, and obliged Sir Thomas Smith, who had farmed them, to refund some of his former profits.[a] This improvement of the revenue was owing to

[r] Winwood, vol. i. p. 29, 54.   [s] Winwood, vol. i. p. 117, 395.   [t] D'Ewes, p. 483.   [u] Camden, p. 167.   [w] Appendix to the earl of Essex's apology. [x] Birch's Memoirs, vol. ii.   [y] Nanton's Regalia, chap. 1.   [z] Franklyn in his annals, p. 9. says that the profit of the kingdom, besides Wards and the dutchy of Lancaster *(which amounted to about 120,000 pounds)* was 188,197 pounds: The crown lands seem to be comprehended in this computation. [a] Camden, p. 558. This account of Camden is difficult or impossible to be reconciled to the state of the customs in the beginning of the subsequent reign, as they appear in the journals of the commons. See Hist. of James, chap. 46.

the suggestions of one Caermarthen; and was opposed by Burleigh, Leicester, and Walsingham: But the queen's perseverance overcame all their opposition. The great undertakings, which she executed with so narrow a revenue, and with such small supplies from her people, prove the mighty effects of wisdom and economy. She received from the parliament, during the course of her whole reign, only twenty subsidies and thirty-nine fifteenths. I pretend not to determine exactly the amount of these supplies; because the value of a subsidy was continually falling; and in the end of her reign it amounted only to eighty thousand pounds,[b] though in the beginning it had been a hundred and twenty thousand. If we suppose, that the supplies, granted Elizabeth during a reign of forty-five years, amounted to three millions, we shall not probably be much wide of the truth.[c] This sum makes only sixty-six thousand six hundred and sixty-six pounds a-year; and it is surprizing, that, while the queen's demands were so moderate, and her expences so well regulated, she should ever have found any

[b] D'Ewes, p. 630.   [c] Lord Salisbury, computed these supplies only at 2,800,000 pounds, Journ. 17 Feb. 1609. King James was certainly mistaken, when he estimated the queen's annual supplies at 137,000 pounds, Franklyn, p. 44. It is curious to observe, that the minister, in the war began in 1754, was, in some periods, allowed to lavish in two months as great a sum as was granted by parliament to queen Elizabeth in forty-five years. The extreme frivolous object of the late war, and the great importance of hers, set this matter in still a stronger light. Money too, we may observe, was in most particulars of the same value in both periods: She payed eight pence a day to every foot soldier. But our late delusions have much exceeded any thing known in history, not even excepting those of the crusades. For, I suppose, there is no mathematical, still less an arithmetical demonstration, that the road to the Holy Land was not the road to Paradise, as there is, that the endless encrease of national debts is the direct road to national ruin. But having now compleatly reached that goal, it is needless at present to reflect on the past. It will be found in the present year, 1776, that all the revenues of this island, north of Trent and west of Reading, are mortgaged or anticipated for ever. Could the small remainder be in a worse condition, were those provinces seized by Austria and Prussia? There is only this difference, that some event might happen in Europe, which would oblige these great monarchs to disgorge their acquisitions. But no imagination can figure a situation, which will induce our creditors to relinquish their claims, or the public to seize their revenues. So egregious indeed has been our folly, that we have even lost all title to compassion, in the numberless calamities that are waiting us.

difficulty in obtaining a supply from parliament, or be reduced to make sale of the crown-lands. But such was the extreme, I had almost said, absurd parsimony of the parliaments during that period. They valued nothing in comparison of their money: The members had no connexion with the court; and the very idea, which they conceived of the trust committed to them, was, to reduce the demands of the crown, and to grant as few supplies as possible. The crown, on the other hand, conceived the parliament in no other light than as a means of supply. Queen Elizabeth made a merit to her people of seldom summoning parliaments.[d] No redress of grievances was expected from these assemblies: They were supposed to meet for no other purpose than to impose taxes.

Before the reign of Elizabeth, the English princes had usually recourse to the city of Antwerp for voluntary loans; and their credit was so low, that, besides paying the high interest of ten or twelve per cent. They were obliged to make the city of London join in the security. Sir Thomas Gresham, that great and enterprizing merchant, one of the chief ornaments of this reign, engaged the company of merchant-adventurers to grant a loan to the queen; and as the money was regularly re-paid, her credit by degrees established itself in the city, and she shook off this dependance on foreigners.[e]

In the year 1559, however, the queen employed Gresham to borrow for her two hundred thousand pounds at Antwerp, in order to enable her to reform the coin, which was at that time extremely debased.[f] She was so impolitic as to make, herself, an innovation in the coin; by dividing a pound of silver into sixty-two shillings, instead of sixty, the former standard. This is the last time that the coin has been tampered with in England.

Commerce.   Queen Elizabeth, sensible how much the defence of her kingdom depended on its naval power, was desirous, to encourage commerce and navigation: But as her monopolies tended to extinguish all domestic industry, which is much more valuable than foreign trade, and is the foundation of it, the general train of her conduct was ill calculated to serve the purpose at which she aimed, much less to promote the riches of her people. The exclusive

[d] Strype, vol. iv. p. 124.   [e] Stowe's Survey of London, book i. p. 286.
[f] MS. of lord Royston's from the paper office, p. 295.

APPENDIX III

companies also were an immediate check on foreign trade. Yet, notwithstanding these discouragements, the spirit of the age was strongly bent on naval enterprizes; and besides the military expeditions against the Spaniards, many attempts were made for new discoveries, and many new branches of foreign commerce were opened by the English. Sir Martin Frobisher undertook three fruitless voyages to discover the north-west passage: Davis, not discouraged by this ill success, made a new attempt, when he discovered the straits, which pass by his name. In the year 1600, the queen granted the first patent to the East-India company: The stock of that company was seventy-two thousand pounds; and they fitted out four ships, under the command of James Lancaster, for this new branch of trade. The adventure was successful; and the ships, returning with a rich cargo, encouraged the company to continue the commerce.

The communication with Muscovy had been opened in queen Mary's time by the discovery of the passage to Archangel: But the commerce to that country did not begin to be carried on to a great extent till about the year 1569. The queen obtained from the czar an exclusive patent to the English for the whole trade of Muscovy;[g] and she entered into a personal, as well as national, alliance with him. This czar was named John Basilides, a furious tyrant, who, continually suspecting the revolt of his subjects, stipulated to have a safe retreat and protection in England. In order the better to ensure this resource, he purposed to marry an English woman; and the queen intended to have sent him lady Anne Hastings, daughter of the earl of Huntingdon: But when the lady was informed of the barbarous manners of the country, she wisely declined purchasing an empire at the expence of her ease and safety.[h]

The English, encouraged by the privileges, which they had obtained from Basilides, ventured farther into those countries, than any Europeans had formerly done. They transported their goods along the river Dwina in boats made of one entire tree, which they towed and rowed up the stream as far as Walogda. Thence they carried their commodities seven days journey by land to Yeraslau, and then down the Volga to Astracan. At Astracan,

[g] Camden, p. 408.   [h] Ibid. p. 493.

they built ships, crossed the Caspian Sea, and distributed their manufactures into Persia. But this bold attempt met with such discouragements, that it was never renewed.[i]

After the death of John Basilides, his son Theodore revoked the patent, which the English enjoyed for a monopoly of the Russian trade: When the queen remonstrated against this innovation, he told her ministers, that princes must carry an indifferent hand, as well between their subjects as between foreigners; and not convert trade, which, by the laws of nations, ought to be common to all, into a monopoly for the private gain of a few.[k] So much juster notions of commerce were entertained by this barbarian, than appear in the conduct of the renowned queen Elizabeth! Theodore, however, continued some privileges to the English, on account of their being the discoverers of the communication between Europe and his country.

The trade to Turkey commenced about the year 1583; and that commerce was immediately confined to a company by queen Elizabeth. Before that time, the grand signior had always conceived England to be a dependant province of France;[l] but having heard of the queen's power and reputation, he gave a good reception to the English, and even granted them larger privileges than he had given to the French.

The merchants of the Hanse-towns complained loudly in the beginning of Elizabeth's reign of the treatment, which they had received in the reigns of Edward and Mary. She prudently replied, that, as she would not innovate any thing, she would still protect them in the immunities and privileges, of which she found them possessed. This answer not contenting them, their commerce was soon after suspended for a time, to the great advantage of the English merchants, who tried what they could themselves effect for promoting their commerce. They took the whole trade into their own hands; and their returns proving successful, they divided themselves into staplers and merchant adventurers; the former residing constantly at one place, the latter trying their fortunes in other towns and states abroad with cloth and other manufactures. This success so enraged the Hanse-towns, that they tried all the methods, which a discontented people could devise, to

[i] Camden, p. 418.   [k] Camden, p. 493.   [l] Birch's Memoirs, vol. i. p. 36.

APPENDIX III

draw upon the English merchants the ill opinion of other nations and states. They prevailed so far as to obtain an imperial edict, by which the English were prohibited all commerce in the empire: The queen, by way of retaliation, retained sixty of their ships, which had been seized in the river Tagus with contraband goods of the Spaniards. These ships the queen intended to have restored, as desiring to have compromised all differences with those trading cities; but when she was informed, that a general assembly was held at Lubec, in order to concert measures for distressing the English trade, she caused the ships and cargoes to be confiscated: Only two of them were released to carry home the news, and to inform these states, that she had the greatest contempt imaginable for all their proceedings.[m]

Henry VIII. in order to fit out a navy, was obliged to hire ships from Hamburgh, Lubec, Dantzick, Genoa, and Venice: But Elizabeth, very early in her reign, put affairs upon a better footing; both by building some ships of her own, and by encouraging the merchants to build large trading vessels, which, on occasion, were converted into ships of war.[n] In the year 1582, the seamen in England were found to be fourteen thousand two hundred and ninety-five men;[o] the number of vessels twelve hundred and thirty-two; of which there were only two hundred and seventeen above eighty tons. Monson pretends, that, though navigation decayed in the first years of James I. by the practice of the merchants, who carried on their trade in foreign bottoms,[p] yet before the year 1640, this number of seamen was tripled in England.[q]

The navy, which the queen left at her decease, appears considerable, when we reflect only on the number of vessels, which were forty-two: But when we consider that none of these ships carried above forty guns; that four only came up to that number; that there were but two ships of a thousand tons; and twenty-three below five hundred, some of fifty, and some even of twenty tons; and that the whole number of guns belonging to the fleet was seven hundred and seventy-four;[r] we must entertain a contemptible idea of the English navy, compared to the force which it has

Military force.

[m] Lives of the Admirals, vol. i. p. 470.   [n] Camden, p. 388.   [o] Monson, p. 256.   [p] Ibid. p. 300.   [q] Ibid. p. 210, 256.   [r] Monson, p. 196. The English navy at present carries about 14,000 guns.

now attained.⁵ In the year 1588, there were not above five vessels, fitted out by the noblemen and sea-ports, which exceeded two hundred tons.ᵗ

In the year 1599, an alarm was given of an invasion by the Spaniards; and the queen equipped a fleet and levied an army in a fortnight to oppose them. Nothing gave foreigners a higher idea of the power of England than this sudden armament. In the year 1575, all the militia in the kingdom were computed at a hundred and eighty-two thousand nine hundred and twenty-nine.ᵘ A distribution was made, in the year 1595, of a hundred and forty thousand men, besides those which Wales could supply.ʷ These armies were formidable by their numbers; but their discipline and experience were not proportionate. Small bodies from Dunkirk and Newport frequently ran over, and plundered the east coast: So unfit was the militia, as it was then constituted, for the defence of the kingdom. The lord lieutenants were first appointed to the counties in this reign.

Mr. Murdenˣ has published from the Salisbury collections a paper, which contains the military force of the nation at the time of the Spanish Armada, and which is somewhat different from the account given by our ordinary historians. It makes all the able-bodied men of the kingdom amount to a hundred and eleven thousand five hundred and thirteen; those armed, to eighty thousand eight hundred and seventy-five; of whom forty-four thousand seven hundred and twenty-seven were trained. It must be supposed that these able-bodied men consisted of such only as were registered, otherwise the small number is not to be accounted for. Yet Sir Edwardʸ Coke said in the house of commons, that he was employed about the same time, together with Popham, chief justice, to take a survey of all the people of England, and that they found them to be 900,000 of all sorts. This number, by the ordinary rules of computation, supposes that there were above 200,000 men able to bear arms. Yet even this number is surprizingly small. Can we suppose that the kingdom is six or seven times more populous at present? And that Murden's was the real number of men, excluding catholics and children and infirm persons?

⁵ See note [JJ] at the end of the volume.   ᵗ Monson, p. 300.   ᵘ Lives of the Admirals, vol. i. p. 432.   ʷ Strype, vol. iv. p. 211.   ˣ p. 608.   ʸ Journ. 25 April, 1621.

APPENDIX III

Harrison says, that in the musters taken in the years 1574 and 1575, the men fit for service amounted to 1,172,674; yet was it believed that a full third was omitted. Such uncertainty and contradiction are there in all these accounts. Notwithstanding the greatness of this number, the same author complains much of the decay of populousness: A vulgar complaint in all places and all ages. Guicciardini makes the inhabitants of England in this reign amount to two millions.

Whatever opinion we may form of the comparative populousness of England in different periods, it must be allowed, that, abstracting from the national debt, there is a prodigious encrease of power, in that, more perhaps than in any other European state, since the beginning of the last century. It would be no paradox to affirm, that Ireland alone could at present exert a greater force than all the three kingdoms were capable of at the death of queen Elizabeth. And we might go farther, and assert, that one good county in England is able to make, at least to support, a greater effort than the whole kingdom was capable of in the reign of Harry V; when the maintainance of a garrison in a small town, like Calais, formed more than a third of the ordinary national expence. Such are the effects of liberty, industry, and good government!

The state of the English manufactures was at this time very low; and foreign wares of almost all kinds had the preference.[z] About the year 1590, there were in London four persons only rated in the subsidy-books so high as four hundred pounds.[a] This computation is not indeed to be deemed an exact estimate of their wealth. In 1567, there were found on enquiry to be four thousand eight hundred and fifty-one strangers of all nations in London: Of whom three thousand eight hundred and thirty-eight were Flemings, and only fifty-eight Scots.[b] The persecutions in France and the Low Countries drove afterwards a greater number of foreigners into England; and the commerce, as well as manufactures of that kingdom, was very much improved by them.[c] It was then that Sir Thomas Gresham built, at his own charge, the magnificent fabric of the Exchange for the reception of the merchants: The queen visited it, and gave it the appellation of the Royal Exchange.

By a lucky accident in language, which has a great effect on men's ideas, the invidious word, usury, which formerly meant

z D'Ewes, p. 505.   [a] Id. p. 497.   [b] Haynes, p. 461, 462.   [c] Stowe, p. 668.

the taking of any interest for money, came now to express only the taking of exorbitant and illegal interest. An act, passed in 1571, violently condemns all usury; but permits ten per cent interest to be payed. Henry IV. of France reduced interest to 6½ per cent: An indication of the great advance of France above England in commerce.

Dr. Howell says[d] that queen Elizabeth in the third of her reign was presented with a pair of black silk knit stockings by her silkwoman, and never wore cloth hose any more. The author of the present State of England, says that about 1577, pocket watches were first brought into England from Germany. They are thought to have been invented at Nuremberg. About 1580, the use of coaches was introduced by the earl of Arundel.[e] Before that time, the queen, on public occasions, rode behind her chamberlain.

Camden says, that in 1581, Randolph, so much employed by the queen in foreign embassies, possessed the office of post-master general of England. It appears, therefore, that posts were then established; though from Charles I.'s regulations in 1635, it would seem, that few post-houses were erected before that time.

In a remonstrance of the Hanse Towns to the diet of the empire in 1582, it is affirmed that England exported annually about 200,000 pieces of cloth.[f] This number seems to be much exaggerated.

In the fifth of this reign was enacted the first law for the relief of the poor.

A judicious author of that age confirms the vulgar observation, that the kingdom was depopulating from the encrease of inclosures and decay of tillage; and he ascribes the reason very justly to the restraints put on the exportation of corn; while full liberty was allowed to export all the produce of pasturage, such as wool, hides, leather, tallow, &c. These prohibitions of exportation were derived from the prerogative, and were very injudicious. The queen, once, on the commencement of her reign, had tried a contrary practice, and with good success. From the same author we learn, that the complaints, renewed in our time, were then very common, concerning the high prices of every thing.[g] There seems,

[d] History of the World, vol. ii. p. 222.   [e] Anderson, vol. i. p. 421.
[f] Anderson, vol. i. p. 424.   [g] A compendious or brief Examination of certain ordinary Complaints of divers of our Countrymen. The author says,

indeed, to have been two periods, in which prices rose remarkably in England, namely, that in queen Elizabeth's reign, when they are computed to have doubled, and that in the present age. Between the two, there seems to have been a stagnation. It would appear that industry, during that intermediate period, encreased as fast as gold and silver, and kept commodities nearly at a par with money.

There were two attempts made in this reign to settle colonies in America; one by Sir Humphrey Gilbert in Newfoundland, another by Sir Walter Raleigh in Virginia: But neither of these projects proved successful. All those noble settlements were made in the following reigns. The current specie of the kingdom, in the end of this reign, is computed at four millions.[h]

The earl of Leicester desired Sir Francis Walsingham, then ambassador in France, to provide him with a riding master in that country, to whom he promises a hundred pounds a-year, beside maintaining himself and servant and a couple of horses. "I know," adds the earl, "that such a man as I want may receive higher wages in France: But let him consider, that a shilling in England goes as far as two shillings in France."[i] It is known that every thing is much changed since that time.

The nobility in this age still supported, in some degree, the ancient magnificence in their hospitality, and in the numbers of their retainers; and the queen found it prudent to retrench, by proclamation, their expences in this last particular.[k] The expence of hospitality, she somewhat encouraged, by the frequent visits she paid her nobility, and the sumptuous feasts, which she received from them.[l] The earl of Leicester gave her an entertainment in

Manners.

that in 20 or 30 years before 1581, commodities had in general risen 50 per cent; some more. Cannot you, neighbour, remember, says he, that, within these 30 years, I could in this town buy the best pig or goose I could lay my hands on for four-pence, which now costeth twelve-pence, a good capon for three pence, or four-pence, a chicken for a penny, a hen for two-pence, p. 35. Yet the price of ordinary labour was then eight-pence a day, p. 31. [h] Lives of the Admirals, vol. i. p. 475. [i] Digges's compleat Ambassador. [k] Strype, vol. iii. Append. p. 54. [l] Harrison, after enumerating the queen's palaces, adds: "But what shall I need to take upon me to repeat all, and tell what houses the queen's majesty hath? Sith all is hers; and when it pleaseth her in the summer season to recreate herself abroad, and view the estate of the country, and hear the complaints of her poor commons injured by her unjust officers or their substitutes, every nobleman's house is

Kenilworth Castle, which was extraordinary for expence and magnificence. Among other particulars, we are told, that three hundred and sixty-five hogsheads of beer were drunk at it.[m] The earl
had fortified this castle at great expence; and it contained arms for
ten thousand men.[n] The earl of Derby had a family consisting of
two hundred and forty servants.[o] Stowe remarks it as a singular
proof of beneficence in this nobleman, that he was contented with
his rent from his tenants, and exacted not any extraordinary services from them: A proof that the great power of the sovereign
(what was almost unavoidable) had very generally countenanced
the nobility in tyrannizing over the people. Burleigh, though he
was frugal, and had no paternal estate, kept a family consisting of
a hundred servants.[p] He had a standing table for gentlemen, and
two other tables for persons of meaner condition, which were
always served alike, whether he were in town or in the country.
About his person he had people of great distinction, insomuch that
he could reckon up twenty gentlemen retainers who had each a
thousand pounds a-year; and as many among his ordinary servants, who were worth from a thousand pounds to three, five, ten,
and twenty thousand pounds.[q] It is to be remarked, that, though
the revenues of the crown were at that time very small, the ministers and courtiers sometimes found means, by employing the
boundless prerogative, to acquire greater fortunes than it is possible for them at present to amass, from their larger salaries, and
more limited authority.

Burleigh entertained the queen twelve several times in his
country house; where she remained three, four, or five weeks at a
time. Each visit cost him two or three thousand pounds.[r] The
quantity of silver plate possessed by this nobleman, is surprising:

her palace, where she continueth during pleasure, and till she return again
to some of her own, in which she remaineth, so long as she pleaseth." Book
ii. chap. xv. Surely one may say of such a guest, what Cicero says to Atticus,
on occasion of a visit payed him by Caesar. Hospes tamen non is cui diceres,
amabo te, eodem ad me cum revertêre. Lib. xiii. Ep. 52. If she relieved the
people from oppressions (to whom it seems the law could give no relief) her
visits were a great oppression on the nobility. [m] Biogr. Brit. vol. iii. p.
1791. [n] Strype, vol. iii. p. 394. [o] Stowe, p. 674. [p] Strype, vol. iii. p.
129. Append. [q] Life of Burleigh published by Collins. [r] Ibid. p. 40.

No less than fourteen or fifteen thousand pounds weight;[s] which, besides the fashion, would be above forty-two thousand pounds sterling in value. Yet Burleigh left only 4000 pounds a-year in land, and 11,000 pounds in money; and as land was then commonly sold at ten years purchase, his plate was nearly equal to all the rest of his fortune. It appears, that little value was then put upon the fashion of the plate, which probably was but rude: The weight was chiefly considered.[t]

But though there were preserved great remains of the ancient customs, the nobility were, by degrees, acquiring a taste for elegant luxury; and many edifices, in particular, were built by them, neat, large, and sumptuous, to the great ornament of the kingdom, says Camden;[u] but to the no less decay of the glorious hospitality of the nation. It is, however, more reasonable to think, that this new turn of expence promoted arts and industry; while the ancient hospitality was the source of vice, disorder, sedition, and idleness.[w]

Among the other species of luxury, that of apparel began much to encrease during this age; and the queen thought proper to restrain it by proclamation.[x] Her example was very little conformable to her edicts. As no woman was ever more conceited of her beauty, or more desirous of making impression on the hearts of beholders, no one ever went to a greater extravagance in apparel, or studied more the variety and richness of her dresses. She appeared almost every day in a different habit; and tried all the several modes, by which she hoped to render herself agreeable. She was also so fond of her cloaths, that she never could part with any of them; and at her death she had in her wardrobe all the different habits, to the number of three thousand, which she had ever worn in her life-time.[y]

The retrenchment of the ancient hospitality, and the diminution of retainers, were favourable to the prerogative of the sovereign; and by disabling the great noblemen from resistance, promoted the execution of the laws, and extended the authority of the

[s] See note [KK] at the end of the volume. [t] This appears from Burleigh's will: He specifies only the number of ounces to be given to each legatee, and appoints a goldsmith to see it weighed out to them, without making any distinction of the pieces. [u] Page 452. [w] See note [LL] at the end of the volume. [x] Camden, p. 452. [y] Carte, vol. iii. p. 702. from Beaumont's Dispatches.

courts of justice. There were many peculiar causes in the situation
and character of Henry VII. which augmented the authority of the
crown: Most of these causes concurred in succeeding princes; together with the factions in religion, and the acquisition of the
supremacy, a most important article of prerogative: But the manners of the age were a general cause, which operated during this
whole period, and which continually tended to diminish the riches,
and still more the influence, of the aristocracy, anciently so formidable to the crown. The habits of luxury dissipated the immense
fortunes of the ancient barons; and as the new methods of expence
gave subsistance to mechanics and merchants, who lived in an
independant manner on the fruits of their own industry, a nobleman, instead of that unlimited ascendant, which he was wont to
assume over those who were maintained at his board, or subsisted
by salaries conferred on them, retained only that moderate influence, which customers have over tradesmen, and which can never
be dangerous to civil government. The landed proprietors also,
having a greater demand for money than for men, endeavoured to
turn their lands to the best account with regard to profit, and
either inclosing their fields, or joining many small farms into a few
large ones, dismissed those useless hands, which formerly were
always at their call in every attempt to subvert the government, or
oppose a neighbouring baron. By all these means the cities encreased; the middle rank of men began to be rich and powerful;
the prince, who, in effect, was the same with the law, was implicitly
obeyed; and though the farther progress of the same causes begat
a new plan of liberty, founded on the privileges of the commons,
yet in the interval between the fall of the nobles and the rise of this
order, the sovereign took advantage of the present situation, and
assumed an authority almost absolute.

Whatever may be commonly imagined, from the authority of
lord Bacon, and from that of Harrington, and later authors, the
laws of Henry VII. contributed very little towards the great revolution, which happened about this period in the English constitution. The practice of breaking entails, by a fine and recovery,
had been introduced in the preceding reigns; and this prince only
gave indirectly a legal sanction to the practice, by reforming some
abuses which attended it. But the settled authority, which he acquired to the crown, enabled the sovereign to encroach on the
separate jurisdictions of the barons, and produced a more general

and regular execution of the laws. The counties palatine underwent the same fate as the feudal powers; and by a statute of Henry
VIII,[z] the jurisdiction of these counties was annexed to the crown,
and all writs were ordained to run in the king's name. But the
change of manners was the chief cause of the secret revolution of
government, and subverted the power of the barons. There appear still in this reign some remains of the ancient slavery of the
boors and peasants,[a] but none afterwards.

Learning, on its revival, was held in high estimation by the
English princes and nobles; and as it was not yet prostituted by
being too common, even the Great deemed it an object of ambition
to attain a character for literature. The four successive sovereigns,
Henry, Edward, Mary, and Elizabeth, may, on one account or
other, be admitted into the class of authors. Queen Catherine Parr
translated a book: Lady Jane Gray; considering her age, and her
sex, and her station, may be regarded as a prodigy of literature. Sir
Thomas Smith was raised from being professor in Cambridge, first
to be ambassador to France, then secretary of state. The dispatches
of those times, and among others those of Burleigh himself, are
frequently interlarded with quotations from the Greek and Latin
classics. Even the ladies of the court valued themselves on knowledge: Lady Burleigh, lady Bacon, and their two sisters, were mis-
tresses of the ancient, as well as modern languages; and placed
more pride in their erudition than in their rank and quality.

Learning.

Queen Elizabeth wrote and translated several books; and she
was familiarly acquainted with the Greek as well as Latin tongue.[b]
It is pretended, that she made an extemporary reply in Greek to
the university of Cambridge, who had addressed her in that language. It is certain, that she answered in Latin without pre-
meditation, and in a very spirited manner, to the Polish ambassador, who had been wanting in respect to her. When she had
finished, she turned about to her courtiers, and said, "God's death,
my lords," (for she was much addicted to swearing) "I have been
forced this day to scour up my old Latin, that hath long lain
rusting."[c] Elizabeth, even after she was queen, did not entirely
drop the ambition of appearing as an author; and next to her
desire of admiration for beauty, this seems to have been the chief

---

[z] 27 Hen. VIII. c. 24. [a] Rymer, tom. xv. p. 731. [b] See note [MM] at the
end of the volume. [c] Speed.

object of her vanity. She translated Boethius of the Consolation of Philosophy; in order, as she pretended, to allay her grief for Henry IV.'s change of religion. As far as we can judge from Elizabeth's compositions, we may pronounce, that, notwithstanding her application, and her excellent parts, her taste in literature was but indifferent: She was much inferior to her successor in this particular, who was himself no perfect model of eloquence.

Unhappily for literature, at least for the learned of this age, the queen's vanity lay more in shining by her own learning, than in encouraging men of genius by her liberality. Spencer himself, the finest English writer of his age, was long neglected; and after the death of Sir Philip Sydney, his patron, was allowed to die almost for want. This poet contains great beauties, a sweet and harmonious versification, easy elocution, a fine imagination: Yet does the perusal of his work become so tedious, that one never finishes it from the mere pleasure which it affords: It soon becomes a kind of task-reading; and it requires some effort and resolution to carry us on to the end of his long performance. This effect, of which every one is conscious, is usually ascribed to the change of manners: But manners have more changed since Homer's age; and yet that poet remains still the favourite of every reader of taste and judgment. Homer copied true natural manners, which, however rough or uncultivated, will always form an agreeable and interesting picture: But the pencil of the English poet was employed in drawing the affectations, and conceits, and fopperies of chivalry, which appear ridiculous as soon as they lose the recommendation of the mode. The tediousness of continued allegory, and that too seldom striking or ingenious has also contributed to render the *Fairy Queen* peculiarly tiresome; not to mention the too great frequency of its descriptions, and the languor of its stanza. Upon the whole, Spencer maintains his place in the shelves among our English classics: But he is seldom seen on the table; and there is scarcely any one, if he dares to be ingenuous, but will confess, that, notwithstanding all the merit of the poet, he affords an entertainment with which the palate is soon satiated. Several writers of late have amused themselves in copying the stile of Spencer; and no imitation has been so indifferent as not to bear a great resemblance to the original: His manner is so peculiar, that it is almost impossible not to transfer some of it into the copy.

NOTES TO THE
FOURTH VOLUME

NOTE [A], p. 12

The parliament also granted the queen the duties of tonnage and pound-age; but this concession was at that time regarded only as a matter of form, and she had levied these duties before they were voted by parliament: But there was another exertion of power, which she practiced, and which peo-ple, in the present age, from their ignorance of ancient practices, may be apt to think a little extraordinary. Her sister, after the commencement of the war with France, had, from her own authority, imposed four marks on each ton of wine imported, and had encreased the poundage a third on all commodities. Queen Elizabeth continued these impositions, as long as she thought convenient. The parliament, who had so good an opportunity of restraining these arbitrary taxes, when they voted the tonnage and pound-age, thought not proper to make any mention of them. They knew, that the sovereign, during that age, pretended to have the sole regulation of foreign trade, and that their intermeddling with that prerogative would have drawn on them the severest reproof, if not chastisement. See Forbes, vol. i. p. 132, 133. We know certainly from the statutes and journals, that no such impo-sitions were granted by parliament.

NOTE [B], p. 22

Knox, p. 127. We shall suggest afterwards some reasons to suspect, that, perhaps, no express promise was ever given. Calumnies easily arise during times of faction, especially those of the religious kind, when men think every art lawful for promoting their purpose. The congregation in their manifesto, in which they enumerate all the articles of the regent's mal-administration, do not reproach her with this breach of promise. It was probably nothing but a rumour spread abroad to catch the populace. If the papists have sometimes maintained, that no faith was to be kept with heretics, their adversaries seem also to have thought, that no truth ought to be told of idolaters.

NOTE [C], p. 25

Spotswood, p. 146. Melvil, p. 29. Knox, p. 225, 228. Lesley, lib. x. That there was really no violation of the capitulation of Perth, appears from the manifesto of the congregation in Knox, p. 184, in which it is not so much as pretended. The companies of Scotch soldiers were, probably, in Scotch pay, since the congregation complains, that the country was oppressed with taxes to maintain armies. Knox, p. 164, 165. And even if they had been in French pay, it had been no breach of the capitulation, since they were national troops, not French. Knox, does not say, p. 139, that any of the inhabitants of Perth were tried or punished for their past offences; but only that they were oppressed with the quartering of soldiers: And the congregation, in their manifesto, say only that many of them had fled for fear. This plain detection of the calumny with regard to the breach of the capitulation of Perth, may make us suspect a like calumny with regard to the pretended promise not to give sentence against the ministers. The affair lay altogether between the regent and the laird of Dun; and that gentleman, though a man of sense and character, might be willing to take some general professions for promises. If the queen, overawed by the power of the congregation, gave such a promise in order to have liberty to proceed to a sentence; How could she expect to have power to execute a sentence so insidiously obtained? And to what purpose could it serve?

NOTE [D], p. 26

Knox, p. 153, 154, 155. This author pretends that this article was agreed to verbally, but that the queen's scribes omitted it in the treaty which was signed. The story is very unlikely, or rather very absurd; and in the mean time it is allowed, that the article is not in the treaty: Nor do the congregation, in their subsequent manifesto insist upon it. Knox, p. 184. Besides, Would the queen regent in an article of a treaty, call her own religion idolatry?

NOTE [E], p. 28

The Scotch lords in their declaration say, "How far we have sought support of England, or of any other prince, and what just cause we had and have so to do, we shall shortly make manifest unto the world, to the praise of God's holy name, and to the confusion of all those that slander us for so doing: For this we fear not to confess, that, as in this enterprize against the devil, against idolatry and the maintainers of the same, we chiefly and only seek God's glory to be notified unto men, sin to be punished, and virtue to be maintained; so where power faileth of ourselves, we will seek it, wheresoever God shall offer the same." Knox, p. 176.

NOTE [F], p. 65

This year the council of Trent was dissolved, which had sitten from 1545. The publication of its decrees excited anew the general ferment in Europe;

while the catholics endeavoured to enforce the acceptance of them, and the protestants rejected them. The religious controversies were too far advanced to expect that any conviction would result from the decrees of this council. It is the only general council which has been held in an age truly learned and inquisitive; and as the history of it has been written with great penetration and judgment, it has tended very much to expose clerical usurpations and intrigues, and may serve us as a specimen of more ancient councils. No one expects to see another general council, till the decay of learning and the progress of ignorance shall again fit mankind for these great impostures.

NOTE [G], p. 72

It appears, however, from Randolf's Letters, (See Keith, p. 290.) that some offers had been made to that minister, of seizing Lenox and Darnley, and delivering them into queen Elizabeth's hands. Melvil confirms the same story, and says, that the design was acknowledged by the conspirators, p. 56. This serves to justify the account given by the queen's party of the Raid of Baith, as it is called. See farther, Goodall, vol. ii. p. 358. The other conspiracy, of which Murray complained, is much more uncertain, and is founded on very doubtful evidence.

NOTE [H], p. 77

Buchanan confesses that Rizzio was ugly; but it may be inferred, from the narration of that author, that he was young. He says, that on the return of the duke of Savoy to Turin, Rizzio was *in adolescentiae vigore;* in the vigour of youth. Now that event happened only a few years before, lib. xvii. cap. 44. That Bothwel was young appears, among many other invincible proofs, from Mary's instructions to the bishop of Dumblain, her ambassador at Paris; where she says, that in 1559, only eight years before, he was *very young.* He might therefore have been about thirty when he married her. See Keith's History, p. 388. From the appendix to the *epistolae regum Scotorum,* it appears, by authentic documents, that Patrick, earl of Bothwel, father to James, who espoused queen Mary, was alive, till near the year 1560. Buchanan, by a mistake, which has been long ago corrected, calls him James.

NOTE [I], p. 88

Mary herself confessed, in her instructions to the ambassadors, whom she sent to France, that Bothwel persuaded all the noblemen, that their application in favour of his marriage was agreeable to her, Keith, p. 389. Anderson, vol. i. p. 94. Murray afterwards produced to queen Elizabeth's commissioners a paper signed by Mary, by which she permitted them to make this application to her. This permission was a sufficient declaration of her intentions, and was esteemed equivalent to a command. Anderson, vol. iv. p. 59. They even asserted, that the house, in which they met, was surrounded with armed men. Goodall, vol. ii. p. 141.

NOTE [J], p. 112

Mary's complaint of the queen's partiality in admitting Murray to a confer-ence was a mere pretext in order to break off the conference. She indeed employs that reason in her order for that purpose (see Goodall, vol. ii. p. 184), but in her private letter, her commissioners are directed to make use of that order to prevent her honour from being attacked, Goodall, vol. ii. p. 183. It was therefore the accusation only she was afraid of. Murray was the least obnoxious of all her enemies: He was abroad when her subjects rebelled and reduced her to captivity: He had only accepted of the regency, when voluntarily proffered him by the nation. His being admitted to queen Elizabeth's presence was therefore a very bad foundation for a quarrel, or for breaking off the conference; and was plainly a mere pretence.

NOTE [K], p. 114

We shall not enter into a long discussion concerning the authenticity of these letters: We shall only remark in general, that the chief objections against them are, that they are supposed to have passed through the earl of Morton's hands, the least scrupulous of all Mary's enemies; and that they are, to the last degree, indecent, and even somewhat inelegant, such as it is not likely she would write. But to these presumptions we may oppose the following considerations. (1.) Though it be not difficult to counterfeit a subscription, it is very difficult, and almost impossible, to counterfeit several pages, so as to resemble exactly the hand-writing of any person. These letters were examined and compared with Mary's hand-writing, by the English privy-council, and by a great many of the nobility, among whom were several partizans of that princess. They might have been exam-ined by the bishop of Ross, Herreis, and others of Mary's commissioners. The regent must have expected, that they would be very critically examined by them: And had they not been able to stand that test, he was only preparing a scene of confusion to himself. Bishop Lesly expressly declines the comparing of the hands, which he calls no legal proof, Goodall, vol. ii. p. 389. (2.) The letters are very long, much longer than they needed to have been, in order to serve the purposes of Mary's enemies; a circumstance, which encreased the difficulty, and exposed any forgery the more to the risk of detection. (3.) They are not so gross and palpable, as forgeries commonly are; for they still left a pretext for Mary's friends to assert, that their meaning was strained to make them appear criminal; see Goodall, vol. ii. p. 361. (4.) There is a long contract of marriage, said to be written by the earl of Huntley, and signed by the queen, before Bothwell's acquital. Would Morton, without any necessity, have thus doubled the difficulties of the forgery, and the danger of detection? (5.) The letters are indiscreet; but such was apparently Mary's conduct at that time: They are inelegant; but they have a careless, natural air, like letters hastily written between familiar friends. (6.) They contain such a variety of particular circumstances, as nobody could have thought of inventing, especially as they must necessarily have afforded her many means of detection. (7.) We have not the originals of the letters, which were in French: We have only a Scotch and Latin translation from the original, and a French translation professedly done from the Latin. Now it is remarkable, that the Scotch translation is full of Gallicisms, and is clearly a translation from a French original: Such as *make fault, faire des fautes; make it seem that I believe, faire semblant de le croire; make brek, faire breche; this is my first journay, c'est ma premiere journée; have you not desire to laugh, n'avez vous pas envie de rire; the place will hald unto the death, la place tiendra jusqu'à la mort; he may not come forth of the house this long time, il ne peut pas sortir du logis de long-tems; to make me advertisement, faire m'avertir; put order to it; mettre ordre a cela; discharge your heart, decharger votre coeur; make gud watch, faites bonne garde, &c.* (8.) There is a conversation which she mentions, between herself and the king one evening: But Murray produced before the English commissioners, the testimony of one Crawford, a gentleman of the Earl of Lenox, who swore, that the king, on her departure from him, gave him an account of the same conversation. (9.) There seems very little reason why Murray and his associates should run the risk of such dangerous forgery, which must have rendered them infamous, if detected; since their cause, from Mary's known conduct, even without these letters, was sufficiently good and justifiable. (10.) Murray exposed these letters to the examination of persons qualified to judge of them: the Scotch council, the Scotch parliament, queen Elizabeth and her council, who were possessed of a great number of Mary's genuine letters. (11.) He gave Mary herself an opportunity of refuting and exposing him, if she had chosen to lay hold of it. (12.) The letters tally so well with all the other parts of her conduct during that transaction, that these proofs throw the strongest light on each other. (13.) The duke of Norfolk, who had examined these papers, and who favoured so much the queen of Scots, that he intended to marry her, and in the end lost his life in her cause, yet believed them authentic, and was fully convinced of her guilt. This appears not only from his letters above mentioned, to queen Elizabeth and her ministers, but by his secret acknowledgment to Banister, his most trusty confident. See State Trials, vol. i. p. 81. In the conferences between the duke, secretary Lidington, and the bishop of Ross, all of them zealous partizans of that princess, the same thing is always taken for granted. Ibid. p. 74, 75. See farther MS. in the Advocate's library. A. 3, 28. p. 314. from Cott. lib. Calig. c. 9. Indeed, the duke's full persuasion of Mary's guilt, without the least doubt or hesitation, could not have had place, if he had found Lidington or the bishop of Ross of a different opinion, or if they had ever told him that these letters were forged. It is to be remarked, that Lidington, being one of the accomplices, knew the whole bottom of the conspiracy against king Henry, and was, besides, a man of such penetration, that nothing could escape him in such interesting events. (14.) I need not repeat the presumption drawn from Mary's refusal to answer. The only excuse for her silence, is, she suspected Elizabeth to be a partial judge: It was not, indeed, the interest of that princess to acquit and justify her rival and competitor; and we accordingly find that Lidington, from the secret information of the duke of Norfolk, informed Mary, by the bishop of Ross, that the queen of England never meant to come to a decision; but only to get into her hands the proofs of Mary's guilt, in order to blast her character: See State Trials, vol. i. p. 77. But this was a better reason for declining the conference altogether than for breaking it off, on frivolous pretences, the very moment the chief accusation was unexpectedly opened against her. Though she could not expect Elizabeth's final decision in her favour, it was of importance to give a satisfactory answer, if she had any, to the accusation of the Scotch commissioners. That answer could have been dispersed for the satisfaction of the public, of foreign nations, and of posterity. And surely after the accusation and proofs were in queen Elizabeth's hands, it could do no harm to give in the answers. Mary's information, that the queen never intended to come to a decision, could be no obstacle to her justification. (15.) The very disappearance of these letters, is a presumption of their authenticity. That event can be accounted for no way but from the care of king James's friends, who were desirous to destroy every proof of his mother's crimes. The disappearance of Morton's narrative, and of Crawford's evidence, from the Cotton library, Calig. c. 1. must have proceeded from a like cause. See MS. in the Advocates' library, A. 3. 29. p. 88.

I find an objection made to the authenticity of the letters, drawn from the vote of the Scotch privy-council, which affirms the letters to be written and subscribed by queen Mary's own hand; whereas the copies given in to the parliament, a few days after, were only written, not subscribed. See Goodall, vol. ii. p. 64, 67. But it is not considered, that this circumstance is of no matter of force: There were certainly letters, true or false, laid before the council; and whether the letters were true or false, this mistake proceeds equally from the inaccuracy or blunder of the clerk. The mistake may be accounted for: The letters were only written by her: The second contract with Bothwell was only subscribed. A proper accurate distinction was not made; and they are all said to be written and subscribed. A late writer, Mr. Goodall, has endeavoured to prove, that these letters clash with chronology, and that the queen was not in the places mentioned in the letters, on the days there assigned: To confirm this, he produces charters and other deeds signed by the queen, where the date and place do not agree with the letters. But it is well known, that the date of charters, and such like grants, is no proof of the real day on which they were signed by the sovereign. Papers of that kind commonly pass through different offices: The date is affixed by the first office; and may precede very long the day of the signature.

The account given by Morton of the manner in which the papers came into his hands, is very natural. When he gave it to the English commissioners, he had reason to think it would be canvassed with all the severity of able adversaries, interested in the highest degree to refute it. It is probable, that he could have confirmed it by many circumstances and testimonies; since they declined the contest.

The sonnets are inelegant; insomuch, that both Brantome and Ronsard, who knew queen Mary's style, were assured, when they saw them, that they could not be of her composition. Jebb, vol. ii. p. 478. But no person is equal in his productions, especially one whose style is so little formed as Mary's must be supposed to be. Not to mention, that such dangerous and criminal enterprizes leave little tranquillity of mind for elegant, poetical compositions.

In a word, queen Mary might easily have conducted the whole conspiracy against her husband, without opening her mind to any one person except Bothwel, and without writing a scrap of paper about it; but it was very difficult to have conducted it so that her conduct should not betray her to men of discernment. In the present case, her conduct was so gross as to betray her to every body; and fortune threw into her enemies' hands, papers by which they could convict her. The same infatuation and imprudence, which happily is the usual attendant of great crimes, will account for both. It is proper to observe, that there is not one circumstance of the foregoing narrative, contained in the history, that is taken from Knox, Buchanan, or even Thuanus, or indeed, from any suspected authority.

NOTE [L], p. 115

Unless we take this angry accusation, advanced by queen Mary, to be an argument of Murray's guilt, there remains not the least presumption which should lead us to suspect him to have been any wise an accomplice in the king's murder. That queen never pretended to give any proof of the charge; and her commissioners affirmed at the time, that they themselves knew of none, though they were ready to maintain its truth by their mistress's orders, and would produce such proof as she should send them. It is remarkable, that, at that time, it was impossible for either her or them to produce any proof; because the conferences before the English commissioners were previously broken off.

It is true, the bishop of Ross, in an angry pamphlet, written by him under a borrowed name (where it is easy to say any thing), affirms, that lord Herreis, a few days after the king's death, charged Murray with the guilt, openly, to his face, at his own table. This latter nobleman, as Lesly relates the matter, affirmed, that Murray riding in Fife with one of his servants, the evening before the commission of that crime, said to him among other talk, *This night 'ere morning the lord Darnley shall lose his life.* See Anderson, vol. i. p. 75. But this is only a hearsay of Lesly's, concerning a hearsay of Herreis's; and contains a very improbable fact. Would Murray, without any use of necessity, communicate to a servant, such a dangerous and important secret, merely by way of conversation? We may also observe, that lord Herreis himself was one of queen Mary's commissioners who accused Murray. Had he ever heard this story, or given credit to it, was not that the time to have produced it? and not have affirmed, as he did, that he, for his part, knew nothing of Murray's guilt. See Goodall, vol. ii. p. 307.

The earls of Huntley and Argyle accuse Murray of this crime; but the reason which they assign is ridiculous. He had given his consent to Mary's

divorce from the king: therefore he was the king's murderer. See Anderson, vol. iv. part 2. p. 192. It is a sure argument, that these earls knew
no better proof against Murray, otherwise they would have produced it,
and not have insisted on so absurd a presumption. Was not this also the
time for Huntley to deny his writing Mary's contract with Bothwel, if that
paper had been a forgery?

Murray could have no motive to commit that crime. The king, indeed,
bore him some ill-will; but the king himself was become so despicable, both
from his own ill conduct and the queen's aversion to him, that he could
neither do good nor harm to any body. To judge by the event, in any case,
is always absurd; especially in the present. The king's murder, indeed,
procured Murray the regency: But much more Mary's ill-conduct and
imprudence, which he could not possibly foresee, and which never would
have happened, had she been entirely innocent.

NOTE [M], p. 115

I believe there is no reader of common sense, who does not see, from the
narrative in the text, that the author means to say, that queen Mary refuses
constantly to answer before the English commissioners, but offers only to
answer in person before queen Elizabeth in person, contrary to her practice
during the whole course of the conference, till the moment the evidence of
her being an accomplice in her husband's murder is unexpectedly produced. It is true, the author having repeated four or five times an account
of this demand of being admitted to Elizabeth's presence, and having
expressed his opinion, that, as it had been refused from the beginning,
even before the commencement of the conferences, she did not expect it
would now be complied with; thought it impossible his meaning could be
misunderstood (as indeed it was impossible), and not being willing to tire
his reader with continual repetitions, he mentions in a passage or two,
simply, that she had refused to make any answer. I believe also, there is no
reader of common sense who peruses Anderson or Goodall's collections,
and does not see, that, agreeably to this narrative, queen Mary insists
unalterably and strenuously on not continuing to answer before the English
commissioners, but insists to be heard in person, by queen Elizabeth in
person; though once or twice, by way of bravado, she says simply, that she
will answer and refute her enemies, without inserting this condition, which
still is understood. But there is a person, that has writ an *Enquiry historical
and critical into the evidence against Mary queen of Scots;* and has attempted to
refute the foregoing narrative. He quotes a single passage of the narrative
in which Mary is said simply to refuse answering; and then a single passage
from Goodall, in which she boasts simply that she will answer; and he very
civilly and almost directly calls the author a liar, on account of this pretended contradiction. That whole Enquiry, from beginning to end, is composed of such scandalous artifices; and from this instance, the reader may
judge of the candour, fair dealing, veracity, and good manners of the

NOTES TO THE FOURTH VOLUME

Enquirer. There are indeed three events in our history, which may be regarded as touchstones of partymen. An English Whig, who asserts the reality of the popish plot, an Irish Catholic, who denies the massacre in 1641, and a Scotch Jacobite, who maintains the innocence of queen Mary, must be considered as men beyond the reach of argument or reason, and must be left to their prejudices.

NOTE [N], p. 133

By Murden's state papers, published after the writing of this history, it appears, that an agreement had been made between Elizabeth and the regent for the delivering up of Mary to him. The queen afterwards sent down Killigrew to the earl of Marre when regent, offering to put Mary into his hands. Killigrew was instructed to take good security from the regent, that that queen should be tried for her crimes, and that the sentence should be executed upon her. It appears that Marre rejected the offer; because we hear no more of it.

NOTE [O], p. 135

Sir James Melvil, p. 108, 109. ascribes to Elizabeth a positive design of animating the Scotch factions against each other; but his evidence is too inconsiderable to counterbalance many other authorities, and is, indeed, contrary to her subsequent conduct, as well as her interest, and the necessity of her situation. It was plainly her interest, that the king's party should prevail, and nothing could have engaged her to stop their progress, or even forbear openly assisting them, but her intention of still amusing the queen of Scots, by the hopes of being peaceably restored to her throne. See farther Strype, vol. ii. Append. p. 20.

NOTE [P], p. 192

That the queen's negociations for marrying the duke Anjou were not feigned nor political, appears clearly from many circumstances; particularly from a passage in Dr. Forbes's manuscript collections, at present in the possession of lord Royston. She there enjoins Walsingham, before he opens the treaty, to examine the person of the duke; and as that prince had lately recovered from the small pox, she desires her ambassador to consider, whether he yet retained so much of his good looks, as that a woman could fix her affections on him. Had she not been in earnest, and had she only meant to amuse the public or the court of France, this circumstance was of no moment.

NOTE [Q], p. 209

D'Ewes, p. 328. The puritanical sect had indeed gone so far, that a book of discipline was secretly subscribed by above five hundred clergymen; and the presbyterian government thereby established in the midst of the

church, notwithstanding the rigour of the prelates and of the high commission. So impossible is it by penal statutes, however severe, to suppress all
religious innovation. See Neal's Hist. of the Puritans, vol. i. p. 483. Strype's
Life of Whitgift, p. 291.

NOTE [R], p. 211

This year, the earl of Northumberland, brother to the earl beheaded some
years before, had been engaged in a conspiracy with lord Paget for the
deliverance of the queen of Scots. He was thrown into the Tower; and
being conscious that his guilt could be proved upon him, at least, that
sentence would infallibly be pronounced against him, he freed himself
from farther prosecution by a voluntary death. He shot himself in the
breast with a pistol. About the same time, the earl of Arundel, son of the
unfortunate duke of Norfolk, having entered into some exceptionable measures, and reflecting on the unhappy fate, which had attended his family,
endeavoured to depart secretly beyond sea, but was discovered and thrown
into the Tower. In 1587 this nobleman was brought to his trial for high
treason; chiefly because he had dropped some expressions of affection to
the Spaniards, and had affirmed that he would have masses said for the
success of the Armada. His peers found him guilty of treason: This severe
sentence was not executed; but Arundel never recovered his liberty. He
died a prisoner in 1595. He carried his religious austerities so far, that they
were believed the immediate cause of his death.

NOTE [S], p. 223

Mary's extreme animosity against Elizabeth may easily be conceived, and it
broke out, about this time, in an incident, which may appear curious. While
the former queen was kept in custody by the earl of Shrewsbury, she lived
during a long time in great intimacy with the countess; but that lady entertaining a jealousy of an amour between her and the earl, their friendship
was converted into enmity; and Mary took a method of revenge, which at
once gratified her spite against the countess and that against Elizabeth. She
wrote to the queen informing her of all the malicious scandalous stories,
which, she said, the countess of Shrewsbury had reported of her: That
Elizabeth had given a promise of marriage to a certain person, whom she
afterwards often admitted to her bed: That she had been equally indulgent
to Simier, the French agent, and to the duke of Anjou: That Hatton was
also one of her paramours, who was even disgusted with her excessive love
and fondness: That though she was on other occasions avaricious to the last
degree, as well as ungrateful, and kind to very few, she spared no expence
in gratifying her amorous passions: That notwithstanding her licentious
amours, she was not made like other women; and all those who courted her
marriage would in the end be disappointed: That she was so conceited of
her beauty, as to swallow the most extravagant flattery from her courtiers,
who could not, on these occasions, forbear even sneering at her for her

folly: That it was usual for them to tell her, that the lustre of her beauty dazzled them like that of the sun, and they could not behold it with a fixed eye: She added, that the countess had said, that Mary's best policy would be to engage her son to make love to the queen; nor was there any danger that such a proposal would be taken for mockery: So ridiculous was the opinion which she had entertained of her own charms. She pretended, that the countess had represented her as no less odious in her temper than profligate in her manners, and absurd in her vanity: That she had so beaten a young woman of the name Scudamore as to break that lady's finger; and in order to cover over the matter, it was pretended, that the accident had proceeded from the fall of a candlestick: That she had cut another across the hand with a knife, who had been so unfortunate as to offend her. Mary added, that the countess had informed her, that Elizabeth had suborned Rolstone to pretend friendship to her, in order to debauch her, and thereby throw infamy on her rival. See Murden's State Papers, p. 558. This imprudent and malicious letter was written a very little before the detection of Mary's conspiracy; and contributed, no doubt, to render the proceedings against her the more rigorous. How far these imputations against Elizabeth can be credited, may perhaps appear doubtful; But her extreme fondness for Leicester, Hatton, and Essex, not to mention Mountjoy and others, with the curious passages between her and admiral Seymour, contained in Haynes, render her chastity very much to be suspected. Her self-conceit with regard to beauty, we know from other undoubted authority, to have been extravagant. Even when she was a very old woman, she allowed her courtiers to flatter her with regard to her excellent beauties. Birch, vol. ii. p. 442, 443. Her passionate temper may also be proved from many lively instances; and it was not unusual with her to beat her maids of honour. See the Sydney Papers, vol. ii. p. 38. The blow she gave to Essex before the privy-council is another instance. There remains in the Museum a letter of the earl of Huntington's, in which he complains grievously of the queen's pinching his wife very sorely, on account of some quarrel between them. Had this princess been born in a private station, she would not have been, very amiable: But her absolute authority, at the same time that it gave an uncontroling swing to her violent passions, enabled her to compensate her infirmities by many great and signal virtues.

NOTE [T], p. 232

Camden, p. 525. This evidence was that of Curle, her secretary, whom she allowed to be a very honest man; and who, as well as Nau, had given proofs of his integrity, by keeping so long such important secrets, from whose discovery he could have reaped the greatest profit. Mary, after all, thought, that she had so little reason to complain of Curle's evidence, that she took care to have him paid a considerable sum by her will, which she wrote the day before her death. Goodall, vol. i. p. 413. Neither did she forget Nau, though less satisfied in other respects with his conduct. Id. ibid.

NOTE [U], p. 233

The detail of this conspiracy is to be found in a letter of the queen of Scots
to Charles Paget, her great confident. This letter is dated the 20th of May
1586, and is contained in Dr. Forbes's manuscript collections, at present in
the possession of lord Royston. It is a copy attested by Curle, Mary's secretary, and indorsed by lord Burleigh. What proves its authenticity beyond
question is that we find in Murden's Collection, p. 516, that Mary actually
wrote that very day a letter to Charles Paget: And farther, she mentions, in
the manuscript letter, a letter of Charles Paget's of the 10th of April: Now
we find by Murden, p. 506, that Charles Paget did actually write her a letter
of that date.

This violence of spirit is very consistent with Mary's character. Her
maternal affection was too weak to oppose the gratification of her passions,
particularly her pride, her ambition, and her bigotry. Her son, having made
some fruitless attempts to associate her with him in the title, and having
found the scheme impracticable, on account of the prejudices of his protestant subjects, at last desisted from that design, and entered into an alliance
with England, without comprehending his mother. She was in such a rage
at this undutiful behaviour, as she imagined it, that she wrote to queen
Elizabeth, that she no longer cared what became of him or herself in the
world; the greatest satisfaction she could have before her death was to see
him and all his adherents become a signal example of tyranny, ingratitude
and impiety, and undergo the vengeance of God for their wickedness. She
would find in Christendom other heirs, and doubted not to put her inheritance in such hands as would retain the firmest hold of it. She cared not,
after taking this revenge, what became of her body: The quickest death
would then be the most agreeable to her. And she assured her, that, if he
persevered, she would disown him for her son, would give him her male-
diction, would disinherit him, as well of his present possessions as of all he
could expect by her; abandoning him not only to her subjects to treat him
as they had done her, but to all strangers to subdue and conquer him. It was
in vain to employ menaces against her: The fear of death or other misfortune would never induce her to make one step or pronounce one syllable
beyond what she had determined: She would rather perish with honour, in
maintaining the dignity, to which God had raised her, than degrade herself
by the least pusillanimity, or act what was unworthy of her station and of
her race. Murden, p. 566, 567.

James said to Courcelles, the French ambassador, that he had seen a
letter under her own hand, in which she threatened to disinherit him, and
said that he might betake him to the lordship of Darnley, For that was all
he had by his father. *Courcelles' Letter, a M S. of Dr. Campbel's.* There is in
Jebb, vol. ii. p. 573, a letter of her's where she throws out the same menace
against him.

We find this scheme of seizing the king of Scots, and delivering him into
the hands of the pope or the king of Spain, proposed by Morgan to Mary.
See Murden, p. 525. A mother must be very violent to whom one would

dare to make such a proposal: But it seems she assented to it. Was not such a woman very capable of murdering her husband, who had so grievously offended her?

NOTE [V], p. 234

The volume of State Papers collected by Mr. Murden, prove beyond controversy, that Mary was long in close correspondence with Babington, p. 513, 516, 532, 533. She entertained a like correspondence with Ballard, Morgan, and Charles Paget, and laid a scheme with them for an insurrection, and for the invasion of England by Spain, p. 528, 531. The same papers show, that there had been a discontinuance of Babington's correspondence, agreeably to Camden's narration. See State Papers, p. 513. where Morgan recommends it to queen Mary to renew her correspondence with Babington. These circumstances prove, that no weight can be laid on Mary's denial of guilt, and that her correspondence with Babington contained particulars, which could not be avowed.

NOTE [W], p. 234

There are three suppositions, by which the letter to Babington may be accounted for, without allowing Mary's concurrence in the conspiracy for assassinating Elizabeth. The first is, that which she seems herself to have embraced, that her secretaries had received Babington's letter, and had, without any treacherous intention, ventured of themselves to answer it, and had never communicated the matter to her: But it is utterly improbable, if not impossible, that a princess of so much sense and spirit should, in an affair of that importance, be so treated by her servants who lived in the house with her, and who had every moment an opportunity of communicating the secret to her. If the conspiracy failed, they must expect to suffer the severest punishment from the court of England; if it succeeded, the lightest punishment, which they could hope for from their own mistress, must be disgrace, on account of their temerity. Not to mention, that Mary's concurrence was in some degree requisite for effecting the design of her escape: It was proposed to attack her guards, while she was employed in hunting: She must therefore concert the time and place with the conspirators. The second supposition is, that these two secretaries were previously traitors; and being gained by Walsingham, had made such a reply in their mistress's cypher, as might involve her in the guilt of the conspiracy. But these two men had lived long with the queen of Scots, had been entirely trusted by her, and had never fallen under suspicion either with her or her partizans. Camden informs us, that Curle afterwards claimed a reward from Walsingham on pretence of some promise; but Walsingham told him, that he owed him no reward, and that he had made no discoveries on his examination, which were not known with certainty from other quarters. The third supposition is, that neither the queen nor the two secretaries, Nau and Curle, ever saw Babington's letter, or made any answer; but that

Walsingham, having decyphered the former, forged a reply. But this supposition implies the falsehood of the whole story, told by Camden, of Gifford's access to the queen of Scots' family, and Paulet's refusal to concur in allowing his servants to be bribed. Not to mention, that as Nau's and Curl's evidence must, on this supposition, have been extorted by violence and terror, they would necessarily have been engaged, for their own justification, to have told the truth afterwards; especially upon the accession of James. But Camden informs us, that Nau, even after that event, persisted still in his testimony.

We must also consider, that the two last suppositions imply such a monstrous criminal conduct in Walsingham, and consequently in Elizabeth (for the matter could be no secret to her) as exceeds all credibility. If we consider the situation of things and the prejudices of the times, Mary's consent to Babington's conspiracy appears much more natural and probable. She believed Elizabeth to be an usurper and a heretic: She regarded her as a personal and a violent enemy: She knew that schemes for assassinating heretics were very familiar in that age, and generally approved of by the court of Rome and the zealous catholics: Her own liberty and sovereignty were connected with the success of this enterprize: And it cannot appear strange, that where men of so much merit as Babington could be engaged, by bigotry alone, in so criminal an enterprize, Mary, who was actuated by the same motive, joined to so many others, should have given her consent to a scheme projected by her friends. We may be previously certain, that, if such a scheme was ever communicated to her, with any probability of success, she would assent to it: And it served the purpose of Walsingham and the English ministry to facilitate the communication of these schemes, as soon as they had gotten an expedient for intercepting her answer, and detecting the conspiracy. Now Walsingham's knowledge of the matter is a supposition necessary to account for the letter delivered to Babington.

As to the not punishing of Nau and Curle by Elizabeth, it never is the practice to punish lesser criminals, who had given evidence against the principal.

But what ought to induce us to reject these three suppositions, is, that they must, all of them, be considered as bare possibilities: The partizans of Mary can give no reason for preferring one to the other: Not the slightest evidence ever appeared to support any one of them: Neither at that time, nor at any time afterwards, was any reason discovered, by the numerous zealots at home and abroad who had embraced Mary's defence, to lead us to the belief of any of these three suppositions; and even her apologists at present seem not to have fixed on any choice among these supposed possibilities. The positive proof of two very credible witnesses, supported by the other very strong circumstances, still remains unimpeached. Babington, who had an extreme interest to have communication with the queen of Scots, believed he had found a means of correspondence with her, and had received an answer from her: He, as well as the other conspirators, died in that belief: There has not occurred, since that time, the least argument to

NOTES TO THE FOURTH VOLUME

prove that they were mistaken: Can there be any reason at present to doubt the truth of their opinion? Camden, though a profest apologist for Mary, is constrained to tell the story in such a manner as evidently supposes her guilt. Such was the impossibility of finding any other consistent account, even by a man of parts, who was a contemporary!

In this light might the question have appeared even during Mary's trial. But what now puts her guilt beyond all controversy is the following passage of her letter to Thomas Morgan, dated the 27th of July 1586. "As to Babington, he hath both kindly and honestly offered himself and all his means to be employed any way I would. Whereupon I hope to have satisfied him by two of my several letters, since I had his; and the rather, for that I opened him the way, whereby I received his with your aforesaid." Murden, p. 533. Babington confessed, that he had offered her to assassinate the queen: It appears by this, that she had accepted the offer: So that all the suppositions of Walsingham's forgery, or the temerity or treachery of her secretaries, fall to the ground.

NOTE [X], p. 238

This parliament granted the queen a supply of a subsidy and two fifteenths. They adjourned, and met again after the execution of the queen of Scots; when there passed some remarkable incidents, which it may be proper not to omit. We shall give them in the words of Sir Simon D'Ewes, p. 410, 411, which are almost wholly transcribed from Townshend's Journal. On Monday the 27th of February, Mr. Cope, first using some speeches touching the necessity of a learned ministry and the amendment of things amiss in the ecclesiastical estate, offered to the house a bill and a book written; the bill containing a petition, that it might be enacted, that all laws now in force touching ecclesiastical government should be void: And that it might be enacted that that book of common prayer now offered, and none other, might be received into the church to be used. The book contained the form of prayer and administration of the sacraments, with divers rites and ceremonies to be used in the church; and he desired that the book might be read. Whereupon Mr. Speaker in effect used this speech: For that her majesty before this time had commanded the house not to meddle with this matter, and that her majesty had promised to take order in those causes, he doubted not but to the good satisfaction of all her people, he desired that it would please them to spare the reading of it. Notwithstanding the house desired the reading of it. Whereupon Mr. Speaker desired the clerk to read. And the court being ready to read it, Mr. Dalton made a motion against the reading of it; saying, that it was not meet to be read, and it did appoint a new form of administration of the sacraments and ceremonies of the church, to the discredit of the book of common prayer and of the whole state; and thought that this dealing would bring her majesty's indignation against the house, thus to enterprize this dealing with those things which her majesty especially had taken into her own charge and direction. Whereupon Mr. Lewkenor spake, shewing the necessity of preaching and of a learned ministry, and thought it very fit that the petition and book should be read. To this purpose spake Mr. Hurleston and Mr. Bainbrigg; and so, the time being passed, the house broke up, and neither the petition nor book read. This done, her majesty sent to Mr. Speaker, as well for this petition and book, as for that other petition and book for the like effect, that was delivered the last session of parliament, which Mr. Speaker sent to her majesty. On Tuesday the 28th of February, her majesty sent for Mr. Speaker, by occasion whereof the house did not sit. On Wednesday the first day of March, Mr. Wentworth delivered to Mr. Speaker certain articles, which contained questions touching the liberties of the house, and to some of which he was to answer, and desired they might be read. Mr. Speaker desired him to spare his motion, until her majesty's pleasure was further known touching the petition and book lately delivered into the house; but Mr. Wentworth would not be so satisfied, but required his articles might be read. Mr. Wentworth introduced his queries by lamenting, that he as well as many others were deterred from speaking, by their want of knowledge and experience in the liberties of the house; and the queries were as follow: Whether this council were not a place for any member of the same here assembled, freely and without controulment of any person or danger of laws, by bill or speech to utter any of the griefs of this commonwealth whatsoever, touching the service of God, the safety of the prince and this noble realm. Whether that great honour may be done unto God, and benefit and service unto the prince and state, without free speech in this council that may be done with it? Whether there be any council which can make, add, or diminish from the laws of the realm but only this council of parliament? Whether it be not against the orders of this council to make any secret or matter of weight, which is here in hand, known to the prince or any other, concerning the high service of God, prince, or state, without the consent of the house? Whether the speaker or any other may interrupt any member of this council in his speech used in this house tending to any of the forenamed services? Whether the speaker may rise when he will, any matter being propounded, without consent of the house or not? Whether the speaker may over-rule the house in any matter or cause there in question, or whether he is to be ruled or over-ruled in any matter or not? Whether the prince and state can continue, and stand, and be maintained, without this council of parliament, not altering the government of the state? At the end of these questions, says Sir Simon D'Ewes, I found set down this short note or memorial ensuing: By which it may be perceived, both what serjeant Puckering, the speaker, did with the said questions after he had received them, and what became also of this business, viz. "These questions Mr. Puckering pocketed up and shewed Sir Thomas Henage, who so handled the matter, that Mr. Wentworth went to the Tower, and the questions not at all moved. Mr. Buckler of Essex herein brake his faith in forsaking the matter, &c. and no more was done." After setting down, continues Sir Simon D'Ewes, the said business of Mr. Wentworth in the original journal book, there follows only this short conclusion of the day

NOTES TO THE FOURTH VOLUME

itself, viz. "This day, Mr. Speaker being sent for to the queen's majesty, the house departed." On Thursday the second of March, Mr. Cope, Mr. Lewkenor, Mr. Hurlston, and Mr. Bainbrigg were sent for to my lord chancellor and by divers of the privy council, and from thence were sent to the Tower. On Saturday, the fourth day of March, Sir John Higham made a motion to this house, for that divers good and necessary members thereof were taken from them, that it would please them to be humble petitioners to her majesty for the restitution of them again to the house. To which speeches Mr. Vice-chamberlain answered, that if the gentlemen were committed for matter within the compass of the privilege of this house, then there might be a petition; but if not, then we should give occasion to her majesty's farther displeasure: And therefore advised to stay until they heard more, which could not be long: And farther, he said touching the book and the petition, her majesty had, for diverse good causes best known to herself, thought fit to suppress the same, without any farther examination thereof; and yet thought it very unfit for her majesty to give any account of her doings.———But whatsoever Mr. Vice-chamberlain pretended, it is most probable these members were committed for intermeddling with matters touching the church, which her majesty had often inhibited, and which had caused so much disputation and so many meetings between the two houses the last parliament.

This is all we find of the matter in Sir Simon D'Ewes and Townsend; and it appears that those members, who had been committed, were detained in custody till the queen thought proper to release them. These questions of Mr. Wentworth are curious; because they contain some faint dawn of the present English constitution; though suddenly eclipsed by the arbitrary government of Elizabeth. Wentworth was indeed, by his puritanism, as well as his love of liberty (for these two characters of such unequal merit, arose and advanced together) the true forerunner of the Hambdens, the Pyms, and the Hollises, who, in the next age, with less courage, because with less danger, rendered their principles so triumphant. I shall only ask, whether it be not sufficiently clear from all these transactions, that in the two succeeding reigns it was the people who encroached upon the sovereign; not the sovereign, who attempted, as is pretended, to usurp upon the people?

NOTE [Y], p. 266

The queen's speech in the camp of Tilbury was in these words: My loving people, we have been persuaded by some, that are careful of our safety, to take heed how we commit ourselves to armed multitudes, for fear of treachery; but assure you, I do not desire to live to distrust my faithful and loving people. Let tyrants fear: I have always so behaved myself, that, under God, I have placed my chiefest strength and safeguard in the loyal hearts and good will of my subjects. And therefore I am come amongst you at this time, not as for my recreation or sport, but being resolved in the midst and heat of the battle to live or die amongst you all; to lay down, for my God, and for my kingdom, and for my people, my honour and my blood, even in the dust. I know I have but the body of a weak and feeble woman, but I have the heart of a king, and of a king of England too; and think foul scorn, that Parma or Spain, or any prince of Europe, should dare to invade the borders of my realms: To which, rather than any dishonour shall grow by me, I myself will take up arms; I myself will be your general, judge, and rewarder of every one of your virtues in the field. I know already, by your forwardness, that you have deserved rewards and crowns; and we do assure you, on the word of a prince, they shall be duly paid you. In the mean time, my lieutenant general shall be in my stead; than whom never prince commanded a more noble and worthy subject; not doubting, by your obedience to my general, by your concord in the camp, and your valour in the field, we shall shortly have a famous victory over those enemies of my God, of my kingdom, and of my people.

NOTE [Z], p. 271

Strype, vol. iii. p. 525. On the fourth of September, soon after the dispersion of the Spanish Armada, died the earl of Leicester, the queen's great, but unworthy, favourite. Her affection for him continued to the last. He had discovered no conduct in any of his military enterprizes; and was suspected of cowardice: Yet she entrusted him with the command of her armies during the danger of the Spanish invasion; a partiality, which might have proved fatal to her, had the duke of Parma been able to land his troops in England. She had even ordered a commission to be drawn for him, constituting him her lieutenant in the kingdoms of England and Ireland; but Burleigh and Hatton represented to her the danger of entrusting such unlimited authority in the hands of any subject, and prevented the execution of that design. No wonder, that a conduct, so unlike the usual jealousy of Elizabeth, gave reason to suspect, that her partiality was founded on some other passion than friendship. But Elizabeth seemed to carry her affection to Leicester no farther than the grave: She ordered his goods to be disposed of at a public sale, in order to reimburse herself of some debt which he owed her; and her usual attention to money was observed to prevail over her regard to the memory of the deceased. This earl was a great hypocrite, a pretender to the strictest religion, an encourager of the puritans, and a founder of hospitals.

NOTE [AA], p. 271

Strype, vol. iii. p. 542. Id. append. p. 239. There are some singular passages in this last speech, which may be worth taking notice of; especially as they came from a member who was no courtier: For he argues against the subsidy. "And first," says he, "for the *necessity* thereof, I cannot deny, but if it were a charge imposed upon us by her majesty's commandment, or a demand proceeding from her majesty by way of request, that I think there is not one among us all, either so disobedient a subject in regard of our duty, or so unthankful a man in respect of the inestimable benefits which, by her or from her, we have received, which would not with frank consent, both of voice and heart, most willingly submit himself thereunto, without any unreverend enquiry into the causes thereof. For it is continually in the mouth of us all, that our lands, goods, and lives are at our prince's disposing. And it agreeth very well with that position of the civil law, which sayeth, *Quod omnia regis sunt.* But how? *Ita tamen ut omnium sint. Ad regem enim potestas omnium pertinet; ad singulos proprietas.* So that although it be most true, that her majesty hath over ourselves and our goods, *potestatem imperandi;* yet it is true, that until that power command (which, no doubt, will not command without very just cause) every subject hath his own *proprietatem possidendi.* Which power and commandment from her majesty, which we have not yet received, I take it (saving reformation) that we are freed from the cause of *necessity.* And the cause of necessity, is the dangerous estate of the commonwealth, &c." The tenor of the speech pleads rather for a general benevolence than a subsidy: For the law of Richard III. against benevolence was never conceived to have any force. The member even proceeds to assert, with some precaution, that it was in the power of a parliament to refuse the king's demand of a subsidy. And that there was an instance of that liberty in Henry III.'s time, near four hundred years before. *Sub fine.*

NOTE [BB], p. 273

We may judge of the extent and importance of these abuses by a speech of Bacon's against purveyors, delivered in the first session of the first parliament of the subsequent reign, by which also we may learn that Elizabeth had given no redress to the grievances complained of. "First," says he, "they take in kind what they ought not to take; secondly, they take in quantity a far greater proportion than cometh to your majesty's use; thirdly, they take in an unlawful manner, in a manner, I say, directly and expressly prohibited by the several laws. For the first, I am a little to alter their name: For instead of takers, they become taxers: Instead of taking provisions for your majesty's service, they tax your people *ad redimendam vexationem;* imposing upon them and extorting from them divers sums of money, sometimes in gross, sometimes in the nature of stipends annually paid, *ne noceant,* to be freed and eased of their oppression. Again, they take trees, which by law they cannot do; timber trees, which are the beauty, countenance, and shelter of men's houses; that men have long spared from their own purse and profit; that men esteem, for their use and delight, above ten times the value; that are a loss which men cannot repair or recover. These, do they take, to the defacing and spoiling of your subjects mansions and dwellings, except they may be compounded with to their own appetites. And if a gentleman be too hard for them while he is at home, they will watch their time when there is but a bailiff or a servant remaining, and put the ax to the root of the tree, ere ever the master can stop it. Again, they use a strange and most unjust exaction in causing the subject to pay poundage of their own debts, due from your majesty unto them: So as a poor man, when he has had his hay or his wood, or his poultry (which perchance he was full loath to part with, and had for the provision of his own family and not to put to sale) taken from him, and that not at a just price, but under the value, and cometh to receive his money, he shall have after the rate of twelve pence in the pound abated for poundage of his due payment upon so hard conditions. Nay farther, they are grown to that extremity (as is affirmed, though it be scarce credible, save that in such persons all things are credible) that they will take double poundage, once when the debenture is made, and again the second time, when the money is paid. For the second point, most gracious sovereign, touching the quantity which they take far above that which is answered to your majesty's use; it is affirmed unto me by divers gentlemen of good report, as a matter which I may safely avouch unto your majesty, that there is no pound profit, which redoundeth unto your majesty in this course, but induceth and begetteth three pound damage upon your subjects, beside the discontentment. And to the end they may make their spoil more securely, what do they? Whereas divers statutes do strictly provide, that whatsoever they take shall be registered and attested, to the end that by making a collation of that which is taken from the country and that which is answered above, their deceits might appear, they, to the end to obscure their deceits, utterly omit the observation of this, which the law prescribeth. And therefore to descend, if it may please your majesty, to the third sort of abuse, which is of the unlawful manner of their taking, whereof this question is a branch; it is so manifold, as it rather asketh an enumeration of some of the particulars than a prosecution of all. For their price, by law they ought to take as they can agree with the subject; by abuse, they take at an imposed and enforced price: By law they ought to make but one apprizement by neighbours in the country; by abuse, they make a second apprizement at the court-gate, and when the subjects cattle come up many miles lean and out of plight by reason of their travel, then they prize them anew at an abated price: By law, they ought to take between sun and sun; by abuse, they take by twilight and in the night-time, a time well chosen for malefactors: By law, they ought not to take in the high-ways (a place by her majesty's high prerogative protected, and by statute by special words excepted); by abuse, they take in the highways: By law, they ought to shew their commission, &c. A number of other particulars there are, &c." Bacon's works, vol. iv. p. 305, 306.

Such were the abuses, which Elizabeth would neither permit her parliaments to meddle with, nor redress herself. I believe it will readily be allowed, that this slight prerogative alone, which has passed almost unobserved amidst other branches of so much greater importance, was sufficient to extinguish all regular liberty. For what elector, or member of parliament, or even juryman, durst oppose the will of the court, while he lay under the lash of such an arbitrary prerogative. For a farther account of the grievous and incredible oppressions of purveyors, see the Journals of the house of commons, vol. i. p. 190. There is a story of a carter, which may be worth mentioning on this occasion. "A carter had three time been at Windsor with his cart to carry away, upon summons of a remove, some part of the stuff of her majesty's wardrobe; and when he had repaired thither once, twice, and the third time, and that they of the wardrobe had told him the third time that the remove held not, the carter, clapping his hand on his thigh, said, *Now I see, that the queen is a woman as well as my wife.* Which words being overheard by her majesty, who then stood at the window, she said, *What a villain is this?* and so sent him three angels to stop his mouth." Birch's Memoirs, vol. i. p. 155.

NOTE [CC], p. 282

This year the nation suffered a great loss, by the death of Sir Francis Walsingham, secretary of state; a man equally celebrated for his abilities and his integrity. He had passed through many employments, had been very frugal in his expence, yet died so poor, that his family was obliged to give him a private burial. He left only one daughter, first married to Sir Philip Sidney, then to the earl of Essex, favourite of queen Elizabeth, and lastly to the earl of Clanricarde of Ireland. The same year died Thomas Randolph, who had been employed by the queen in several embassies to Scotland; as did also the earl of Warwic, elder brother to Leicester.

NOTE [DD], p. 284

This action of Sir Richard Greenville is so singular, as to merit a more particular relation. He was engaged alone with the whole Spanish fleet of fifty-three sail, which had ten thousand men on board; and from the time the fight began, which was about three in the afternoon, to the break of day next morning, he repulsed the enemy fifteen times, though they continually shifted their vessels, and boarded with fresh men. In the beginning of the action he himself received a wound; but he continued doing his duty above deck till eleven at night, when receiving a fresh wound, he was carried down to be dressed. During this operation he received a shot in the head, and the surgeon was killed by his side. The English began now to want powder; all their small arms were broken or become useless; of this number, which were but a hundred and three at first, forty were killed, and almost all the rest wounded; their masts were beat overboard, their tackle cut in pieces, and nothing but a hulk left, unable to move one way or other. In this situation Sir Richard proposed to the ship's company, to trust to the mercy of God, not to that of the Spaniards, and to destroy the ship with themselves, rather than yield to the enemy. The master gunner, and many of the seamen, agreed to this desperate resolution; but others opposed it, and obliged Greenville to surrender himself prisoner. He died a few days after; and his last words were: "Here die I, Richard Greenville, with a joyful and quiet mind; for that I have ended my life as a true soldier ought to do, fighting for his country, Queen, religion, and honour: My soul willingly departing from this body, leaving behind the lasting fame of having behaved as every valiant soldier is in his duty bound to do." The Spaniards lost in this sharp though unequal action, four ships, and about a thousand men. And Greenville's vessel perished soon after, with two hundred Spaniards in her. Hackluyt's Voyages, vol. ii. part 2. p. 169. Camden, p. 565.

NOTE [EE], p. 302

It is usual for the speaker to disqualify himself for the office; but the reasons employed by this speaker are so singular, that they may be worth transcribing. "My estate," said he, "is nothing correspondent for the maintenance of this dignity: For my father dying left me a younger brother; and nothing to me but my bare annuity. Then growing to man's estate and some small practice of the law, I took a wife, by whom I have had many children; the keeping of us all being a great impoverishing to my estate, and the daily living of us all nothing but my daily industry. Neither from my person nor my nature doth this choice arise: For he that supplieth this place ought to be a man big and comely, stately and well-spoken, his voice great, his carriage majestical, his nature haughty, and his purse plentiful and heavy: But contrarily, the stature of my body is small, myself not so well-spoken, my voice low, my carriage lawyer-like, and of the common fashion, my nature soft and bashful, my purse thin, light, and never yet plentiful. ———If *Demosthenes,* being so learned and eloquent as he was, one whom none surpassed, trembled to speak before *Phocion* at *Athens* ; how much more shall I, being unlearned and unskilful to supply the place of dignity, charge, and trouble, to speak before so many *Phocions* as here be? Yea, which is the greatest, before the unspeakable majesty and sacred personage of our dread and dear sovereign: The terror of whose countenance will appal and abase even the stoutest hearts; yea, whose very name will pull down the greatest courage. For how mightily do the estate and name of a prince deject the haughtiest stomach even of their greatest subjects?" D'Ewes, p. 459.

NOTE [FF], p. 307

Cabbala, p. 234. Birch's Memoirs, vol. ii. p. 386. Speed, p. 877. The whole letter of Essex is so curious and so spirited, that the reader may not be displeased to read it. "My very good lord; Though there is not that man this day living, whom I would sooner make judge of any question that might concern me than yourself, yet you must give me leave to tell you, that in some cases I must appeal from all earthly judges: And if any, then surely in this, when the highest judge on earth has imposed on me the heaviest punishment without trial or hearing. Since then I must either answer your lordship's argument, or else forsake mine own just defence, I will force mine aching head to do me service for an hour. I must first deny my discontent, which was forced, to be an humorous discontent; and that it was unseasonable or is of so long continuing, your lordship should rather condole with me than expostulate: Natural seasons are expected here below; but violent and unreasonable storms come from above: There is no tempest equal to the passionate indignation of a prince; nor yet at any time so unseasonable as when it lighteth on those that might expect a harvest of their careful and painful labours. He that is once wounded, must needs feel smart, till his hurt is cured, or the part hurt become senseless: But cure I expect none, her majesty's heart being obdurate against me; and be without sense I cannot, being of flesh and blood. But, say you, I may aim at the end: I do more than aim; for I see an end of all my fortunes, I have set an end to all my desires. In this course do I any thing for my enemies? When I was at court, I found them absolute; and, therefore, I had rather they should triumph alone, than have me attendant upon their chariots. Or do I leave my friends? When I was a courtier, I could yield them no fruit of my love unto them; and now, that I am a hermit, they shall bear no envy, for their love towards me. Or do I forsake myself, because I do enjoy myself? Or do I overthrow my fortunes, because I build not a fortune of paper walls, which every puff of wind bloweth down? Or do I ruinate mine honour, because I leave following the pursuit, or wearing the false badge or mark of the shadow of honour? Do I give courage or comfort to the foreign foe, because I reserve myself to encounter with him? Or because I keep my heart from business, though I cannot keep my fortune from declining? No, no, my good lord, I give every one of these considerations its due weight; and the more I weigh them, the more I find myself justified from offending in any of them. As for the two last objections, that I forsake my country, when it hath most need of me, and fail in that indissoluble duty which I owe to my sovereign; I answer, that if my country had at this time any need of my public service, her majesty that governeth it, would not have driven me to a private life. I am tied to my country by two bonds; one public, to discharge carefully and industriously that trust which is committed to me; the other private, to sacrifice for it my life and carcase, which hath been nourished in it. Of the first I am free, being dismissed, discharged, and disabled by her majesty: Of the other, nothing can free me but death; and therefore no occasion of my performance shall sooner offer itself but I shall meet it half way. The indissoluble duty which I owe unto her majesty, is only the duty of allegiance, which I never have, nor never can fail in: The duty of attendance, is no indissoluble duty. I owe her majesty the duty of an earl and of lord marshal of England. I have been content to do her majesty the service of a clerk; but I can never serve her as a villain or slave. But yet you say I must give way unto the time. So I do; for now that I see the storm come, I have put myself into the harbour. *Seneca* saieth, we must give way to Fortune: I know that Fortune is both blind and strong, and therefore I go as far as I can out of her way. You say the remedy is not to strive: I neither strive nor seek for remedy. But, you say, I must yield and submit: I can neither yield myself to be guilty, nor allow the imputation laid upon me to be just: I owe so much to the Author of all truth, as I can never yield truth to be falsehood, nor falsehood to be truth. Have I given cause, you ask; and yet take a scandal when I have done? No: I gave no cause, not so much as *Fimbria's* complaint against me; for I did *totum telum corpore recipere:* Receive the whole sword into my body. I patiently bear all, and sensibly feel all that I then received, when this scandal was given me. Nay more, when the vilest of all indignities are done unto me," &c. This noble letter, Bacon afterwards, in pleading against Essex, called bold and pre-sumptuous, and derogatory to her majesty. Birch's Memoirs, vol. ii. p. 388.

NOTE [GG], p. 330

Most of queen Elizabeth's courtiers feigned love and desire towards her, and addressed themselves to her in the stile of passion and gallantry. Sir Walter Raleigh, having fallen into disgrace, wrote the following letter to his friend Sir Robert Cecil, with a view, no doubt, of having it shewn to the queen. "My heart was never broke till this day, that I hear the queen goes away so far off, whom I have followed so many years, with so great love and desire, in so many journeys, and am now left behind her in a dark prison all alone. While she was yet near at hand, that I might hear of her once in two or three days, my sorrows were the less; but even now my heart is cast into the depth of all misery. I, that was wont to behold her riding like *Alexander,* hunting like *Diana,* walking like *Venus,* the gentle wind blowing her fair hair about her pure cheeks, like a nymph, sometimes sitting in the shade like a Goddess, sometimes singing like an Angel, sometimes playing like *Orpheus;* behold the sorrow of this world! once amiss hath bereaved me of all. O glory that only shineth in misfortune, what is become of thy assurance? All wounds have scars but that of fantasie: All affections their relenting but that of womankind. Who is the judge of friendship but adversity, or when is grace witnessed but in offences? There were no divinity but by reason of compassion: For revenges are brutish and mortal. All those times past, the loves, the sighs, the sorrows, the desires, cannot they weigh down one frail misfortune? Cannot one drop of gall be hid in so great heaps of sweetness? I may then conclude, *Spes & fortuna, valete.* She is gone in whom I trusted; and of me hath not one thought of mercy, nor any respect of that which was. Do with me now therefore what you list. I am more weary of life than they are desirous I should perish; which, if it had been for her, as it is by her, I had been too happily born." *Murden, 657.* It is to be remarked, that this Nymph, Venus, Goddess, Angel, was then about sixty. Yet five or six years after, she allowed the same language to be held to her. Sir Henry Unton, her ambassador in France, relates to her a conversation which he had with Henry IV. The monarch, after having introduced Unton to his mistress, the fair Gabrielle, asked him how he liked her. "I answered sparingly in her praise," said the minister, "and told him, that if, without offence, I might speak it, I had the picture of a far more excellent mistress, and yet did her picture come far short of her perfection of beauty. As you love me, said he, shew it me, if you have it about you. I made some difficulties; yet upon his importunity offered it to his view very secretly, holding it still in my hand: He beheld it with passion and admiration, saying, that I had reason, *Je me rends,* protesting, that he had never seen the like; so, with great reverence, he kissed it twice or thrice, I detaining it still in my hand. In the end, with some kind of contention, he took it from me, vowing, that I might take my leave of it: For he would not forego it for any treasure: And that to possess the favour of the lively picture, he would forsake all the world, and hold himself most happy; with many other most passionate speeches." *Murden,* p. 718. For farther particulars on this head, see the ingenious author of the Catalogue of royal and noble Authors, article *Essex.*

NOTES TO THE FOURTH VOLUME

NOTE [HH], p. 346

It may not be amiss to subjoin some passages of these speeches; which may serve to give us a just idea of the government of that age, and of the political principles, which prevailed during the reign of Elizabeth. Mr. Laurence Hyde proposed a bill, entituled, An act for the explanation of the common law in certain cases of letters patent. Mr. Spicer said, This bill may touch the prerogative royal, which, as I learned the last parliament, is so transcendent, that the———of the subject may not aspire thereunto. Far be it therefore from me, that the state and prerogative royal of the prince should be tied by me, or by the act of any other subject. Mr. Francis Bacon said, As to the prerogative-royal of the prince, for my own part, I ever allowed of it; and it is such as I hope will never be discussed. The queen, as she is our sovereign, hath both an enlarging and restraining power. For by her prerogative she may set at liberty things restrained by statute law or otherwise, and secondly, by her prerogative she may restrain things which be at liberty. For the first, she may grant a *non obstante* contrary to the penal laws.———With regard to monopolies and such like cases, the case hath ever been to humble ourselves unto her majesty, and by petition desire to have our grievances remedied, especially when the remedy toucheth her so nigh in point of prerogative———I say, and I say it again, that we ought not to deal, to judge, or meddle with her majesty's prerogative. I wish therefore every man to be careful of this business. Dr. Bennet said, He that goeth about to debate her majesty's prerogative had need to walk warily. Mr. Laurence Hyde said, For the bill itself, I made it, and I think I understand it: And far be it from this heart of mine to think, this tongue to speak, or this hand to write any thing either in prejudice or derogation of her majesty's prerogative-royal and the state.———Mr. Speaker, quoth Serjeant Harris, for ought I see, the house moveth to have this bill in the nature of a petition. It must then begin with more humiliation. And truly, Sir, the bill is good of itself, but the penning of it is somewhat out of course. Mr. Montagu said, The matter is good and honest, and I like this manner of proceeding by bill well enough in this matter. The grievances are great, and I would note only unto you thus much, that the last parliament we proceeded by way of petition, which had no successful effect. Mr. Francis More said, I know the queen's prerogative is a thing curious to be dealt withal: yet all grievances are not comparable. I cannot utter with my tongue or conceive with my heart the great grievances that the town and country, for which I serve, suffereth by some of these monopolies. It bringeth the general profit into a private hand, and the end of all this is beggary and bondage to the subjects. We have a law for the true and faithful currying of leather: There is a patent sets all at liberty, notwithstanding that statute. And to what purpose is it to do any thing by act of parliament, when the queen will undo the same by her prerogative? Out of the spirit of humiliation, Mr. Speaker, I do speak it, there is no act of her's that hath been or is more derogatory to her own majesty, more odious to the subject, more dangerous to the commonwealth than the granting of these monopolies. Mr. Martin said, I do speak for a town that grieves and pines, for a country

that groaneth and languisheth under the burden of monstrous and uncon-
scionable substitutes to the monopolitans of starch, tin, fish, cloth, oil,
vinegar, salt, and I know not what; nay, what not? The principalest commodities both of my town and country are engrost into the hands of these
blood-suckers of the commonwealth. If a body, Mr. Speaker, being let
blood, be left still languishing without any remedy, how can the good estate
of that body still remain? Such is the state of my town and country; the
traffic is taken away, the inward and private commodities are taken away,
and dare not be used without the license of these monopolitans. If these
blood-suckers be still let alone to suck up the best and principalest commodities, which the earth there hath given us, what will become of us, from
whom the fruits of our own soil and the commodities of our own labour,
which with the sweat of our brows, even up to the knees in mire and dirt,
we have laboured for, shall be taken by warrant of supreme authority,
which the poor subject dare not gainsay? Mr. George Moore said, We know
the power of her majesty cannot be restrained by any act: why therefore
should we thus talk? Admit we should make this statute with a *non obstante:*
yet the queen may grant a patent with a *non obstante,* to cross this *non
obstante.* I think therefore it agreeth more with the gravity and wisdom of
this house to proceed with all humbleness by petition than bill. Mr. Down-
land said, As I would be no let or over-vehement in any thing, so I am not
sottish or senseless of the common grievance of the commonwealth. If we
proceed by way of petition, we can have no more gracious answer, than we
had the last parliament to our petition. But since that parliament, we have
no reformation. Sir Robert Wroth said, I speak, and I speak it boldly, these
patentees are worse than ever they were. Mr. Hayward Townsend proposed, that they should make suit to her majesty, not only to repeal all
monopolies grievous to the subject, but also that it would please her majesty
to give the parliament leave to make an act that they might be of no more
force, validity, or effect, than they are at the common law, without the
strength of her prerogative. Which though we might now do, and the act
being so reasonable, we might assure ourselves her majesty would not delay
the passing thereof, yet we, her loving subjects, &c. would not offer without
her privity and consent (the cause so nearly touching her prerogative) or go
about to do any such act.

On a subsequent day, the bill against monopolies was again introduced,
and Mr. Spicer said, It is to no purpose to offer to tie her majesty's hands
by act of parliament, when she may loosen herself at her pleasure. Mr.
Davies said, God hath given that power to absolute princes, which he
attributes to himself. *Dixi quod Dii estis.* (N. B. This axiom he applies to the
kings of England.) Mr. secretary Cecil said, I am servant to the queen, and
before I would speak and give consent to a case that should debase her
prerogative, or abridge it, I would wish that my tongue were cut out of my
head, I am sure there were law-makers before there were laws: (Meaning,
I suppose, that the sovereign was above the laws.) One gentleman went
about to possess us, with the execution of the law in an ancient record of

5 or 7 of Edward the third. Likely enough to be true in that time, when the king was afraid of the subject. If you stand upon the law, and dispute of the prerogative, hark ye what Bracton says, *Praerogativam nostram nemo audeat disputare.* And for my own part, I like not these courses should be taken. And you, Mr. Speaker, should perform the charge her majesty gave unto you, in the beginning of this parliament, not to receive bills of this nature: For her majesty's ears be open to all grievances, and her hands stretched out to every man's petitions.————When the prince dispenses with a penal law, that is left to the alteration of sovereignty, that is good and irrevocable. Mr. Montague said, I am loth to speak what I know, lest, perhaps, I should displease. The prerogative-royal is that which is now in question, and which the laws of the land have ever allowed and maintained. Let us therefore apply by petition to her majesty.

After the speaker told the house that the queen had annulled many of the patents, Mr. Francis More said, I must confess, Mr. Speaker, I moved the house both the last parliament and this, touching this point; but I never meant (and I hope the house thinketh so) to set limits and bounds to the prerogative royal. He proceeds to move, that thanks should be given to her majesty; and also, that whereas divers speeches have been moved extravagantly in the house, which doubtless have been told her majesty, and perhaps ill conceived of by her, Mr. Speaker would apologize, and humbly crave pardon for the same. N. B. These extracts were taken by Townsend, a member of the house, who was no courtier; and the extravagance of the speeches seems rather to be on the other side: It will certainly appear strange to us that this liberty should be thought extravagant. However, the queen, notwithstanding her cajoling the house, was so ill satisified with these proceedings, that she spoke of them peevishly in her concluding speech, and told them, that she perceived that private respects with them were privately masqued under public presence. D'Ewes, p. 619.

There were some other topics, in favour of prerogative, still more extravagant, advanced in the house this parliament. When the question of the subsidy was before them, Mr. Serjeant Heyle said, Mr. Speaker, I marvel much that the house should stand upon granting of a subsidy or the time of payment, when all we have is her majesty's, and she may lawfully at her pleasure take it from us: Yea, she hath as much right to all our lands and goods as to any revenue of her crown. At which all the house hemmed, and laughed and talked. Well, quoth serjeant Heyle, all your hemming shall not put me out of countenance. So Mr. Speaker stood up and said, It is a great disorder, that this house should be used————So the said serjeant proceeded, and when he had spoken a little while the house hemmed again; and so he sat down. In his latter speech, he said, he could prove his former position by precedents in the time of Henry the third, king John, king Stephen, &c. which was the occasion of their hemming. D'Ewes, p. 633. It is observable, that Heyle was an eminent lawyer, a man of character. Winwood, vol. i. p. 290. And though the house in general shewed their disapprobation, no one cared to take him down, or oppose these monstrous positions. It was also asserted this session, that in the same manner as the Roman consul was possessed of the power of rejecting or admitting motions in the senate, the speaker might either admit or reject bills in the house. D'Ewes, p. 677. The house declared themselves against this opinion; but the very proposal of it is a proof at what a low ebb liberty was at that time in England.

In the year 1591, the judges made a solemn decree, that England was an absolute empire, of which the king was the head. In consequence of this opinion, they determined, that even if the act of the first of Elizabeth had never been made, the king was supreme head of the church; and might have erected, by his prerogative, such a court as the ecclesiastical commission: For that he was the head of all his subjects. Now that court was plainly arbitrary: The inference is, that his power was equally absolute over the laity. See Coke's Reports, p. 5. Caudrey's case.

NOTE [II], p. 369

We have remarked before that Harrison, in book ii. chap. 11. says, that in the reign of Henry VIII. there were hanged seventy-two thousand thieves and rogues *(besides other malefactors);* this makes about two thousand a year: But in queen Elizabeth's time, the same author says, there were only between three and four hundred a year hanged for theft and robbery: So much had the times mended. But in our age, there are not forty a year hanged for those crimes in all England. Yet Harrison complains of the relaxation of the laws, that there were so few such rogues punished in his time. Our vulgar prepossession, in favour of the morals of former and rude ages, is very absurd, and ill-grounded. The same author says, chap. 10. that there were computed to be 10,000 gypsies in England; a species of banditti, introduced about the reign of Henry VIII.; and he adds, that there will be no way of extirpating them, by the ordinary course of justice: The queen must employ martial law against them. That race has now almost totally disappeared in England and even in Scotland, where there were some remains of them a few years ago. However arbitrary the exercise of martial law, in the crown, it appears, that no body in the age of Elizabeth entertained any jealousy of it.

NOTE [JJ], p. 378

Harrison, *in his Description of Britain, printed in 1577, has the following passage,* chap. 13. Certes there is no prince in Europe that hath a more beautiful sort of ships than the queen's majesty of England at this present; and those generally are of such exceeding force, that two of them being well appointed and furnished as they ought, will not let to encounter with three or four of them of other countries, and either bowge them or put them to flight, if they may not bring them home.—The queen's highness hath at this present already made and furnished to the number of one and twenty great ships, which lie for the most part in Gillingham rode. Beside these, her grace hath other in hand also, of whom hereafter, as their turns do come about, I will not let to leave some farther remembrance. She hath likewise three notable gallies, the Speedwell, the Tryeright, and the Black Galley, with the sight whereof, and the rest of the navy-royal, it is incredible to say how marvellously her grace is delighted; and not with out great cause, sith by their means her coasts are kept in quiet, and sundry foreign enemies put back, which otherwise would invade us. *After speaking of the merchant ships, which he says are commonly estimated at 17 or 18 hundred, he continues.* I add, therefore, to the end all men shoud understand somewhat of the *great masses of treasure,* daily employed upon our navy, how there are few of those ships of the first and second sort, (that is of the merchant ships), that being apparelled and made ready to sail, are not worth one thousand pounds or three thousand duckats at the least, if they should presently be sold. What shall we then think of the navy-royal, of which some one vessel is worth two of the other, as the shipwright has often told me.————It is possible that some covetous person, hearing this report, will either not credit at all, or suppose money so employed to be nothing profitable to the queen's coffers; as a good husband said once when he heard that provisions should be made for armour, wishing the queen's money to be rather laid out to some speedier return of gain unto her grace: But if he wist that the good-keeping of the sea is the safeguard of our land, he would alter his censure, and soon give over his judgment. *Speaking of the forests, this author says,* An infinite deal of wood hath been destroyed within these few years, and I dare affirm, that, if wood do go so fast to decay in the next hundred years of grace, as they have done, or are like to do in this, it is to be feared, that sea-coal will be good merchandize even in the city of London. Harrison's prophecy was fulfilled in a very few years: For about 1615, there were 200 sail employed in carrying coal to London. See Anderson, vol. i. p. 494.

NOTE [KK], p. 383

Life of Burleigh published by Collins, p. 44. The author hints, that this quantity of plate was considered only as small in a man of Burleigh's rank. His words are *his plate was not above fourteen or fifteen thousand pounds:* That he means pounds weight is evident. For, by Burleigh's will, which is annexed to his life, that nobleman gives away in legacies, to friends and relations, near four thousand pounds weight, which would have been above twelve thousand pounds sterling in value. The remainder he orders to be divided into two equal portions; the half to his eldest son and heir; the other half to be divided equally among his second son and three daughters. Were we therefore to understand the whole value of his plate to be only 14 or 15,000 pounds sterling, he left not the tenth of it to the heir of his family.

NOTE [LL], p. 383

Harrison says, "the greatest part of our building in the cities and good towns of England consisteth only of timber, cast over with thick clay to keep

HISTORY OF ENGLAND

out the wind. Certes, this rude kind of building made the Spaniards in queen Mary's days to wonder; but chiefly when they saw that large diet was used in many of these so homely cottages, insomuch that one of no small reputation amongst them, said, after this manner; These English, quoth he, have their houses made of sticks and dirt, but they fare commonly so well as the king. Whereby it appeareth, that he liked better of our good fare in such coarse cabins, than of their own thin diet in their princely habitations and palaces. The clay with which our houses are commonly impannelled is either white, red, or blue." Book ii. chap. 12. The author adds, that the new houses of the nobility are commonly of brick or stone, and that glass windows were beginning to be used in England.

NOTE [MM], p. 385

The following are the words of Roger Ascham, the queen's preceptor. "It is your shame (I speak to you all, you young gentlemen of England), that one maid should go beyond ye all in excellency of learning and knowledge of divers tongues. Point out six of the best given gentlemen of this court, and all they together show not so much good will, spend not so much time, bestow not so many hours daily, orderly, and constantly, for the encrease of learning and knowledge as doth the queen's majesty herself. Yea I believe, that besides her perfect readiness in Latin, Italian, French, and Spanish, she readeth here now at Windsor more Greek every day, than some prebendary of this church doth Latin in a whole week.—Amongst all benefits which God had blessed me withal, next the knowledge of Christ's true religion, I count this the greatest, that it pleased God to call me to be one poor minister in setting forward these excellent gifts of learning," &c. Page 242. Truly, says Harrison, it is a rare thing with us now to hear of a courtier which hath but his own language; and to say how many gentle-women and ladies there are that, besides sound knowledge of the Greek and Latin tongues, are thereto no less skilful in the Spanish, Italian, and French, or in some one of them, it resteth not in me, sith I am persuaded, that as the noblemen and gentlemen do surmount, in this behalf, so these come little or nothing at all behind them, for their parts; which industry God continue.————The stranger, that entereth in the court of England upon the sudden, shall rather imagine himself to come into some public school of the university, where many give ear to one that readeth unto them, than into a prince's palace, if you confer thus with those of other nations. Description of Britain, book ii. chap. 15. By this account, the court had profited by the example of the queen: The sober way of life practised by the ladies of Elizabeth's court appears from the same author. Reading, spinning, and needle work occupied the elder; music the younger. Id. ibid.

END OF THE FOURTH VOLUME.

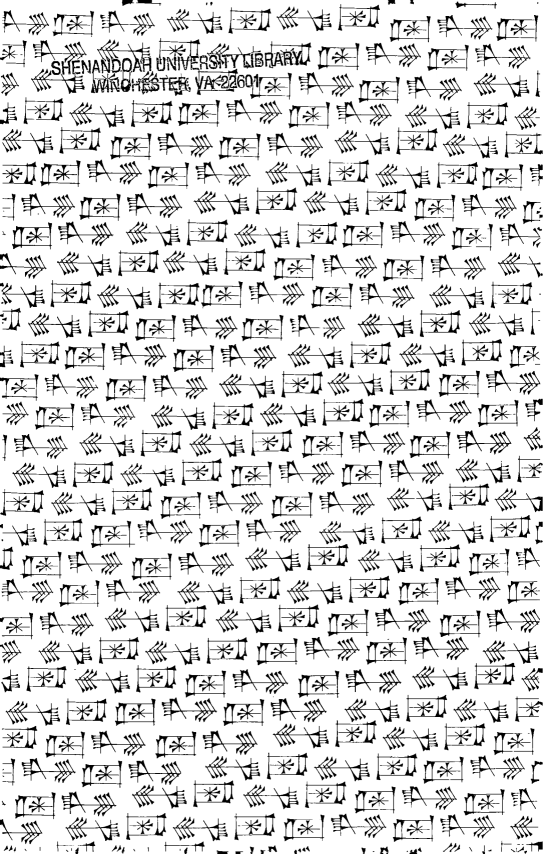